Yuto Tsukuda

Thank you for all the Valentine's Day chocolates you sent to the *Food Wars!* characters this year! The majority went to Takumi, to no one's surprise. Eizan had a really strong year too. Oh, what's this? Asahi Saiba got quite a few as well! It looks like Asahi's subordinate—the one in a kimono and glasses—also got some. Now, that one was a surprise. This is so much fun every year. I really appreciate it. Thanks!

Shun Saeki

I moved! Having some nice greenery around really makes a room feel so much nicer.

About the authors

Yuto Tsukuda won the 34th Jump Juniketsu Newcomers' Manga Award for his one-shot story *Kiba ni Naru*. He made his *Weekly Shonen Jump* debut in 2010 with the series *Shonen Shikku*. His follow-up series, *Food Wars!: Shokugeki no Soma*, is his first English-language release.

Shun Saeki made his *Jump NEXT!* debut in 2011 with the one-shot story *Kimi to Watashi no Renai Soudan*. *Food Wars!: Shokugeki no Soma* is his first *Shonen Jump* series.

Food Wars!
SHOKUGEKI NO SOMA

Volume 34
Shonen Jump Manga Edition
Story by Yuto Tsukuda, Art by Shun Saeki
Contributor Yuki Morisaki

Translation: Adrienne Beck
Touch-Up Art & Lettering: James Gaubatz, Mara Coman
Design: Alice Lewis
Editor: Jennifer LeBlanc

Printed in the U.S.A.

Published by VIZ Media, LLC
P.O. Box 77010
San Francisco, CA 94107

10 9 8 7 6 5 4 3 2 1
First printing, February 2020

ratings.viz.com RATED T+ OLDER TEEN

PARENTAL ADVISORY
FOOD WARS! is rated T+ for Older Teen and is recommended for ages 16 and up. This volume contains sexual situations/humor.

VIZ MEDIA
viz.com

SHONEN JUMP
shonenjump.com

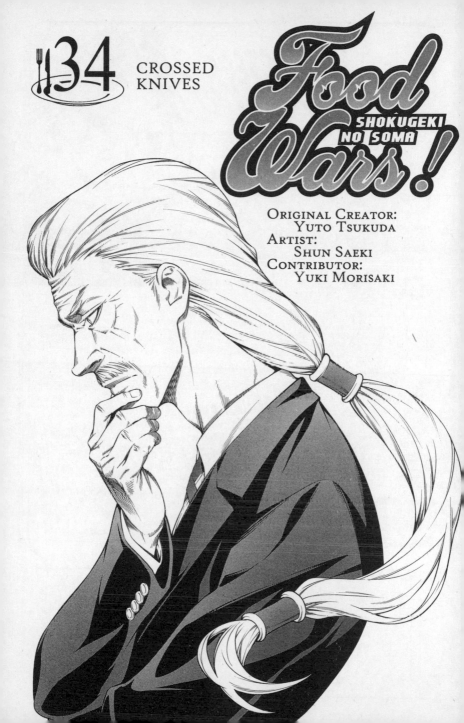

34 CROSSED KNIVES

Food Wars!
SHOKUGEKI NO SOMA

Original Creator:
  Yuto Tsukuda
Artist:
  Shun Saeki
Contributor:
  Yuki Morisaki

CHARACTERS

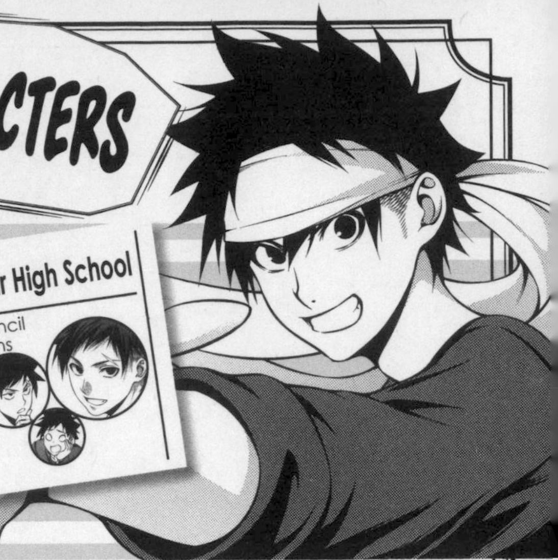

SOMA YUKIHIRA Second Year High School

The current first seat on Totsuki's Council of Ten. Unbound by traditional notions and with a natural inquisitiveness and passion for cooking, his fresh take on cuisine leads him to create dishes no one has ever thought of before. Resides in Polaris Dormitory.

Shokugeki no SOMA

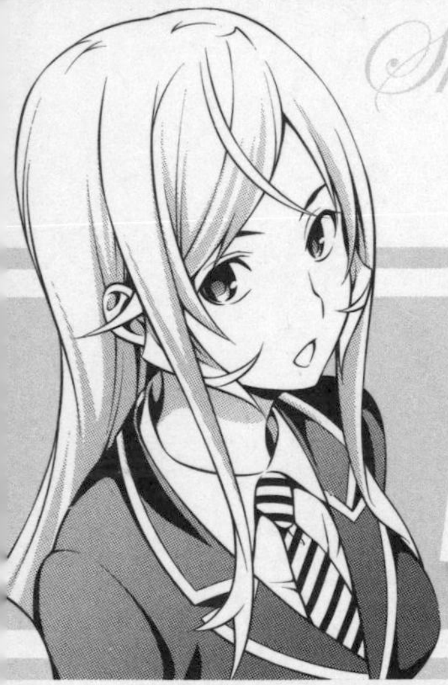

ERINA NAKIRI Second Year High School

The current dean of Totsuki Institute and granddaughter of former dean Senzaemon Nakiri. Her sense of taste is so refined it's known as "the Divine Tongue." Though normally strict and proper, she has a girly side and loves shojo manga.

STORY

Soma grew up helping to cook at his family's restaurant, Yukihira. But one day his father enrolls him in Japan's premier culinary school, Totsuki Institute. Having met other students as skilled as he is and with similar goals, Soma has grown a little as a chef.

Soma, Megumi and Takumi have been invited to participate in the illustrious Blue, a gourmet competition for the best of the world's young chefs. But this year's tournament is drastically different from the standard format, and many traditional chefs quickly fail. Soma and company, however, manage to win their way to the third gate, where they find out that the judge they must impress is a noir?!

Shokugeki no SOMA

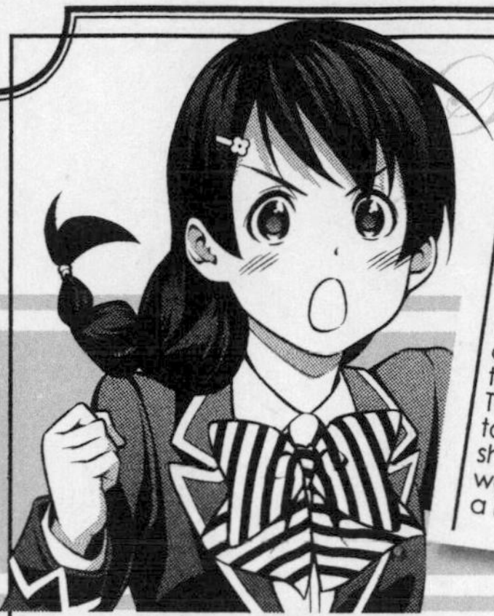

MEGUMI TADOKORO Second Year High School

Coming to the big city from the countryside, she now holds the tenth seat on Totsuki's Council of Ten. Using the privileges granted to her as a council member, she has traveled the globe learning world cultures and cuisines. Currently a Polaris dormitory resident.

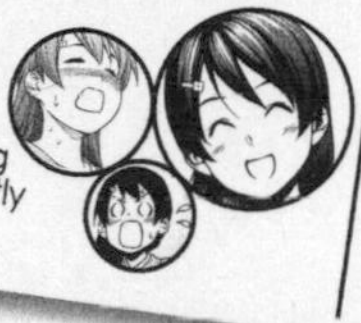

TAKUMI ALDINI Second Year High School

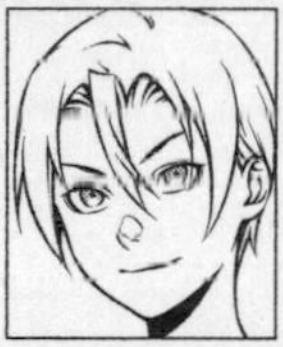

The current seventh seat on Totsuki's Council of Ten. He left his family's trattoria in Italy to attend Japan's Totsuki Institute. Isami is his younger twin brother.

EISHI TSUKASA

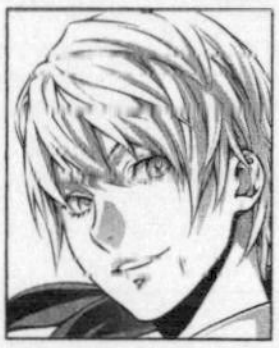

A Totsuki Institute graduate and former first seat, he has a powerful talent for bringing out the best qualities of ingredients.

JOICHIRO YUKIHIRA

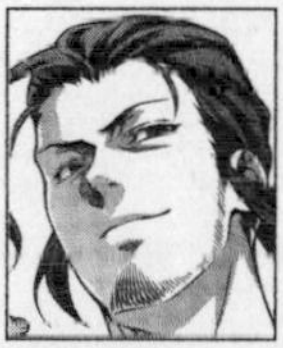

Totsuki alumnus and Soma's father, he was once the second seat on the Council of Ten. Now he's a globe-trotting chef who's famous to those in the know in the culinary world.

UNE

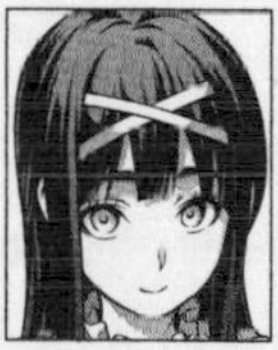

A first-rank adjudicator with the WGO, the organization that publishes *the Book*, a periodical that rates all gourmet restaurants in the world.

SARGE

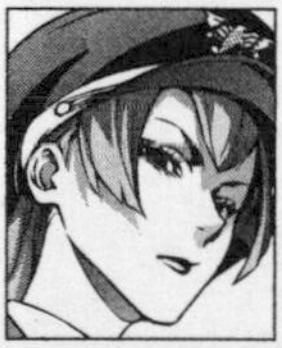

A noir whose signature cooking implement is her chain carving knife, which looks like a chainsaw.

ASAHI SAIBA

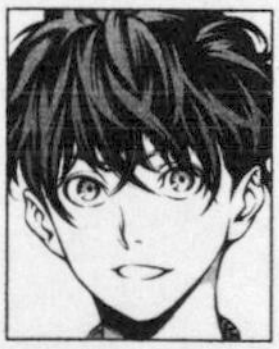

Thanks to information squeezed out of some reluctant cuisiniers noir, it's believed he's involved with the recent shokugeki incidents around Japan. Supposedly an excellent chef.

Food Wars! SHOKUGEKI NO SOMA

34

Table of Contents

129 FREAKISHLY TALENTED CHEFS

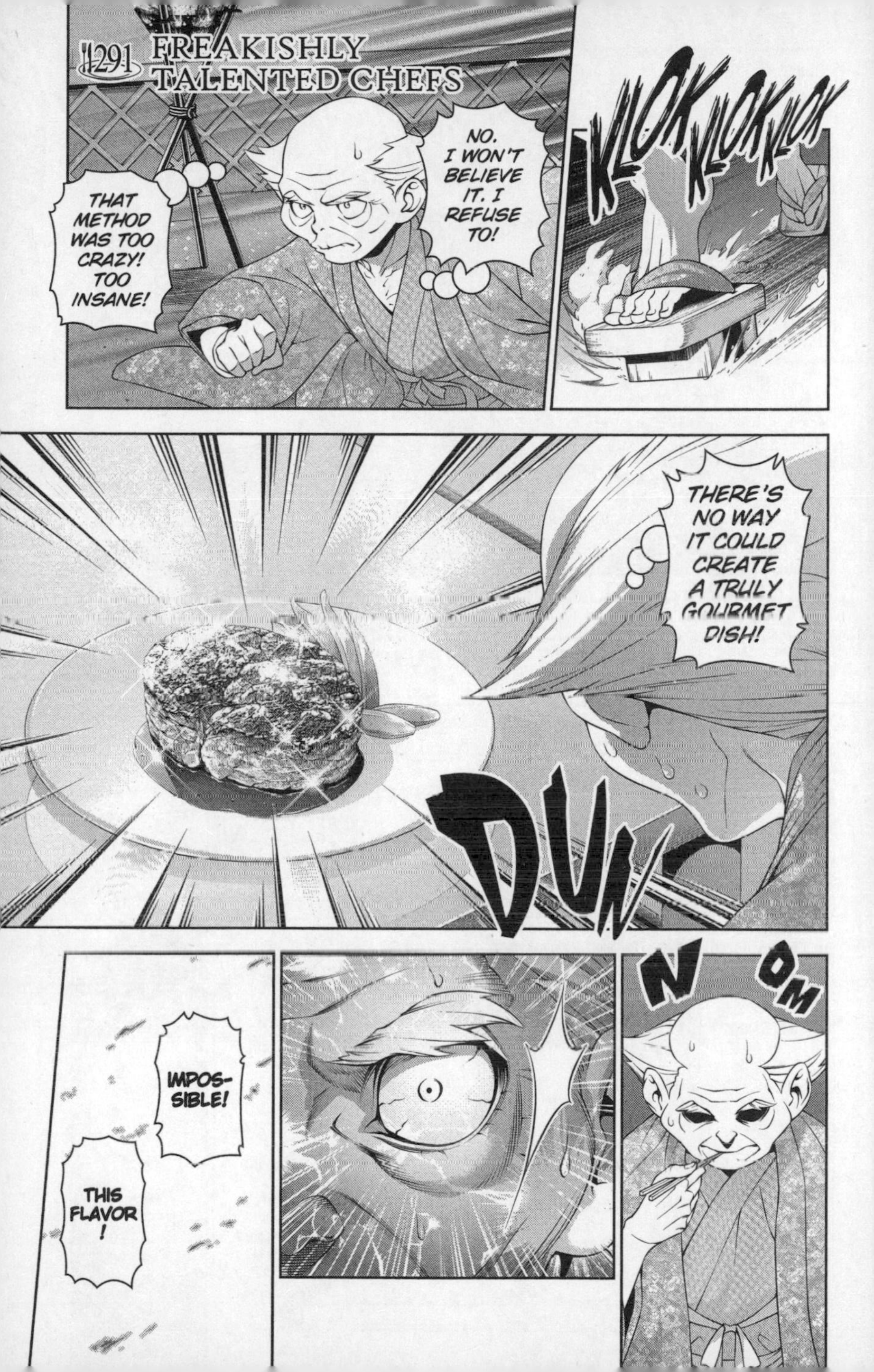
KLOK KLOK KLOK
NO. I WON'T BELIEVE IT. I REFUSE TO!
THAT METHOD WAS TOO CRAZY! TOO INSANE!
THERE'S NO WAY IT COULD CREATE A TRULY GOURMET DISH!
DUN
N OM
IMPOS-SIBLE!
THIS FLAVOR!

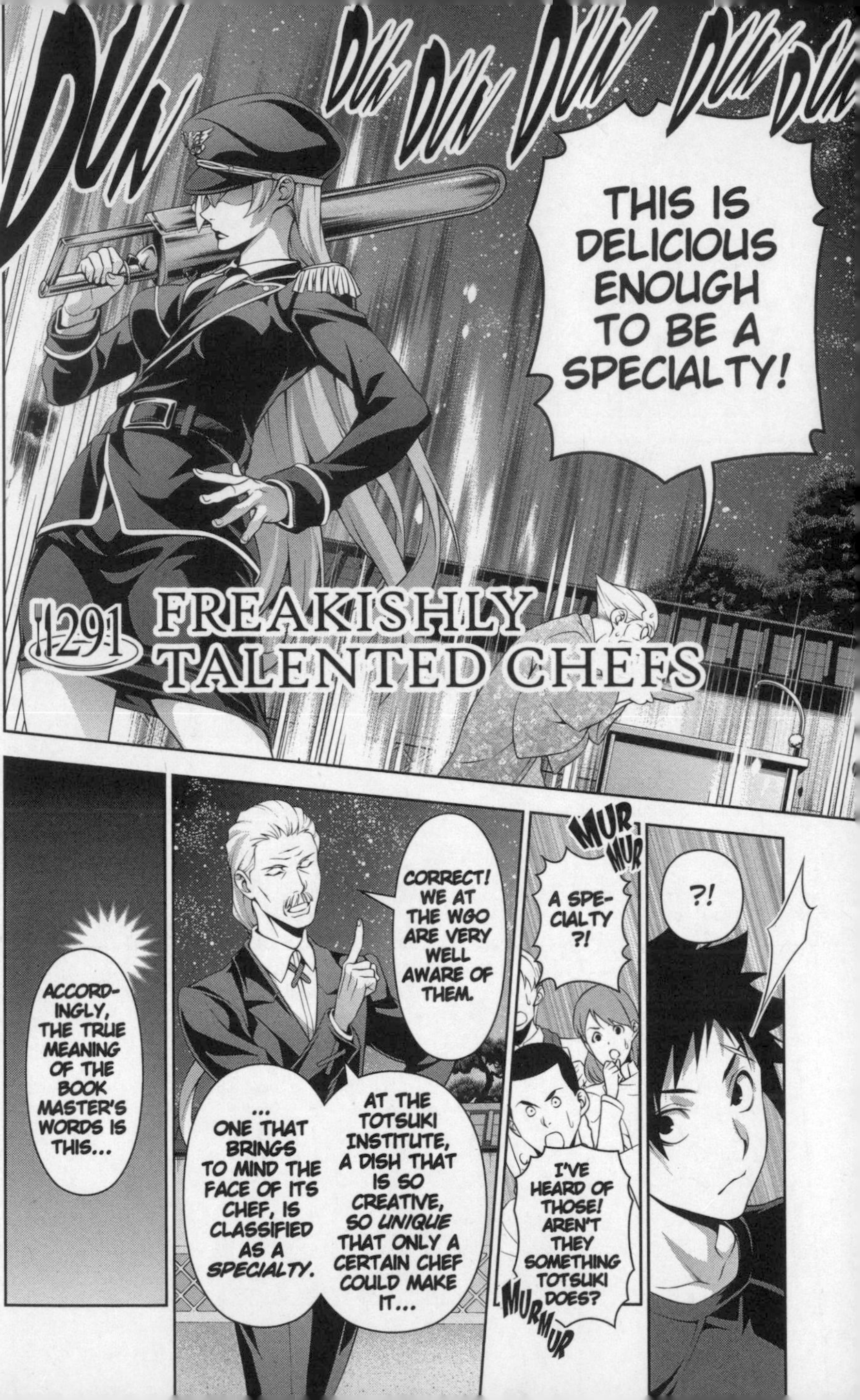
DUN DUN DUN DUN DUN DUN DUN
THIS IS DELICIOUS ENOUGH TO BE A SPECIALTY!
291 FREAKISHLY TALENTED CHEFS
?!
MUR MUR
A SPE-CIALTY ?!
I'VE HEARD OF THOSE! AREN'T THEY SOMETHING TOTSUKI DOES?
MURMUR
CORRECT! WE AT THE WGO ARE VERY WELL AWARE OF THEM.
AT THE TOTSUKI INSTITUTE, A DISH THAT IS SO CREATIVE, SO *UNIQUE* THAT ONLY A CERTAIN CHEF COULD MAKE IT...
... ONE THAT BRINGS TO MIND THE FACE OF ITS CHEF, IS CLASSIFIED AS A *SPECIALTY.*
ACCORD-INGLY, THE TRUE MEANING OF THE BOOK MASTER'S WORDS IS THIS...

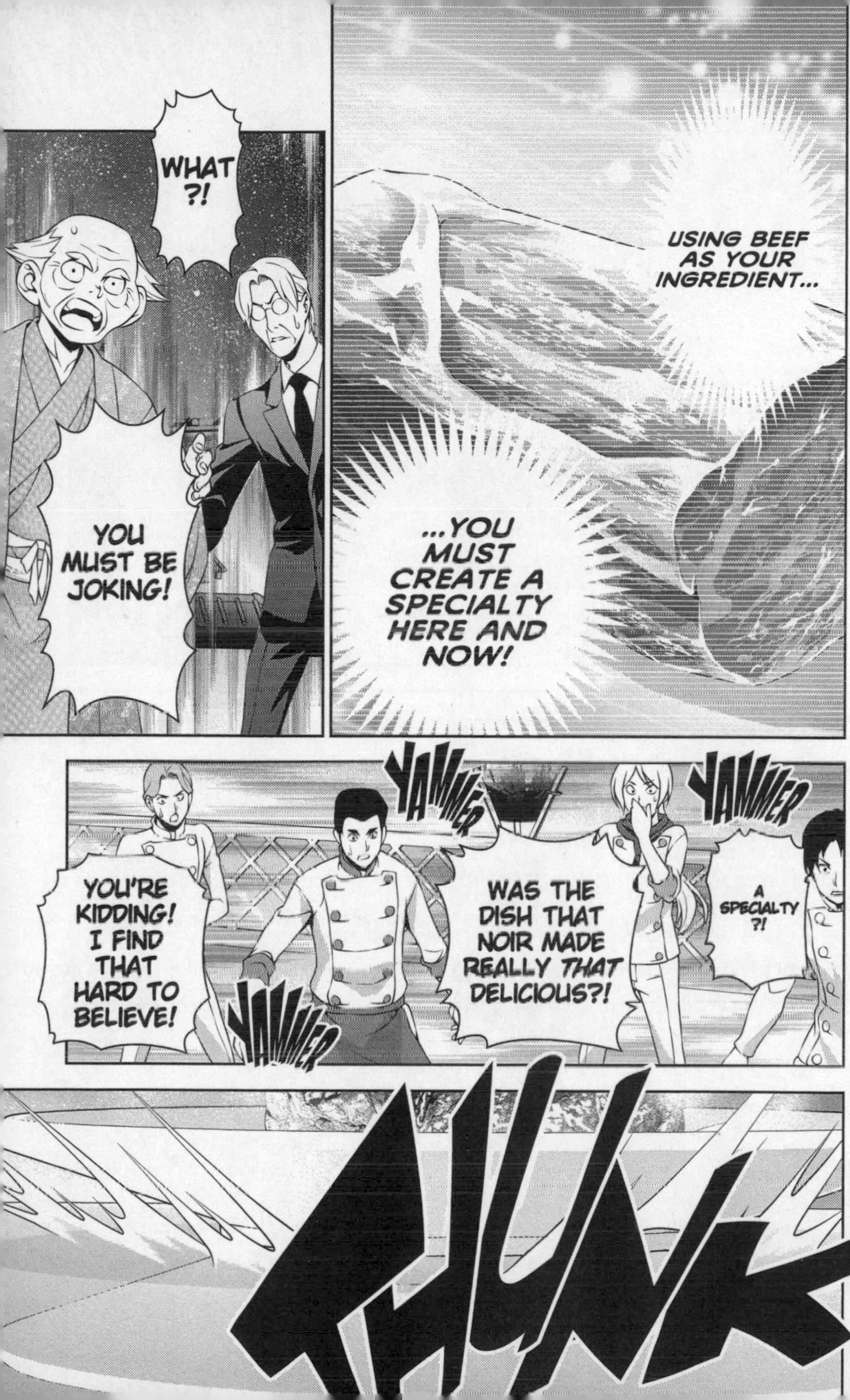

USING BEEF AS YOUR INGREDIENT...
...YOU MUST CREATE A SPECIALTY HERE AND NOW!
WHAT ?!
YOU MUST BE JOKING!
YAMMER
A SPECIALTY ?!
YAMMER
WAS THE DISH THAT NOIR MADE REALLY *THAT* DELICIOUS?!
YAMMER
YOU'RE KIDDING! I FIND THAT HARD TO BELIEVE!
YAMMER
THUNK

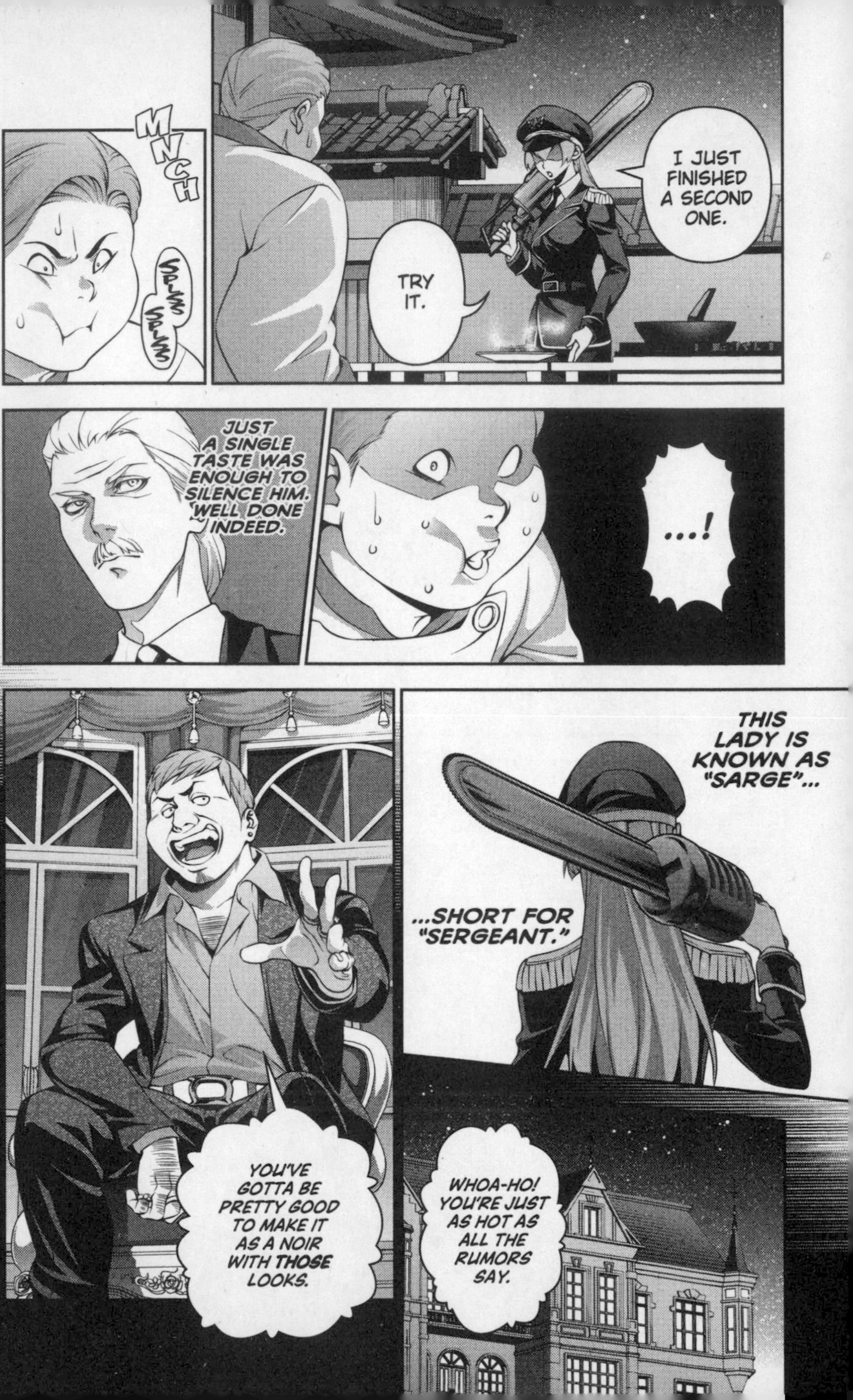
I JUST FINISHED A SECOND ONE.
TRY IT.
MNCH
JUST A SINGLE TASTE WAS ENOUGH TO SILENCE HIM. WELL DONE INDEED.
...!
THIS LADY IS KNOWN AS "SARGE"...
...SHORT FOR "SERGEANT."
WHOA-HO! YOU'RE JUST AS HOT AS ALL THE RUMORS SAY.
YOU'VE GOTTA BE PRETTY GOOD TO MAKE IT AS A NOIR WITH THOSE LOOKS.

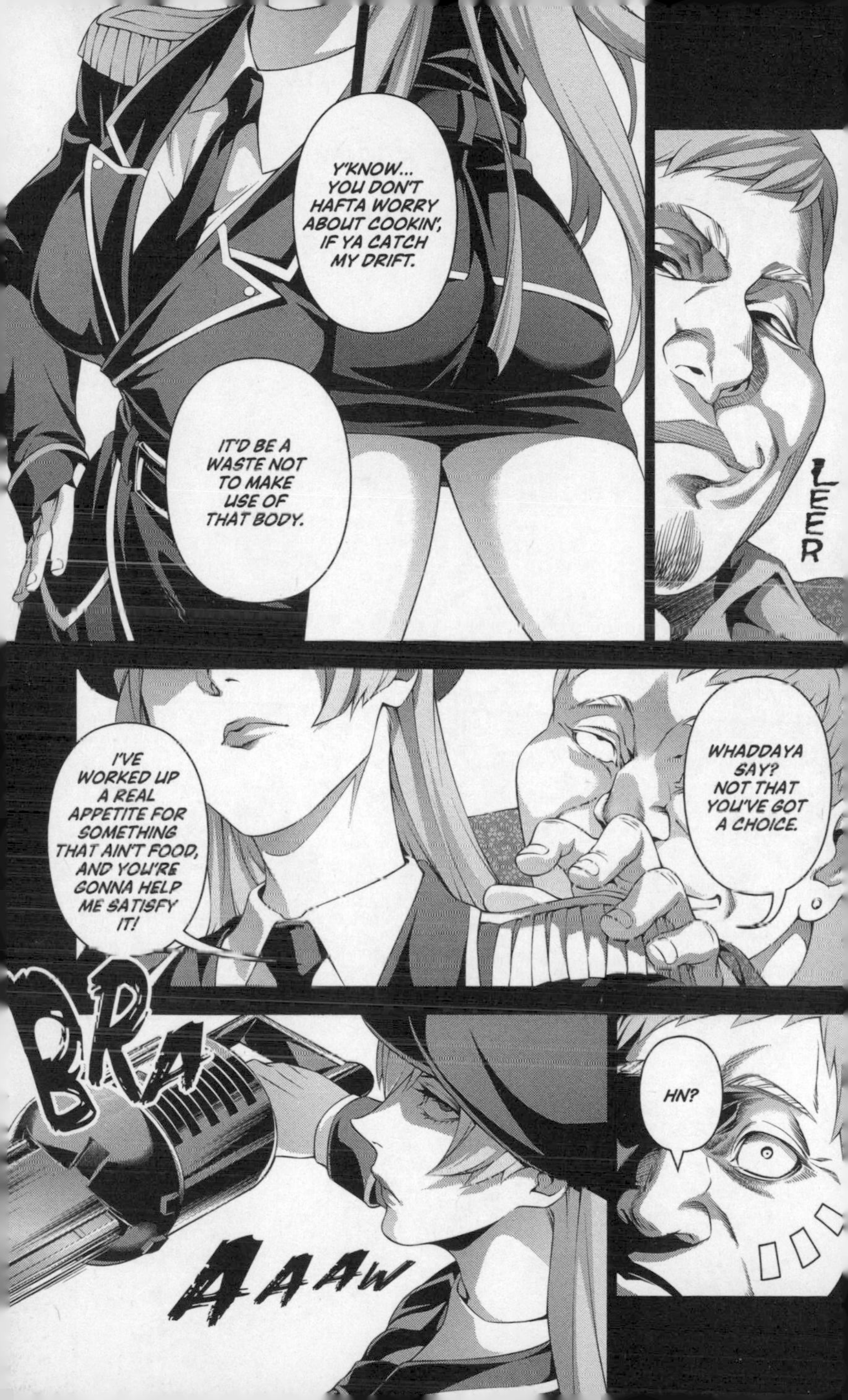
LEER
Y'KNOW... YOU DON'T HAFTA WORRY ABOUT COOKIN', IF YA CATCH MY DRIFT.
IT'D BE A WASTE NOT TO MAKE USE OF THAT BODY.
WHADDAYA SAY? NOT THAT YOU'VE GOT A CHOICE.
I'VE WORKED UP A REAL APPETITE FOR SOMETHING THAT AIN'T FOOD, AND YOU'RE GONNA HELP ME SATISFY IT!
HN?
BRAAAAW

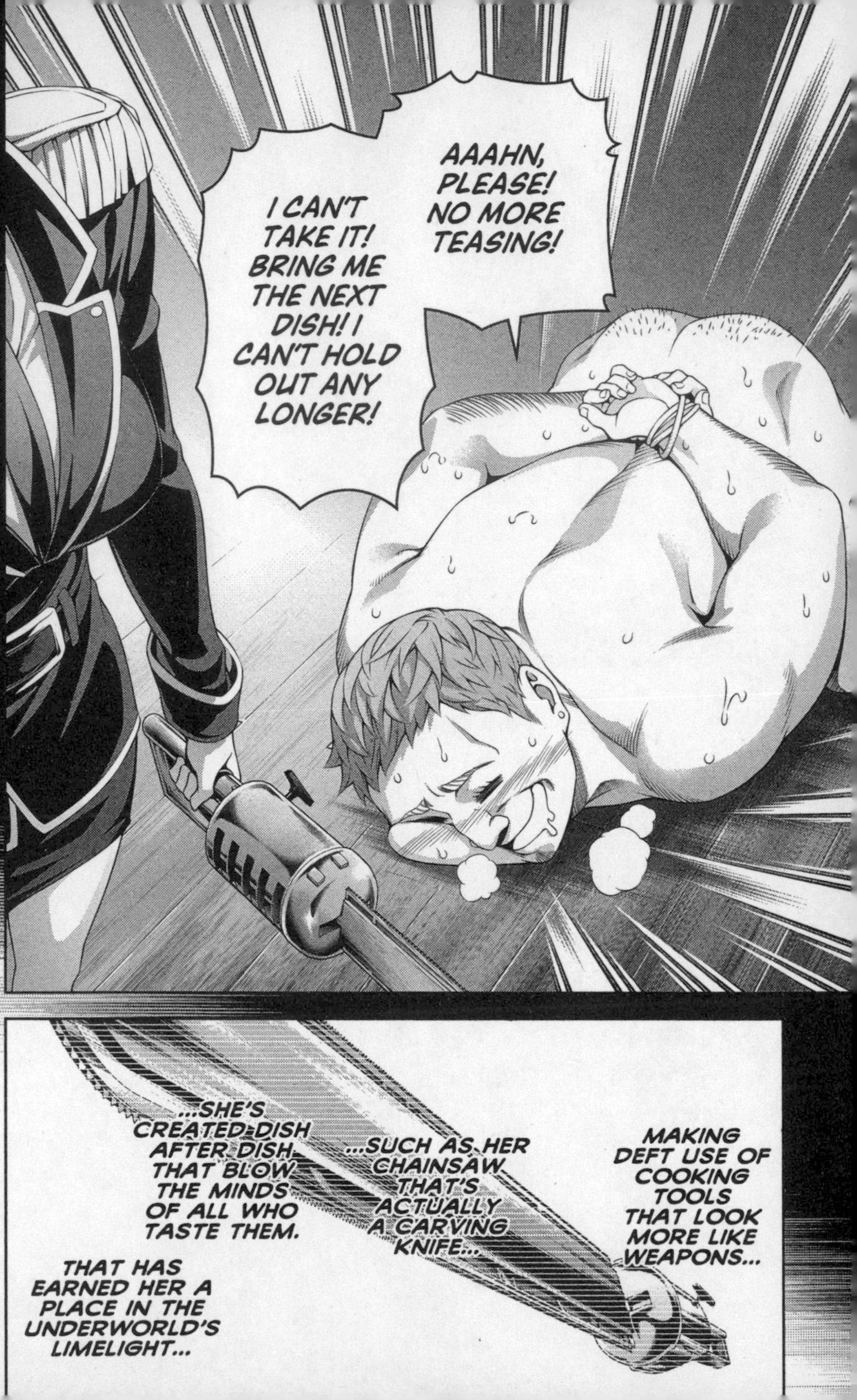
AAAHN, PLEASE! NO MORE TEASING!
I CAN'T TAKE IT! BRING ME THE NEXT DISH! I CAN'T HOLD OUT ANY LONGER!
MAKING DEFT USE OF COOKING TOOLS THAT LOOK MORE LIKE WEAPONS...
...SUCH AS HER CHAINSAW THAT'S ACTUALLY A CARVING KNIFE...
...SHE'S CREATED DISH AFTER DISH THAT BLOW THE MINDS OF ALL WHO TASTE THEM.
THAT HAS EARNED HER A PLACE IN THE UNDERWORLD'S LIMELIGHT...

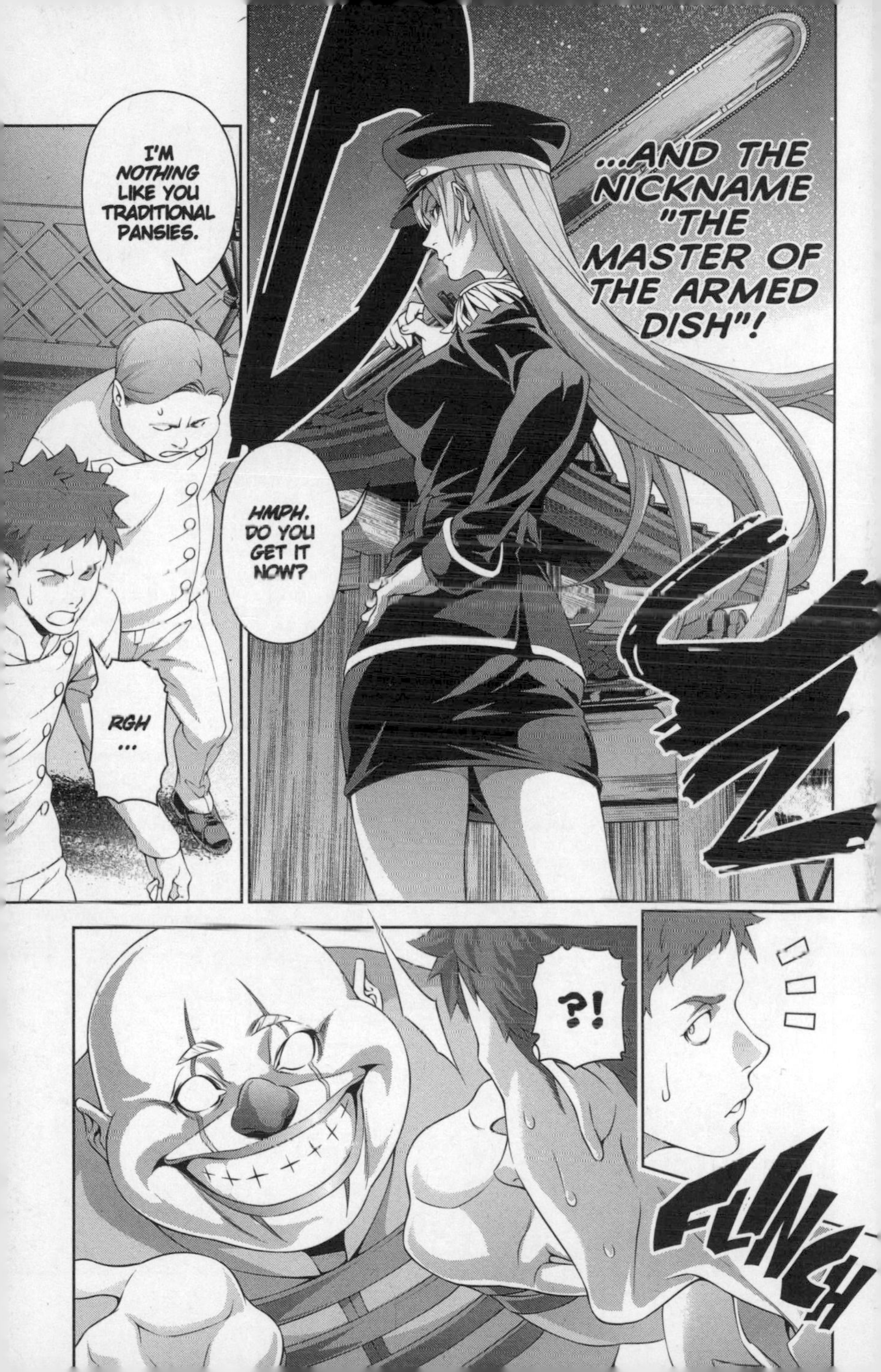
...AND THE NICKNAME "THE MASTER OF THE ARMED DISH"!
I'M NOTHING LIKE YOU TRADITIONAL PANSIES.
HMPH. DO YOU GET IT NOW?
RGH...
?!
FLINCH

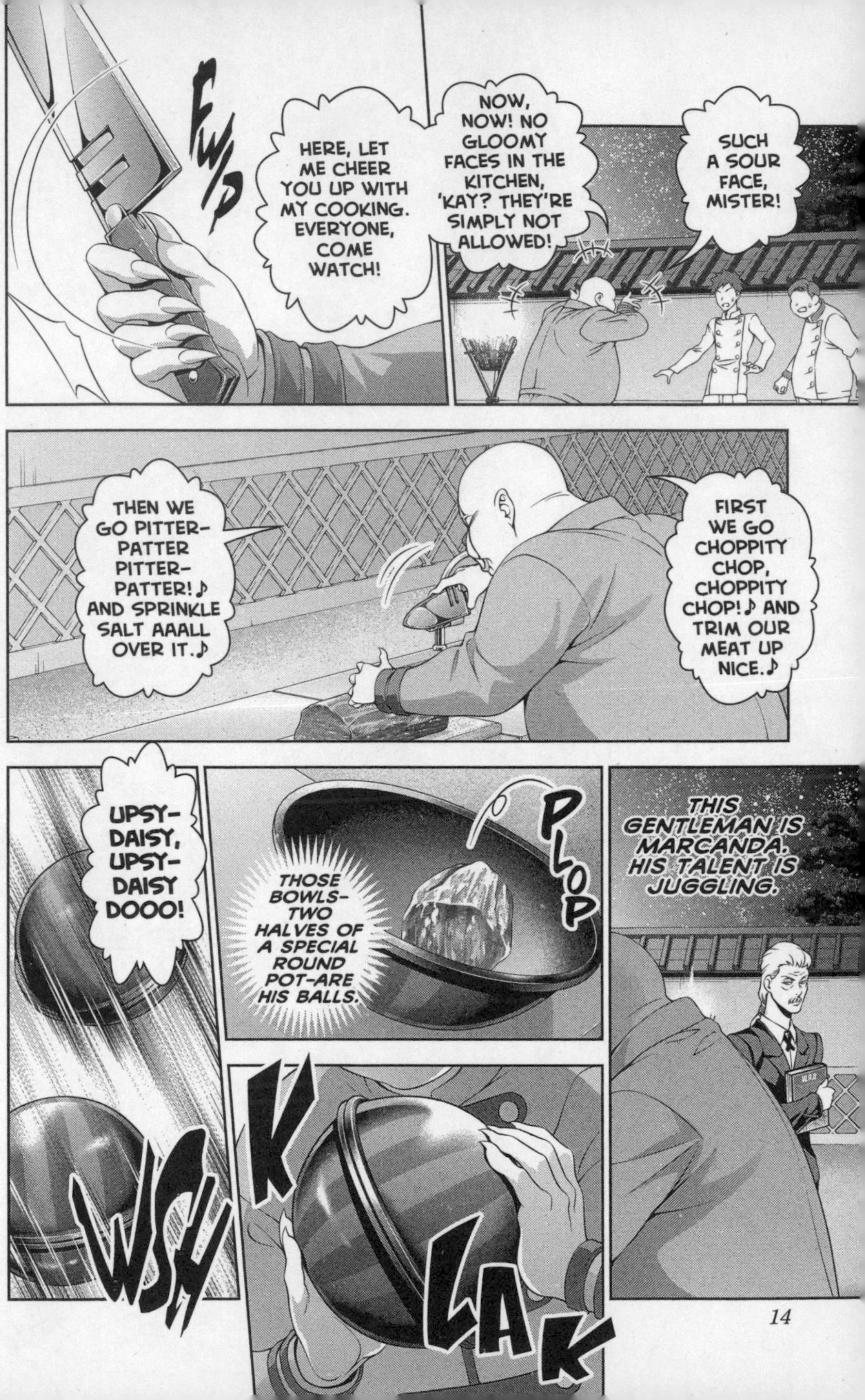
SUCH A SOUR FACE, MISTER!
NOW, NOW! NO GLOOMY FACES IN THE KITCHEN, 'KAY? THEY'RE SIMPLY NOT ALLOWED!
HERE, LET ME CHEER YOU UP WITH MY COOKING. EVERYONE, COME WATCH!
FWIP
FIRST WE GO CHOPPITY CHOP, CHOPPITY CHOP!♪ AND TRIM OUR MEAT UP NICE.♪
THEN WE GO PITTER-PATTER PITTER-PATTER!♪ AND SPRINKLE SALT AAALL OVER IT.♪
THIS GENTLEMAN IS MARCANDA. HIS TALENT IS JUGGLING.
PLOP
THOSE BOWLS—TWO HALVES OF A SPECIAL ROUND POT—ARE HIS BALLS.
K
LAK
UPSY-DAISY, UPSY-DAISY DOOO!
WSH

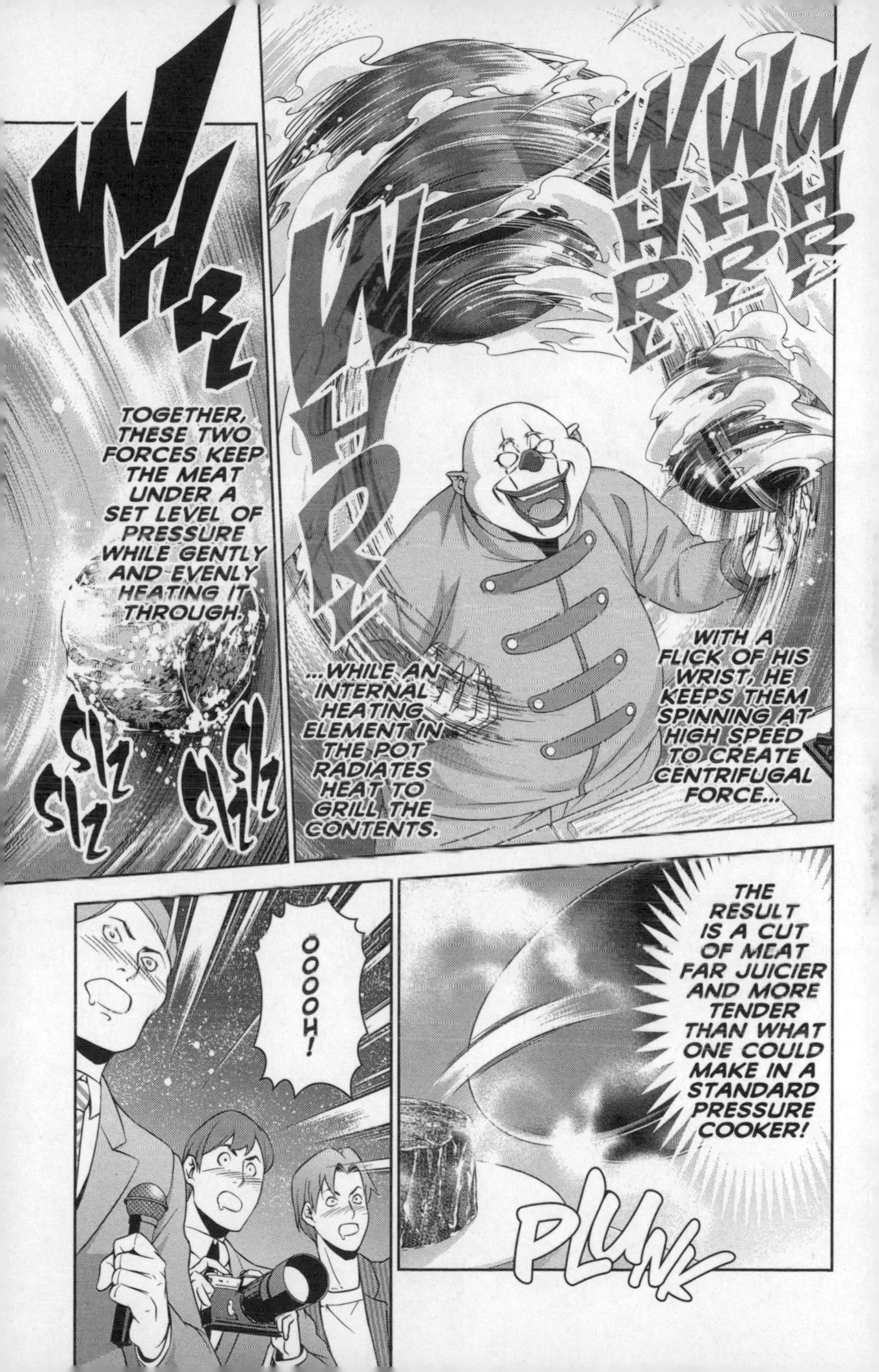
WITH A FLICK OF HIS WRIST, HE KEEPS THEM SPINNING AT HIGH SPEED TO CREATE CENTRIFUGAL FORCE...
WHRR
...WHILE AN INTERNAL HEATING ELEMENT IN THE POT RADIATES HEAT TO GRILL THE CONTENTS.
WHRL
TOGETHER, THESE TWO FORCES KEEP THE MEAT UNDER A SET LEVEL OF PRESSURE WHILE GENTLY AND EVENLY HEATING IT THROUGH.
SHK SHK
SHK SHK
THE RESULT IS A CUT OF MEAT FAR JUICIER AND MORE TENDER THAN WHAT ONE COULD MAKE IN A STANDARD PRESSURE COOKER!
PLUNK
OOOOOH!

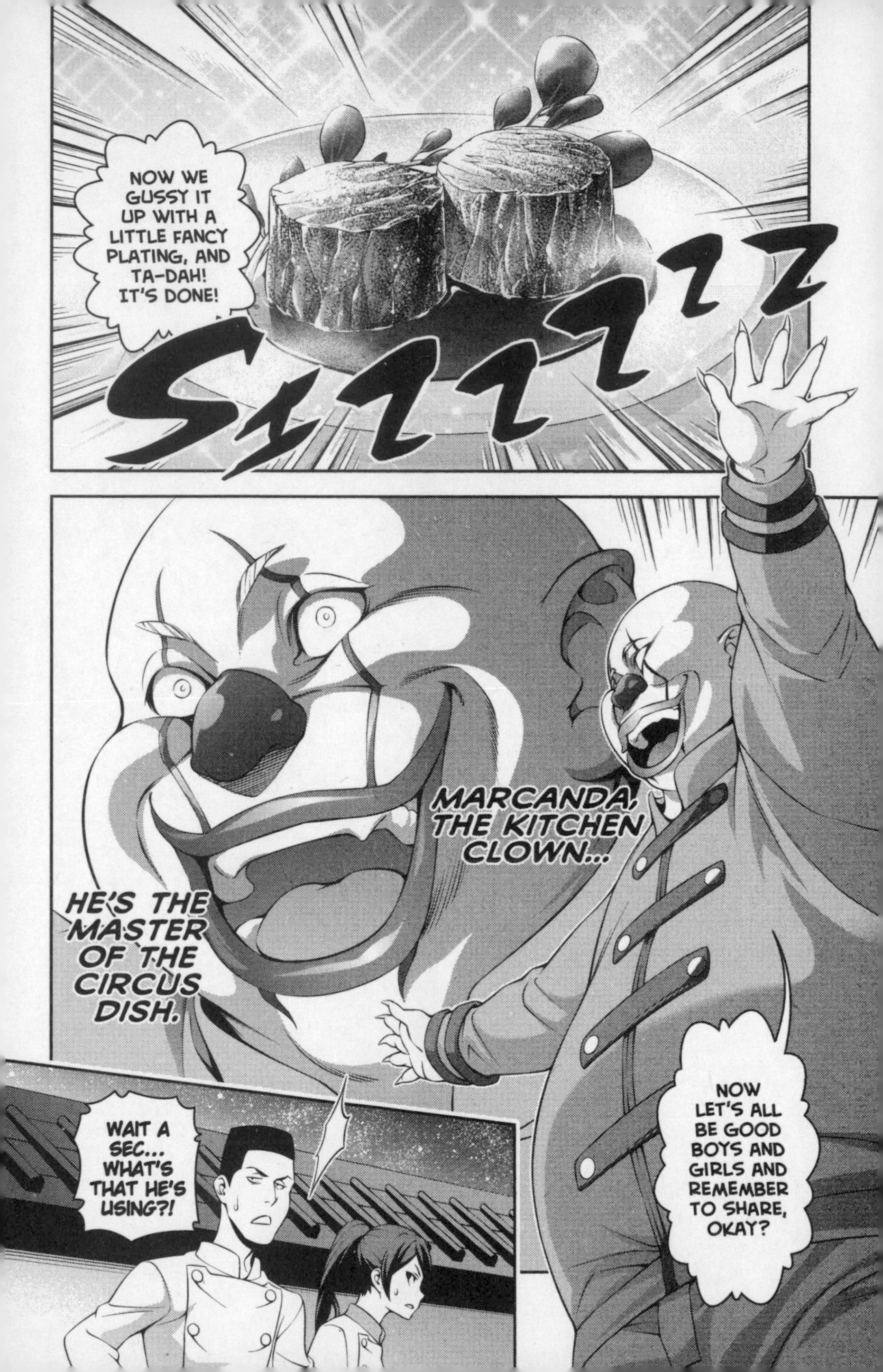
NOW WE GUSSY IT UP WITH A LITTLE FANCY PLATING, AND TA-DAH! IT'S DONE!
MARCANDA, THE KITCHEN CLOWN...
HE'S THE MASTER OF THE CIRCUS DISH.
NOW LET'S ALL BE GOOD BOYS AND GIRLS AND REMEMBER TO SHARE, OKAY?
WAIT A SEC... WHAT'S THAT HE'S USING?!

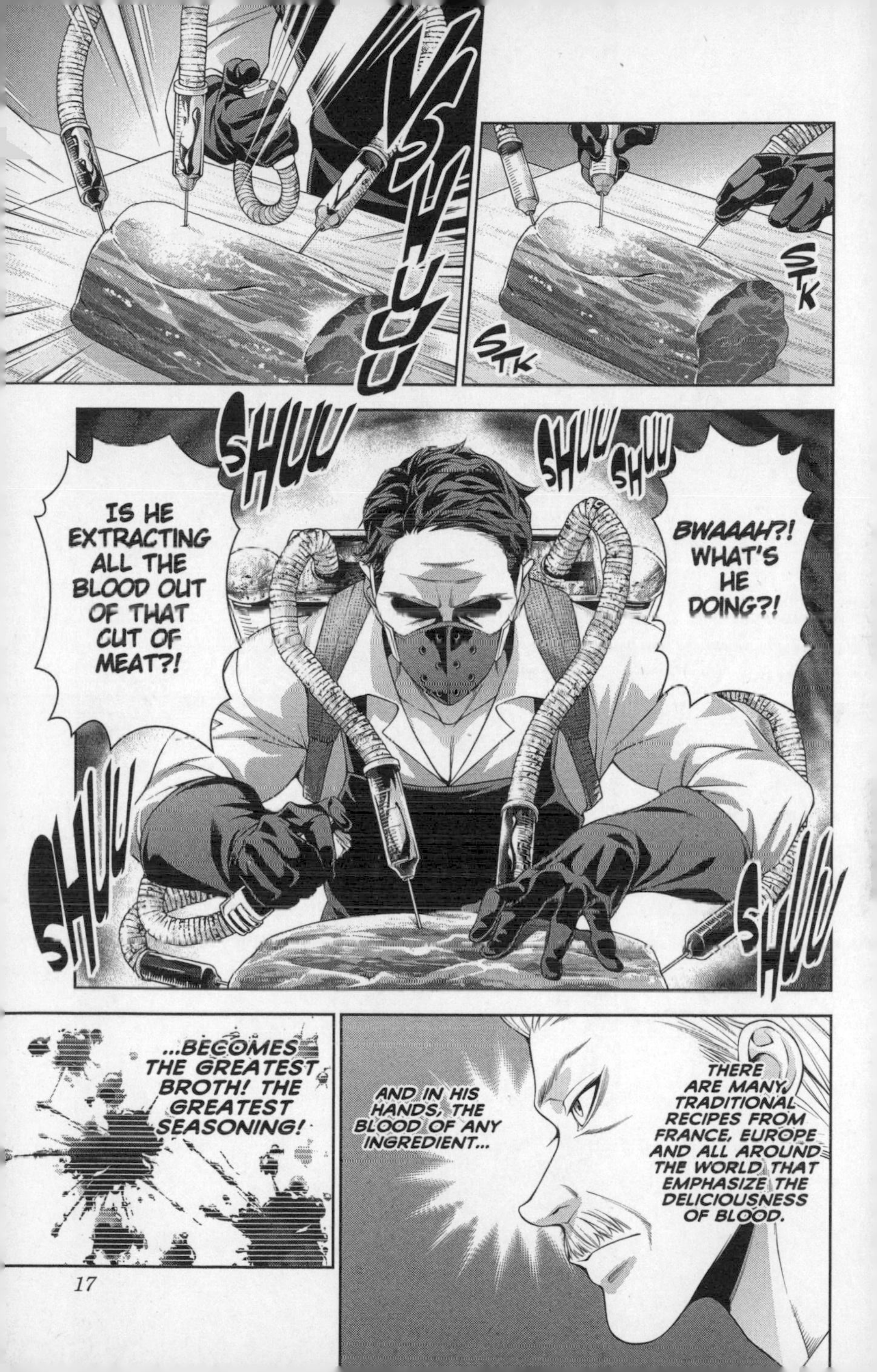
STK
STK
SHUUUU
SHUU SHUU
BWAAAH?! WHAT'S HE DOING?!
SHUU
IS HE EXTRACTING ALL THE BLOOD OUT OF THAT CUT OF MEAT?!
SHUU
SHUU
THERE ARE MANY TRADITIONAL RECIPES FROM FRANCE, EUROPE AND ALL AROUND THE WORLD THAT EMPHASIZE THE DELICIOUSNESS OF BLOOD.
AND IN HIS HANDS, THE BLOOD OF ANY INGREDIENT...
...BECOMES THE GREATEST BROTH! THE GREATEST SEASONING!

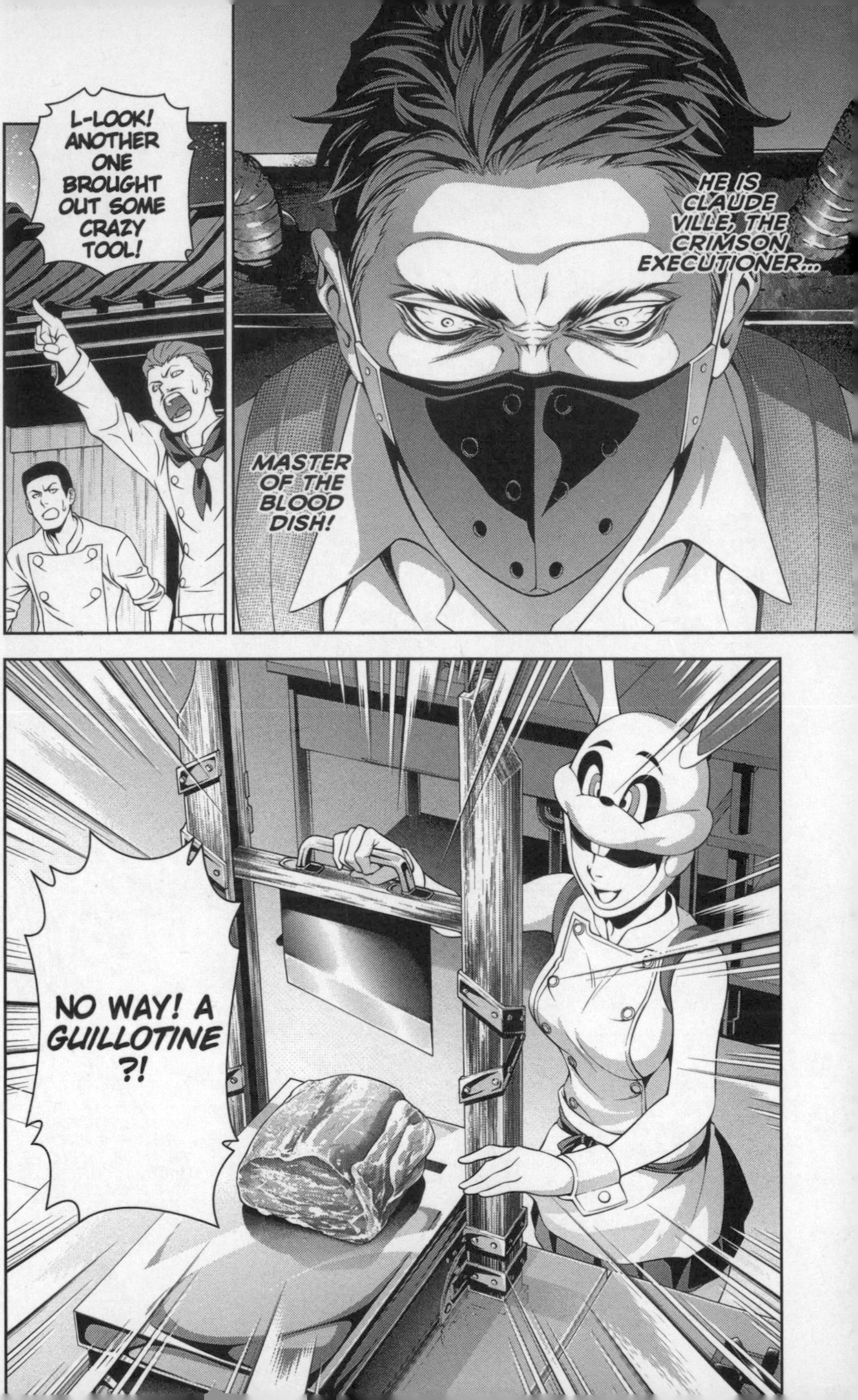
HE IS CLAUDE VILLE, THE CRIMSON EXECUTIONER...
MASTER OF THE BLOOD DISH!
L-LOOK! ANOTHER ONE BROUGHT OUT SOME CRAZY TOOL!
NO WAY! A GUILLOTINE ?!

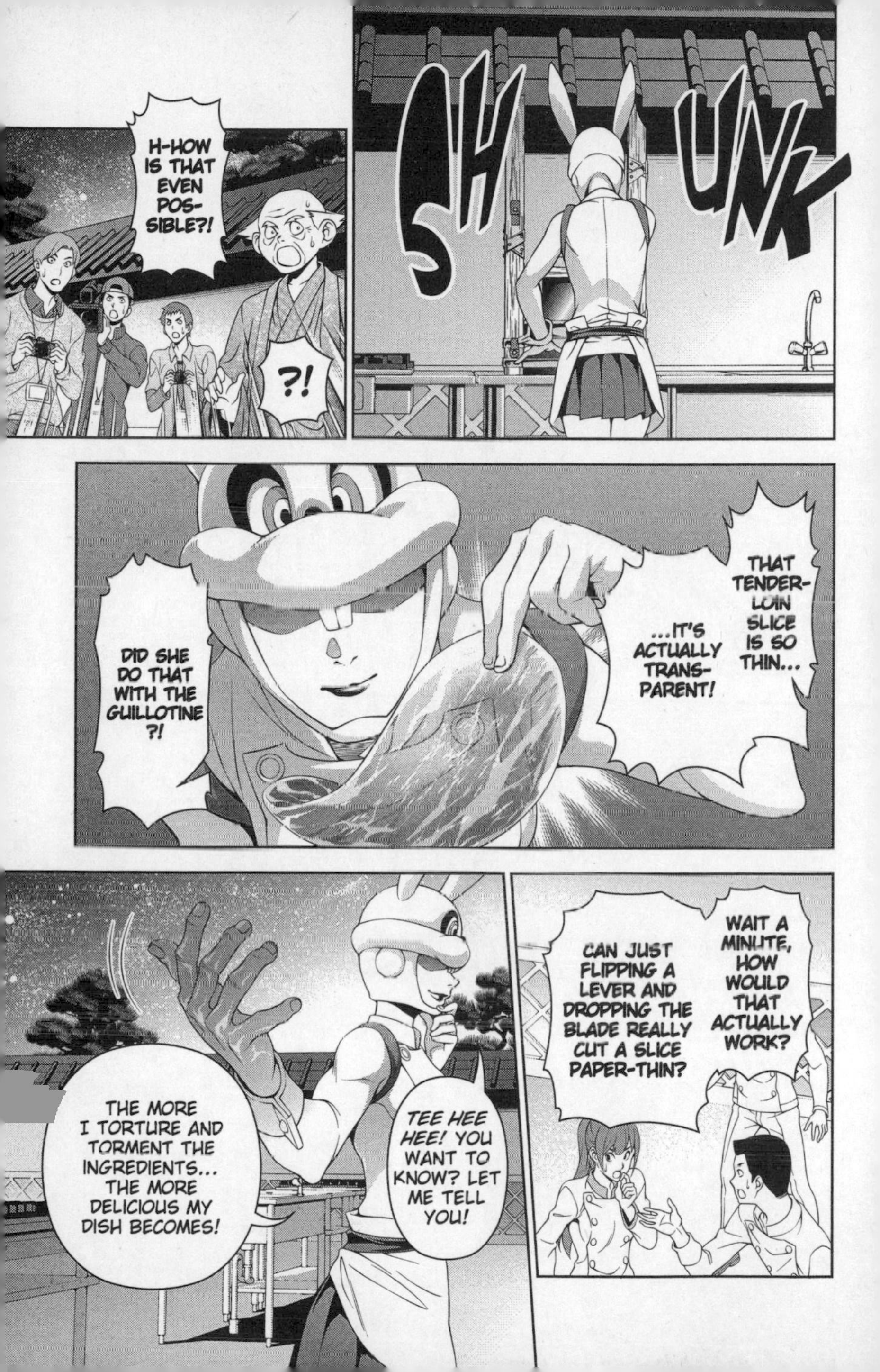
SHUNK
H-HOW IS THAT EVEN POS-SIBLE?!
?!
THAT TENDER-LOIN SLICE IS SO THIN...
...IT'S ACTUALLY TRANS-PARENT!
DID SHE DO THAT WITH THE GUILLOTINE ?!
WAIT A MINUTE, HOW WOULD THAT ACTUALLY WORK?
CAN JUST FLIPPING A LEVER AND DROPPING THE BLADE REALLY CUT A SLICE PAPER-THIN?
TEE HEE HEE! YOU WANT TO KNOW? LET ME TELL YOU!
THE MORE I TORTURE AND TORMENT THE INGREDIENTS... THE MORE DELICIOUS MY DISH BECOMES!

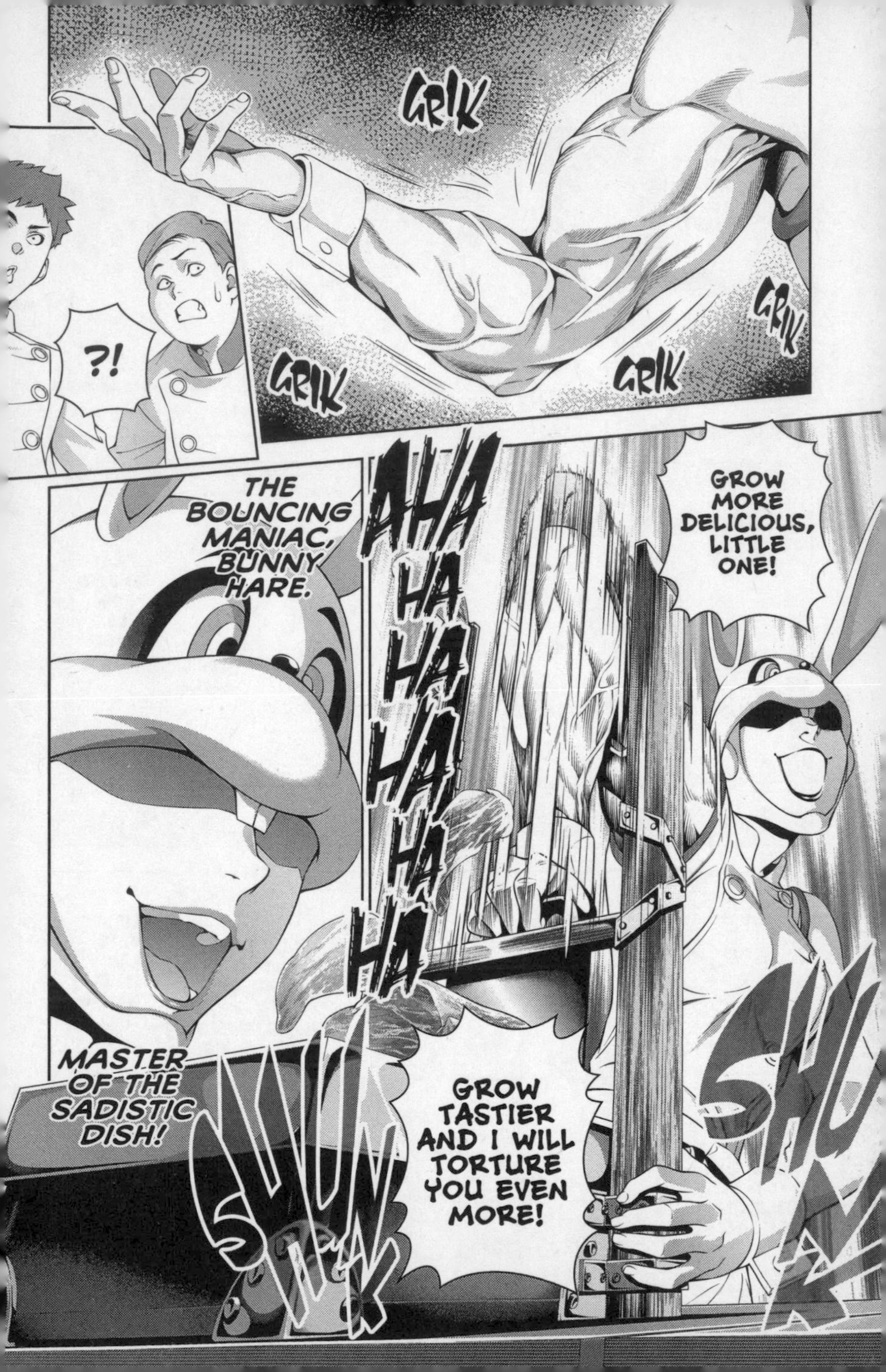
GRIK
GRIK
GRIK
GRIK
?!
GROW MORE DELICIOUS, LITTLE ONE!
AHAHAHAHAHAHA
THE BOUNCING MANIAC, BUNNY HARE.
GROW TASTIER AND I WILL TORTURE YOU EVEN MORE!
MASTER OF THE SADISTIC DISH!

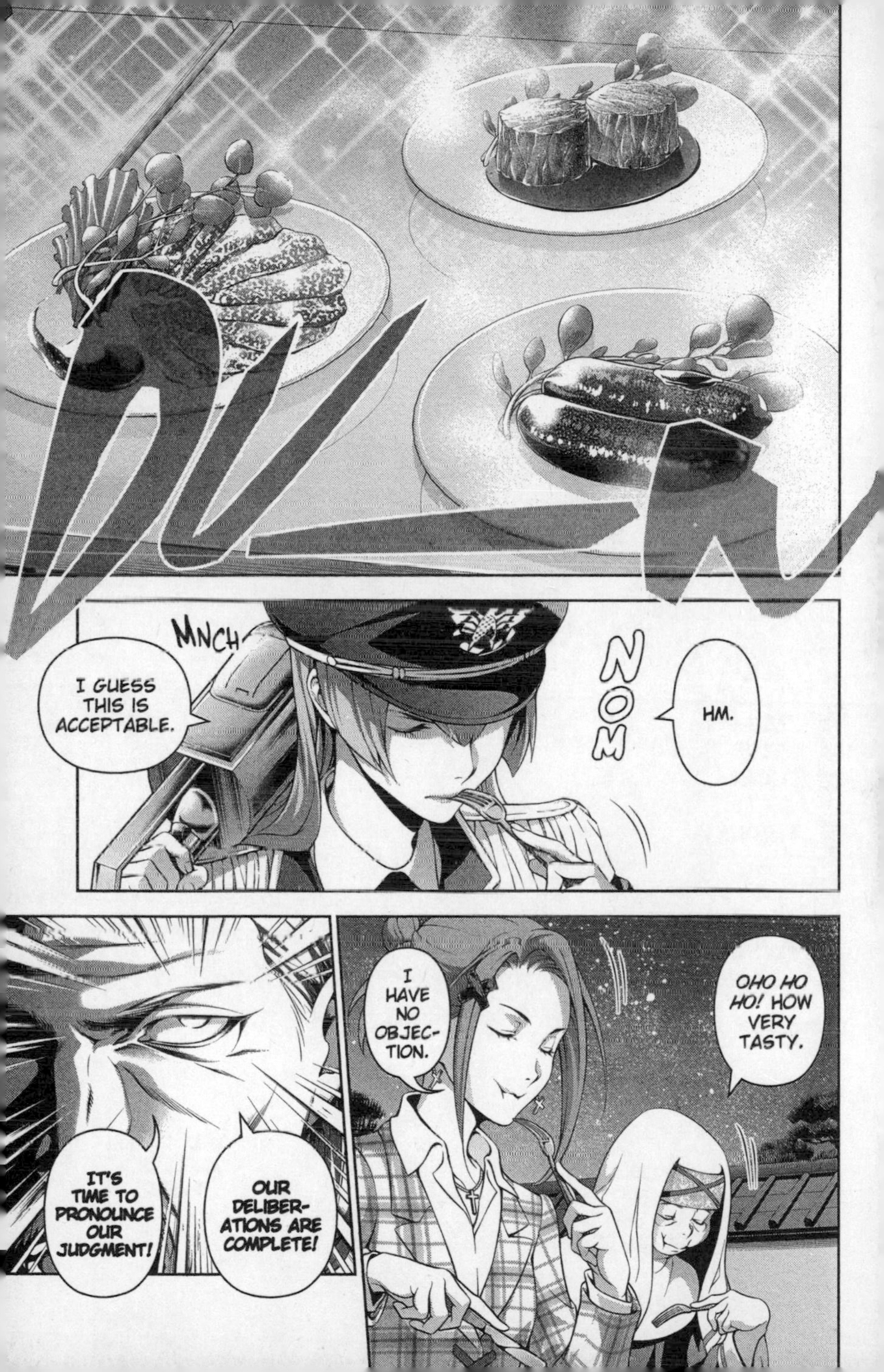
HM.
NOM
MNCH
I GUESS THIS IS ACCEPTABLE.
OHO HO HO! HOW VERY TASTY.
I HAVE NO OBJECTION.
OUR DELIBERATIONS ARE COMPLETE!
IT'S TIME TO PRONOUNCE OUR JUDGMENT!

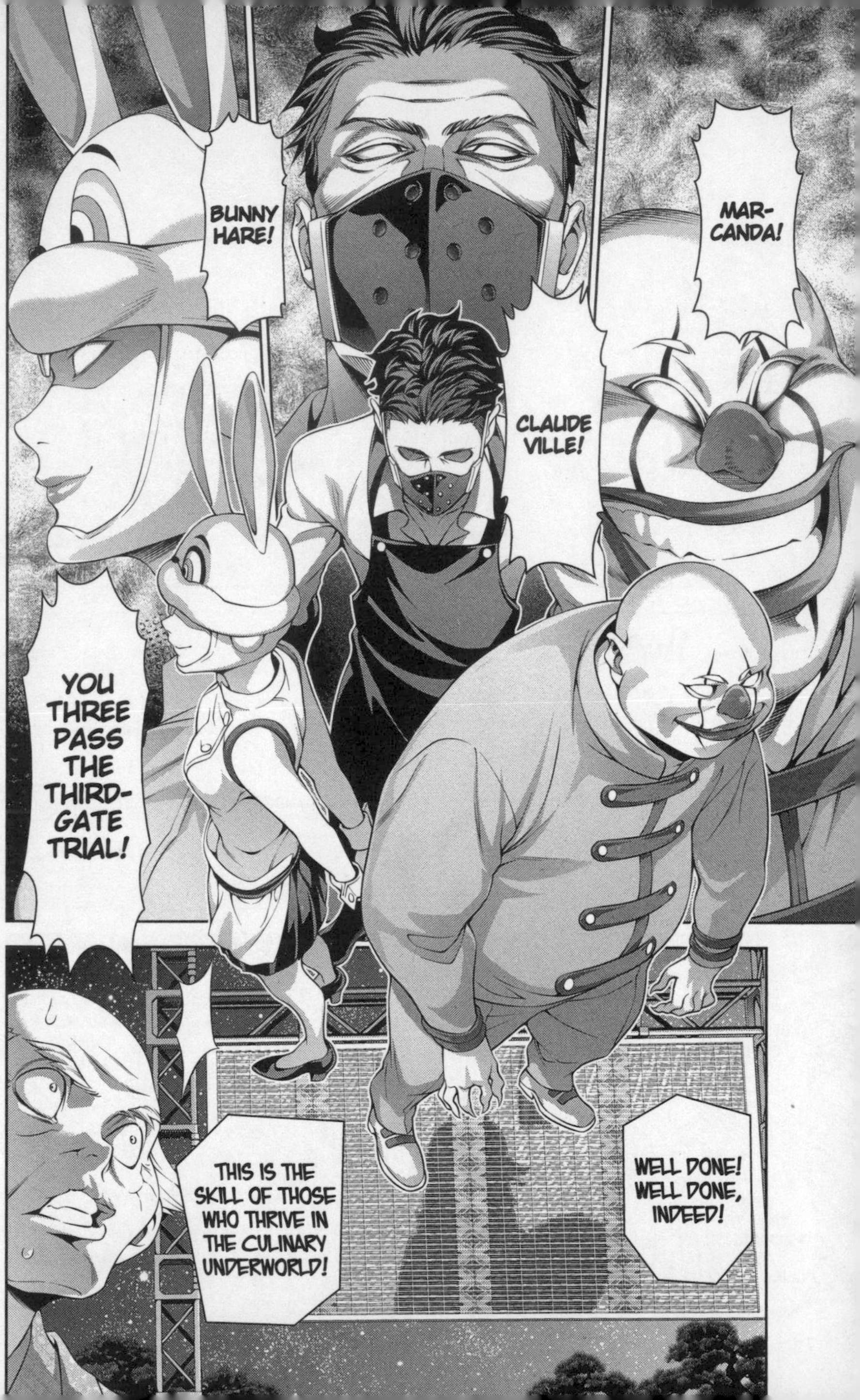
MAR-CANDA!
CLAUDE VILLE!
BUNNY HARE!
YOU THREE PASS THE THIRD-GATE TRIAL!
WELL DONE! WELL DONE, INDEED!
THIS IS THE SKILL OF THOSE WHO THRIVE IN THE CULINARY UNDERWORLD!

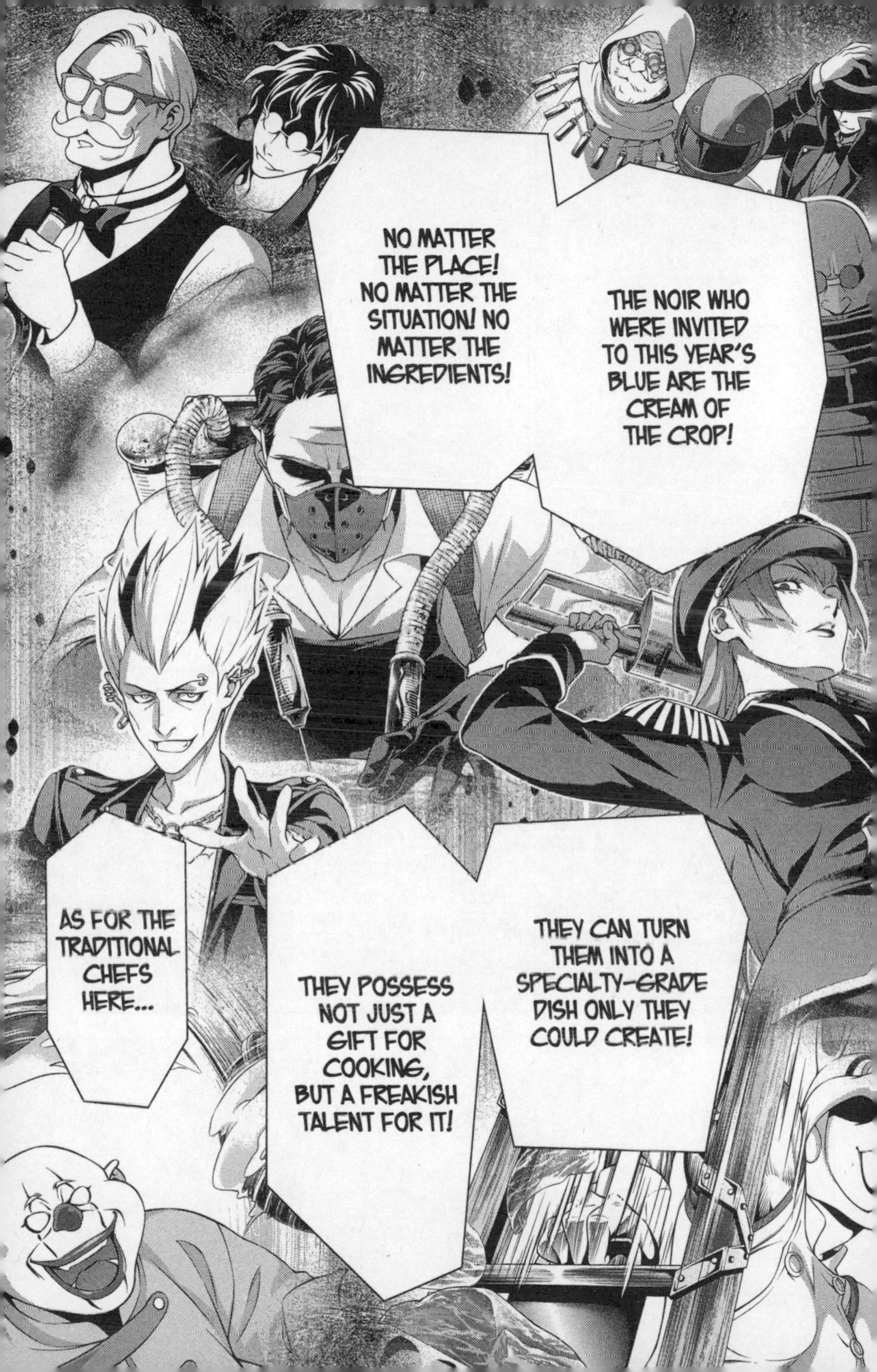
THE NOIR WHO WERE INVITED TO THIS YEAR'S BLUE ARE THE CREAM OF THE CROP!
NO MATTER THE PLACE! NO MATTER THE SITUATION! NO MATTER THE INGREDIENTS!
THEY CAN TURN THEM INTO A SPECIALTY-GRADE DISH ONLY THEY COULD CREATE!
THEY POSSESS NOT JUST A GIFT FOR COOKING, BUT A FREAKISH TALENT FOR IT!
AS FOR THE TRADITIONAL CHEFS HERE...

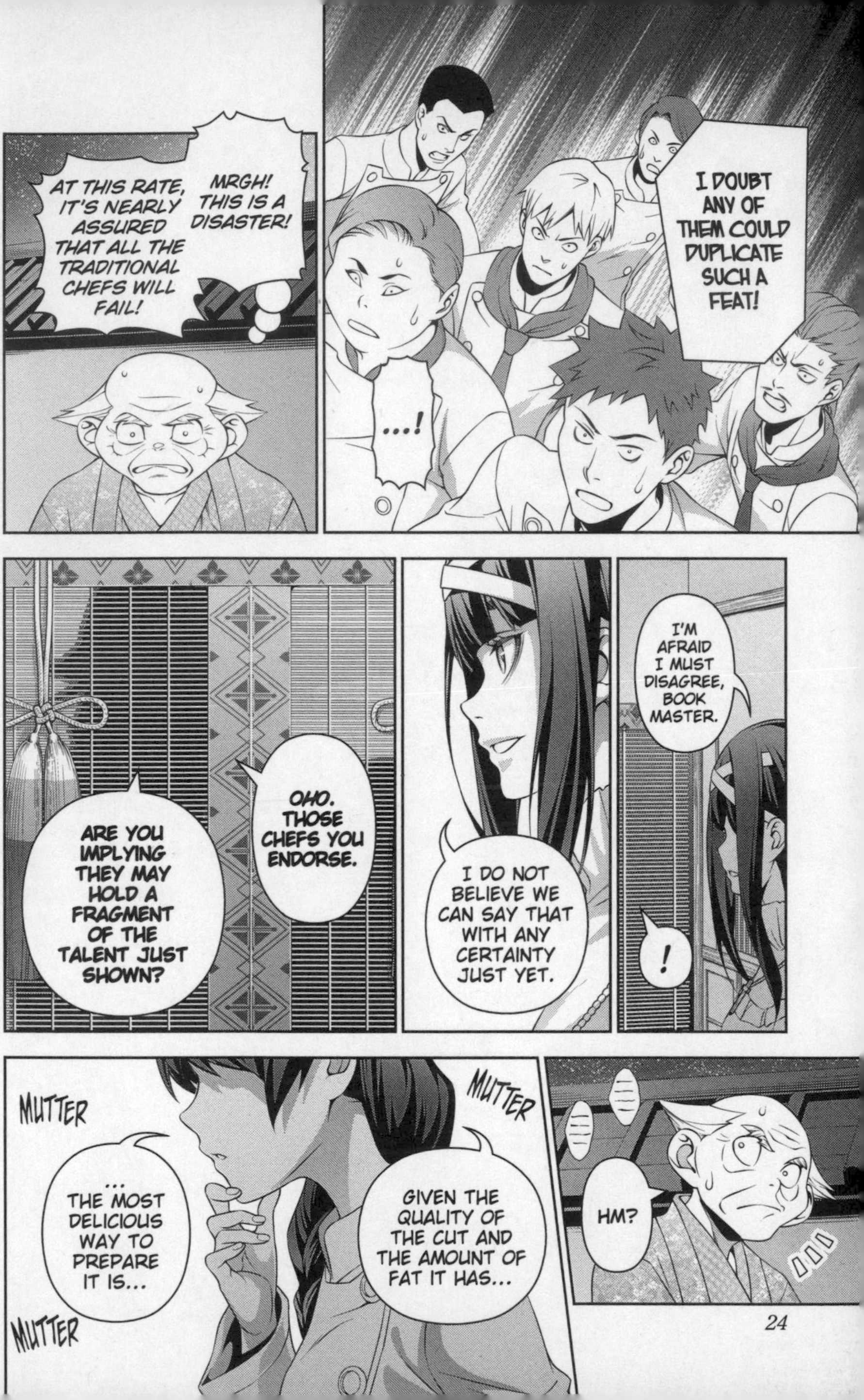
I DOUBT ANY OF THEM COULD DUPLICATE SUCH A FEAT!
...!
MRGH! THIS IS A DISASTER!
AT THIS RATE, IT'S NEARLY ASSURED THAT ALL THE TRADITIONAL CHEFS WILL FAIL!
I'M AFRAID I MUST DISAGREE, BOOK MASTER.
!
I DO NOT BELIEVE WE CAN SAY THAT WITH ANY CERTAINTY JUST YET.
OHO. THOSE CHEFS YOU ENDORSE.
ARE YOU IMPLYING THEY MAY HOLD A FRAGMENT OF THE TALENT JUST SHOWN?
HM?
MUTTER
GIVEN THE QUALITY OF THE CUT AND THE AMOUNT OF FAT IT HAS...
MUTTER
... THE MOST DELICIOUS WAY TO PREPARE IT IS...
MUTTER

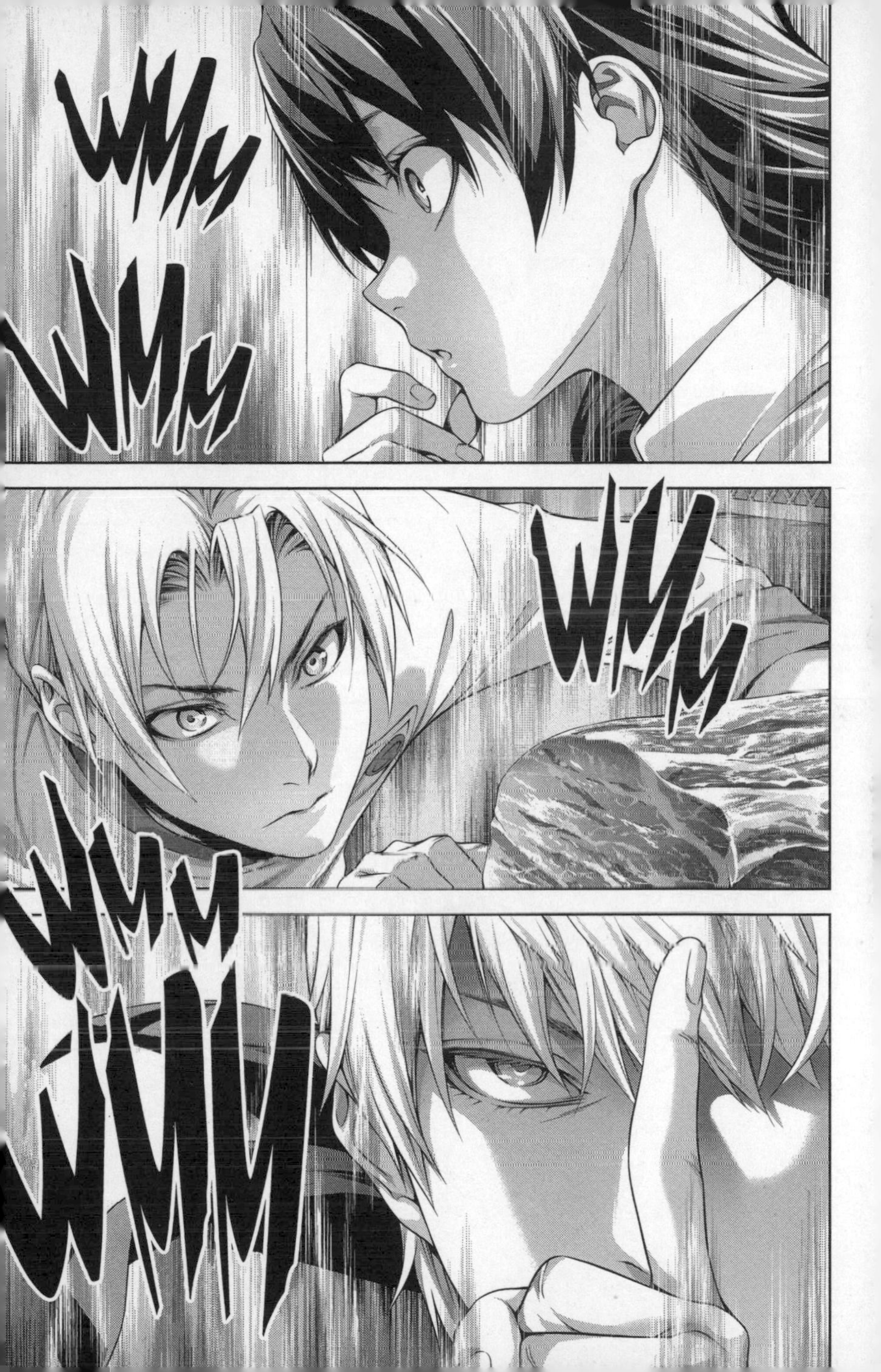
WMM
WMM
WMM
WMM
WMM

EASILY FITS ON
THE BACK FOR
CONVENIENT
TRANSPORT!

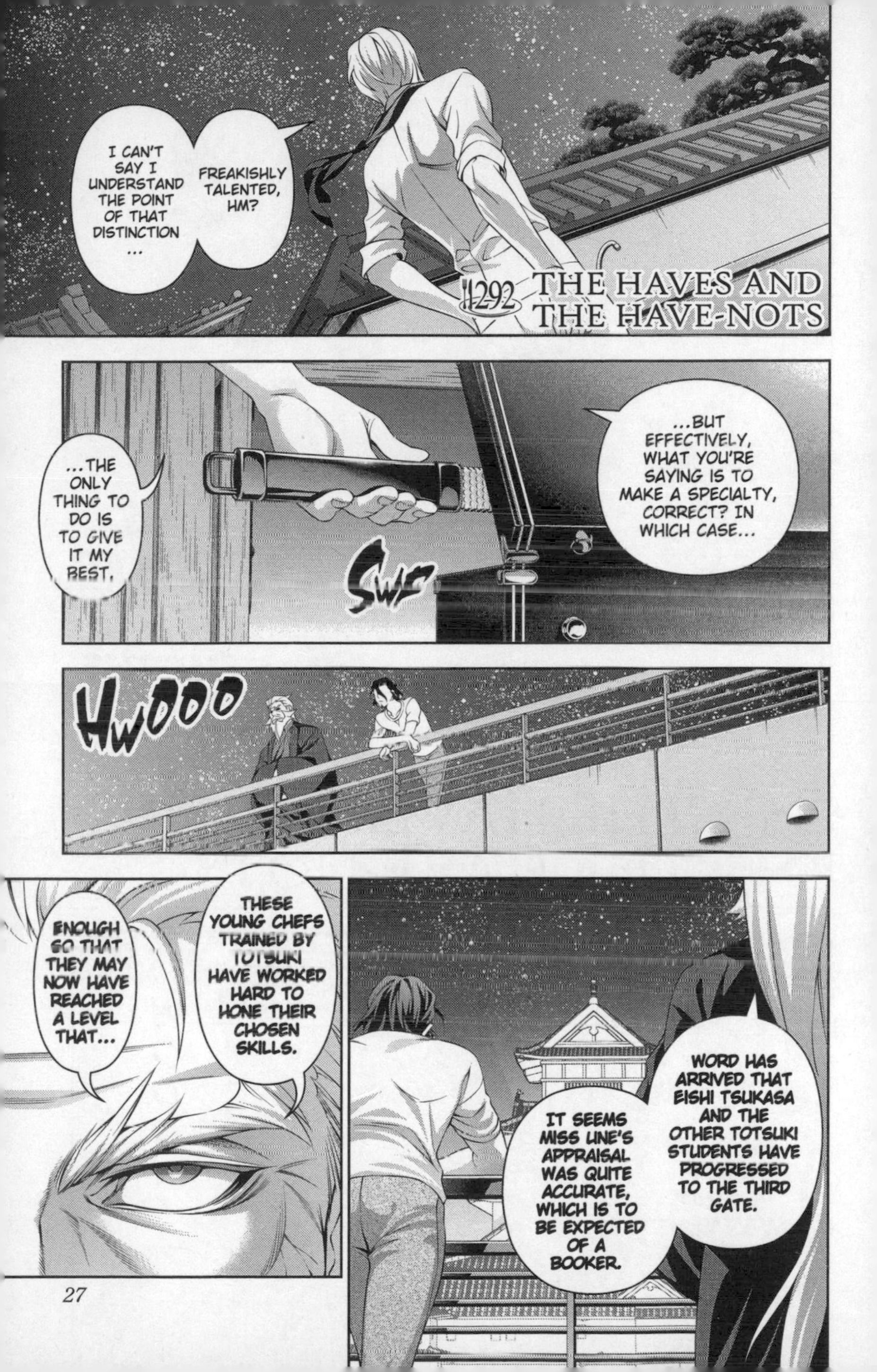
FREAKISHLY TALENTED, HM?
I CAN'T SAY I UNDERSTAND THE POINT OF THAT DISTINCTION ...
292 THE HAVES AND THE HAVE-NOTS
...BUT EFFECTIVELY, WHAT YOU'RE SAYING IS TO MAKE A SPECIALTY, CORRECT? IN WHICH CASE...
SWF
...THE ONLY THING TO DO IS TO GIVE IT MY BEST.
HWOOO
WORD HAS ARRIVED THAT EISHI TSUKASA AND THE OTHER TOTSUKI STUDENTS HAVE PROGRESSED TO THE THIRD GATE.
IT SEEMS MISS UNE'S APPRAISAL WAS QUITE ACCURATE, WHICH IS TO BE EXPECTED OF A BOOKER.
THESE YOUNG CHEFS TRAINED BY TOTSUKI HAVE WORKED HARD TO HONE THEIR CHOSEN SKILLS.
ENOUGH SO THAT THEY MAY NOW HAVE REACHED A LEVEL THAT...

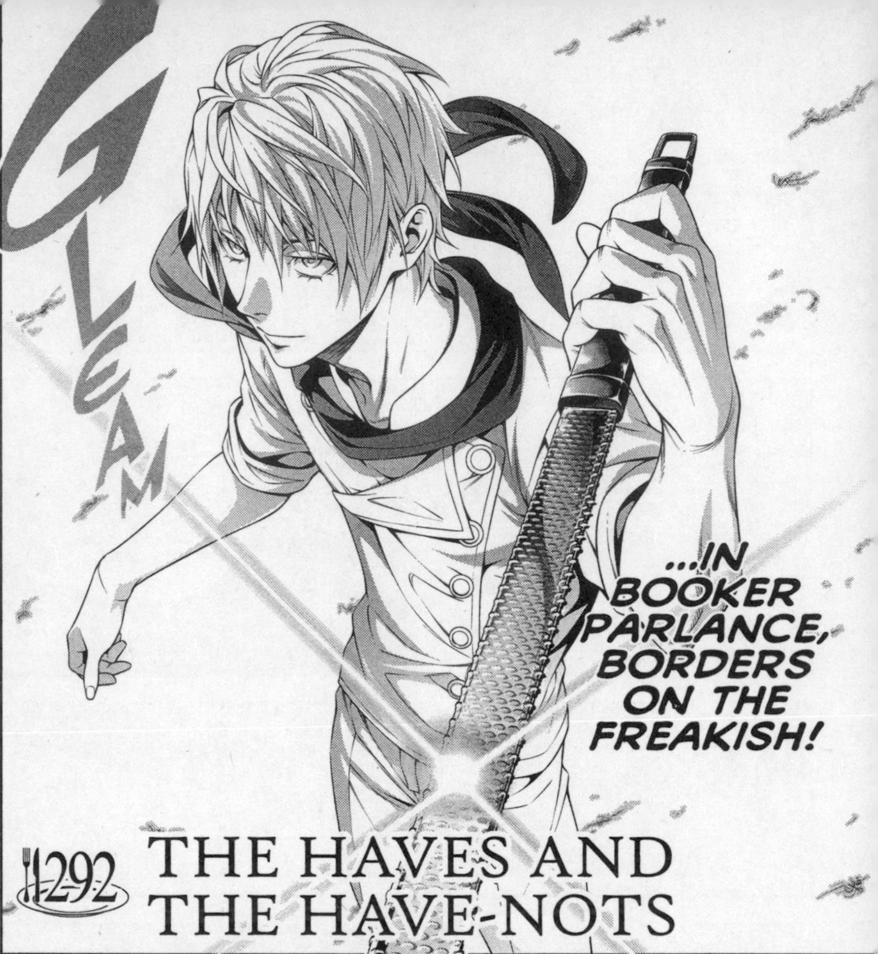
GLEAM
...IN BOOKER PARLANCE, BORDERS ON THE FREAKISH!

292 THE HAVES AND THE HAVE-NOTS

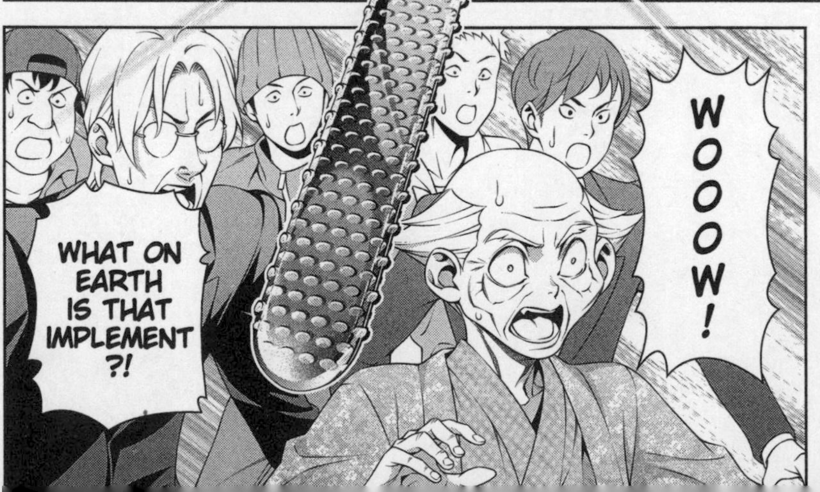
WOOOOW!
WHAT ON EARTH IS THAT IMPLEMENT?!

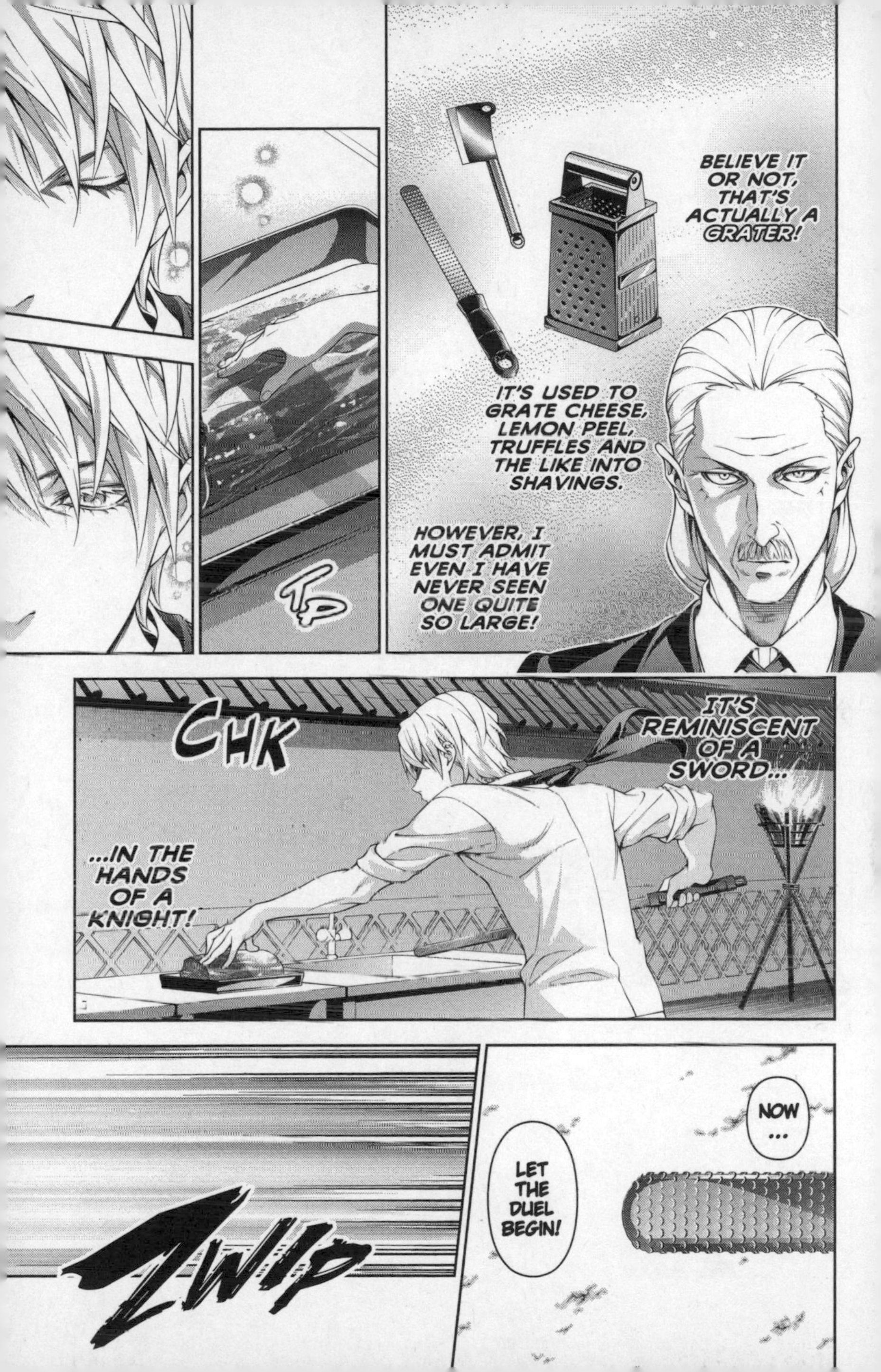
BELIEVE IT OR NOT, THAT'S ACTUALLY A GRATER!
IT'S USED TO GRATE CHEESE, LEMON PEEL, TRUFFLES AND THE LIKE INTO SHAVINGS.
HOWEVER, I MUST ADMIT EVEN I HAVE NEVER SEEN ONE QUITE SO LARGE!
TP
IT'S REMINISCENT OF A SWORD...
CHK
...IN THE HANDS OF A KNIGHT!
NOW ...
LET THE DUEL BEGIN!
ZWIP

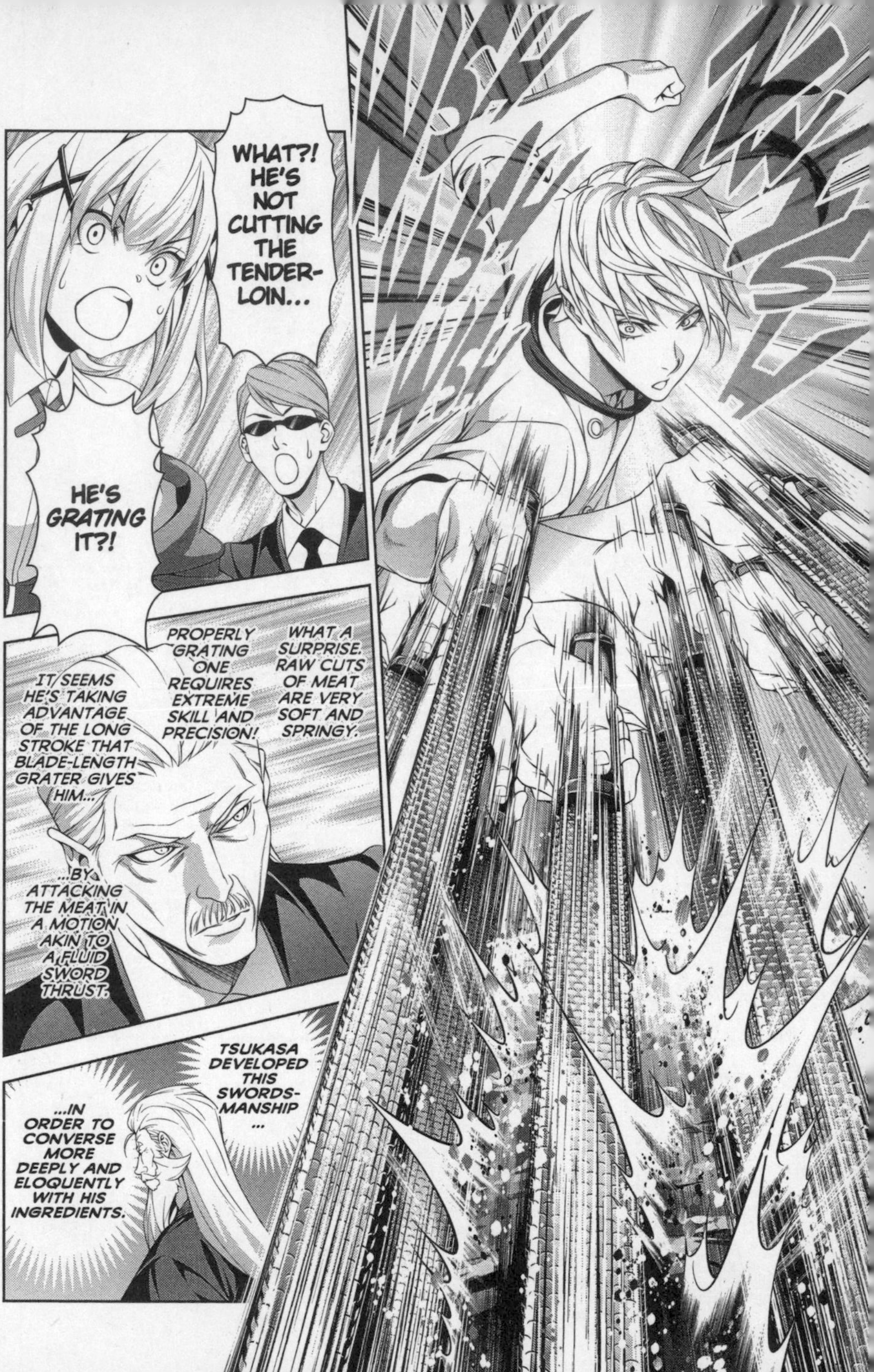
WHAT?! HE'S NOT CUTTING THE TENDER-LOIN...
HE'S GRATING IT?!
WHAT A SURPRISE. RAW CUTS OF MEAT ARE VERY SOFT AND SPRINGY.
PROPERLY GRATING ONE REQUIRES EXTREME SKILL AND PRECISION!
IT SEEMS HE'S TAKING ADVANTAGE OF THE LONG STROKE THAT BLADE-LENGTH GRATER GIVES HIM...
...BY ATTACKING THE MEAT IN A MOTION AKIN TO A FLUID SWORD THRUST.
TSUKASA DEVELOPED THIS SWORDS-MANSHIP...
...IN ORDER TO CONVERSE MORE DEEPLY AND ELOQUENTLY WITH HIS INGREDIENTS.

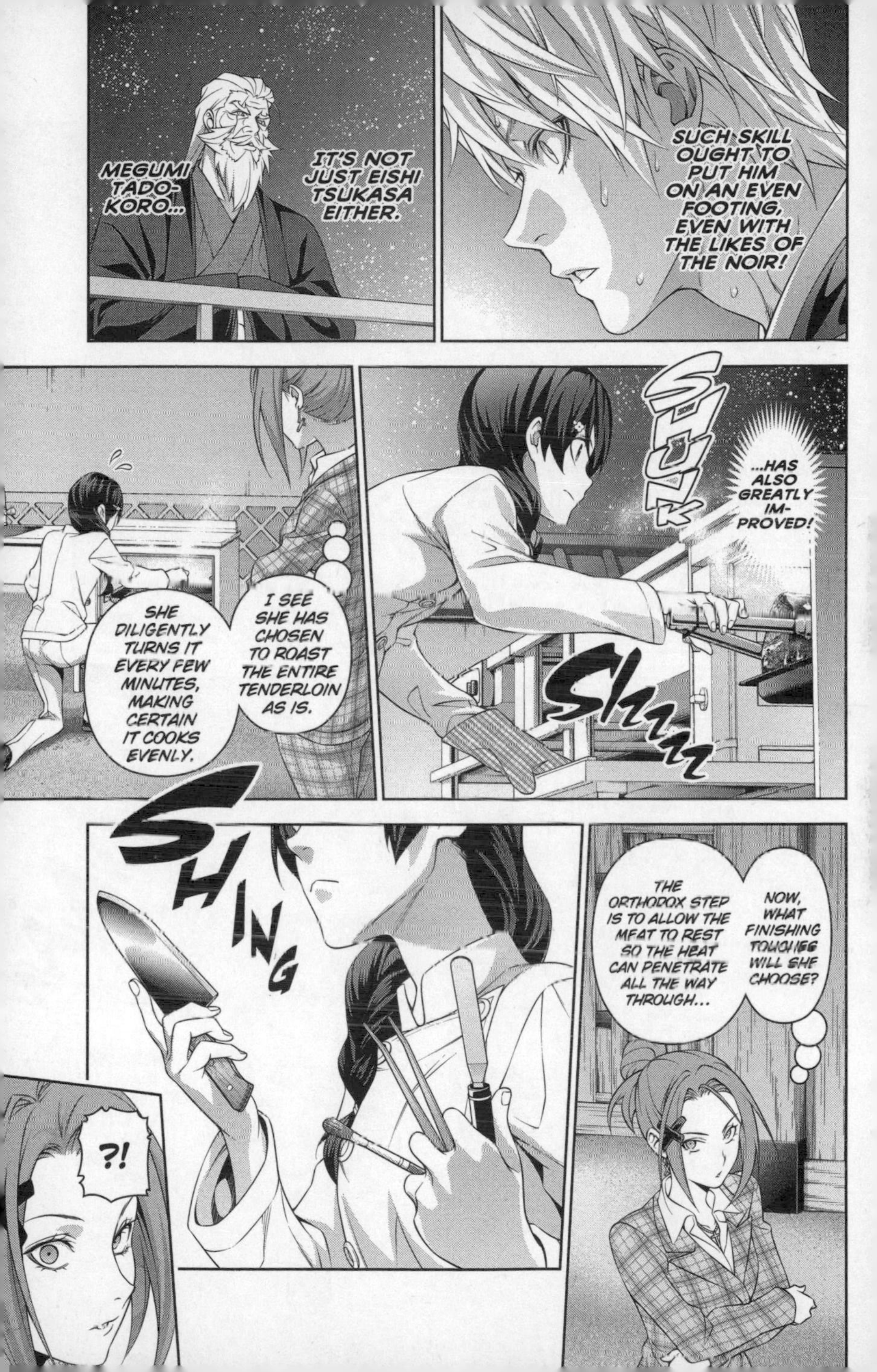
SUCH SKILL OUGHT TO PUT HIM ON AN EVEN FOOTING, EVEN WITH THE LIKES OF THE NOIR!
IT'S NOT JUST EISHI TSUKASA EITHER.
MEGUMI TADO-KORO...
SHUNK
...HAS ALSO GREATLY IM-PROVED!
SHZZZZ
I SEE SHE HAS CHOSEN TO ROAST THE ENTIRE TENDERLOIN AS IS.
SHE DILIGENTLY TURNS IT EVERY FEW MINUTES, MAKING CERTAIN IT COOKS EVENLY.
NOW, WHAT FINISHING TOUCHES WILL SHE CHOOSE?
THE ORTHODOX STEP IS TO ALLOW THE MEAT TO REST SO THE HEAT CAN PENETRATE ALL THE WAY THROUGH...
SHING
?!

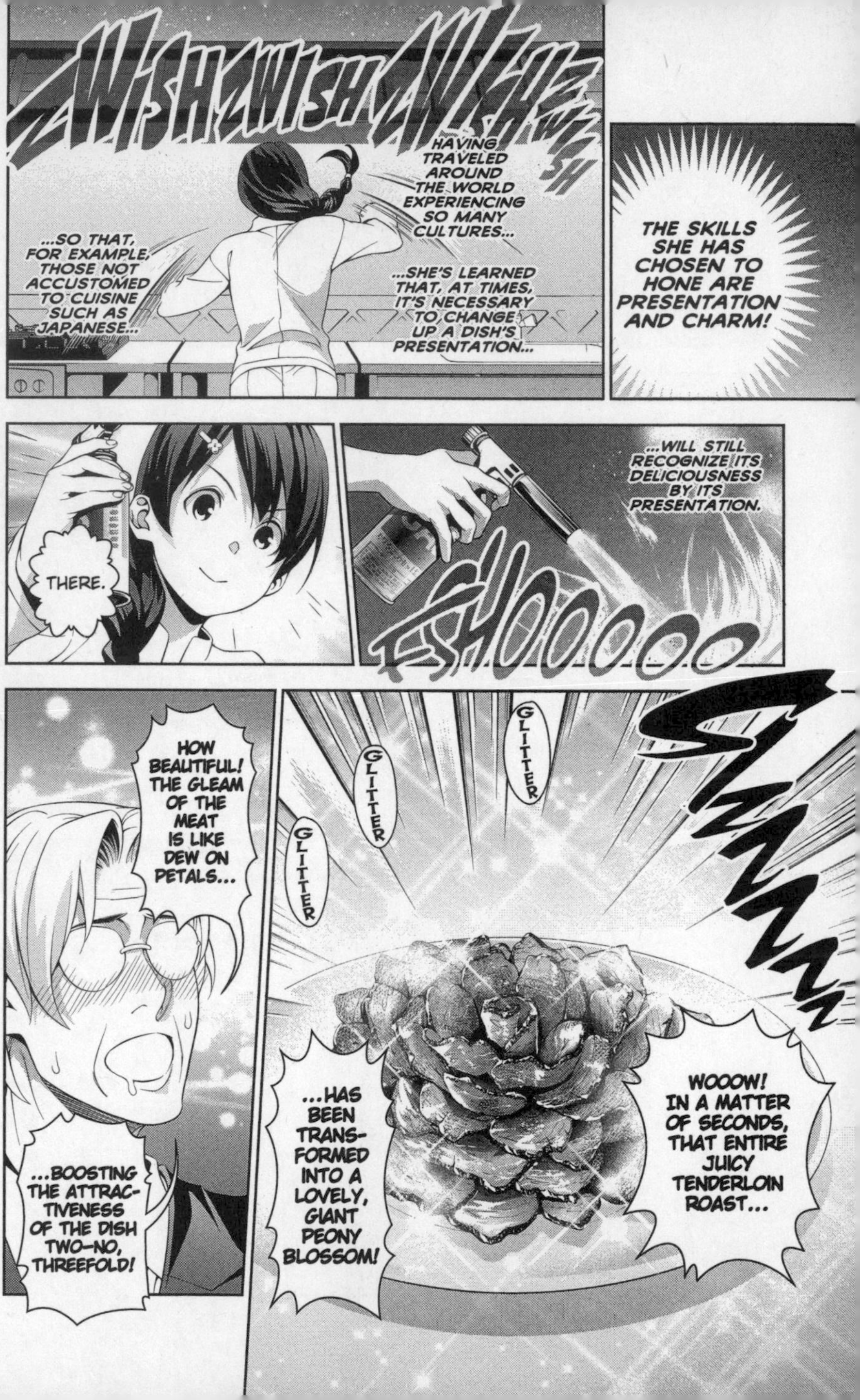
THE SKILLS SHE HAS CHOSEN TO HONE ARE PRESENTATION AND CHARM!
WISH WISH
HAVING TRAVELED AROUND THE WORLD EXPERIENCING SO MANY CULTURES...
...SHE'S LEARNED THAT, AT TIMES, IT'S NECESSARY TO CHANGE UP A DISH'S PRESENTATION...
...SO THAT, FOR EXAMPLE, THOSE NOT ACCUSTOMED TO CUISINE SUCH AS JAPANESE...
...WILL STILL RECOGNIZE ITS DELICIOUSNESS BY ITS PRESENTATION.
FSHOOOOOO
THERE.
GLITTER
GLITTER
GLITTER
WOOOW! IN A MATTER OF SECONDS, THAT ENTIRE JUICY TENDERLOIN ROAST...
...HAS BEEN TRANSFORMED INTO A LOVELY, GIANT PEONY BLOSSOM!
HOW BEAUTIFUL! THE GLEAM OF THE MEAT IS LIKE DEW ON PETALS...
...BOOSTING THE ATTRACTIVENESS OF THE DISH TWO—NO, THREEFOLD!

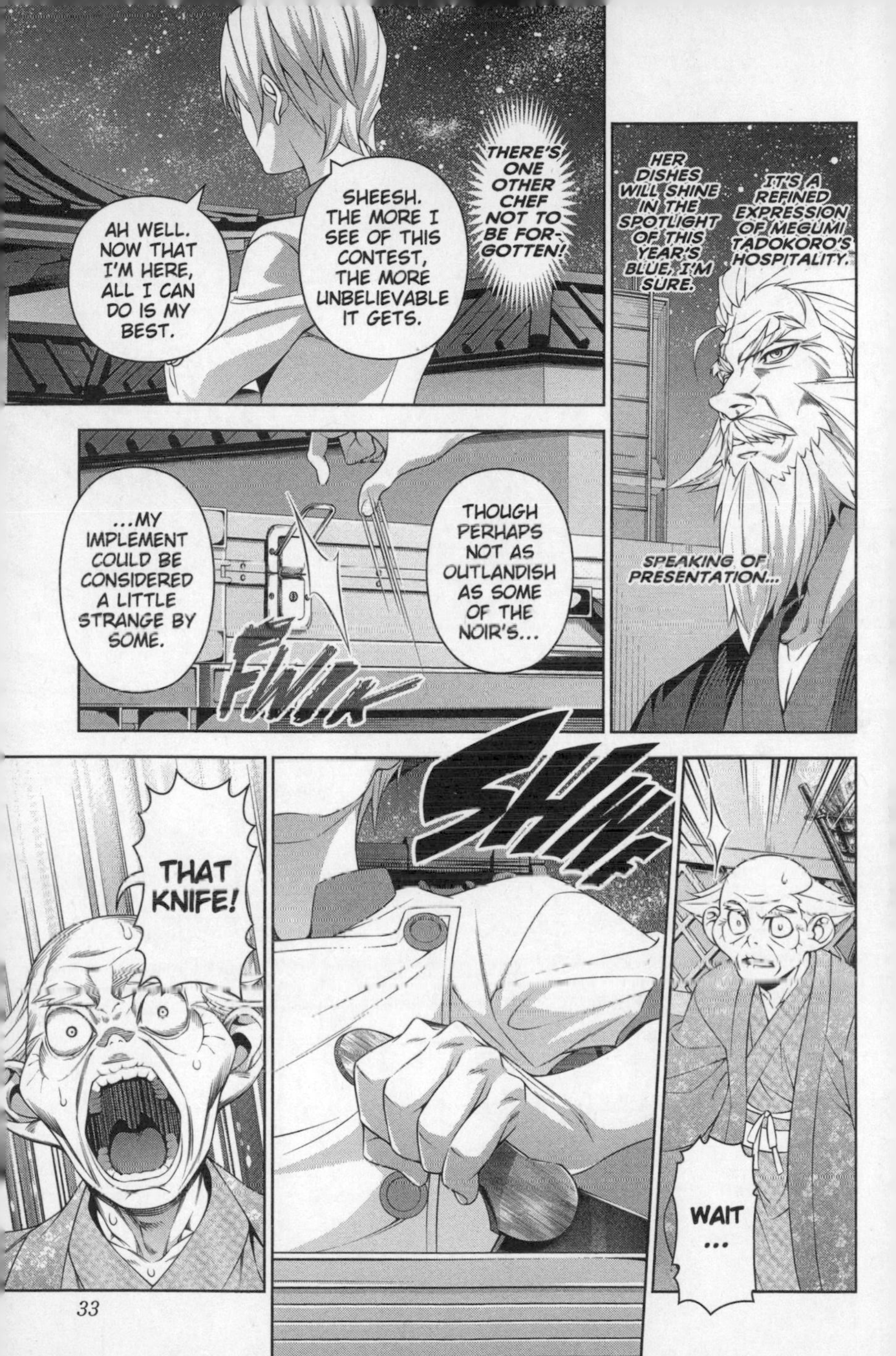
IT'S A REFINED EXPRESSION OF MEGUMI TADOKORO'S HOSPITALITY.
HER DISHES WILL SHINE IN THE SPOTLIGHT OF THIS YEAR'S BLUE, I'M SURE.
SPEAKING OF PRESENTATION...
THERE'S ONE OTHER CHEF NOT TO BE FOR-GOTTEN!
SHEESH. THE MORE I SEE OF THIS CONTEST, THE MORE UNBELIEVABLE IT GETS.
AH WELL. NOW THAT I'M HERE, ALL I CAN DO IS MY BEST.
THOUGH PERHAPS NOT AS OUTLANDISH AS SOME OF THE NOIR'S...
...MY IMPLEMENT COULD BE CONSIDERED A LITTLE STRANGE BY SOME.
FWIK
WAIT ...
THAT KNIFE!

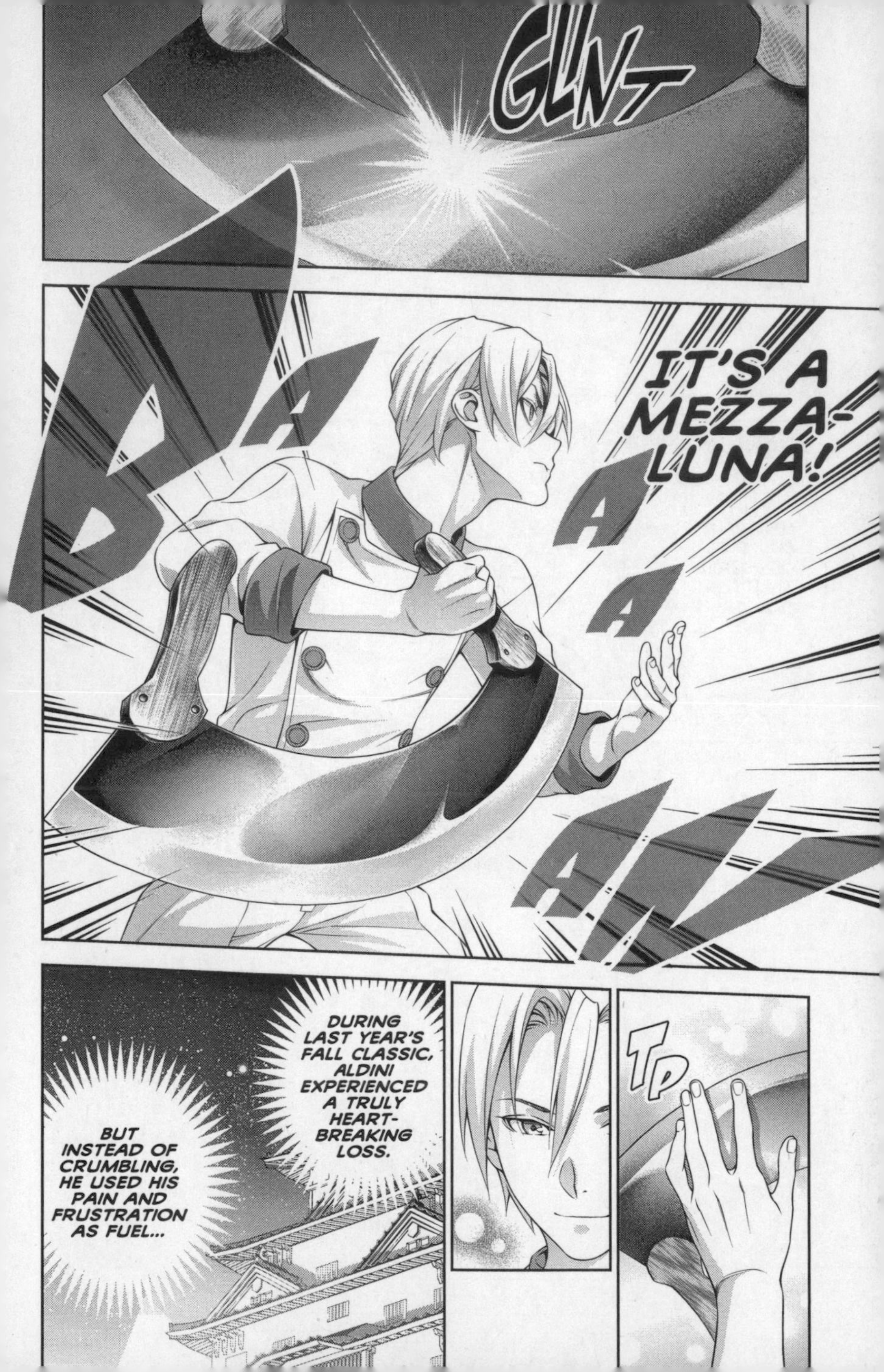
GLINT
BAAAAA
IT'S A MEZZA-LUNA!
TP
DURING LAST YEAR'S FALL CLASSIC, ALDINI EXPERIENCED A TRULY HEART-BREAKING LOSS.
BUT INSTEAD OF CRUMBLING, HE USED HIS PAIN AND FRUSTRATION AS FUEL...

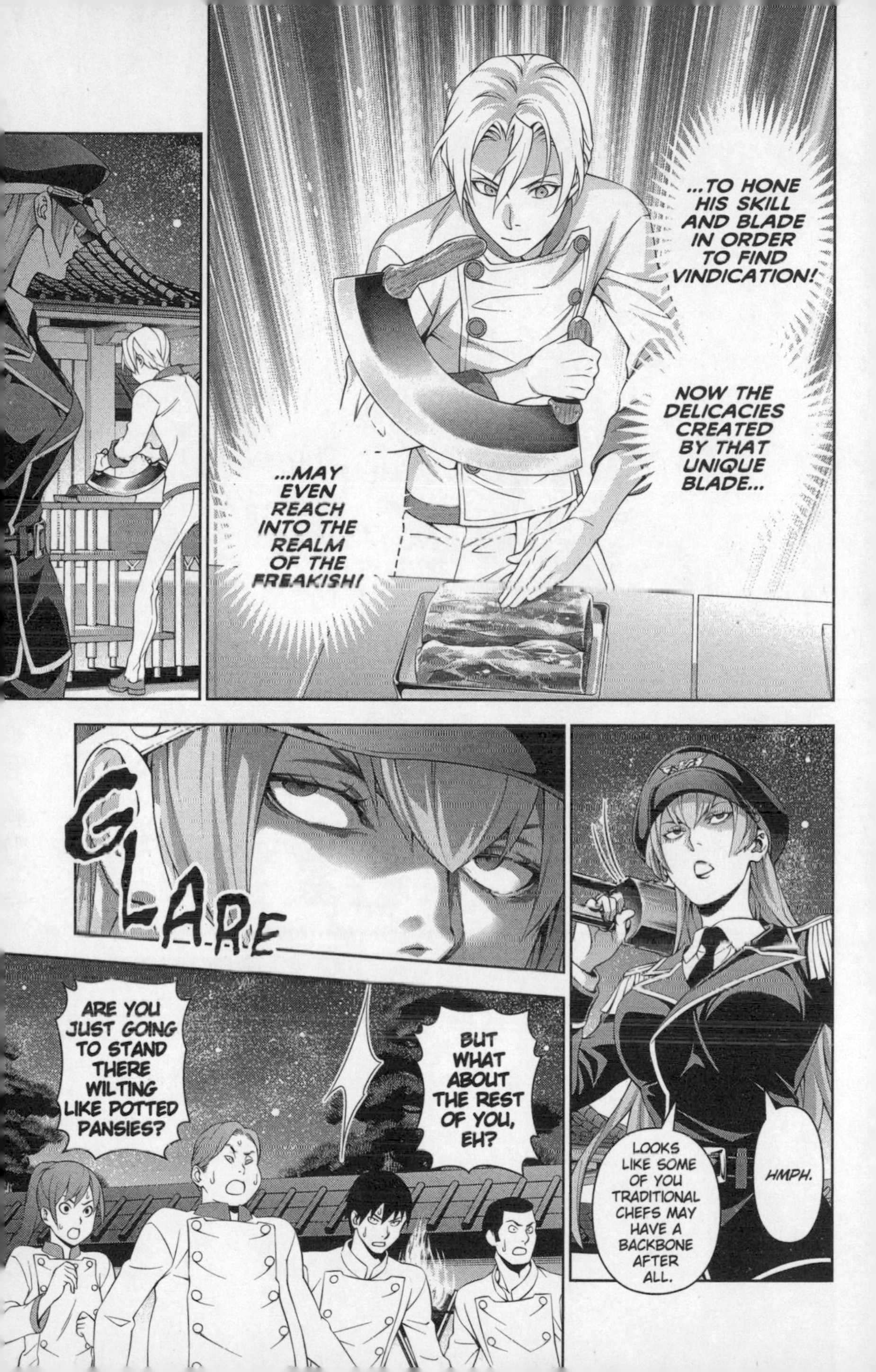
...TO HONE HIS SKILL AND BLADE IN ORDER TO FIND VINDICATION!
NOW THE DELICACIES CREATED BY THAT UNIQUE BLADE...
...MAY EVEN REACH INTO THE REALM OF THE FREAKISH!
HMPH.
LOOKS LIKE SOME OF YOU TRADITIONAL CHEFS MAY HAVE A BACKBONE AFTER ALL.
GLARE
BUT WHAT ABOUT THE REST OF YOU, EH?
ARE YOU JUST GOING TO STAND THERE WILTING LIKE POTTED PANSIES?

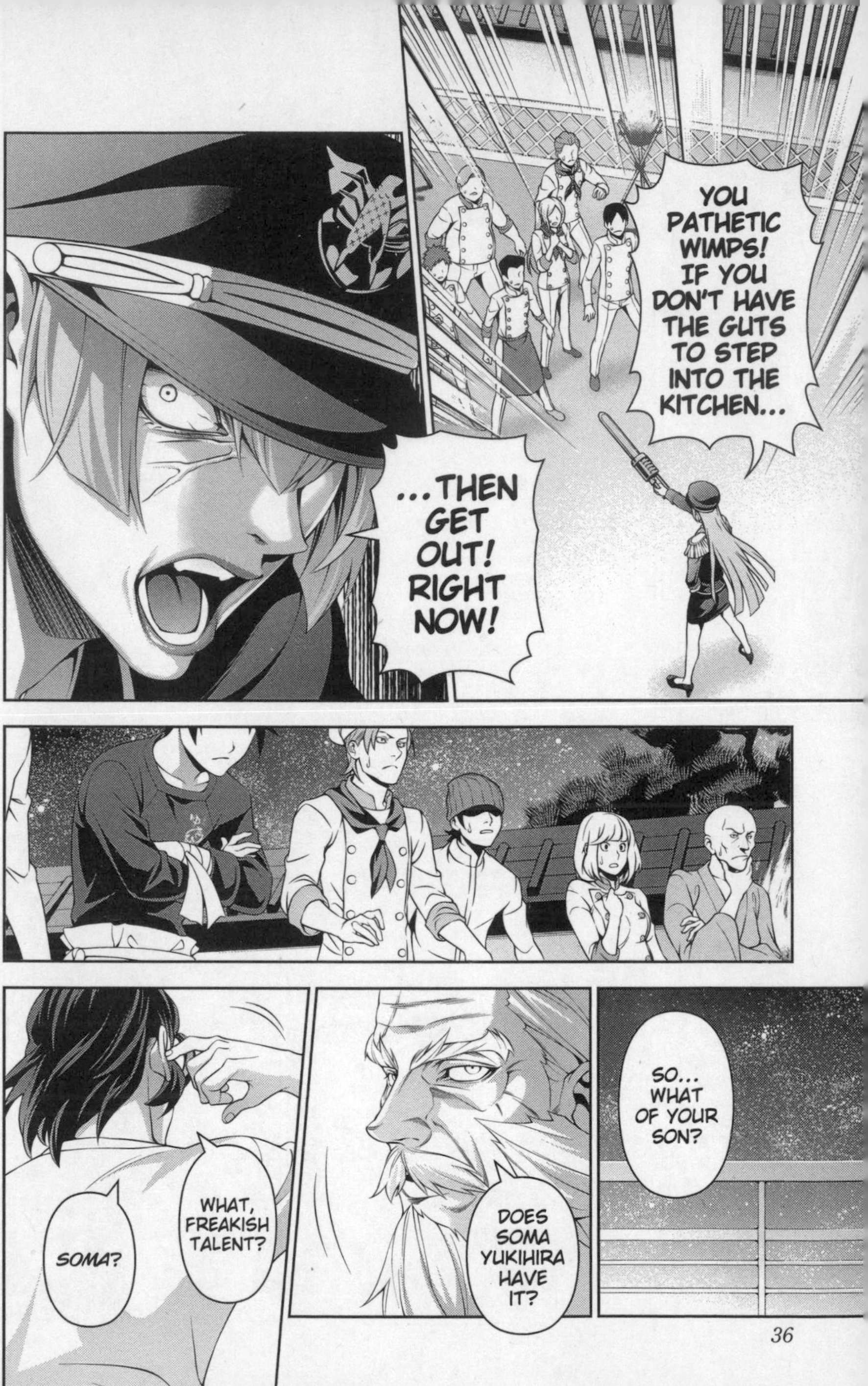
YOU PATHETIC WIMPS! IF YOU DON'T HAVE THE GUTS TO STEP INTO THE KITCHEN...
...THEN GET OUT! RIGHT NOW!
SO... WHAT OF YOUR SON?
DOES SOMA YUKIHIRA HAVE IT?
WHAT, FREAKISH TALENT?
SOMA?

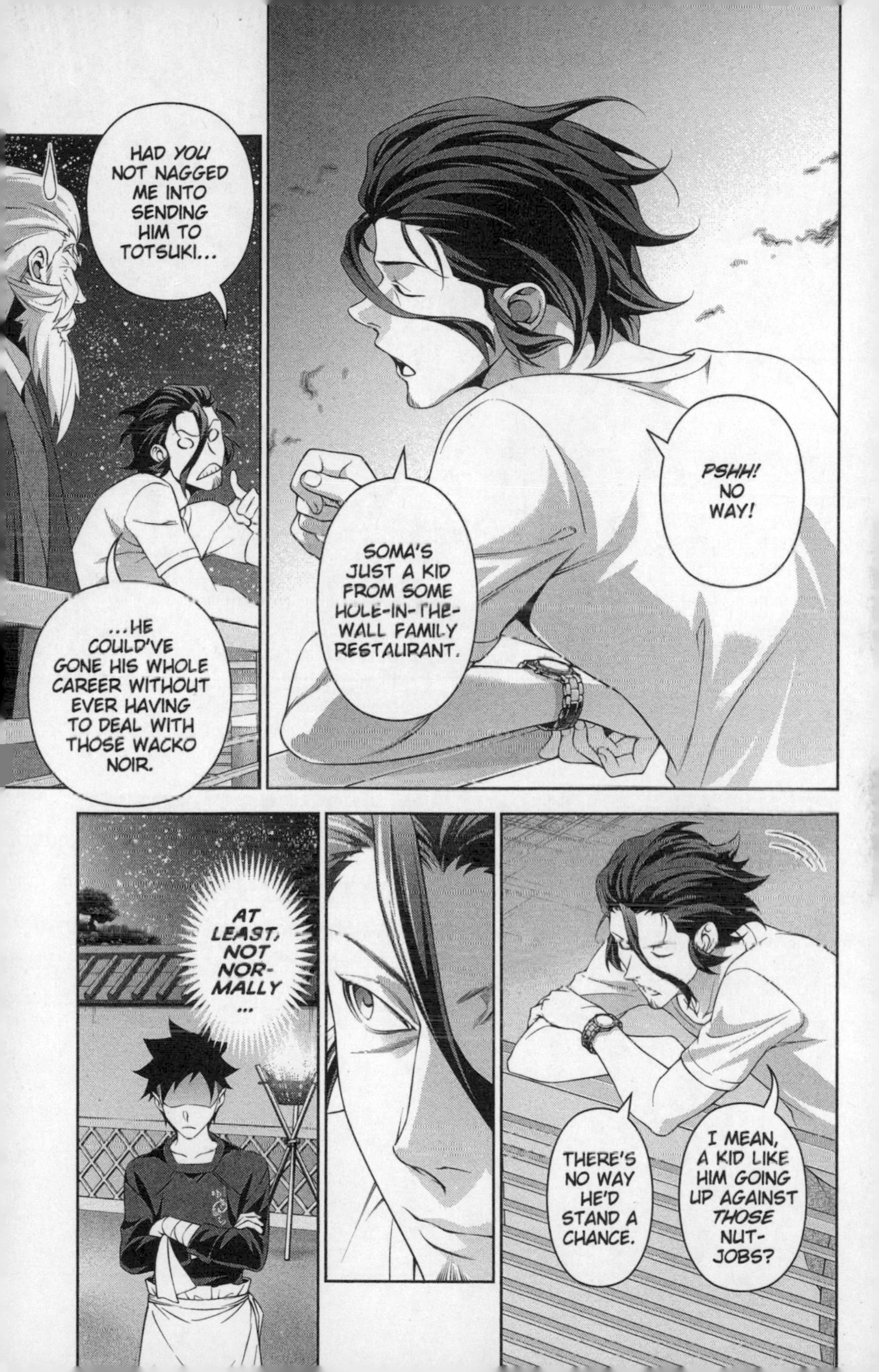

PSHH! NO WAY!
SOMA'S JUST A KID FROM SOME HOLE-IN-THE-WALL FAMILY RESTAURANT.
HAD YOU NOT NAGGED ME INTO SENDING HIM TO TOTSUKI...
...HE COULD'VE GONE HIS WHOLE CAREER WITHOUT EVER HAVING TO DEAL WITH THOSE WACKO NOIR.
I MEAN, A KID LIKE HIM GOING UP AGAINST THOSE NUT-JOBS?
THERE'S NO WAY HE'D STAND A CHANCE.
AT LEAST, NOT NORMALLY...

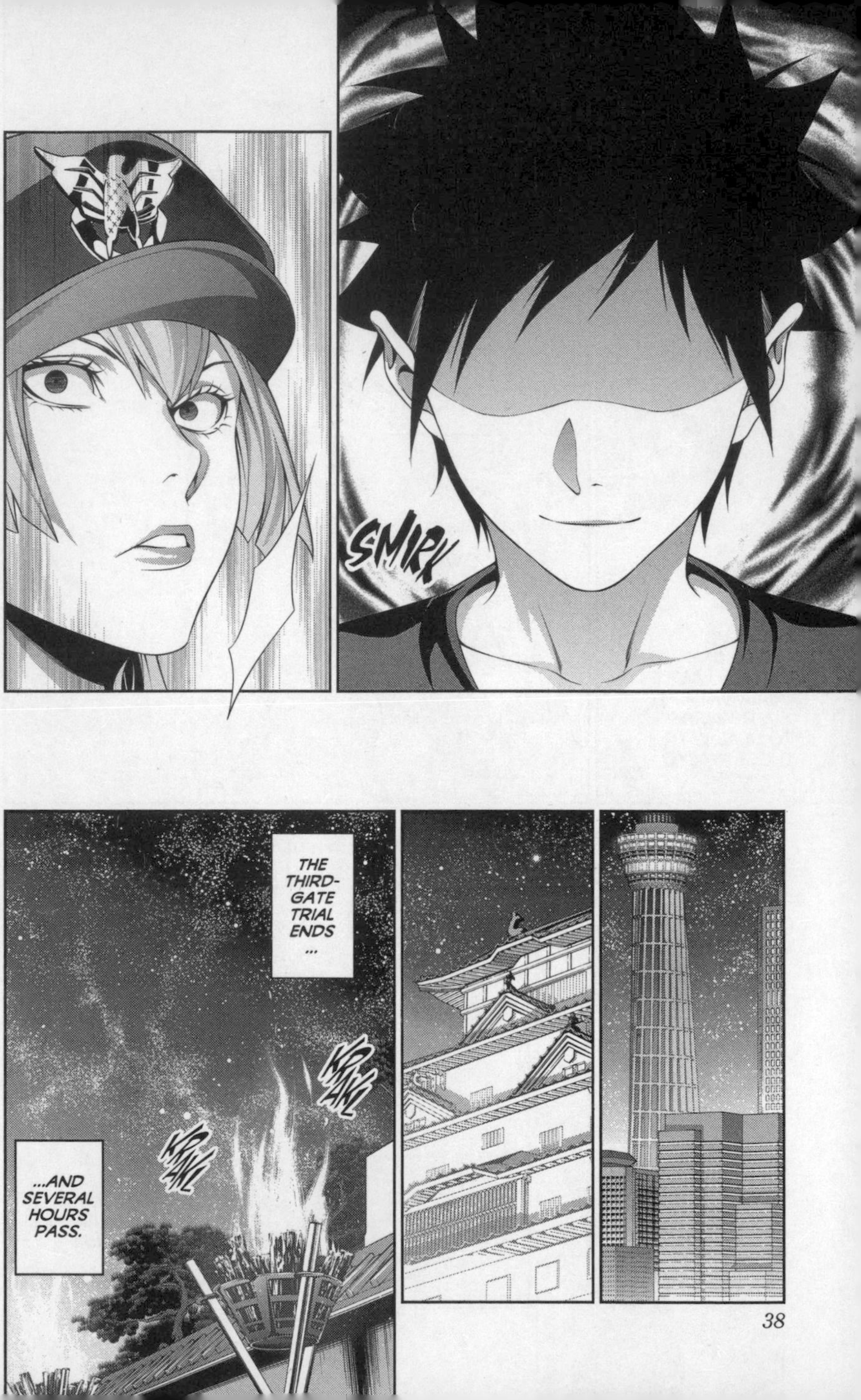
SMIRK
THE THIRD-GATE TRIAL ENDS...
KRAKL
KRAKL
...AND SEVERAL HOURS PASS.

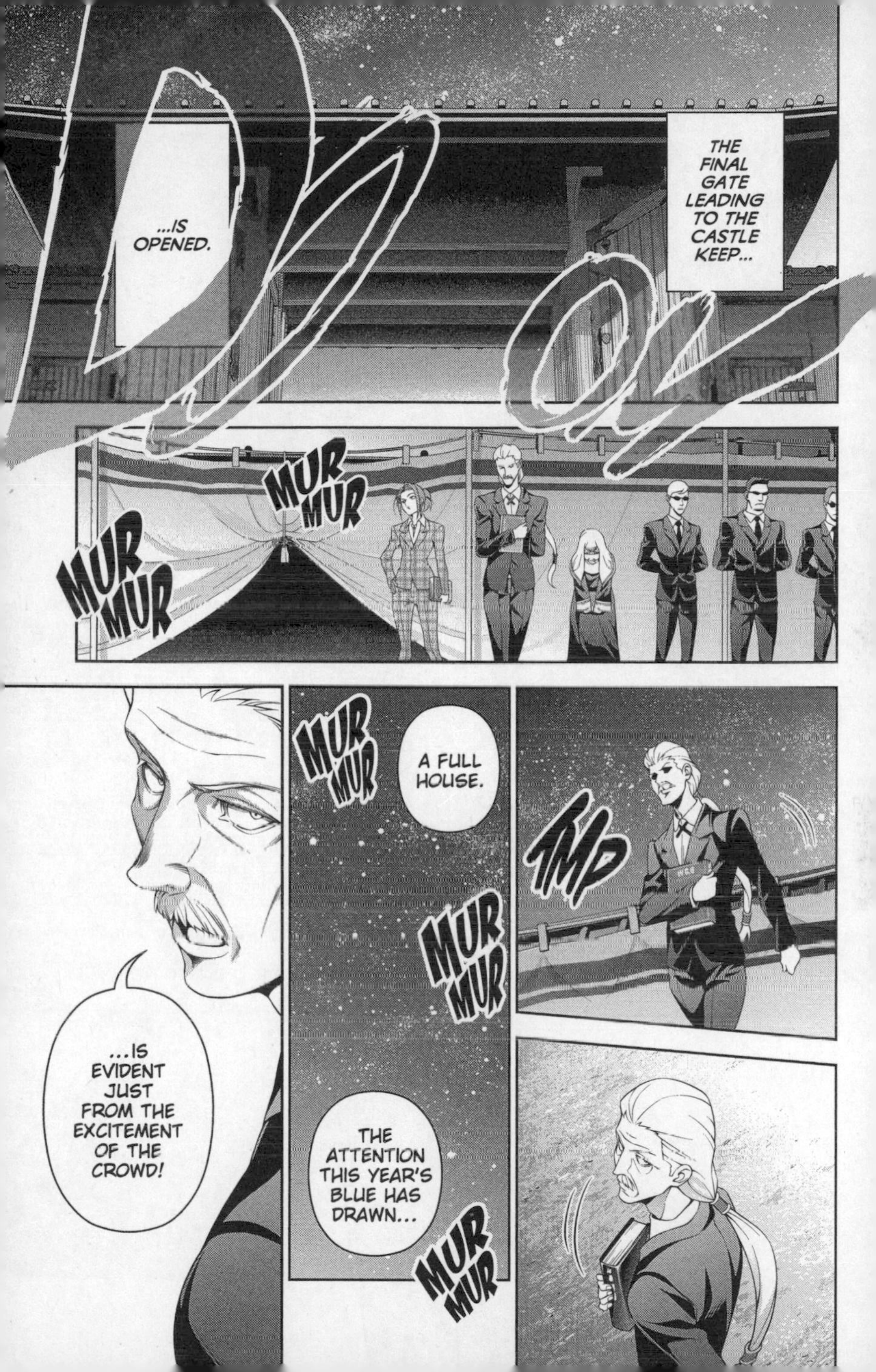
THE FINAL GATE LEADING TO THE CASTLE KEEP...
...IS OPENED.
MUR MUR
MUR MUR
TMP
MUR MUR
MUR MUR
A FULL HOUSE.
THE ATTENTION THIS YEAR'S BLUE HAS DRAWN...
MUR MUR
...IS EVIDENT JUST FROM THE EXCITEMENT OF THE CROWD!

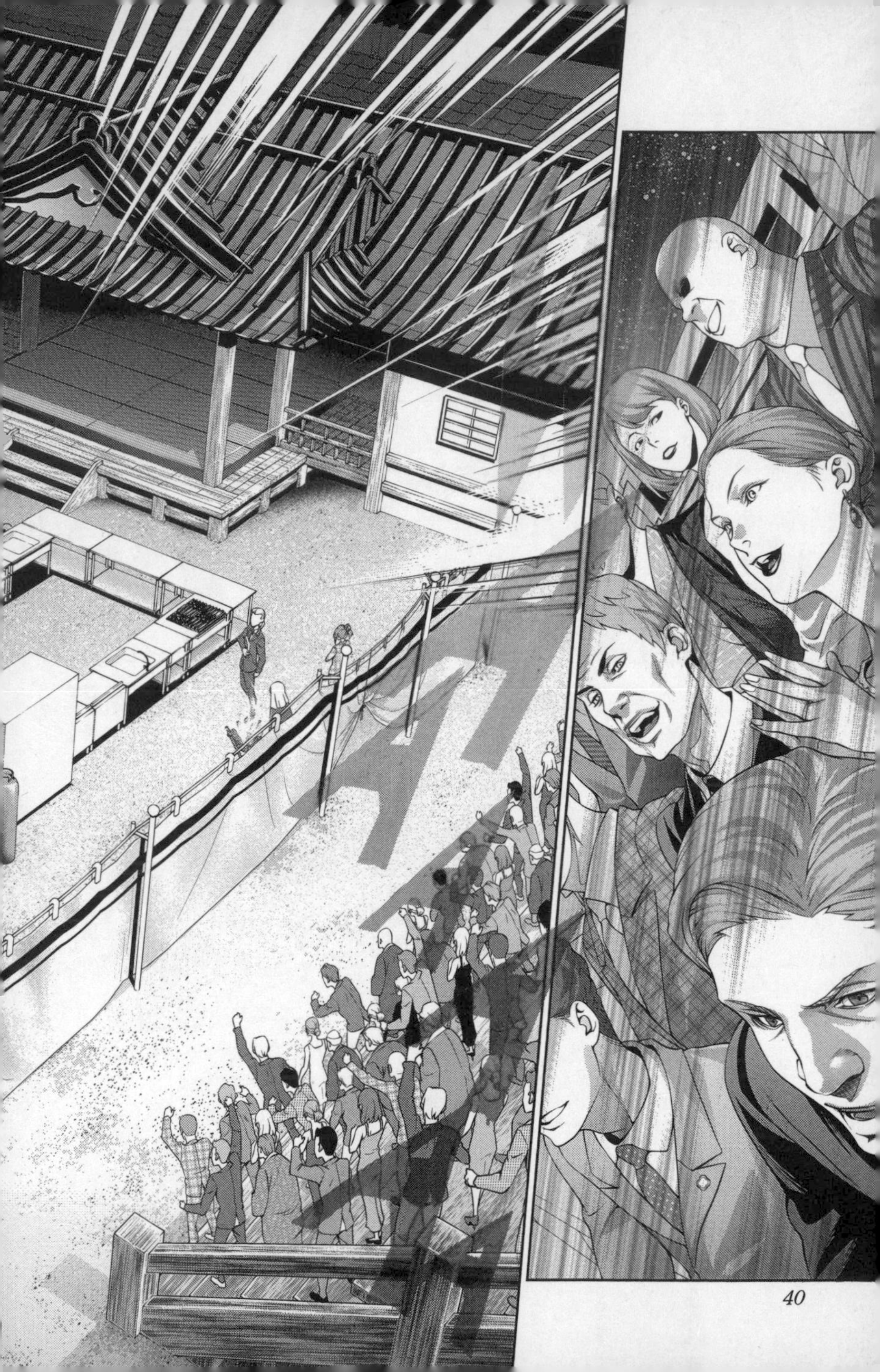

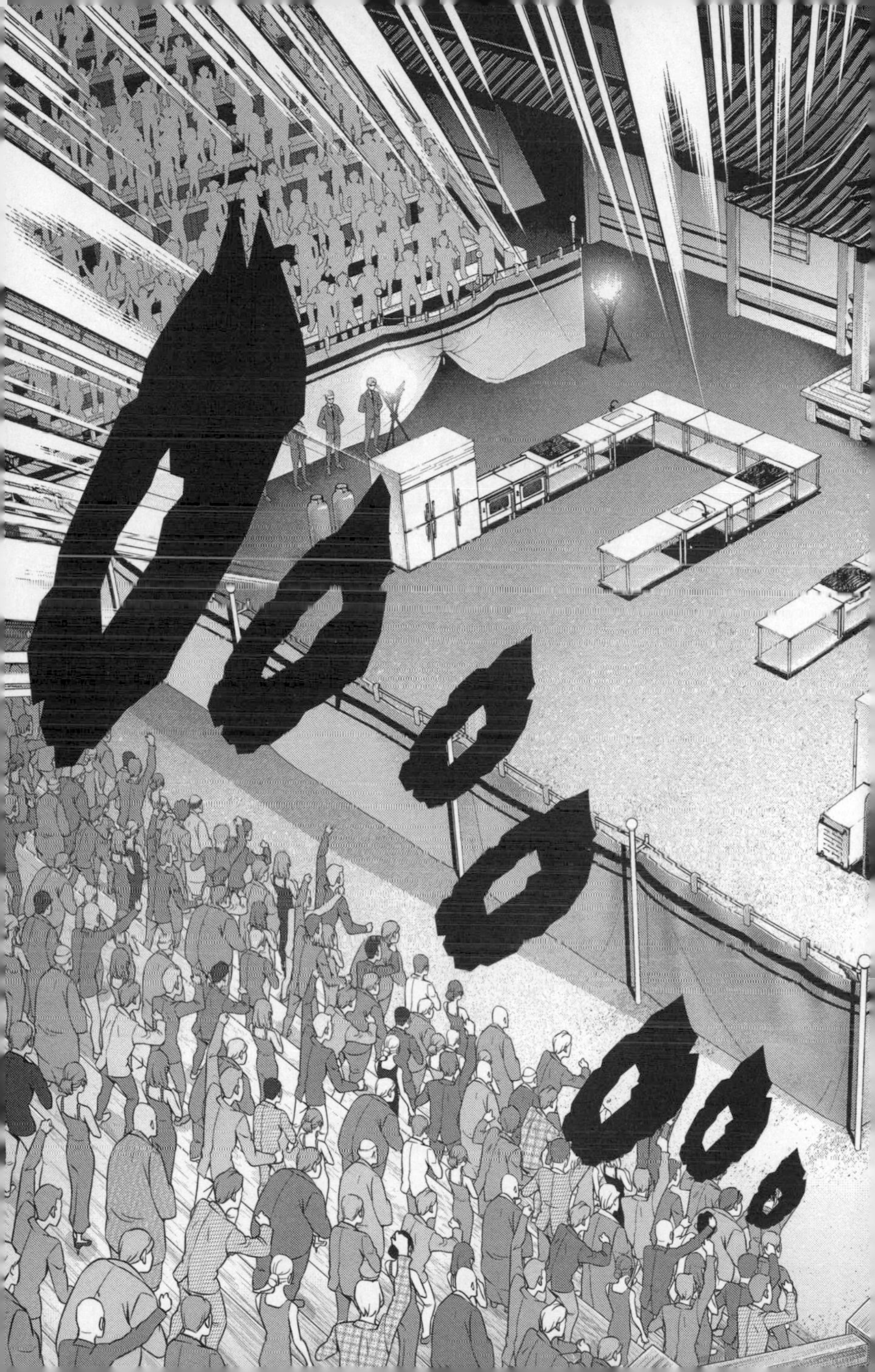

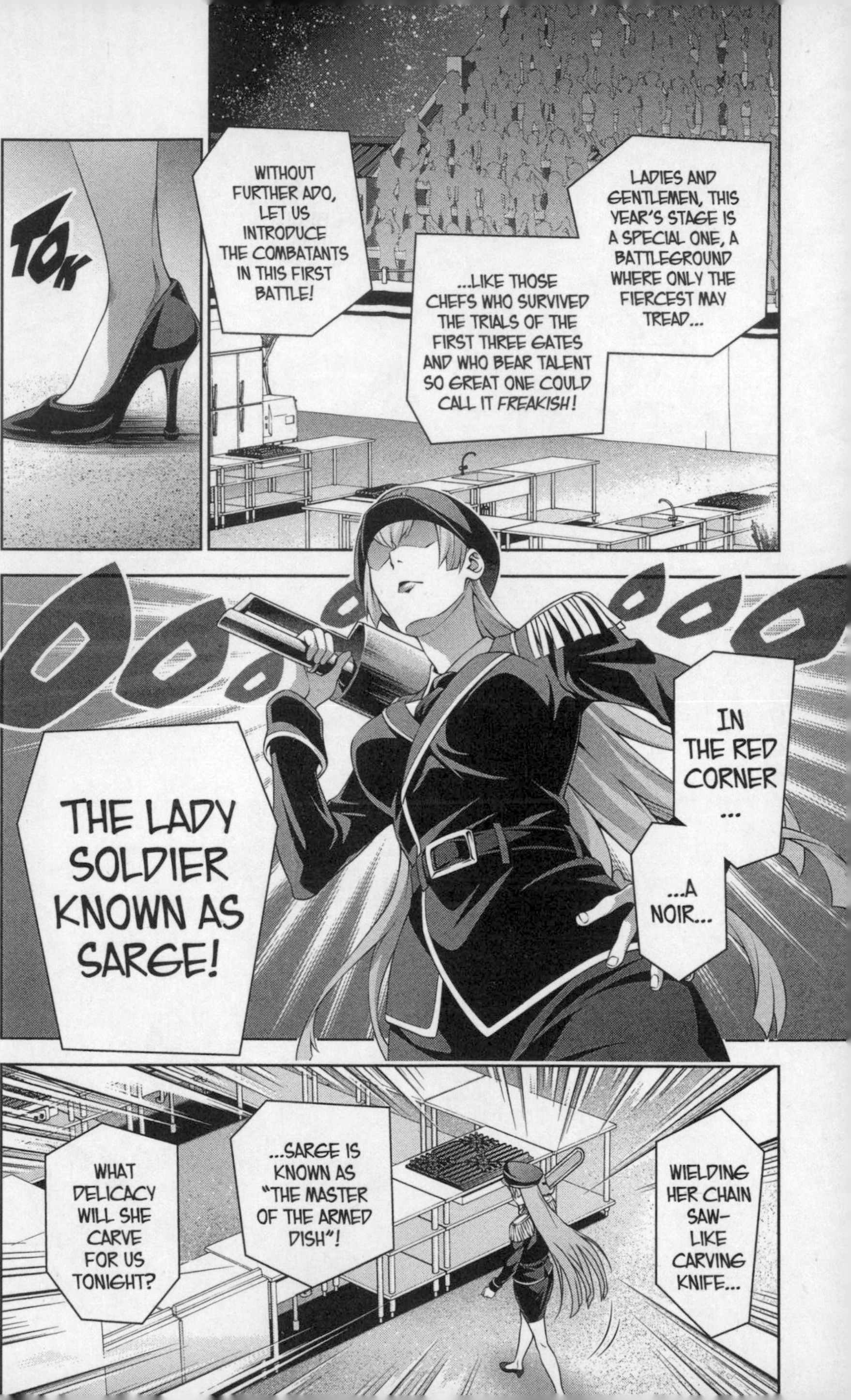
LADIES AND GENTLEMEN, THIS YEAR'S STAGE IS A SPECIAL ONE, A BATTLEGROUND WHERE ONLY THE FIERCEST MAY TREAD...
...LIKE THOSE CHEFS WHO SURVIVED THE TRIALS OF THE FIRST THREE GATES AND WHO BEAR TALENT SO GREAT ONE COULD CALL IT *FREAKISH*!
WITHOUT FURTHER ADO, LET US INTRODUCE THE COMBATANTS IN THIS FIRST BATTLE!
TOK
IN THE RED CORNER ...
...A NOIR...
THE LADY SOLDIER KNOWN AS SARGE!
WIELDING HER CHAIN SAW-LIKE CARVING KNIFE...
...SARGE IS KNOWN AS "THE MASTER OF THE ARMED DISH"!
WHAT DELICACY WILL SHE CARVE FOR US TONIGHT?

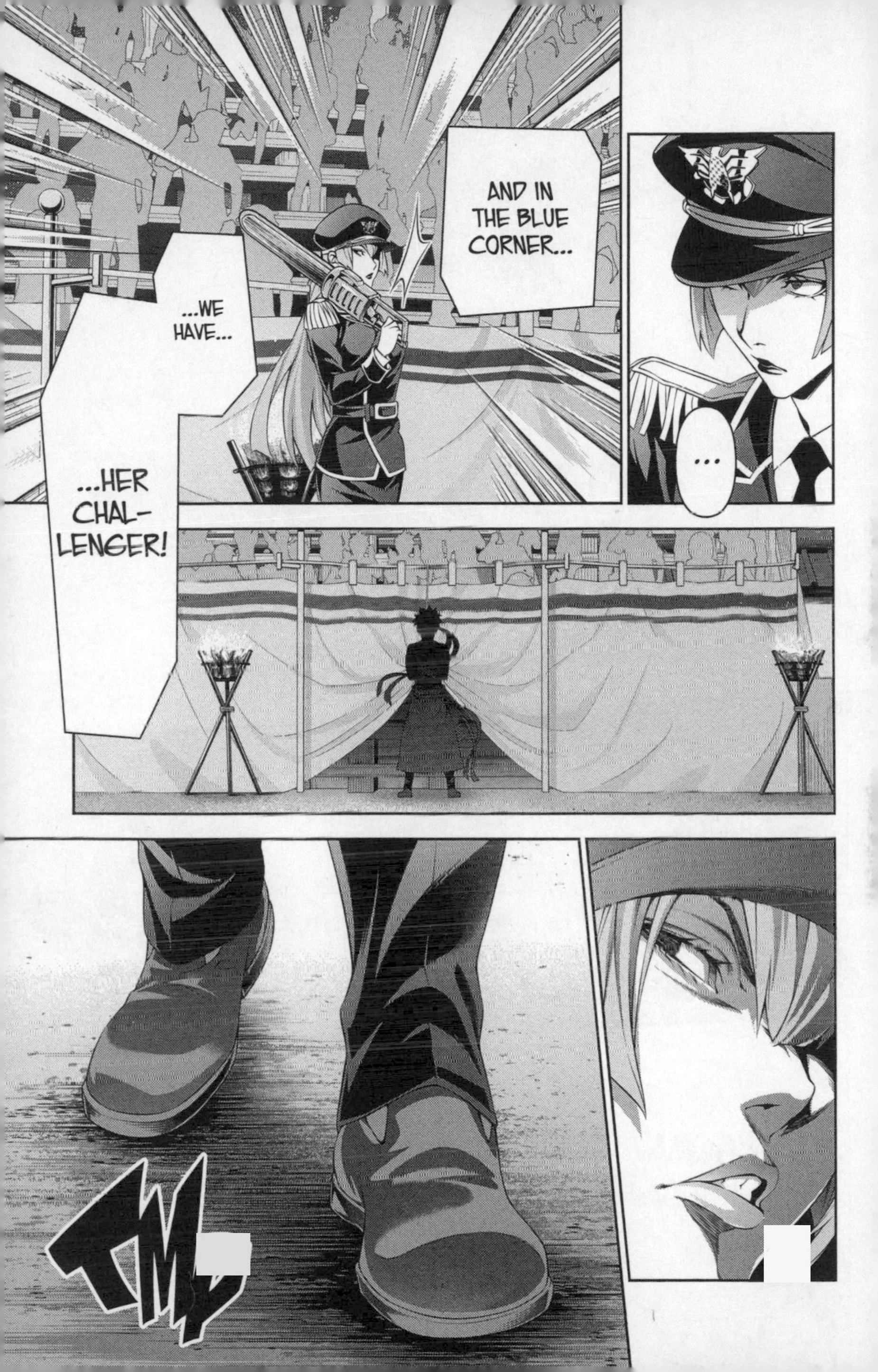
...
AND IN THE BLUE CORNER...
...WE HAVE...
...HER CHAL-LENGER!

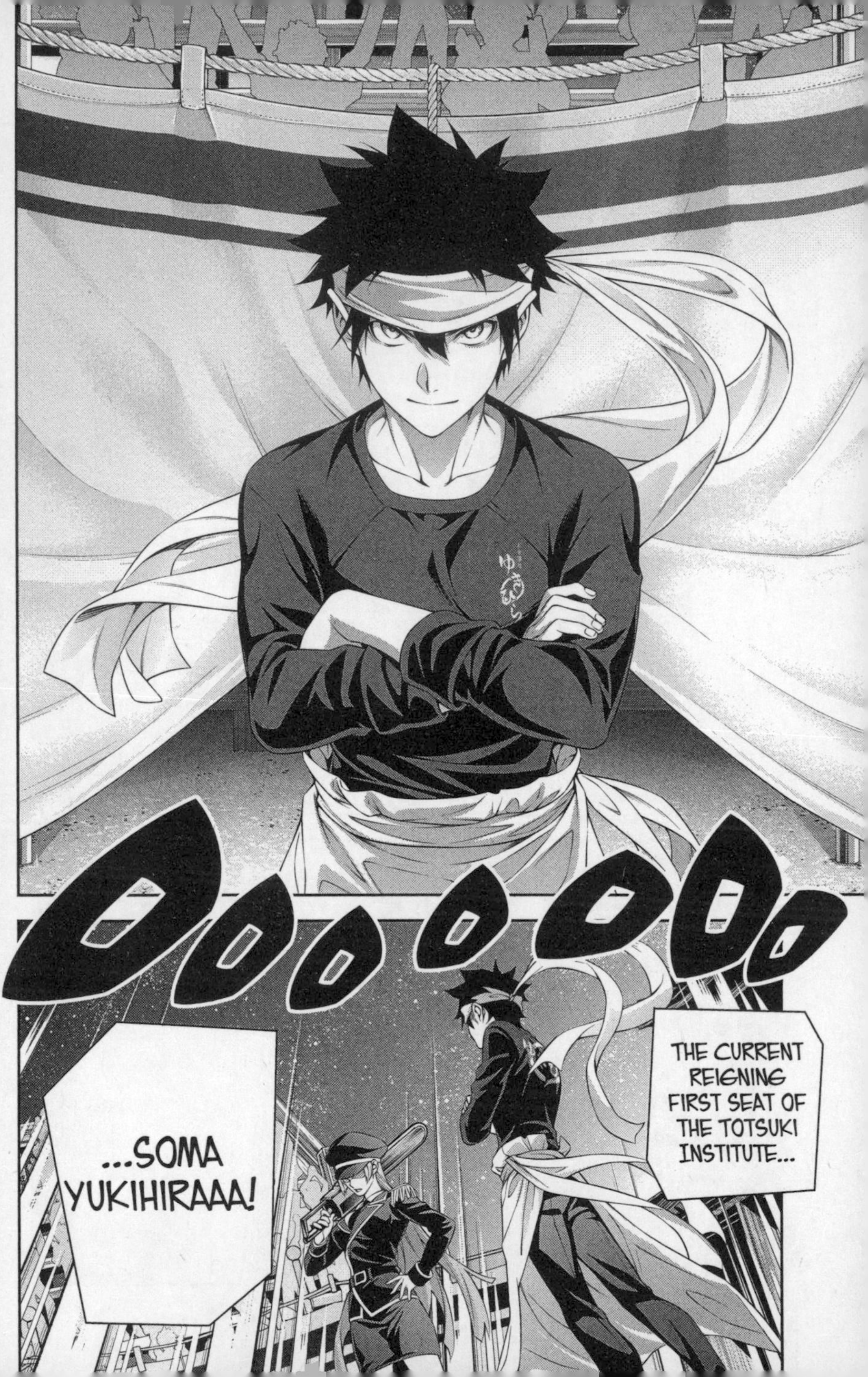
DOOOOOO
THE CURRENT REIGNING FIRST SEAT OF THE TOTSUKI INSTITUTE...
...SOMA YUKIHIRAAA!

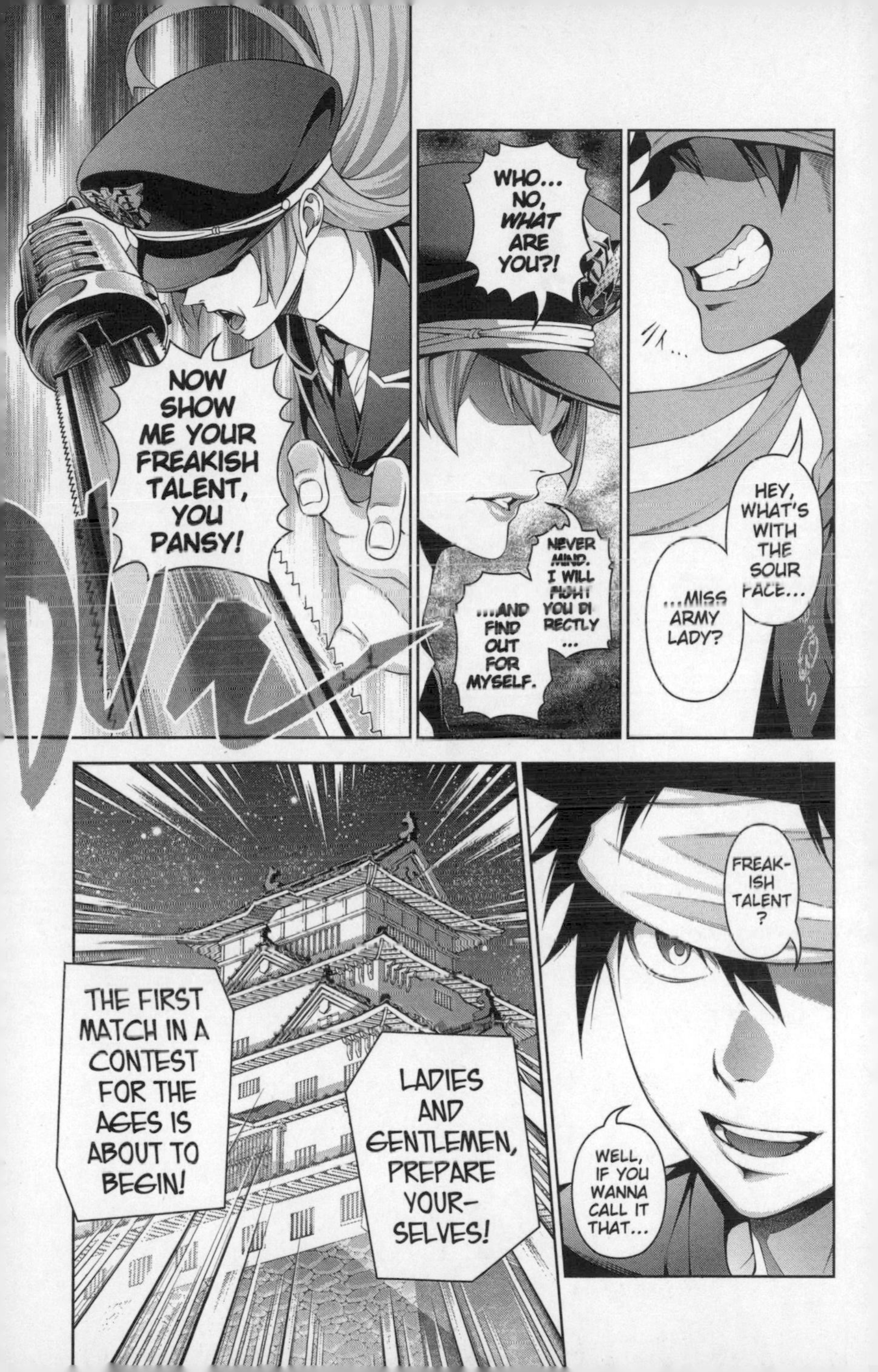
HEY, WHAT'S WITH THE SOUR FACE...
...MISS ARMY LADY?
WHO... NO, WHAT ARE YOU?!
NEVER MIND. I WILL FIGHT YOU DIRECTLY...
...AND FIND OUT FOR MYSELF.
NOW SHOW ME YOUR FREAKISH TALENT, YOU PANSY!
FREAKISH TALENT?
WELL, IF YOU WANNA CALL IT THAT...
LADIES AND GENTLEMEN, PREPARE YOURSELVES!
THE FIRST MATCH IN A CONTEST FOR THE AGES IS ABOUT TO BEGIN!

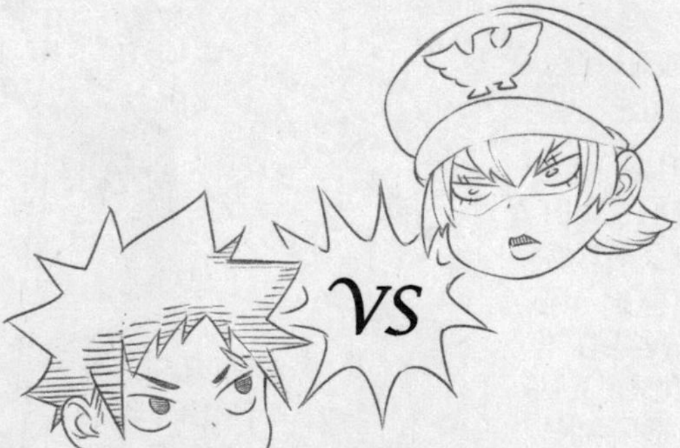
VS

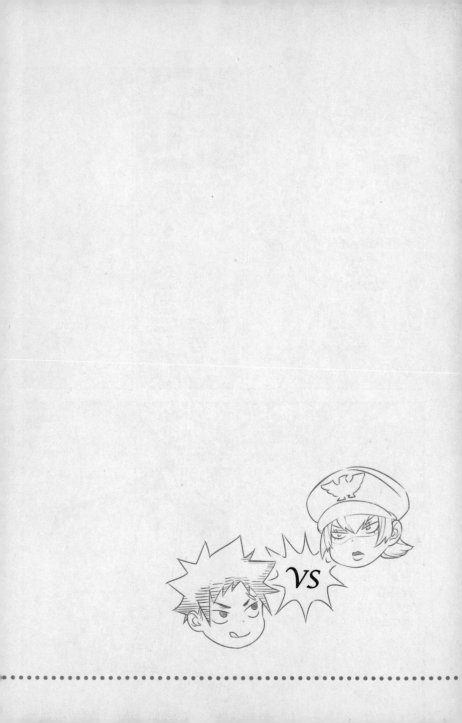

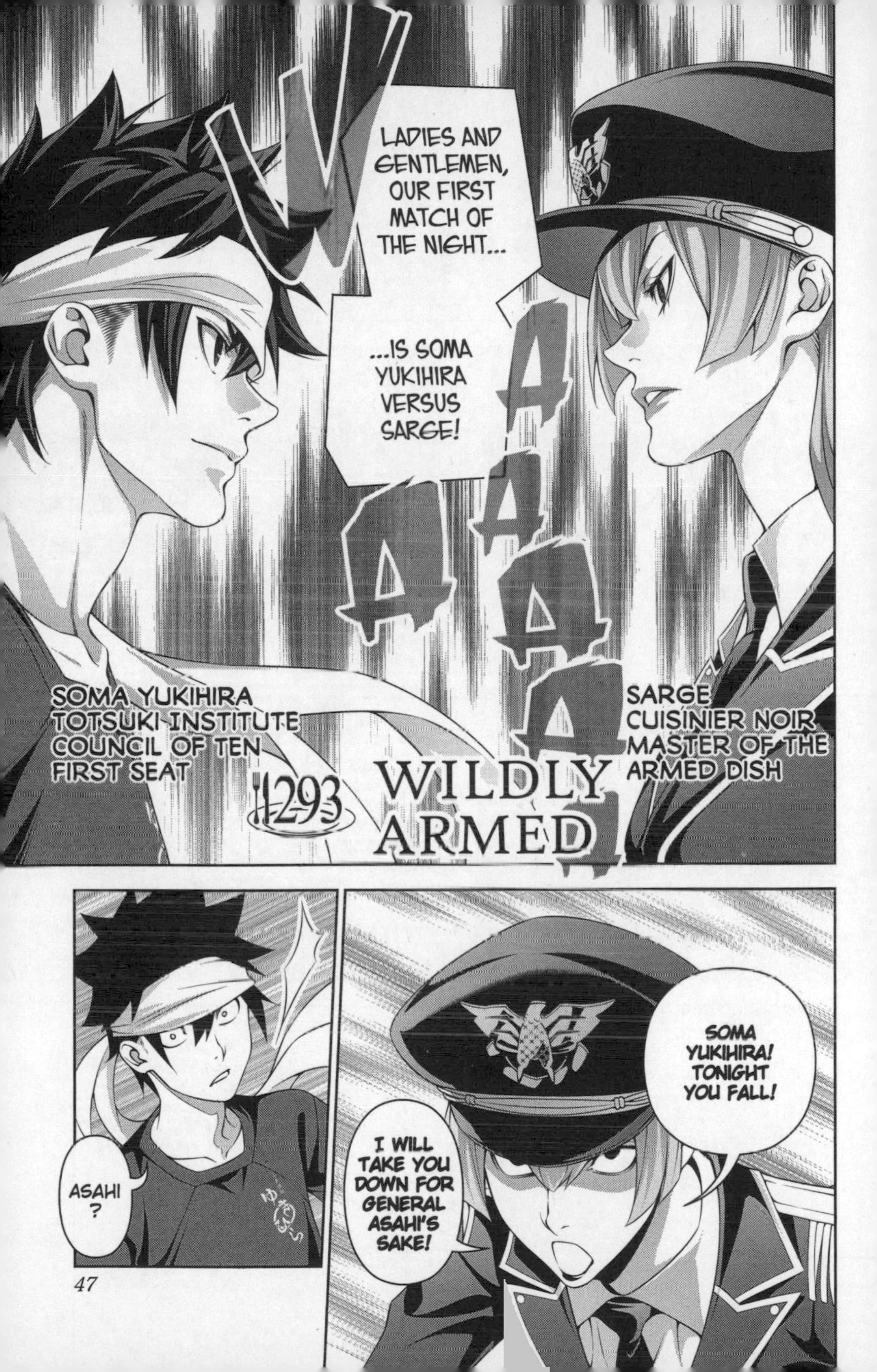
LADIES AND GENTLEMEN, OUR FIRST MATCH OF THE NIGHT...
...IS SOMA YUKIHIRA VERSUS SARGE!
SARGE CUISINIER NOIR MASTER OF THE ARMED DISH
293 WILDLY ARMED
SOMA YUKIHIRA TOTSUKI INSTITUTE COUNCIL OF TEN FIRST SEAT
SOMA YUKIHIRA! TONIGHT YOU FALL!
I WILL TAKE YOU DOWN FOR GENERAL ASAHI'S SAKE!
ASAHI ?

WAA
WAA
WAIT A SEC, YOU KNOW ASAHI SAIBA?
HMPH. THAT'S NONE OF YOUR BUSINESS.
YO! I'VE ALREADY CHALLENGED SOMA YUKIHIRA.
SERIOUSLY. I TRIPPED OVER HIM THE VERY FIRST DAY I INFILTRATED THE INSTITUTE. HOW LUCKY IS THAT?
TOO BAD HE WASN'T ALL THAT IMPRESSIVE.
HECK, HE WAS A TOTAL SCRUB!
AH WELL, TIME FOR BED!
THAT WAS GENERAL ASAHI'S JUDGMENT OF HIM, BUT SOMEHOW...
...HE STILL PASSED THE THIRD-GATE TRIAL.
GENERAL ASAHI IS MY COMMANDING OFFICER. I WILLINGLY RESPECT AND OBEY HIS EVERY ORDER.
MURMUR
BUT COULD IT BE POSSIBLE THAT HIS JUDGMENT WAS... WRONG?
NO! IMPOSSIBLE! HE CAN'T BE WRONG. HE'S NEVER WRONG!

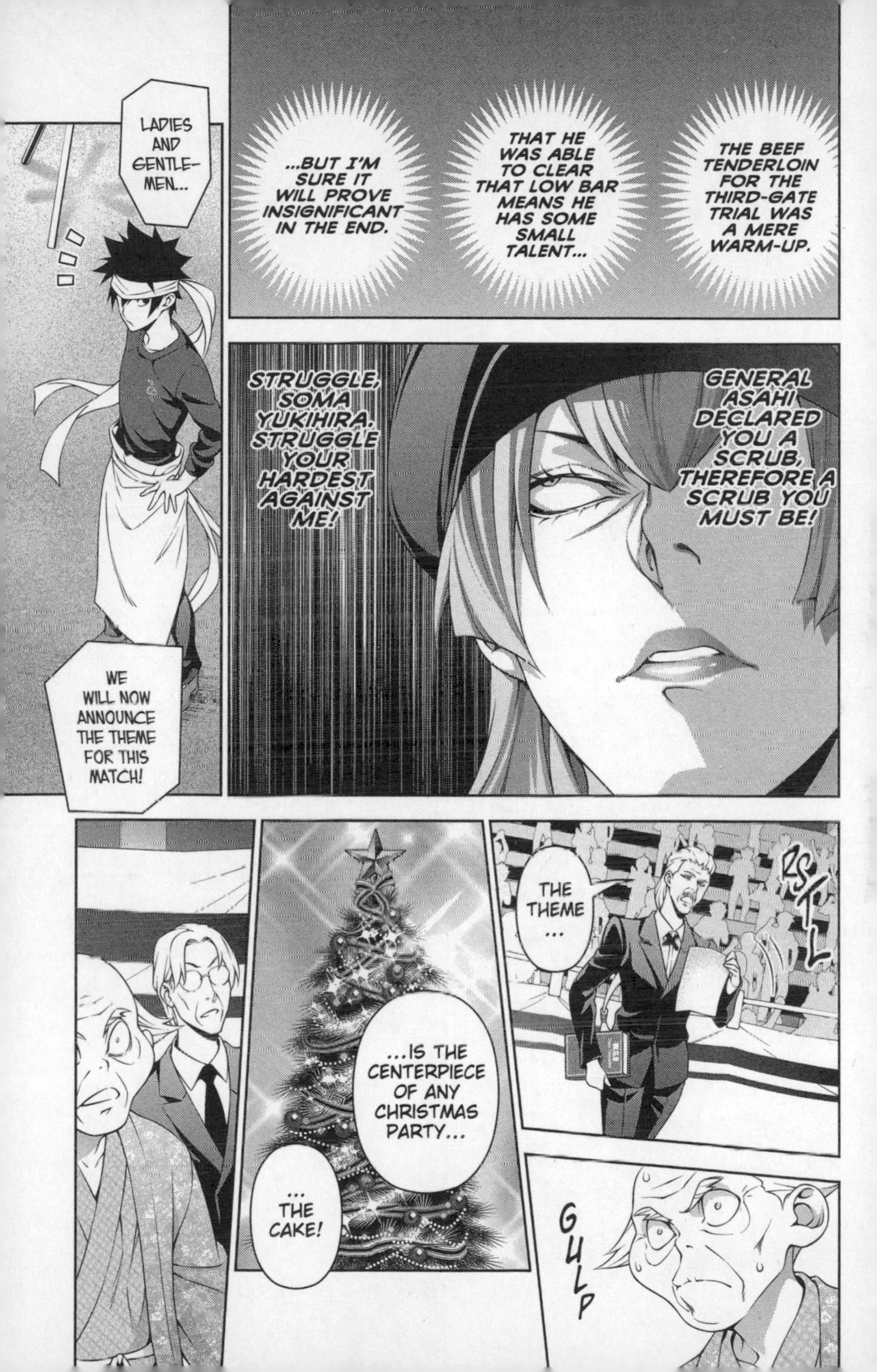
THE BEEF TENDERLOIN FOR THE THIRD-GATE TRIAL WAS A MERE WARM-UP.
THAT HE WAS ABLE TO CLEAR THAT LOW BAR MEANS HE HAS SOME SMALL TALENT...
...BUT I'M SURE IT WILL PROVE INSIGNIFICANT IN THE END.
GENERAL ASAHI DECLARED YOU A SCRUB, THEREFORE A SCRUB YOU MUST BE!
STRUGGLE, SOMA YUKIHIRA. STRUGGLE YOUR HARDEST AGAINST ME!
LADIES AND GENTLE-MEN...
WE WILL NOW ANNOUNCE THE THEME FOR THIS MATCH!
THE THEME...
RSTL
GULP
...IS THE CENTERPIECE OF ANY CHRISTMAS PARTY...
... THE CAKE!

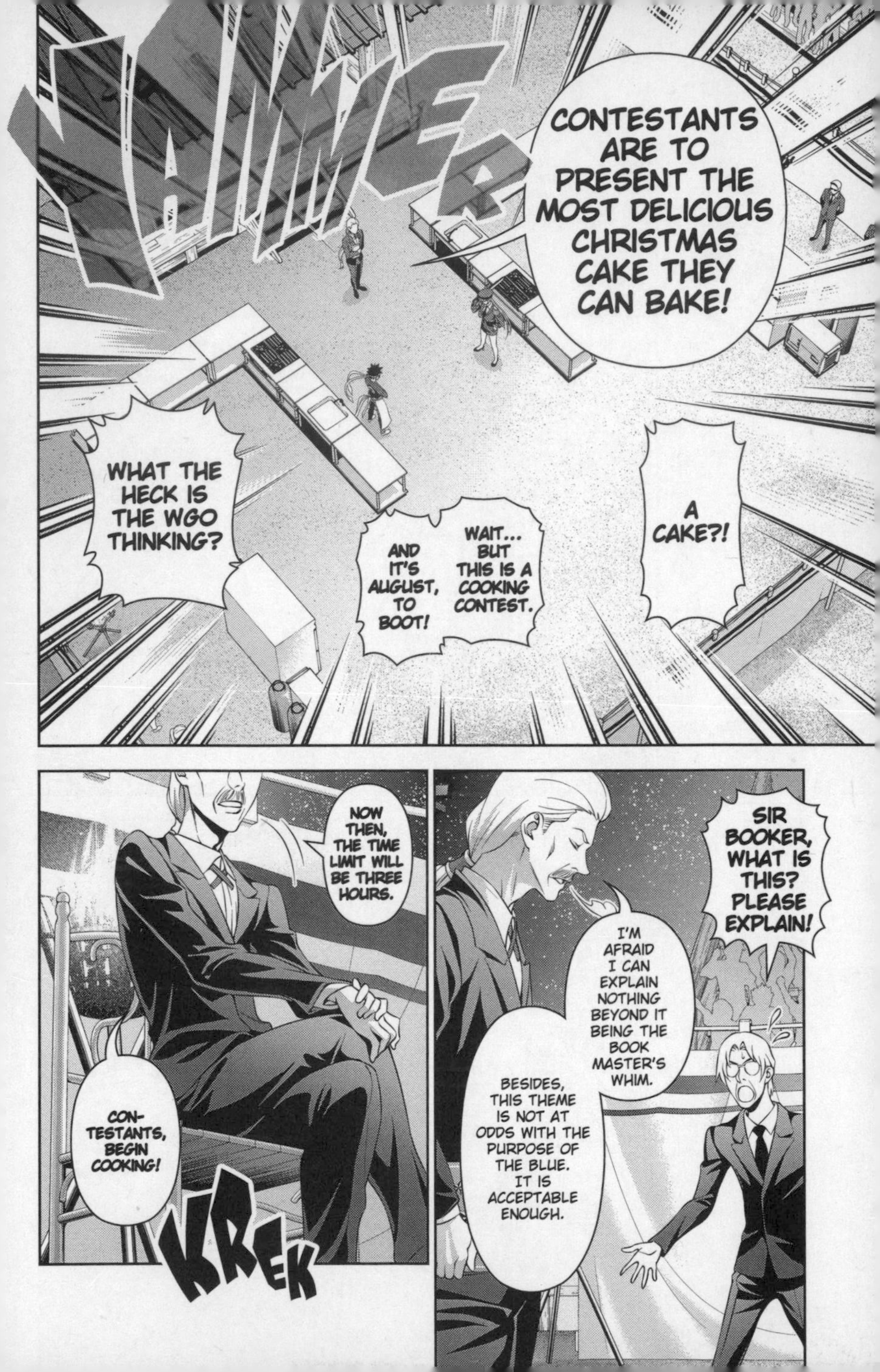
CONTESTANTS ARE TO PRESENT THE MOST DELICIOUS CHRISTMAS CAKE THEY CAN BAKE!
A CAKE?!
WAIT... BUT THIS IS A COOKING CONTEST.
AND IT'S AUGUST, TO BOOT!
WHAT THE HECK IS THE WGO THINKING?
SIR BOOKER, WHAT IS THIS? PLEASE EXPLAIN!
I'M AFRAID I CAN EXPLAIN NOTHING BEYOND IT BEING THE BOOK MASTER'S WHIM.
BESIDES, THIS THEME IS NOT AT ODDS WITH THE PURPOSE OF THE BLUE. IT IS ACCEPTABLE ENOUGH.
NOW THEN, THE TIME LIMIT WILL BE THREE HOURS.
CON-TESTANTS, BEGIN COOKING!
KREK

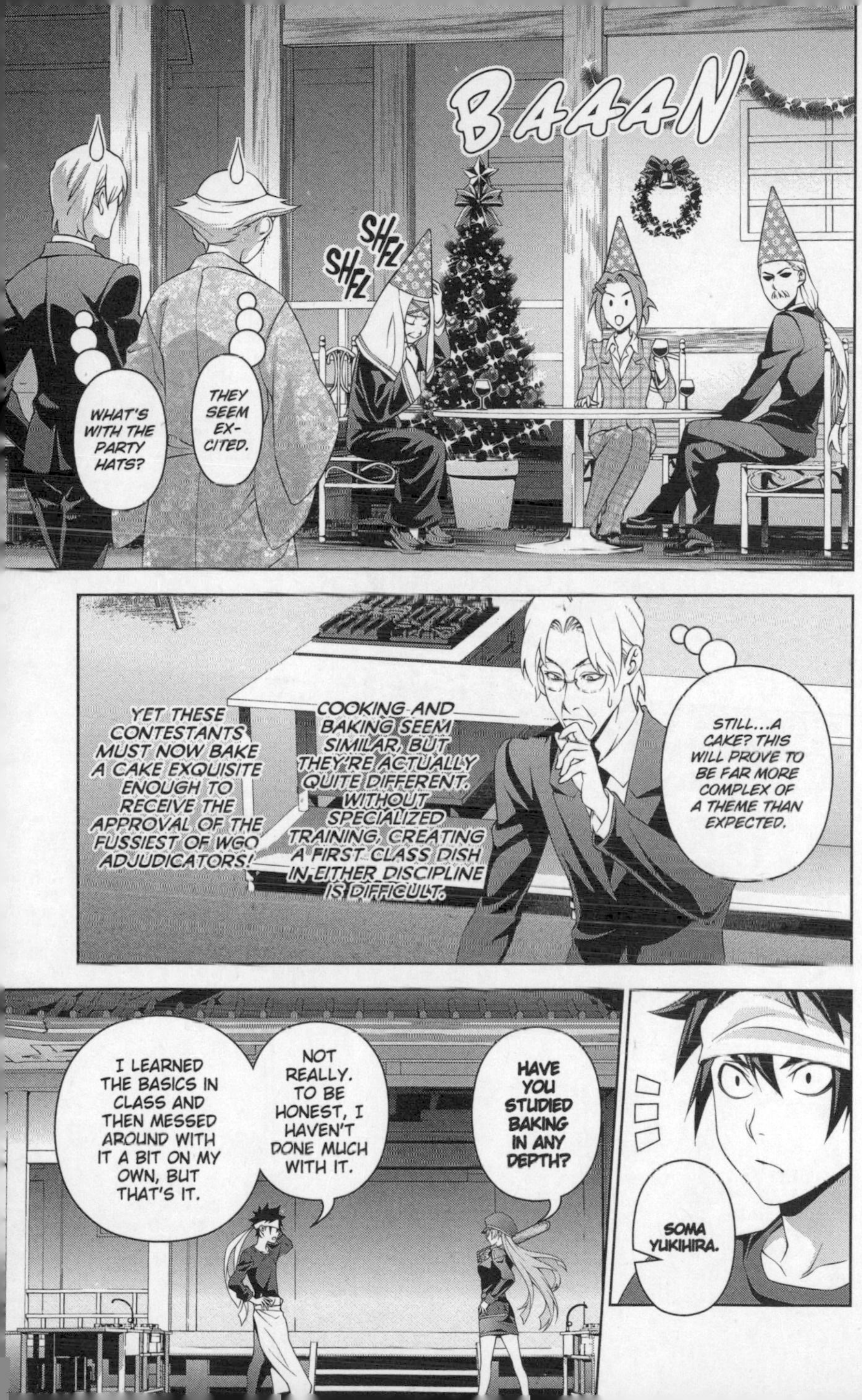
BAAAN
SHFL SHFL
THEY SEEM EX-CITED.
WHAT'S WITH THE PARTY HATS?
STILL...A CAKE? THIS WILL PROVE TO BE FAR MORE COMPLEX OF A THEME THAN EXPECTED.
COOKING AND BAKING SEEM SIMILAR, BUT THEY'RE ACTUALLY QUITE DIFFERENT. WITHOUT SPECIALIZED TRAINING, CREATING A FIRST CLASS DISH IN EITHER DISCIPLINE IS DIFFICULT.
YET THESE CONTESTANTS MUST NOW BAKE A CAKE EXQUISITE ENOUGH TO RECEIVE THE APPROVAL OF THE FUSSIEST OF WGO ADJUDICATORS!
SOMA YUKIHIRA.
HAVE YOU STUDIED BAKING IN ANY DEPTH?
NOT REALLY. TO BE HONEST, I HAVEN'T DONE MUCH WITH IT.
I LEARNED THE BASICS IN CLASS AND THEN MESSED AROUND WITH IT A BIT ON MY OWN, BUT THAT'S IT.

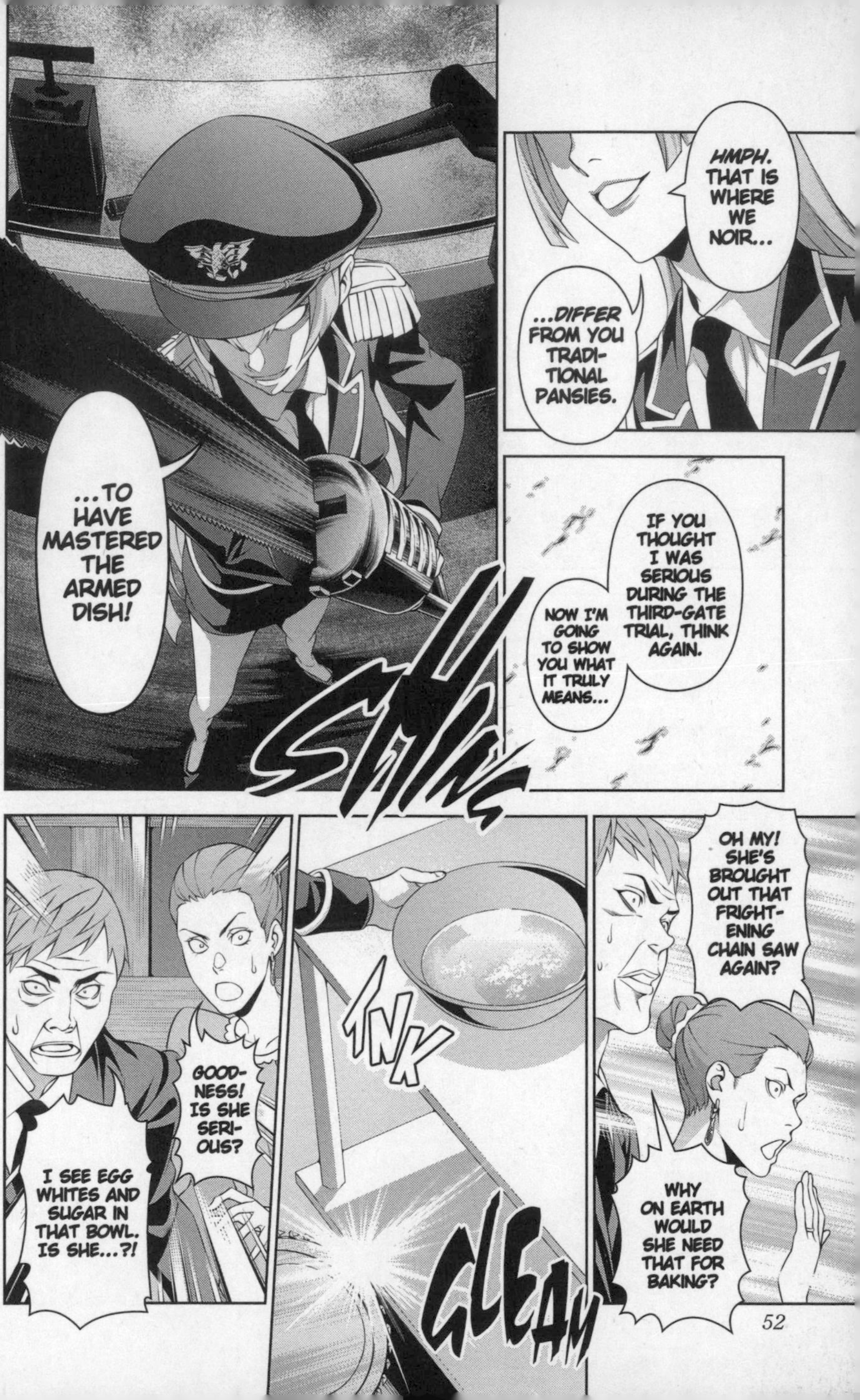
HMPH. THAT IS WHERE WE NOIR...
...DIFFER FROM YOU TRADI-TIONAL PANSIES.
IF YOU THOUGHT I WAS SERIOUS DURING THE THIRD-GATE TRIAL, THINK AGAIN.
NOW I'M GOING TO SHOW YOU WHAT IT TRULY MEANS...
...TO HAVE MASTERED THE ARMED DISH!
SHING
OH MY! SHE'S BROUGHT OUT THAT FRIGHT-ENING CHAIN SAW AGAIN?
WHY ON EARTH WOULD SHE NEED THAT FOR BAKING?
TINK
GLEAM
GOOD-NESS! IS SHE SERI-OUS?
I SEE EGG WHITES AND SUGAR IN THAT BOWL. IS SHE...?!

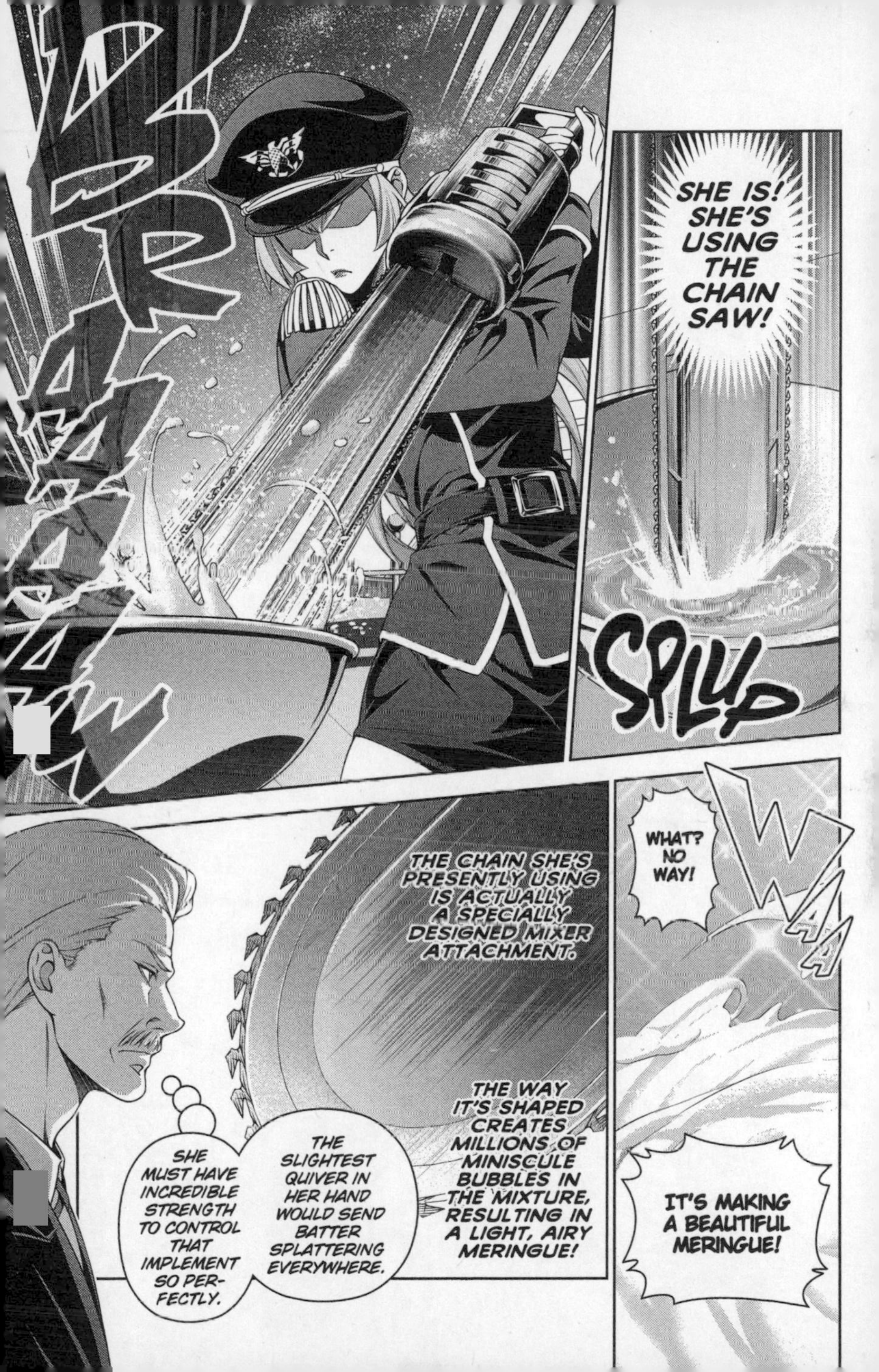
SHE IS! SHE'S USING THE CHAIN SAW!
SPLUP
WHAT? NO WAY!
WAAA
IT'S MAKING A BEAUTIFUL MERINGUE!
THE CHAIN SHE'S PRESENTLY USING IS ACTUALLY A SPECIALLY DESIGNED MIXER ATTACHMENT.
THE WAY IT'S SHAPED CREATES MILLIONS OF MINISCULE BUBBLES IN THE MIXTURE, RESULTING IN A LIGHT, AIRY MERINGUE!
THE SLIGHTEST QUIVER IN HER HAND WOULD SEND BATTER SPLATTERING EVERYWHERE.
SHE MUST HAVE INCREDIBLE STRENGTH TO CONTROL THAT IMPLEMENT SO PER-FECTLY.

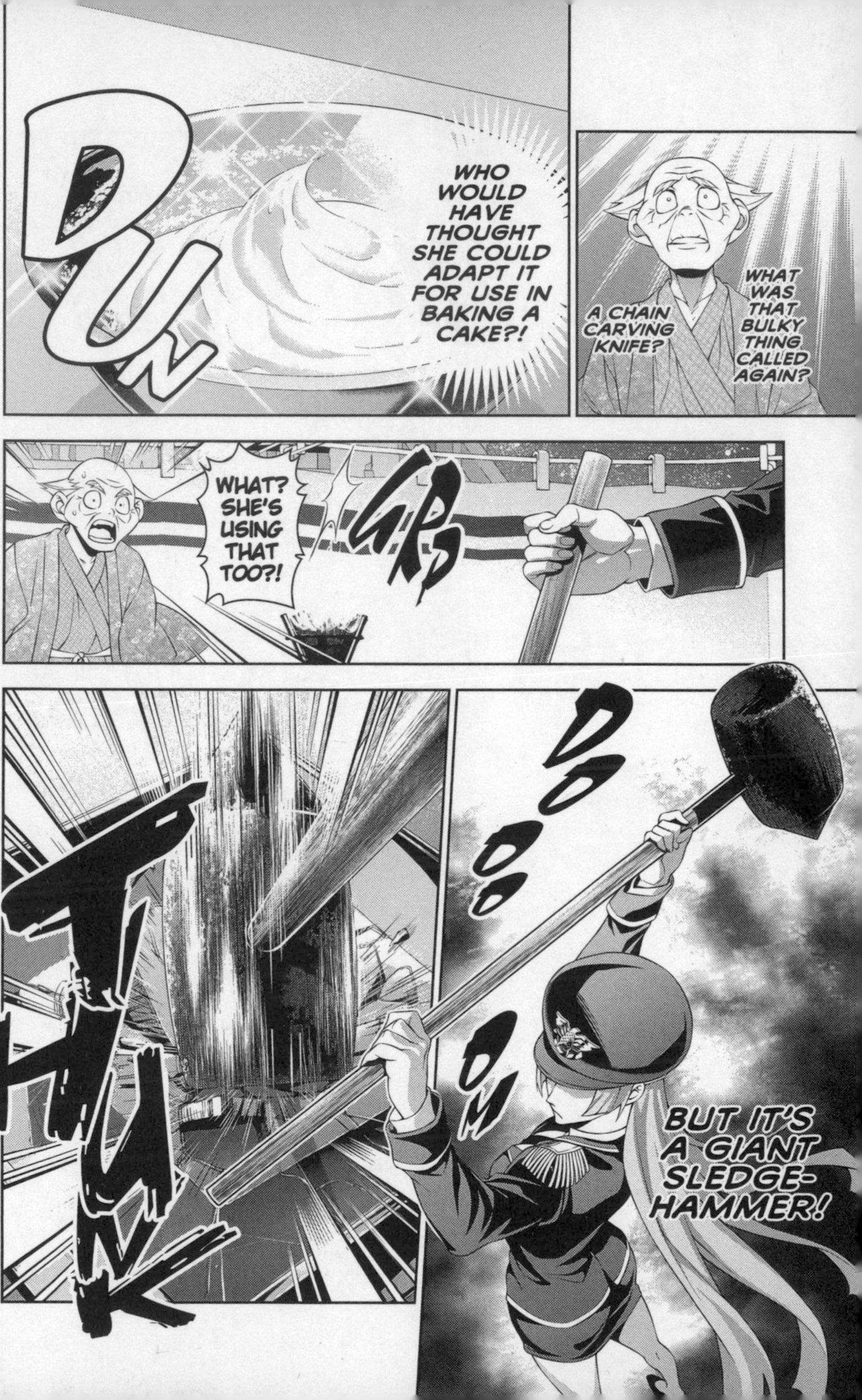
WHAT WAS THAT BULKY THING CALLED AGAIN?
A CHAIN CARVING KNIFE?
WHO WOULD HAVE THOUGHT SHE COULD ADAPT IT FOR USE IN BAKING A CAKE?!
DUN
WHAT? SHE'S USING THAT TOO?!
BUT IT'S A GIANT SLEDGE-HAMMER!

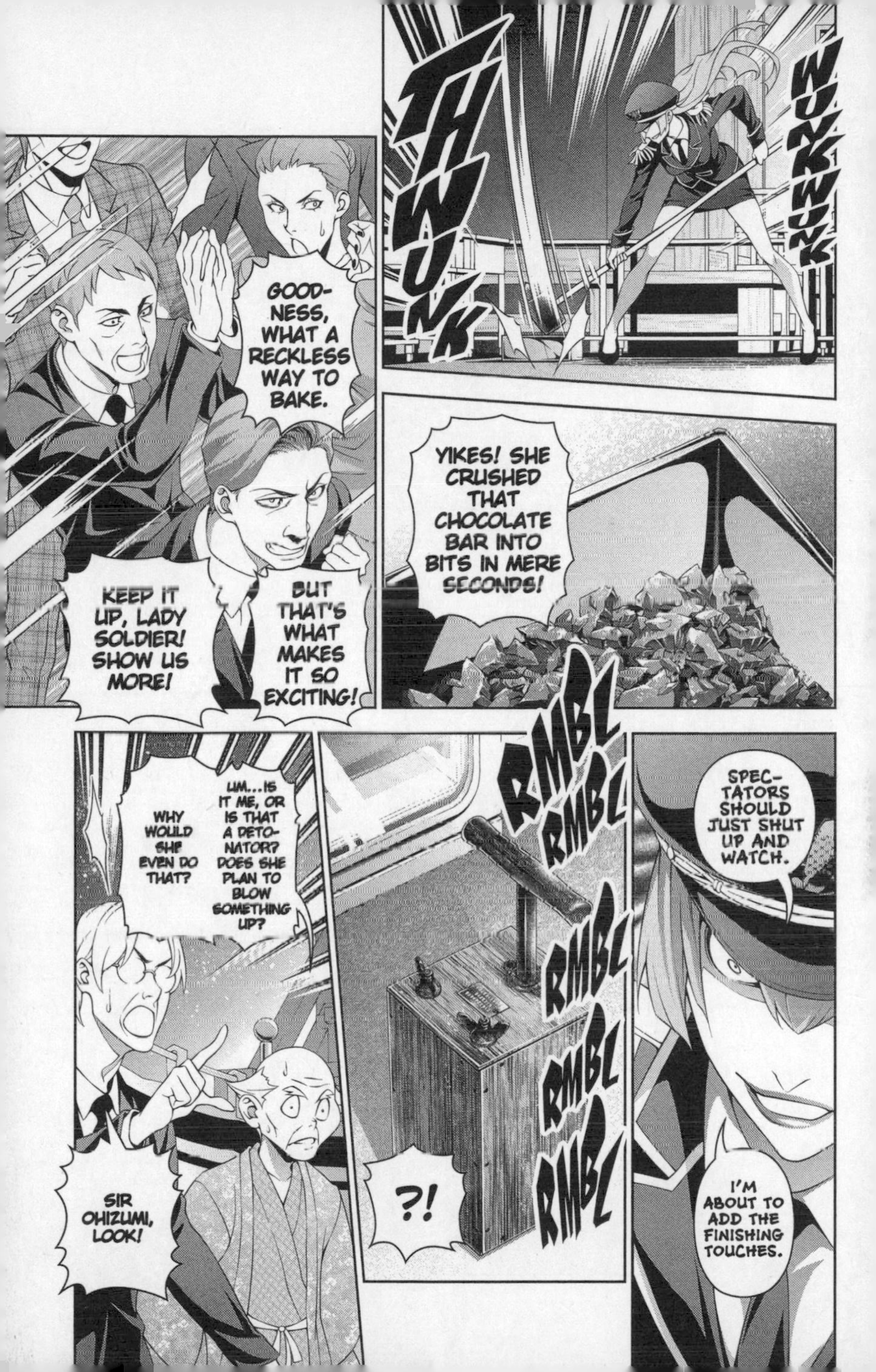
WUNKWUNK
THWUNK
YIKES! SHE CRUSHED THAT CHOCOLATE BAR INTO BITS IN MERE SECONDS!
GOOD-NESS, WHAT A RECKLESS WAY TO BAKE.
BUT THAT'S WHAT MAKES IT SO EXCITING!
KEEP IT UP, LADY SOLDIER! SHOW US MORE!
SPEC-TATORS SHOULD JUST SHUT UP AND WATCH.
I'M ABOUT TO ADD THE FINISHING TOUCHES.
RMBL RMBL
RMBL RMBL RMBL
?!
UM...IS IT ME, OR IS THAT A DETO-NATOR? DOES SHE PLAN TO BLOW SOMETHING UP?
WHY WOULD SHE EVEN DO THAT?
SIR OHIZUMI, LOOK!

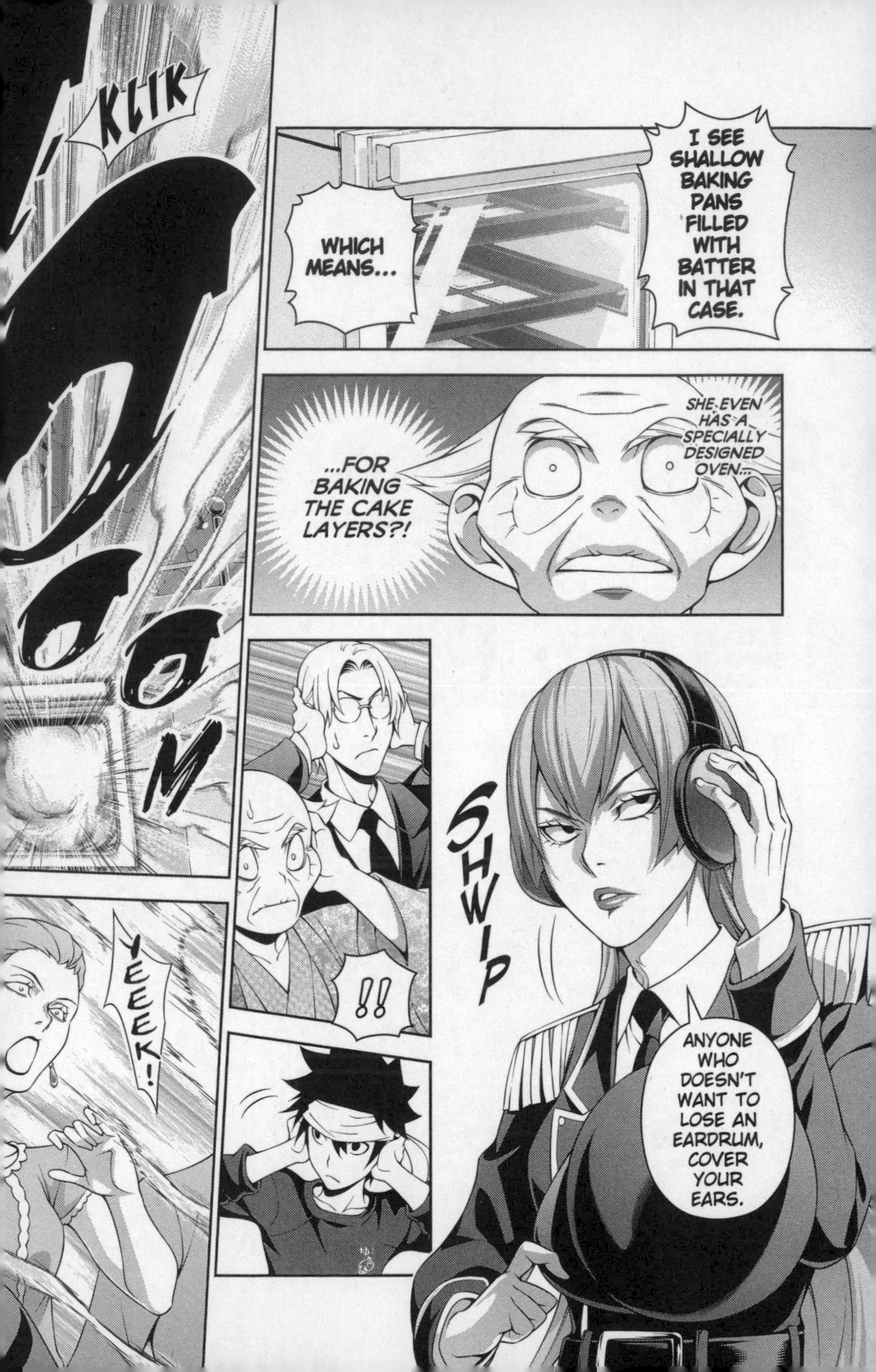
I SEE SHALLOW BAKING PANS FILLED WITH BATTER IN THAT CASE.
WHICH MEANS...
SHE EVEN HAS A SPECIALLY DESIGNED OVEN...
...FOR BAKING THE CAKE LAYERS?!
SHWIP
ANYONE WHO DOESN'T WANT TO LOSE AN EARDRUM, COVER YOUR EARS.
!!
KLIK
BOOM
YEEEK!

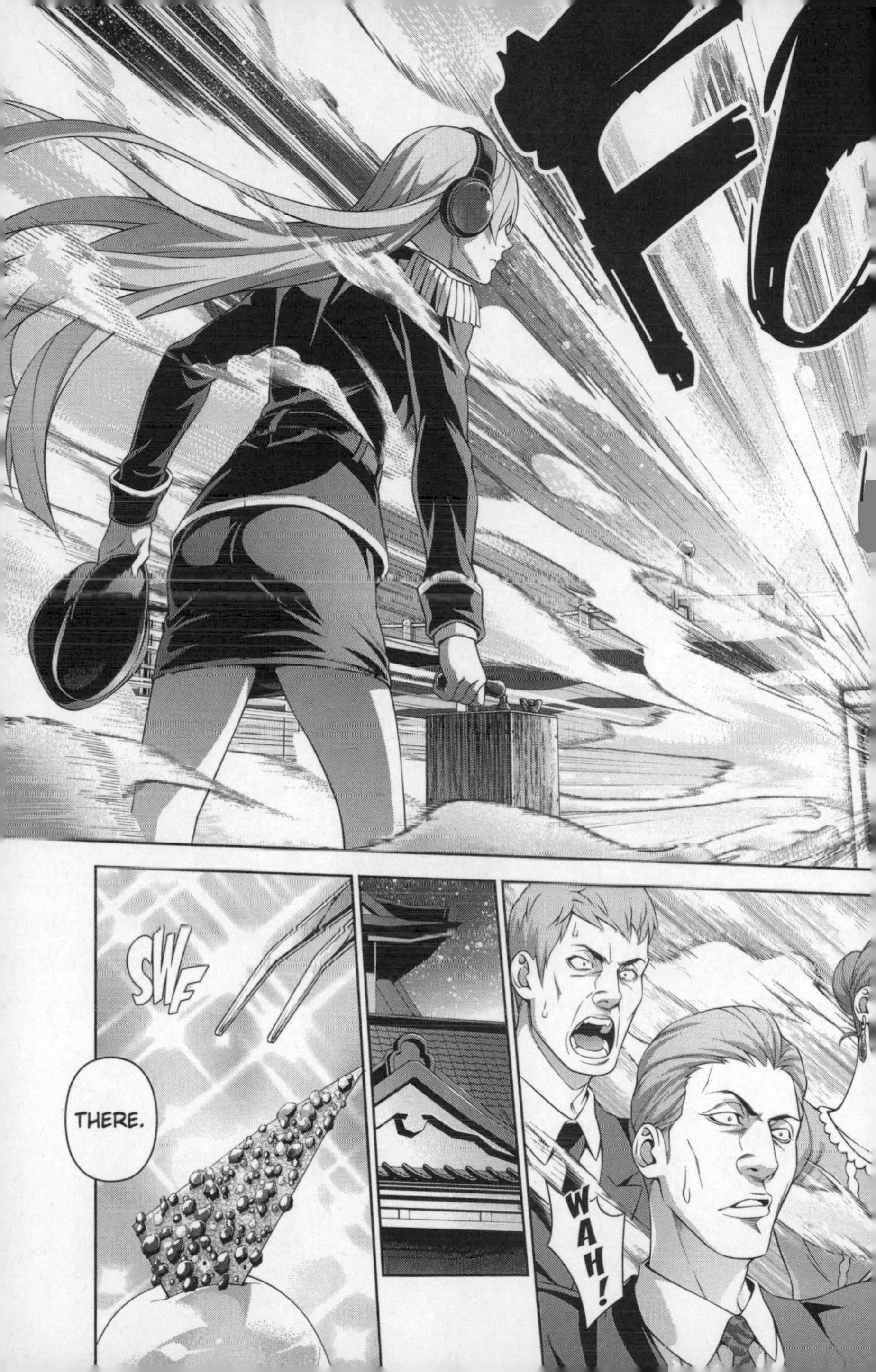
WAH!
SWF
THERE.

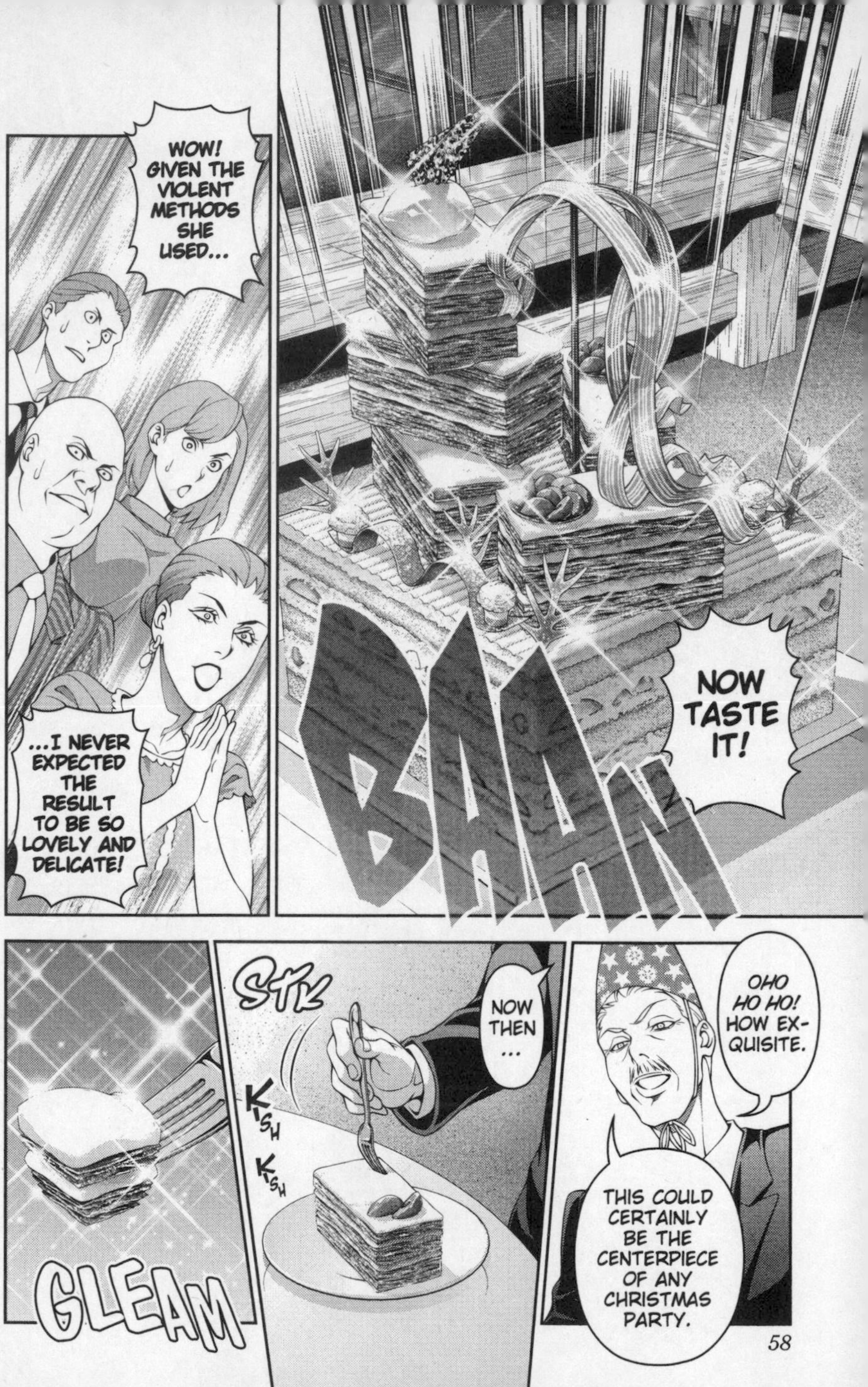
BAAN
NOW TASTE IT!
WOW! GIVEN THE VIOLENT METHODS SHE USED...
...I NEVER EXPECTED THE RESULT TO BE SO LOVELY AND DELICATE!
OHO HO HO! HOW EXQUISITE.
THIS COULD CERTAINLY BE THE CENTERPIECE OF ANY CHRISTMAS PARTY.
STK
NOW THEN ...
KISH
KISH
GLEAM

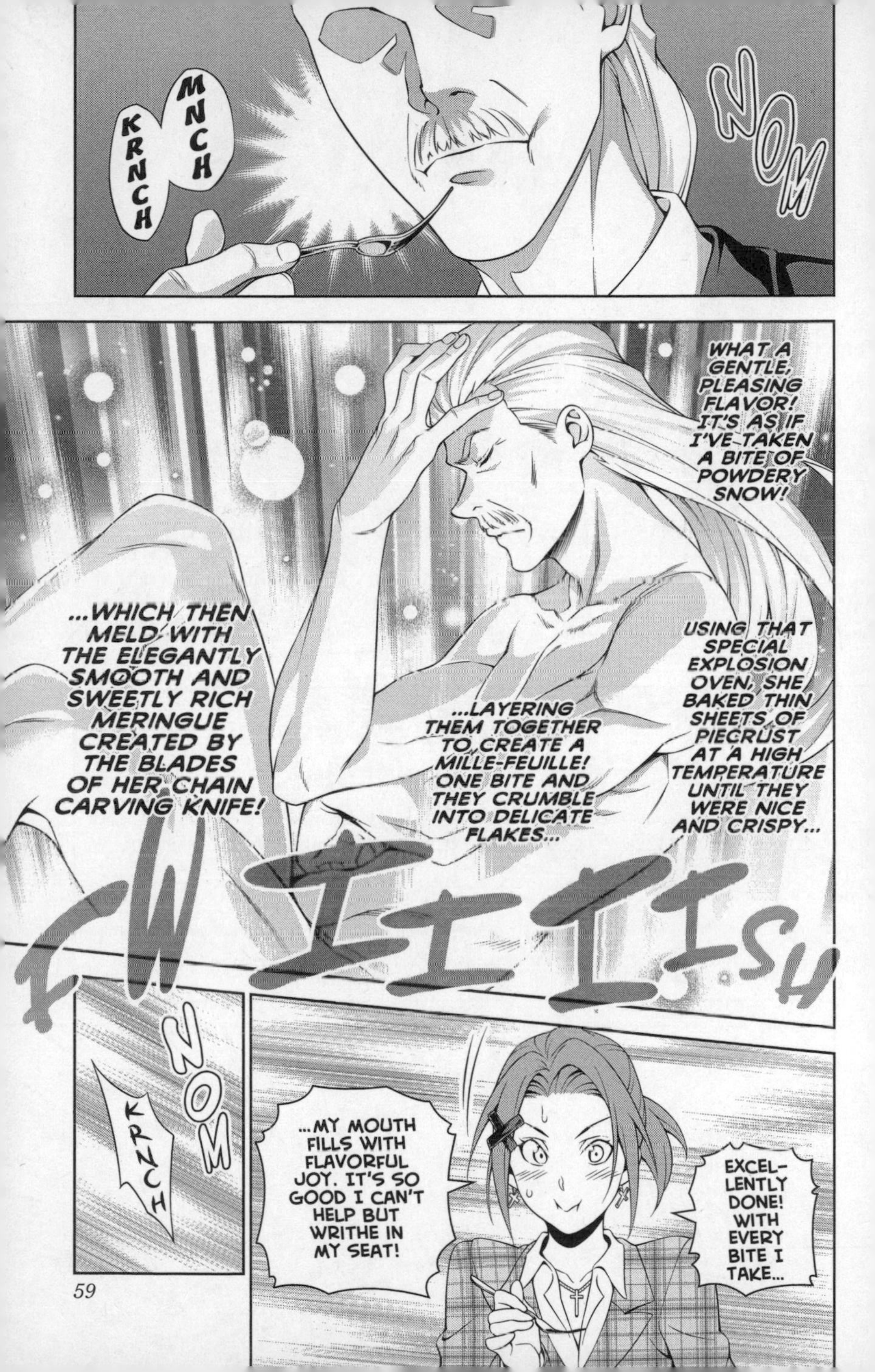
NOM
MNCH
KRNCH
WHAT A GENTLE, PLEASING FLAVOR! IT'S AS IF I'VE TAKEN A BITE OF POWDERY SNOW!
USING THAT SPECIAL EXPLOSION OVEN, SHE BAKED THIN SHEETS OF PIECRUST AT A HIGH TEMPERATURE UNTIL THEY WERE NICE AND CRISPY...
...LAYERING THEM TOGETHER TO CREATE A MILLE-FEUILLE! ONE BITE AND THEY CRUMBLE INTO DELICATE FLAKES...
...WHICH THEN MELD WITH THE ELEGANTLY SMOOTH AND SWEETLY RICH MERINGUE CREATED BY THE BLADES OF HER CHAIN CARVING KNIFE!
FWIIISH
EXCEL-LENTLY DONE! WITH EVERY BITE I TAKE...
...MY MOUTH FILLS WITH FLAVORFUL JOY. IT'S SO GOOD I CAN'T HELP BUT WRITHE IN MY SEAT!
NOM
KRNCH

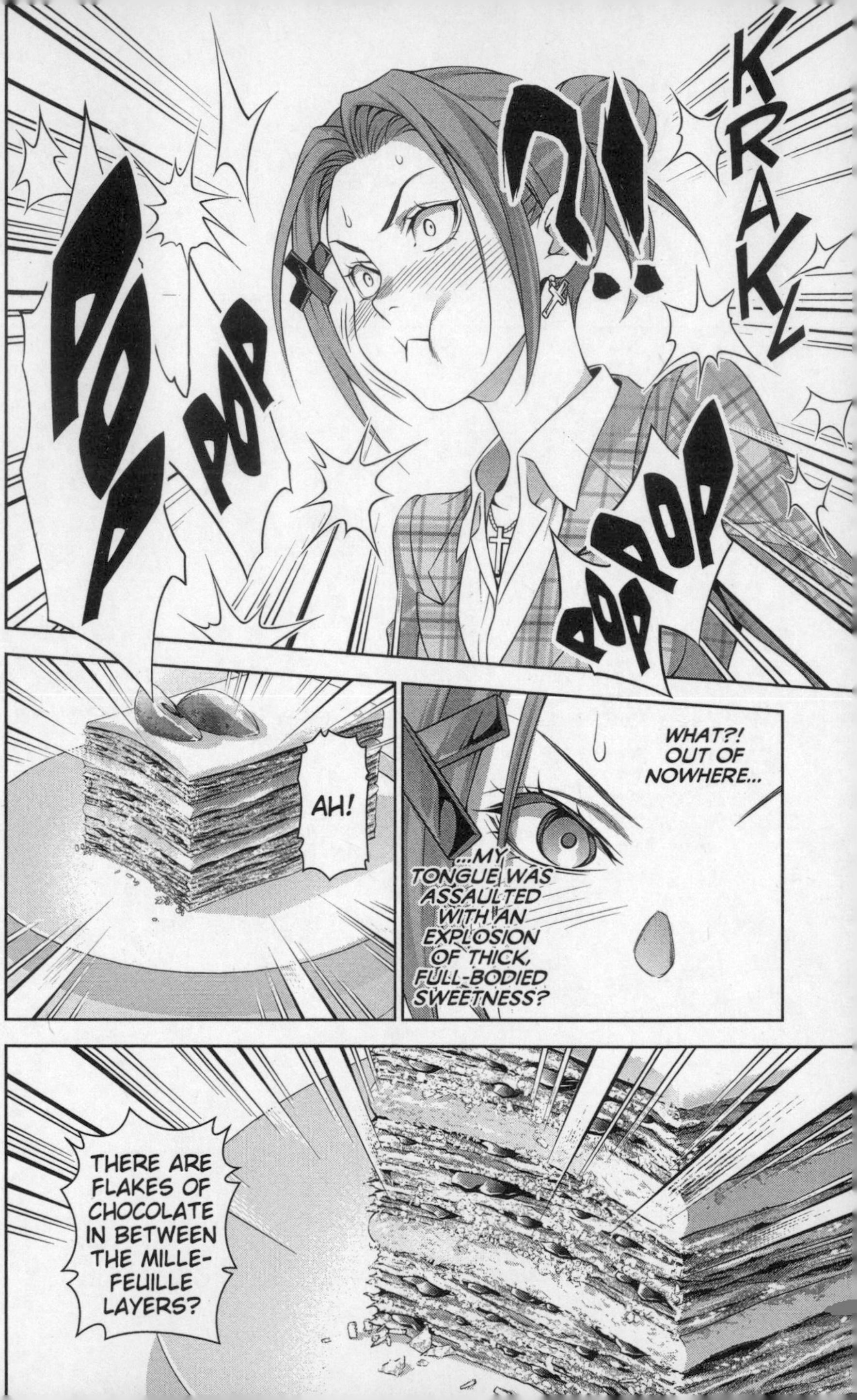
KRAK
?!!
POP POP POP
POP POP
WHAT?! OUT OF NOWHERE...
...MY TONGUE WAS ASSAULTED WITH AN EXPLOSION OF THICK, FULL-BODIED SWEETNESS?
AH!
THERE ARE FLAKES OF CHOCOLATE IN BETWEEN THE MILLE-FEUILLE LAYERS?

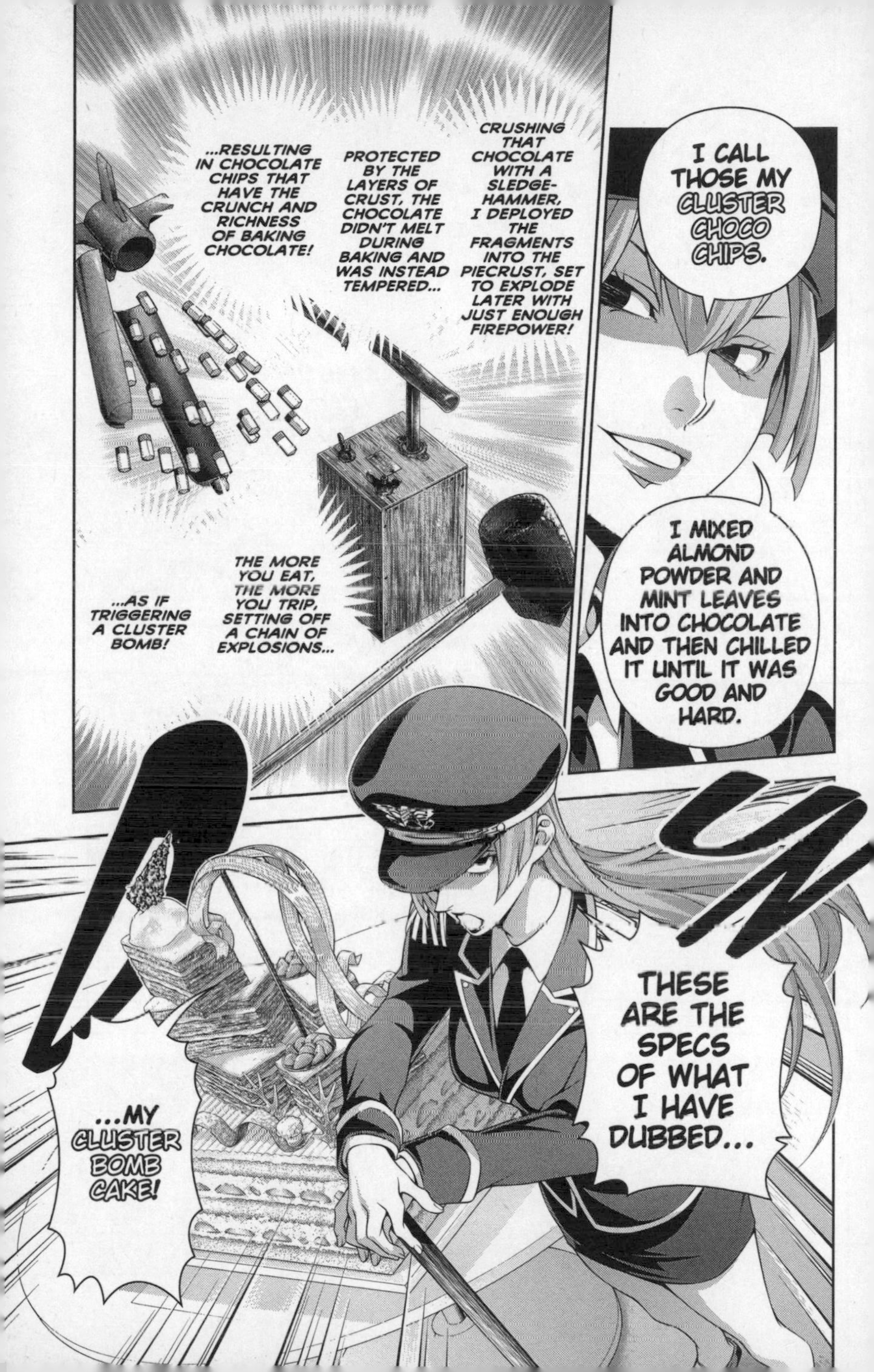
I CALL THOSE MY CLUSTER CHOCO CHIPS.
I MIXED ALMOND POWDER AND MINT LEAVES INTO CHOCOLATE AND THEN CHILLED IT UNTIL IT WAS GOOD AND HARD.
CRUSHING THAT CHOCOLATE WITH A SLEDGE-HAMMER, I DEPLOYED THE FRAGMENTS INTO THE PIECRUST, SET TO EXPLODE LATER WITH JUST ENOUGH FIREPOWER!
PROTECTED BY THE LAYERS OF CRUST, THE CHOCOLATE DIDN'T MELT DURING BAKING AND WAS INSTEAD TEMPERED...
...RESULTING IN CHOCOLATE CHIPS THAT HAVE THE CRUNCH AND RICHNESS OF BAKING CHOCOLATE!
THE MORE YOU EAT, THE MORE YOU TRIP, SETTING OFF A CHAIN OF EXPLOSIONS...
...AS IF TRIGGERING A CLUSTER BOMB!
THESE ARE THE SPECS OF WHAT I HAVE DUBBED...
...MY CLUSTER BOMB CAKE!

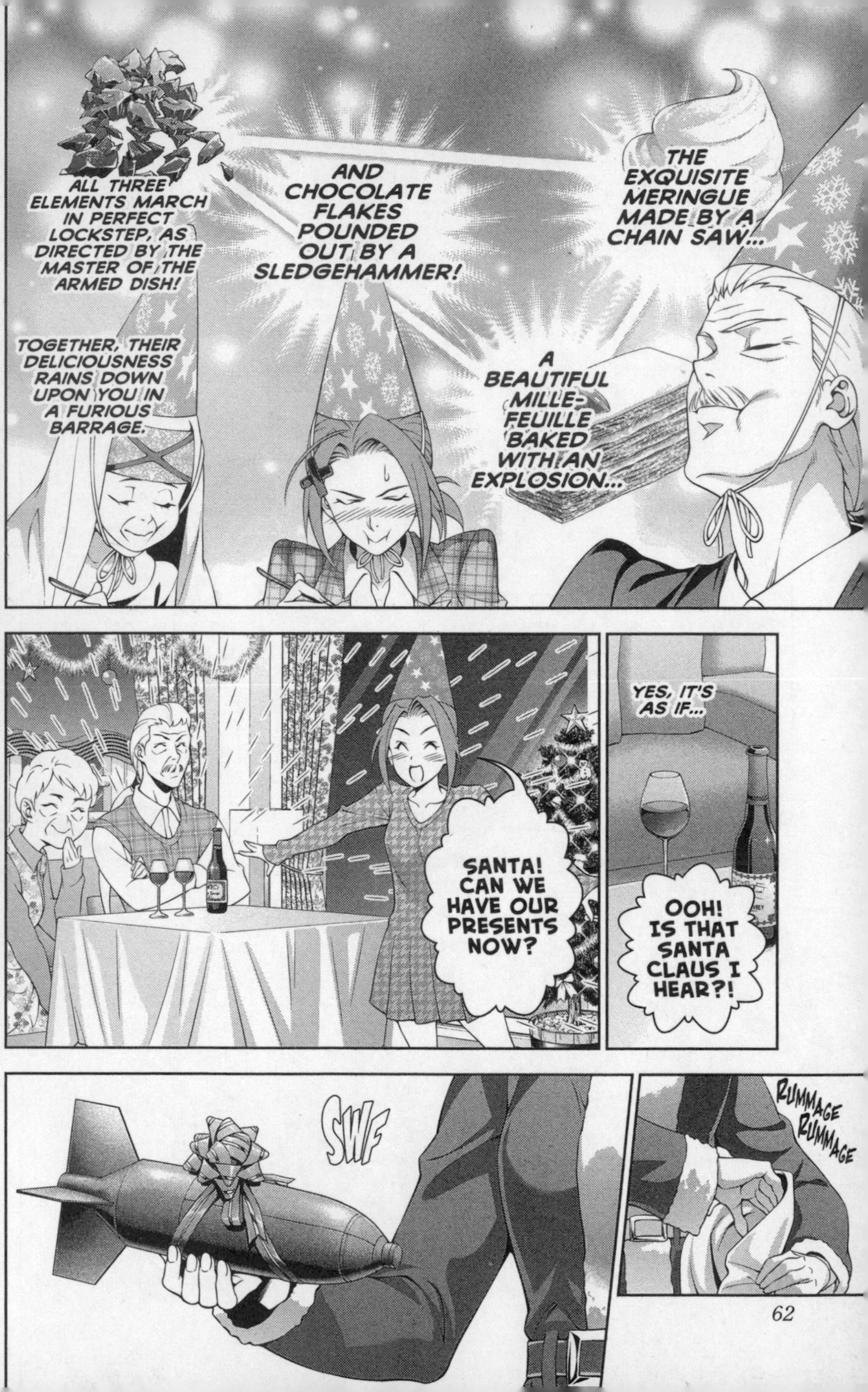
THE EXQUISITE MERINGUE MADE BY A CHAIN SAW...
A BEAUTIFUL MILLE-FEUILLE BAKED WITH AN EXPLOSION...
AND CHOCOLATE FLAKES POUNDED OUT BY A SLEDGEHAMMER!
ALL THREE ELEMENTS MARCH IN PERFECT LOCKSTEP, AS DIRECTED BY THE MASTER OF THE ARMED DISH!
TOGETHER, THEIR DELICIOUSNESS RAINS DOWN UPON YOU IN A FURIOUS BARRAGE.
YES, IT'S AS IF...
OOH! IS THAT SANTA CLAUS I HEAR?!
SANTA! CAN WE HAVE OUR PRESENTS NOW?
RUMMAGE RUMMAGE
SWF

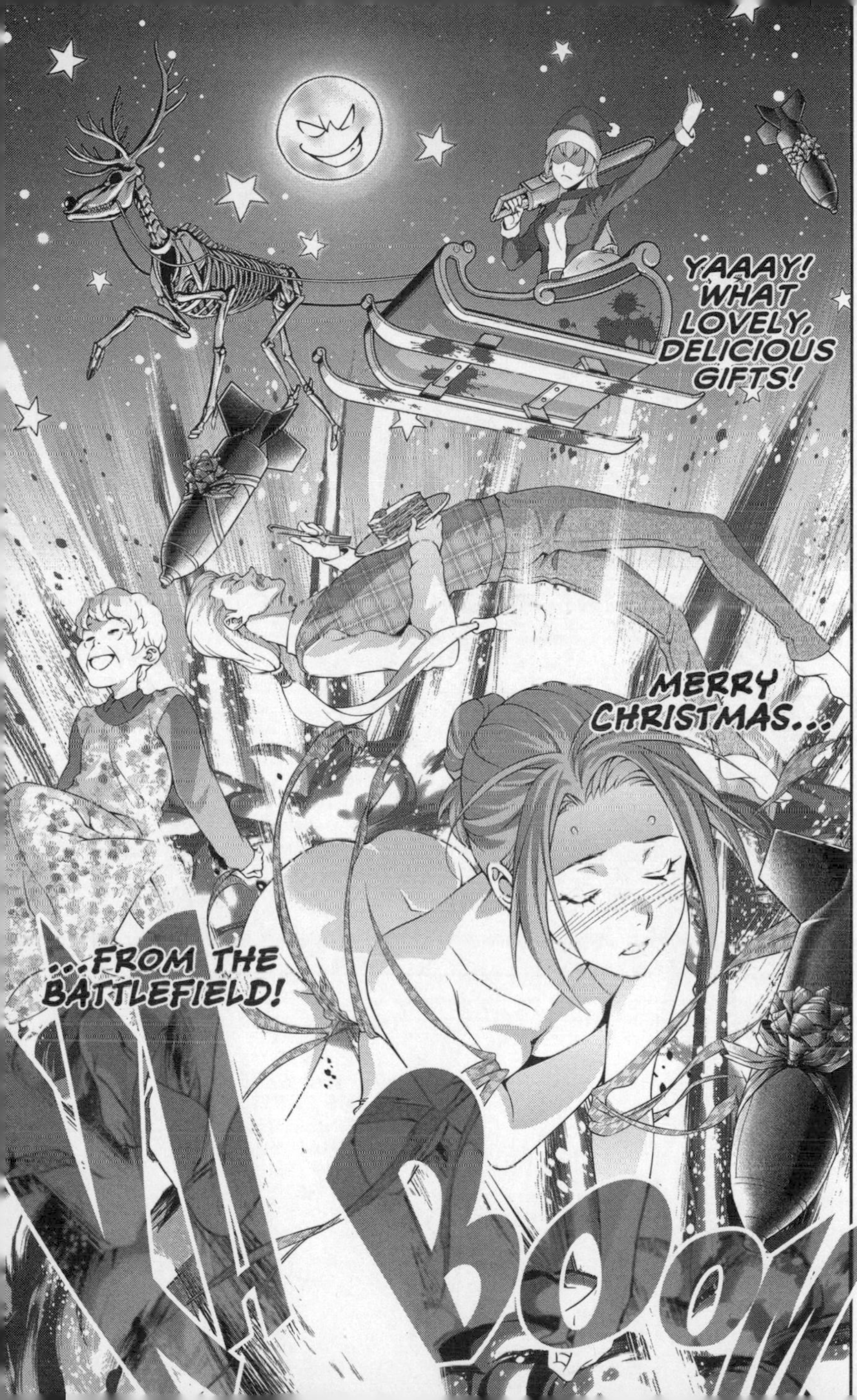
YAAAY! WHAT LOVELY, DELICIOUS GIFTS!
MERRY CHRISTMAS...
...FROM THE BATTLEFIELD!
BOOM

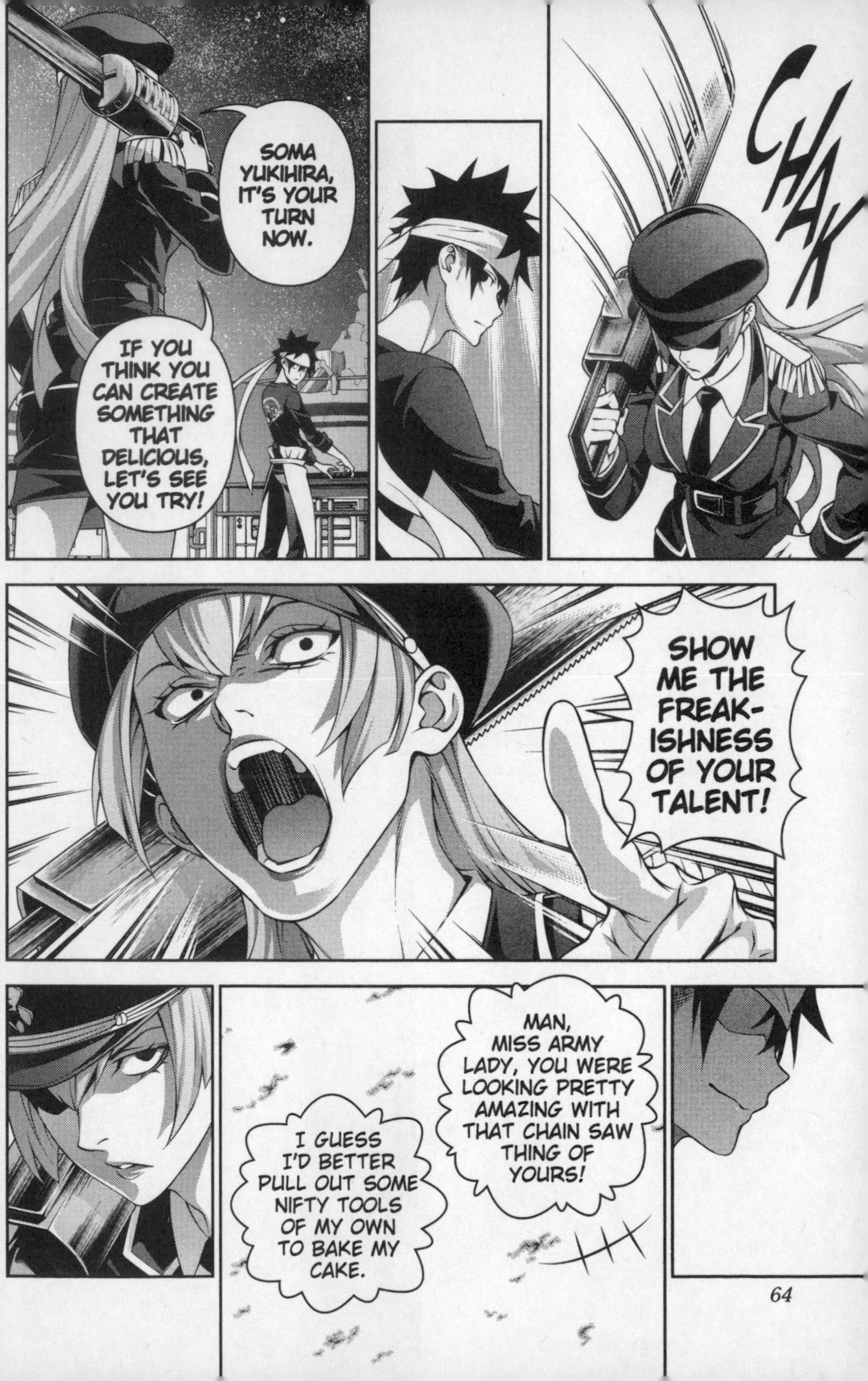
CHAK
SOMA YUKIHIRA, IT'S YOUR TURN NOW.
IF YOU THINK YOU CAN CREATE SOMETHING THAT DELICIOUS, LET'S SEE YOU TRY!
SHOW ME THE FREAK-ISHNESS OF YOUR TALENT!
MAN, MISS ARMY LADY, YOU WERE LOOKING PRETTY AMAZING WITH THAT CHAIN SAW THING OF YOURS!
I GUESS I'D BETTER PULL OUT SOME NIFTY TOOLS OF MY OWN TO BAKE MY CAKE.

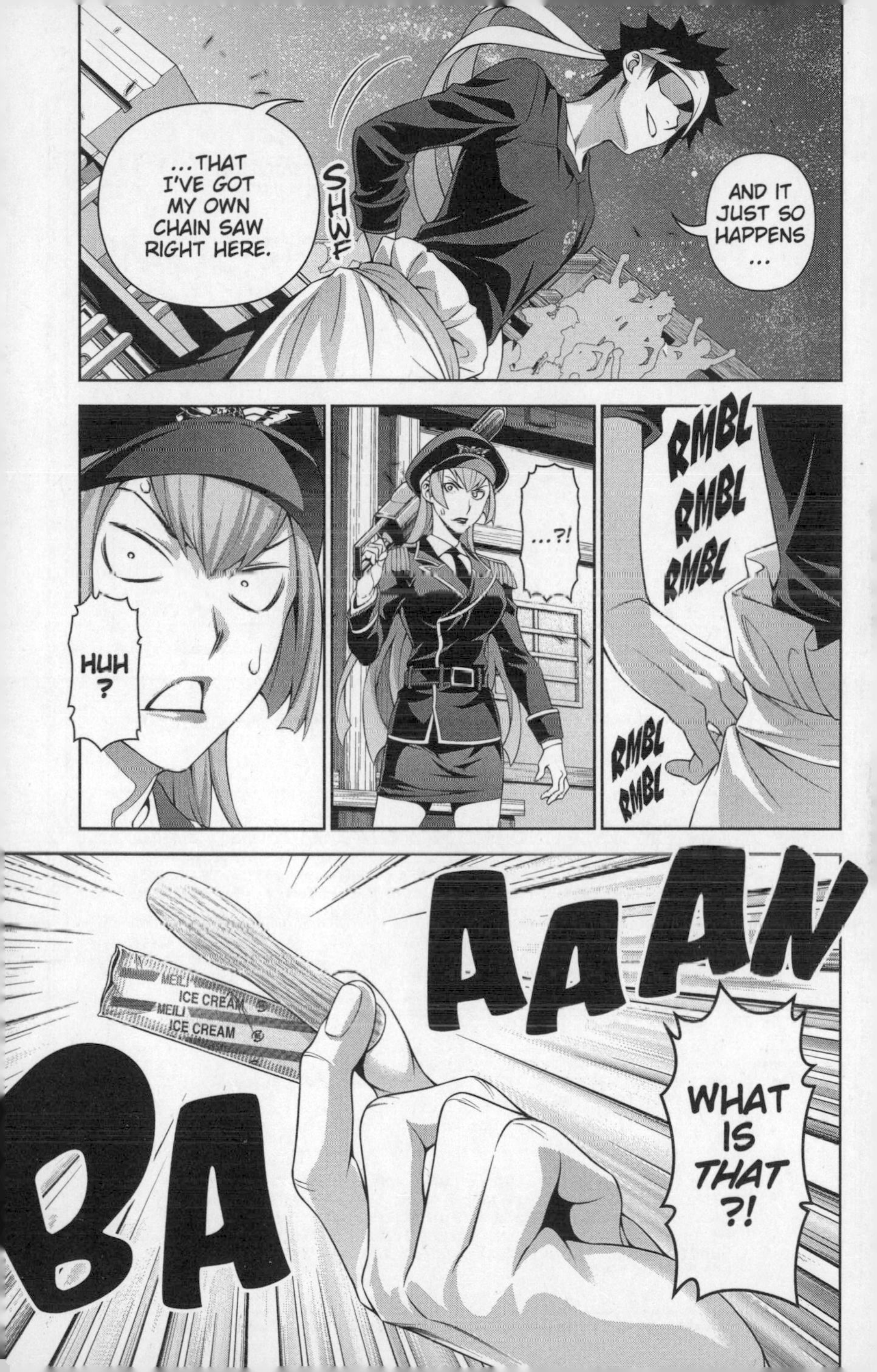
AND IT JUST SO HAPPENS ...
SHWF
...THAT I'VE GOT MY OWN CHAIN SAW RIGHT HERE.
RMBL RMBL RMBL
RMBL RMBL
...?!
HUH ?
WHAT IS THAT ?!
AAAN
MEILI ICE CREAM
MEILI ICE CREAM
BA

ARTIST: YUTO TSUKUDA RECIPE BY: YUKI MORISAKI

VOLUME 34
SPECIAL SUPPLEMENT!

PRACTICAL RECIPE #1

GLARE
MS. SARGE

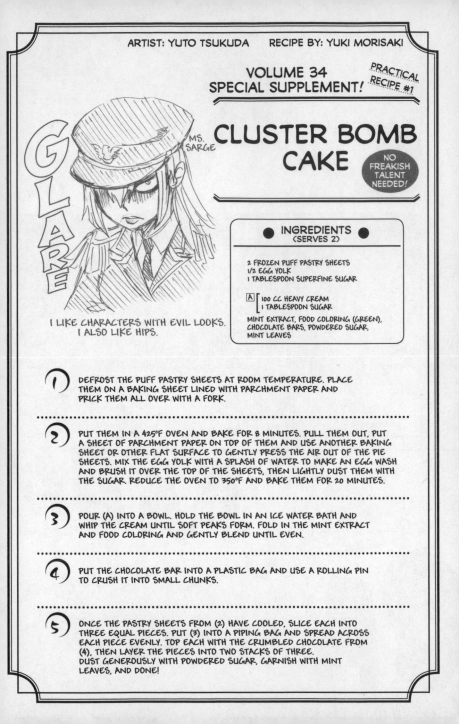

I LIKE CHARACTERS WITH EVIL LOOKS.
I ALSO LIKE HIPS.

CLUSTER BOMB CAKE

NO FREAKISH TALENT NEEDED!

INGREDIENTS
(SERVES 2)

2 FROZEN PUFF PASTRY SHEETS
1/2 EGG YOLK
1 TABLESPOON SUPERFINE SUGAR

A [100 CC HEAVY CREAM
1 TABLESPOON SUGAR

MINT EXTRACT, FOOD COLORING (GREEN), CHOCOLATE BARS, POWDERED SUGAR, MINT LEAVES

1. DEFROST THE PUFF PASTRY SHEETS AT ROOM TEMPERATURE. PLACE THEM ON A BAKING SHEET LINED WITH PARCHMENT PAPER AND PRICK THEM ALL OVER WITH A FORK.

2. PUT THEM IN A 425°F OVEN AND BAKE FOR 8 MINUTES. PULL THEM OUT, PUT A SHEET OF PARCHMENT PAPER ON TOP OF THEM AND USE ANOTHER BAKING SHEET OR OTHER FLAT SURFACE TO GENTLY PRESS THE AIR OUT OF THE PIE SHEETS. MIX THE EGG YOLK WITH A SPLASH OF WATER TO MAKE AN EGG WASH AND BRUSH IT OVER THE TOP OF THE SHEETS, THEN LIGHTLY DUST THEM WITH THE SUGAR. REDUCE THE OVEN TO 350°F AND BAKE THEM FOR 20 MINUTES.

3. POUR (A) INTO A BOWL. HOLD THE BOWL IN AN ICE WATER BATH AND WHIP THE CREAM UNTIL SOFT PEAKS FORM. FOLD IN THE MINT EXTRACT AND FOOD COLORING AND GENTLY BLEND UNTIL EVEN.

4. PUT THE CHOCOLATE BAR INTO A PLASTIC BAG AND USE A ROLLING PIN TO CRUSH IT INTO SMALL CHUNKS.

5. ONCE THE PASTRY SHEETS FROM (2) HAVE COOLED, SLICE EACH INTO THREE EQUAL PIECES. PUT (3) INTO A PIPING BAG AND SPREAD ACROSS EACH PIECE EVENLY. TOP EACH WITH THE CRUMBLED CHOCOLATE FROM (4), THEN LAYER THE PIECES INTO TWO STACKS OF THREE.
DUST GENEROUSLY WITH POWDERED SUGAR, GARNISH WITH MINT LEAVES, AND DONE!

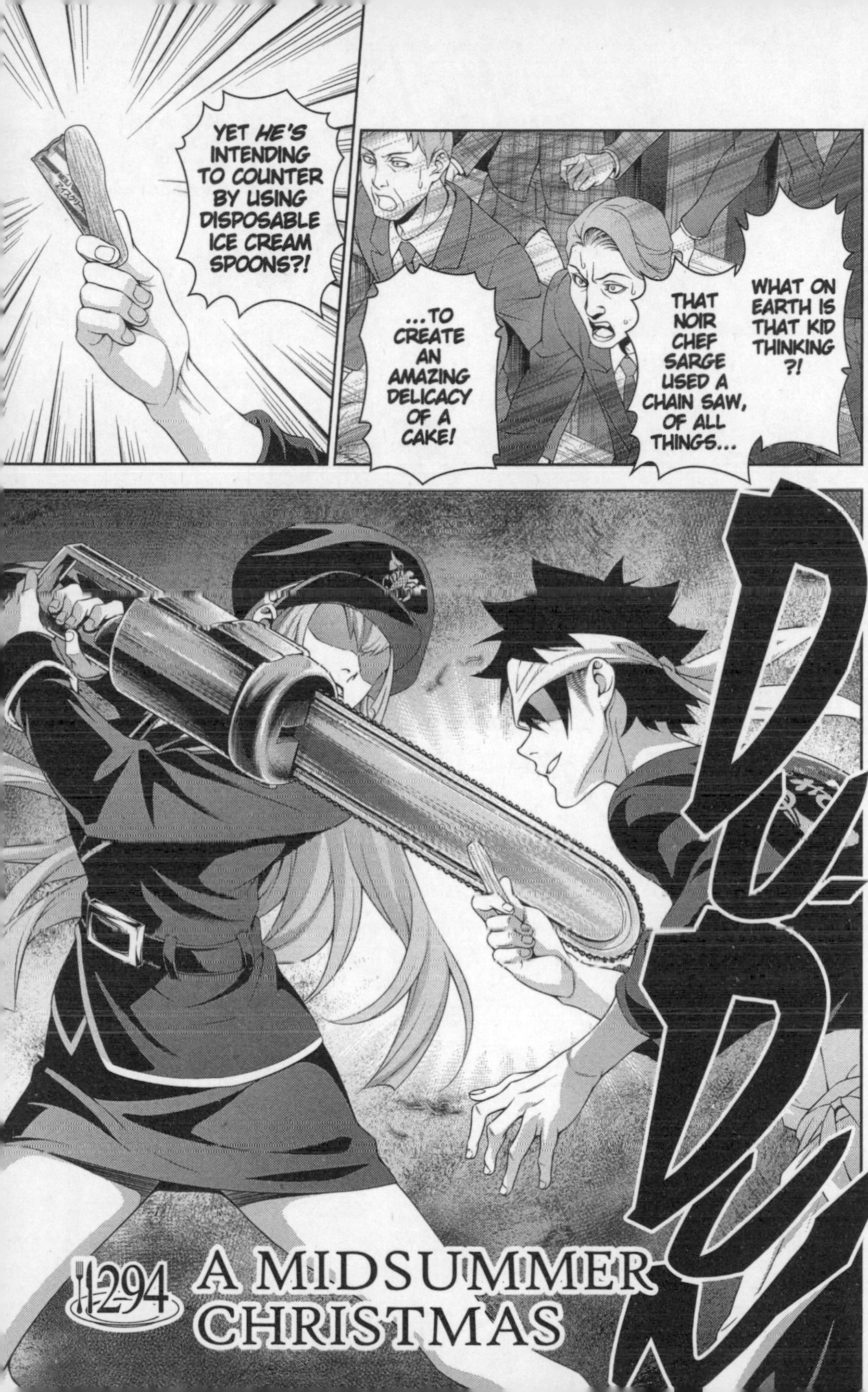
WHAT ON EARTH IS THAT KID THINKING?!
THAT NOIR CHEF SARGE USED A CHAIN SAW, OF ALL THINGS...
...TO CREATE AN AMAZING DELICACY OF A CAKE!
YET HE'S INTENDING TO COUNTER BY USING DISPOSABLE ICE CREAM SPOONS?!
294 A MIDSUMMER CHRISTMAS

294 A MIDSUMMER CHRISTMAS

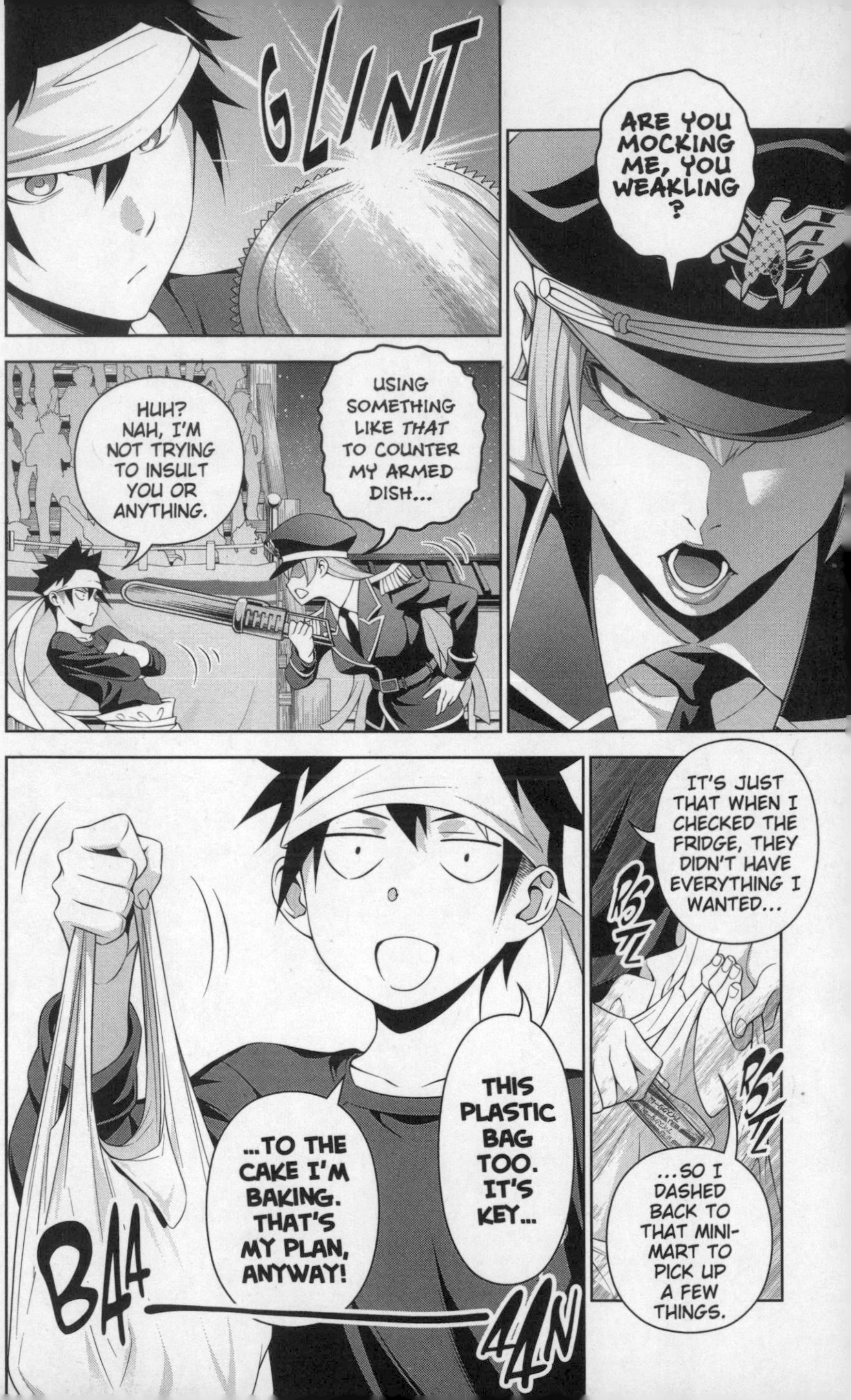
ARE YOU MOCKING ME, YOU WEAKLING?
GLINT
USING SOMETHING LIKE *THAT* TO COUNTER MY ARMED DISH...
HUH? NAH, I'M NOT TRYING TO INSULT YOU OR ANYTHING.
IT'S JUST THAT WHEN I CHECKED THE FRIDGE, THEY DIDN'T HAVE EVERYTHING I WANTED...
RSTL
RSTL
...SO I DASHED BACK TO THAT MINI-MART TO PICK UP A FEW THINGS.
THIS PLASTIC BAG TOO. IT'S KEY...
...TO THE CAKE I'M BAKING. THAT'S MY PLAN, ANYWAY!
BAAAAN

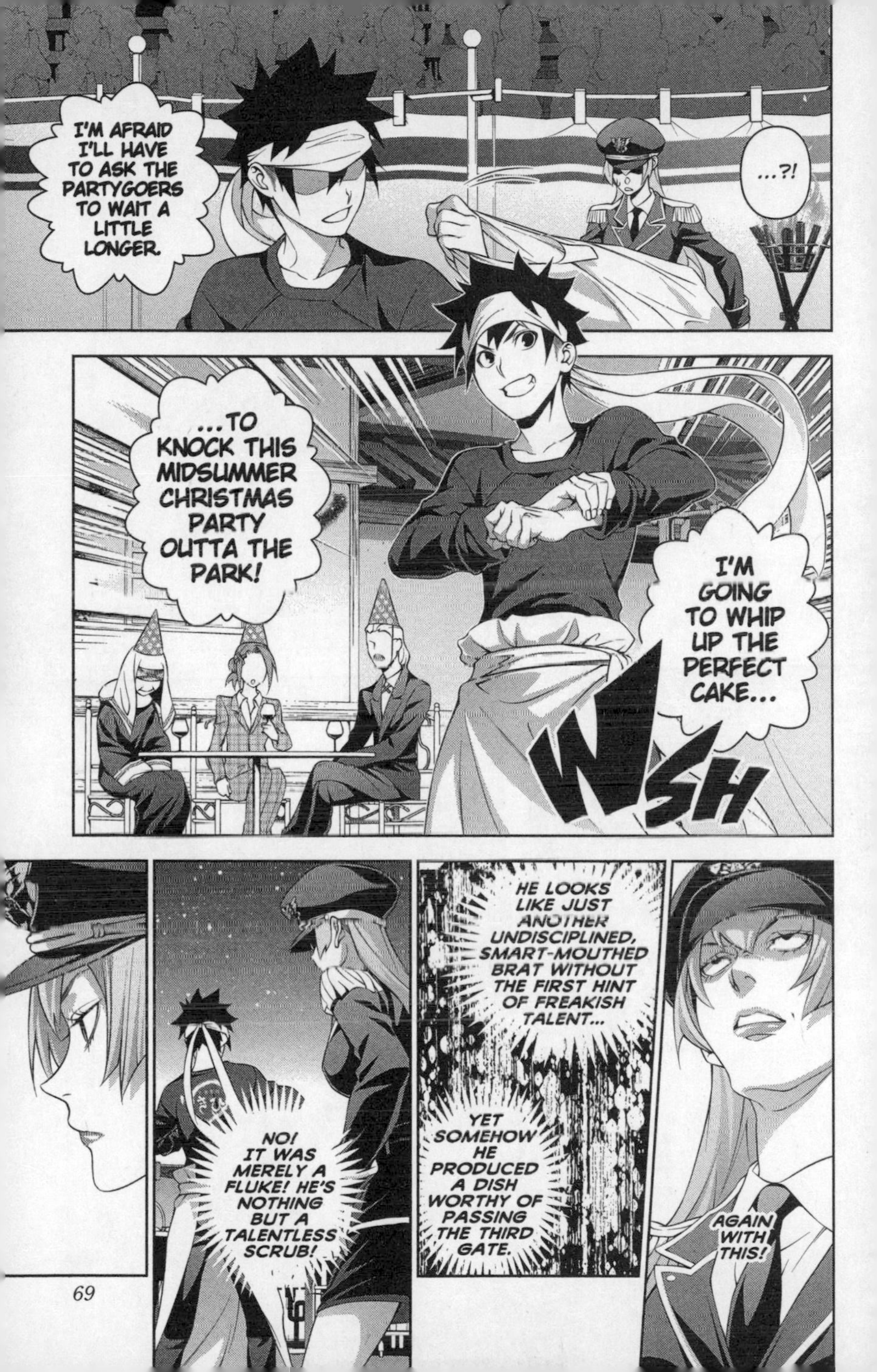
I'M AFRAID I'LL HAVE TO ASK THE PARTYGOERS TO WAIT A LITTLE LONGER.
...?!
I'M GOING TO WHIP UP THE PERFECT CAKE...
...TO KNOCK THIS MIDSUMMER CHRISTMAS PARTY OUTTA THE PARK!
WSH
AGAIN WITH THIS!
HE LOOKS LIKE JUST ANOTHER UNDISCIPLINED, SMART-MOUTHED BRAT WITHOUT THE FIRST HINT OF FREAKISH TALENT...
YET SOMEHOW HE PRODUCED A DISH WORTHY OF PASSING THE THIRD GATE.
NO! IT WAS MERELY A FLUKE! HE'S NOTHING BUT A TALENTLESS SCRUB!

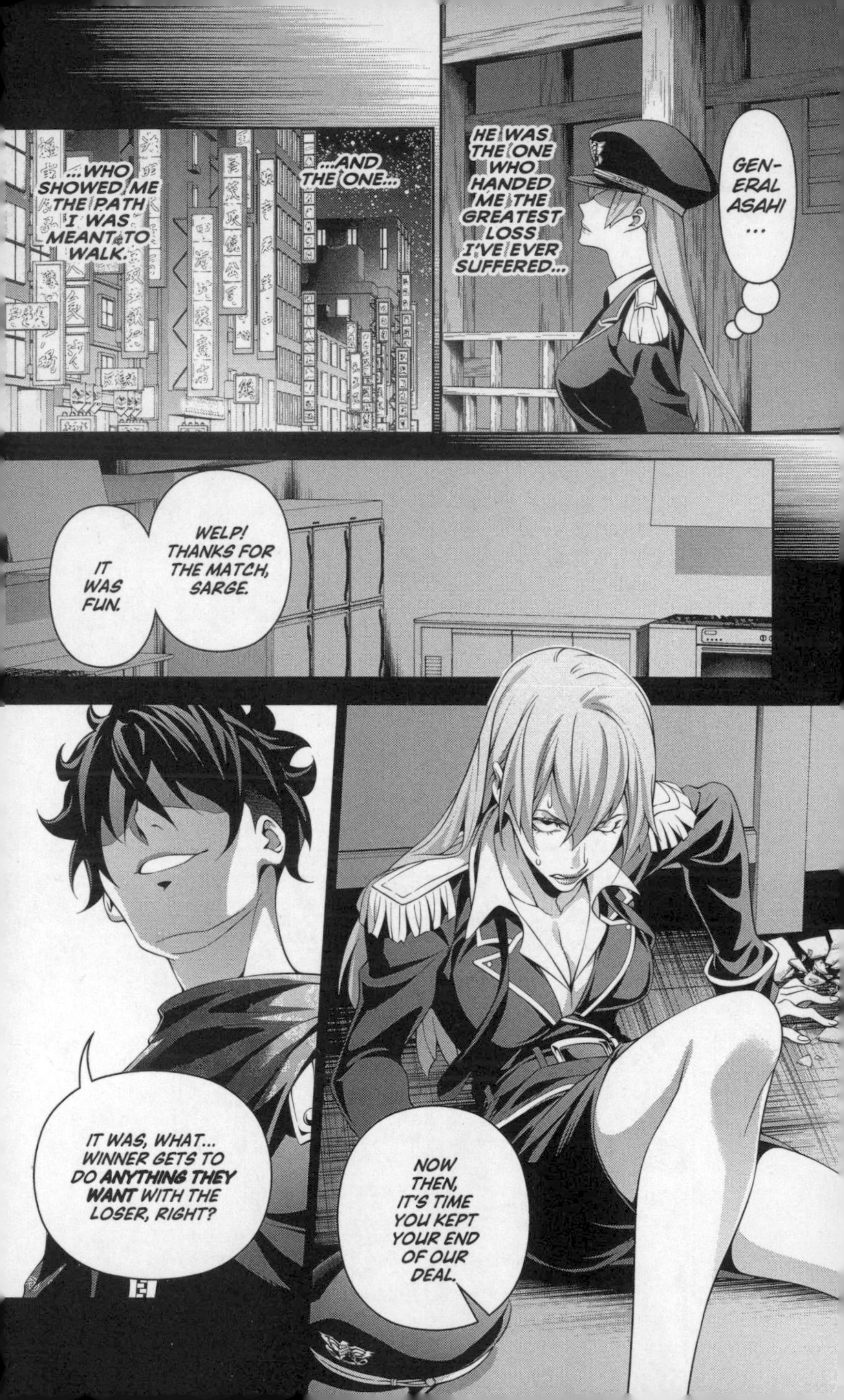
GEN-ERAL ASAHI...
HE WAS THE ONE WHO HANDED ME THE GREATEST LOSS I'VE EVER SUFFERED...
...AND THE ONE...
...WHO SHOWED ME THE PATH I WAS MEANT TO WALK.
WELP! THANKS FOR THE MATCH, SARGE.
IT WAS FUN.
NOW THEN, IT'S TIME YOU KEPT YOUR END OF OUR DEAL.
IT WAS, WHAT... WINNER GETS TO DO **ANYTHING THEY WANT** WITH THE LOSER, RIGHT?

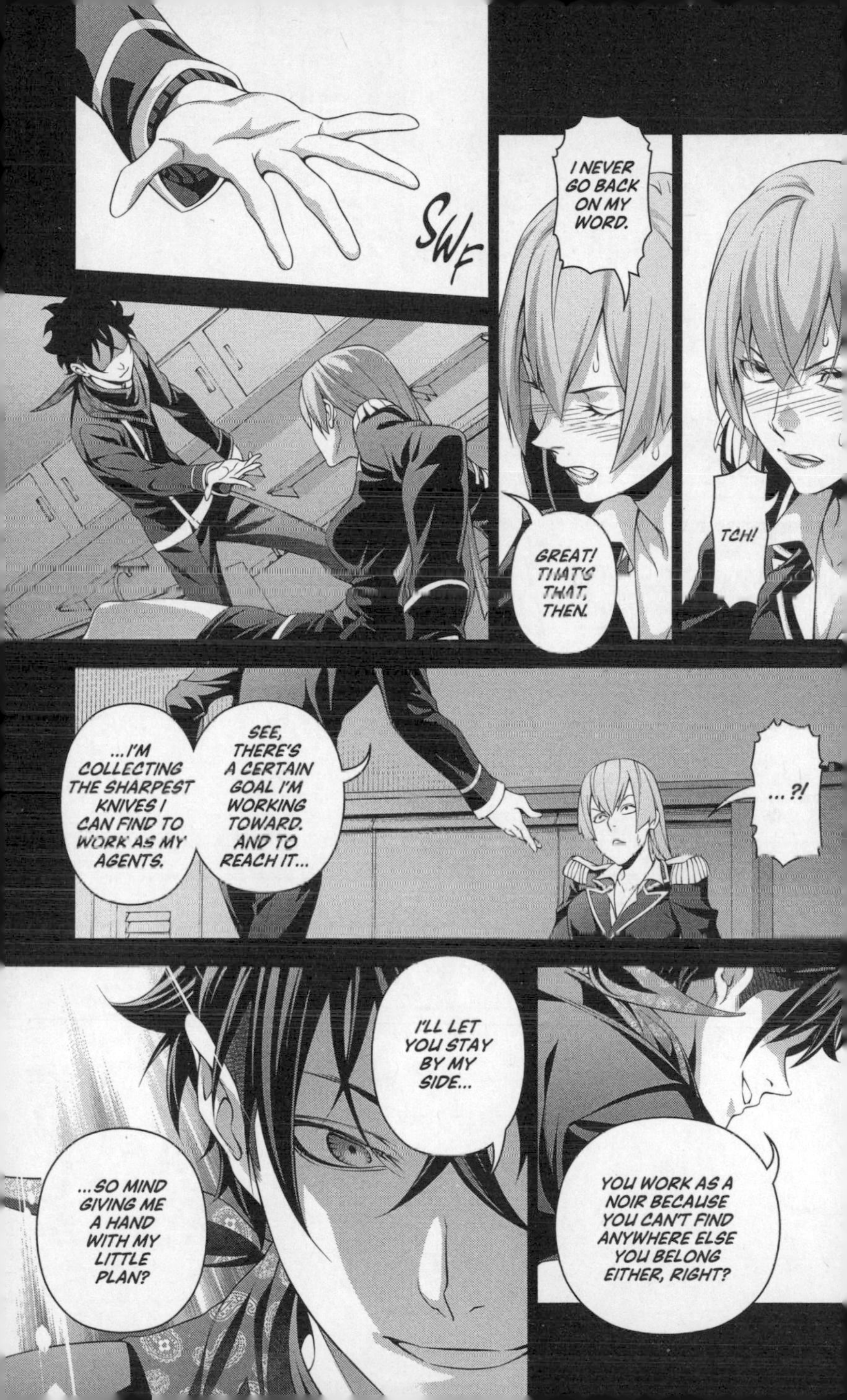
TCH!
I NEVER GO BACK ON MY WORD.
GREAT! THAT'S THAT, THEN.
SWF
...?!
SEE, THERE'S A CERTAIN GOAL I'M WORKING TOWARD. AND TO REACH IT...
...I'M COLLECTING THE SHARPEST KNIVES I CAN FIND TO WORK AS MY AGENTS.
YOU WORK AS A NOIR BECAUSE YOU CAN'T FIND ANYWHERE ELSE YOU BELONG EITHER, RIGHT?
I'LL LET YOU STAY BY MY SIDE...
...SO MIND GIVING ME A HAND WITH MY LITTLE PLAN?

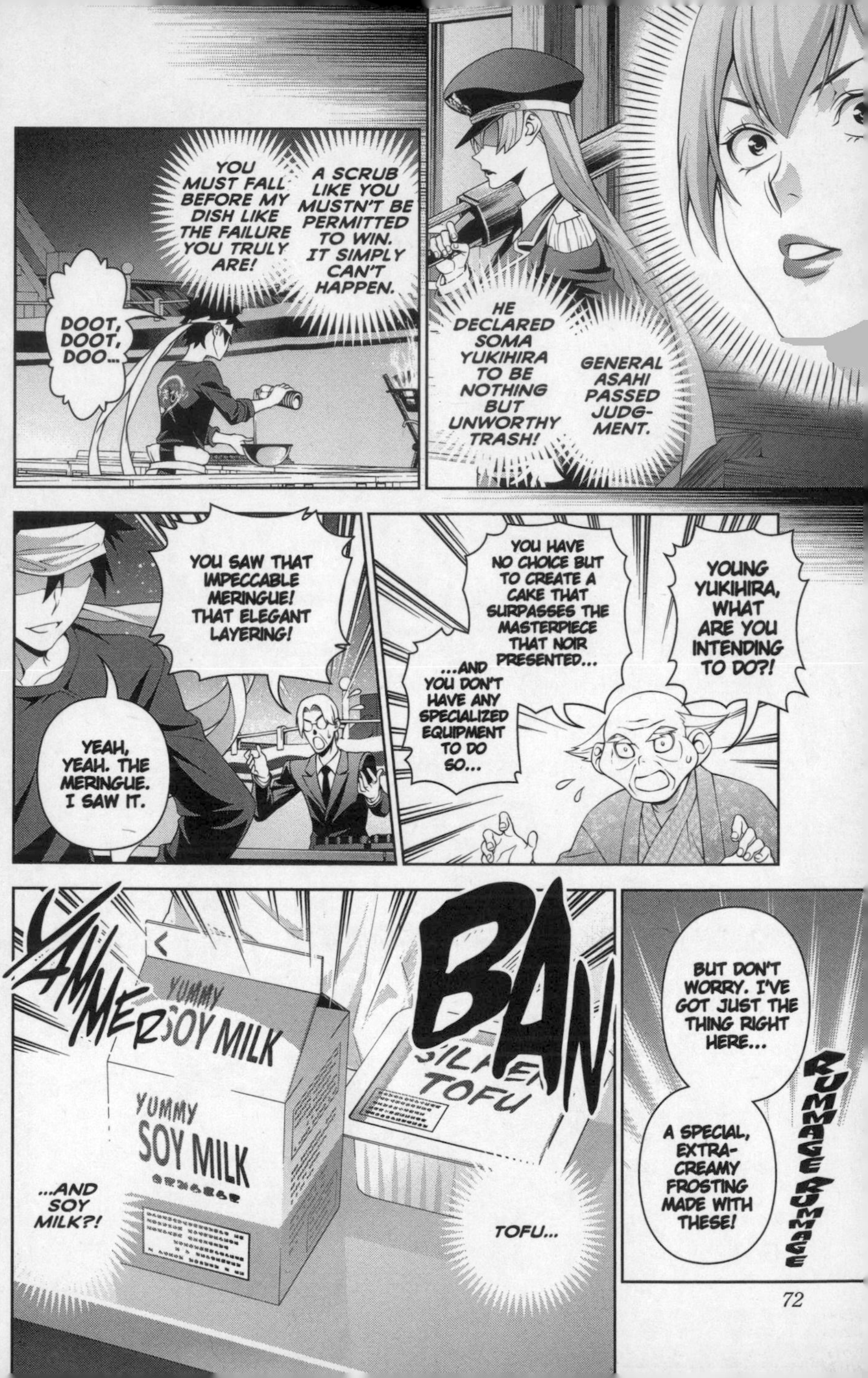
GENERAL ASAHI PASSED JUDG-MENT.
HE DECLARED SOMA YUKIHIRA TO BE NOTHING BUT UNWORTHY TRASH!
A SCRUB LIKE YOU MUSTN'T BE PERMITTED TO WIN. IT SIMPLY CAN'T HAPPEN.
YOU MUST FALL BEFORE MY DISH LIKE THE FAILURE YOU TRULY ARE!
DOOT, DOOT, DOO...
YOUNG YUKIHIRA, WHAT ARE YOU INTENDING TO DO?!
YOU HAVE NO CHOICE BUT TO CREATE A CAKE THAT SURPASSES THE MASTERPIECE THAT NOIR PRESENTED...
...AND YOU DON'T HAVE ANY SPECIALIZED EQUIPMENT TO DO SO...
YOU SAW THAT IMPECCABLE MERINGUE! THAT ELEGANT LAYERING!
YEAH, YEAH. THE MERINGUE. I SAW IT.
RUMMAGE RUMMAGE
BUT DON'T WORRY. I'VE GOT JUST THE THING RIGHT HERE...
A SPECIAL, EXTRA-CREAMY FROSTING MADE WITH THESE!
BAM
TOFU
TOFU...
YUMMY SOY MILK
YUMMY SOY MILK
...AND SOY MILK?!
YAMMER

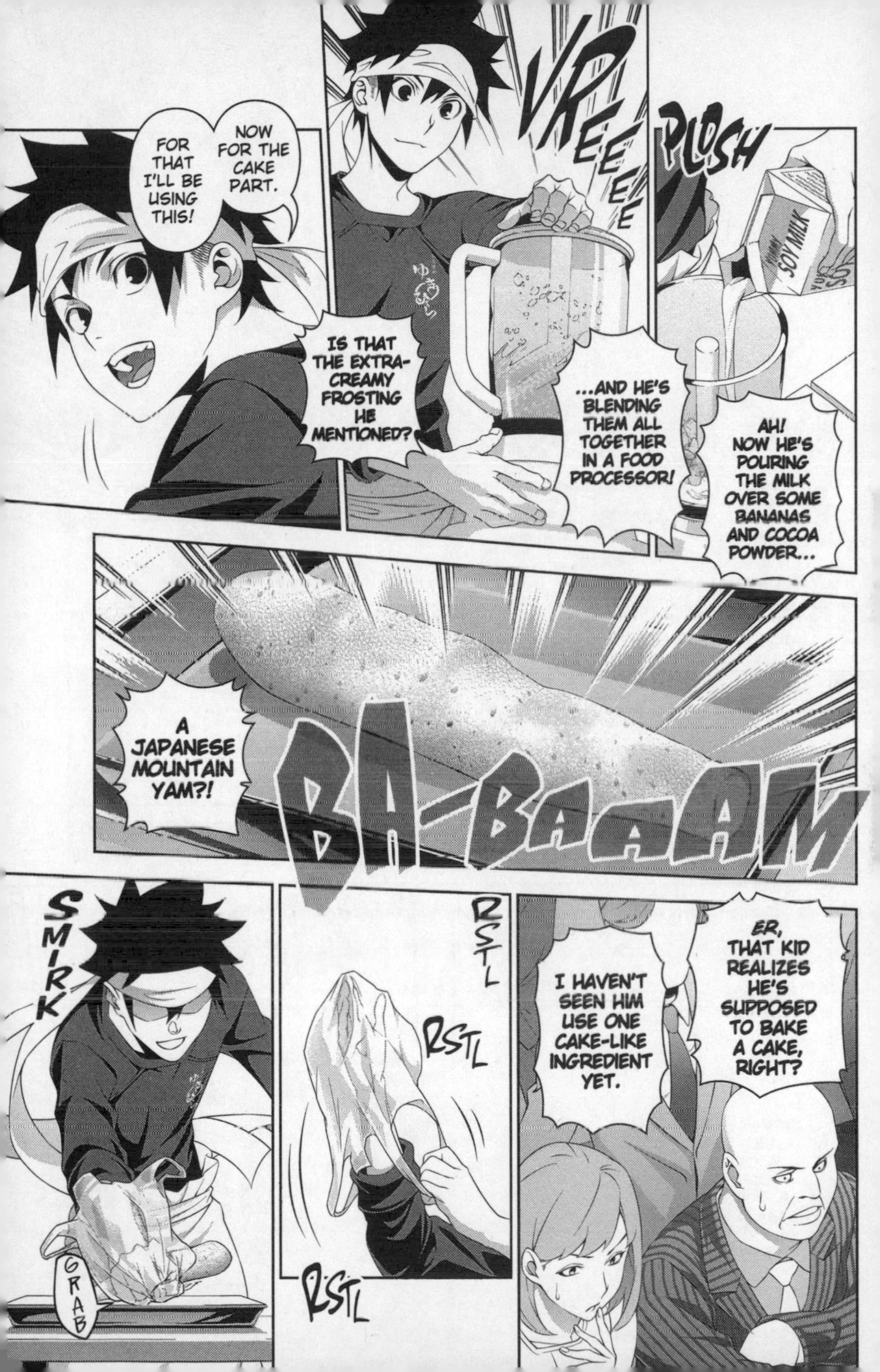
PLOSH
SOY MILK
AH! NOW HE'S POURING THE MILK OVER SOME BANANAS AND COCOA POWDER...
VREEEEE
...AND HE'S BLENDING THEM ALL TOGETHER IN A FOOD PROCESSOR!
IS THAT THE EXTRA-CREAMY FROSTING HE MENTIONED?
NOW FOR THE CAKE PART.
FOR THAT I'LL BE USING THIS!
A JAPANESE MOUNTAIN YAM?!
BA-BAAAM
ER, THAT KID REALIZES HE'S SUPPOSED TO BAKE A CAKE, RIGHT?
I HAVEN'T SEEN HIM USE ONE CAKE-LIKE INGREDIENT YET.
RSTL
RSTL
RSTL
SMIRK
GRAB

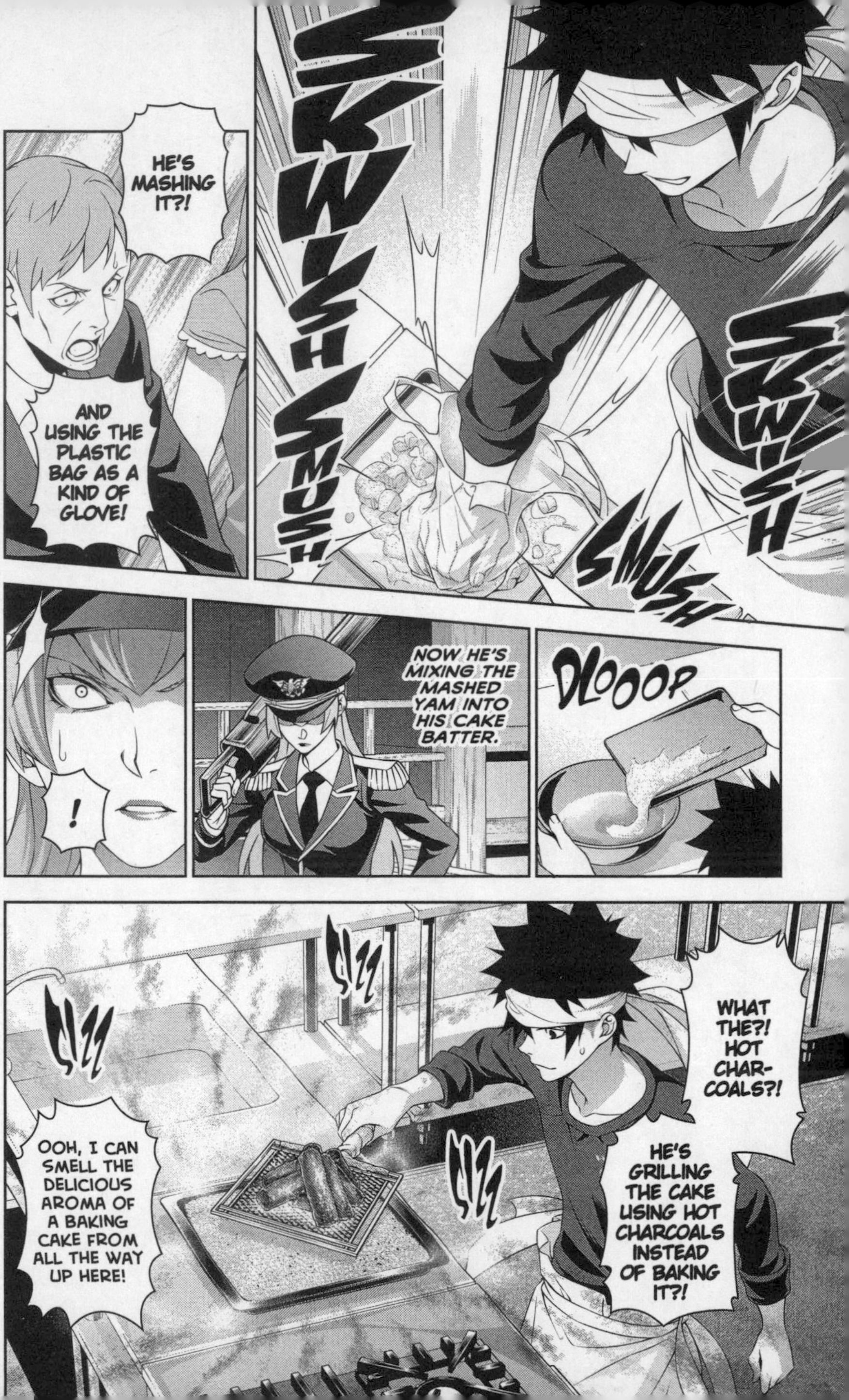

SMUSH
SMUSH
SMUSH
SMUSH
HE'S MASHING IT?!
AND USING THE PLASTIC BAG AS A KIND OF GLOVE!
DLOOOP
NOW HE'S MIXING THE MASHED YAM INTO HIS CAKE BATTER.
!
SIZZ
SIZZ
SIZZ
WHAT THE?! HOT CHAR-COALS?!
HE'S GRILLING THE CAKE USING HOT CHARCOALS INSTEAD OF BAKING IT?!
OOH, I CAN SMELL THE DELICIOUS AROMA OF A BAKING CAKE FROM ALL THE WAY UP HERE!

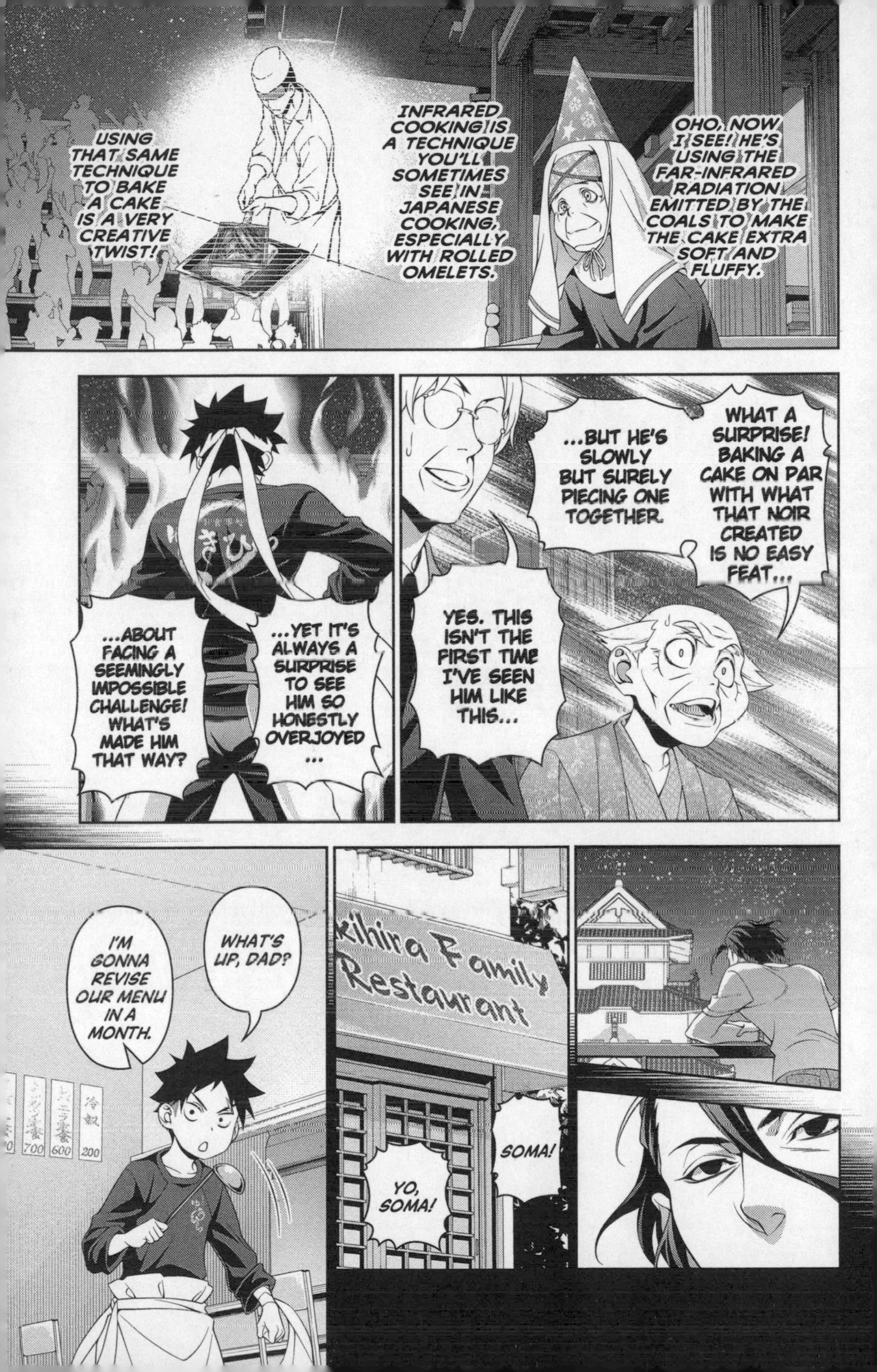
OHO, NOW I SEE! HE'S USING THE FAR-INFRARED RADIATION EMITTED BY THE COALS TO MAKE THE CAKE EXTRA SOFT AND FLUFFY.
INFRARED COOKING IS A TECHNIQUE YOU'LL SOMETIMES SEE IN JAPANESE COOKING, ESPECIALLY WITH ROLLED OMELETS.
USING THAT SAME TECHNIQUE TO BAKE A CAKE IS A VERY CREATIVE TWIST!
WHAT A SURPRISE! BAKING A CAKE ON PAR WITH WHAT THAT NOIR CREATED IS NO EASY FEAT...
...BUT HE'S SLOWLY BUT SURELY PIECING ONE TOGETHER.
YES. THIS ISN'T THE FIRST TIME I'VE SEEN HIM LIKE THIS...
...YET IT'S ALWAYS A SURPRISE TO SEE HIM SO HONESTLY OVERJOYED...
...ABOUT FACING A SEEMINGLY IMPOSSIBLE CHALLENGE! WHAT'S MADE HIM THAT WAY?
kihira Family Restaurant
SOMA!
YO, SOMA!
WHAT'S UP, DAD?
I'M GONNA REVISE OUR MENU IN A MONTH.
700
600
200

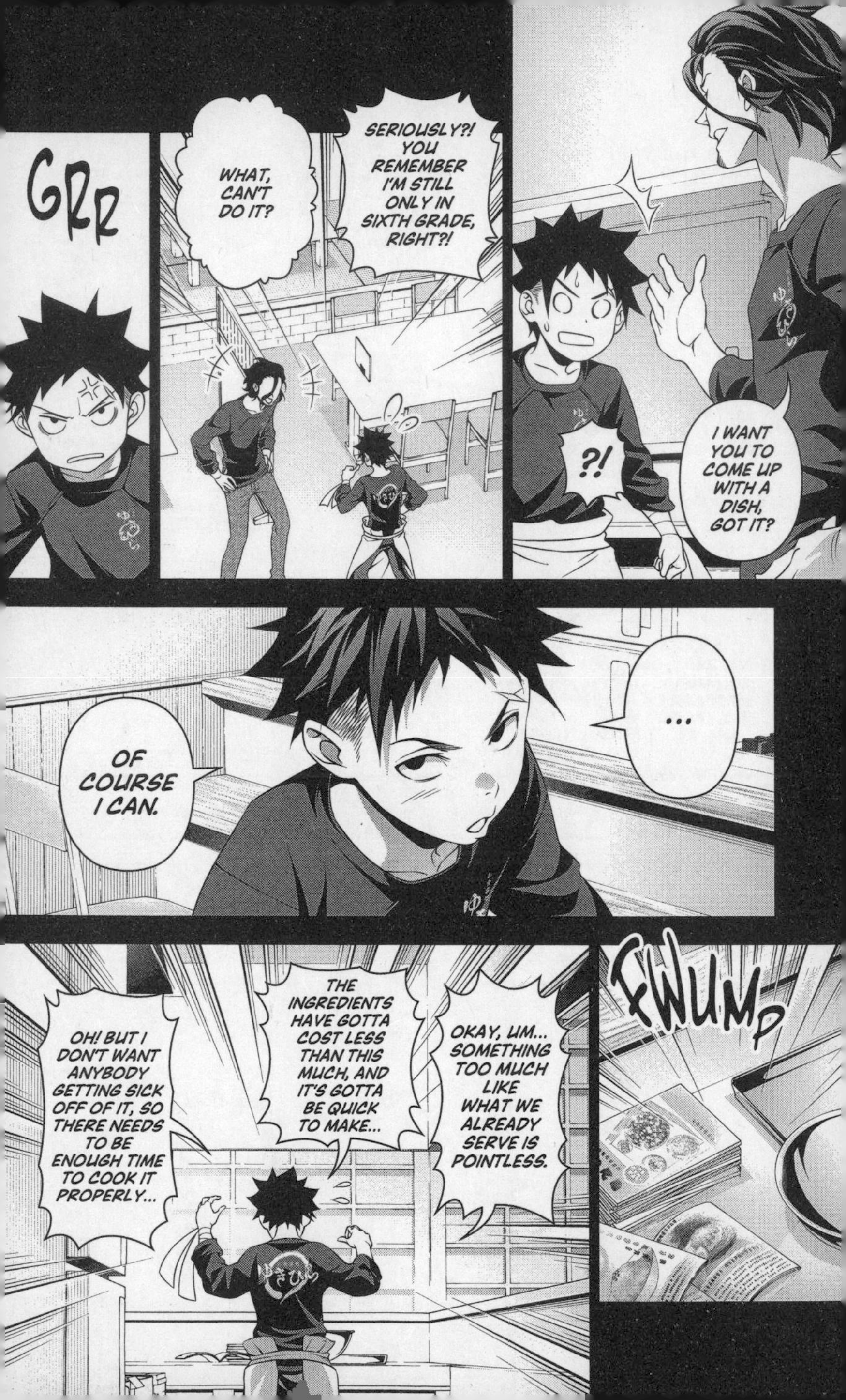
I WANT YOU TO COME UP WITH A DISH, GOT IT?
?!
SERIOUSLY?! YOU REMEMBER I'M STILL ONLY IN SIXTH GRADE, RIGHT?!
WHAT, CAN'T DO IT?
GRR
...
OF COURSE I CAN.
FWUMP
OKAY, UM... SOMETHING TOO MUCH LIKE WHAT WE ALREADY SERVE IS POINTLESS.
THE INGREDIENTS HAVE GOTTA COST LESS THAN THIS MUCH, AND IT'S GOTTA BE QUICK TO MAKE...
OH! BUT I DON'T WANT ANYBODY GETTING SICK OFF OF IT, SO THERE NEEDS TO BE ENOUGH TIME TO COOK IT PROPERLY...

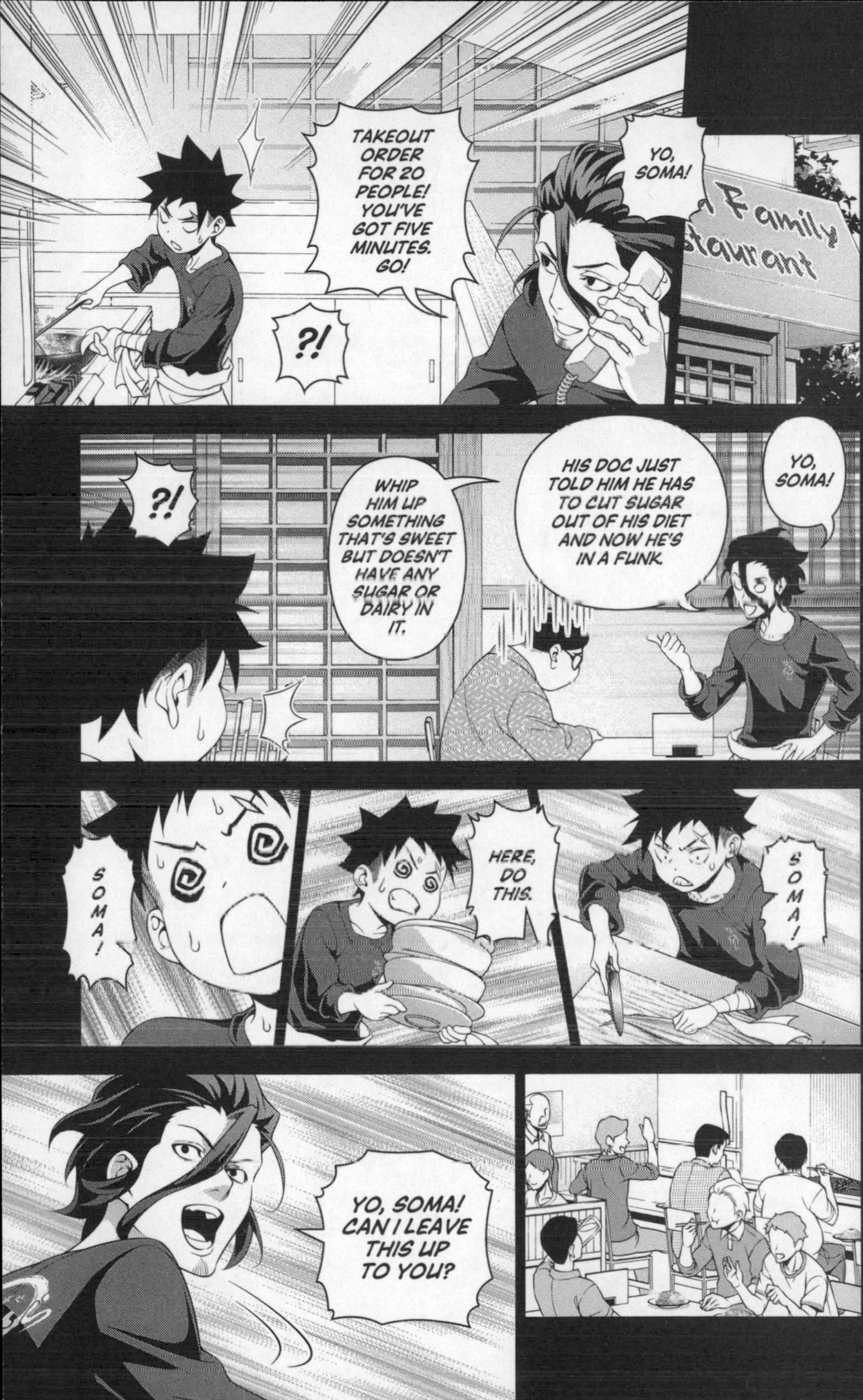
YO, SOMA!
TAKEOUT ORDER FOR 20 PEOPLE! YOU'VE GOT FIVE MINUTES. GO!
?!
YO, SOMA!
HIS DOC JUST TOLD HIM HE HAS TO CUT SUGAR OUT OF HIS DIET AND NOW HE'S IN A FUNK.
WHIP HIM UP SOMETHING THAT'S SWEET BUT DOESN'T HAVE ANY SUGAR OR DAIRY IN IT.
?!
SOMA!
HERE, DO THIS.
SOMA!
YO, SOMA! CAN I LEAVE THIS UP TO YOU?

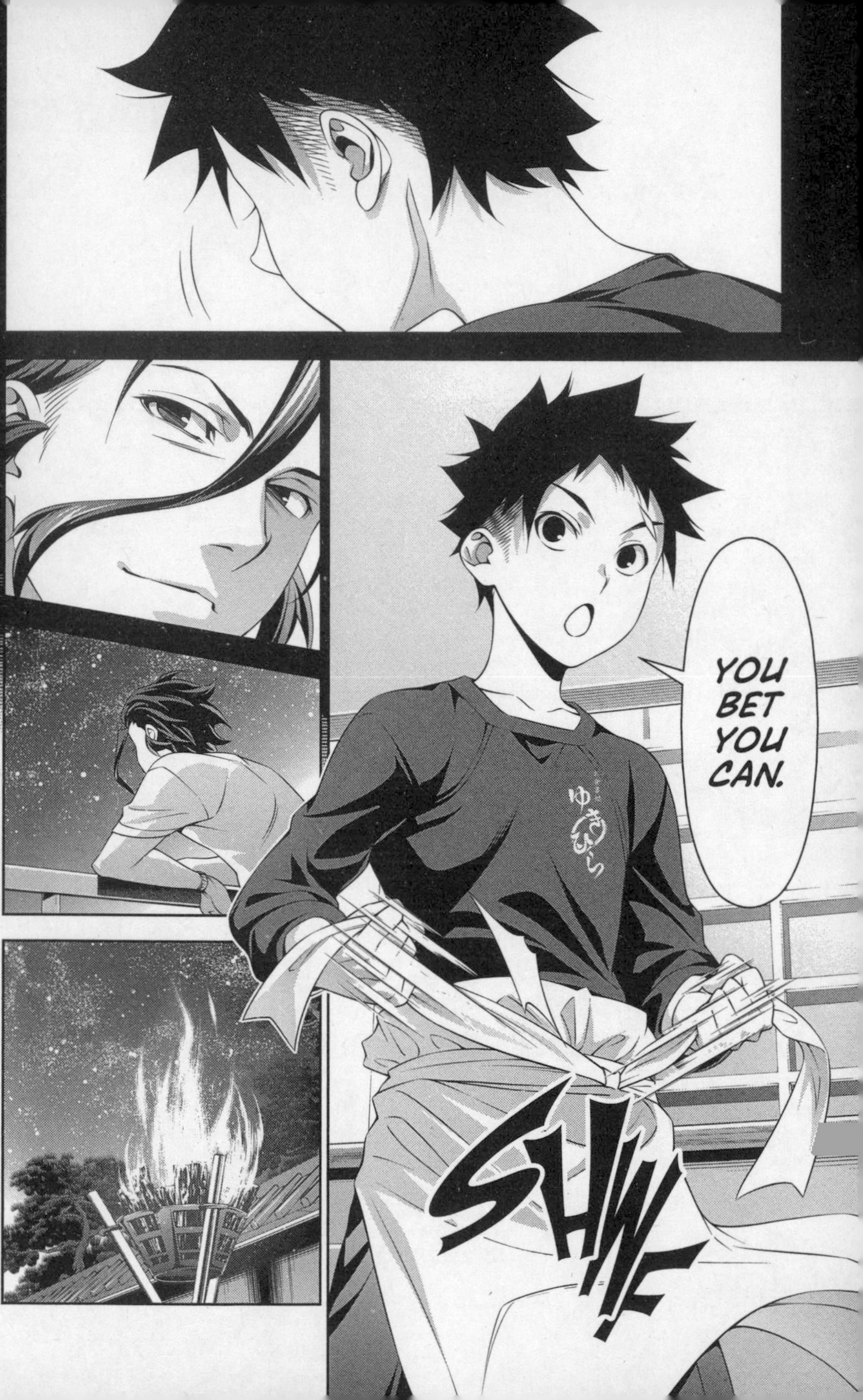
YOU BET YOU CAN.
SHWF

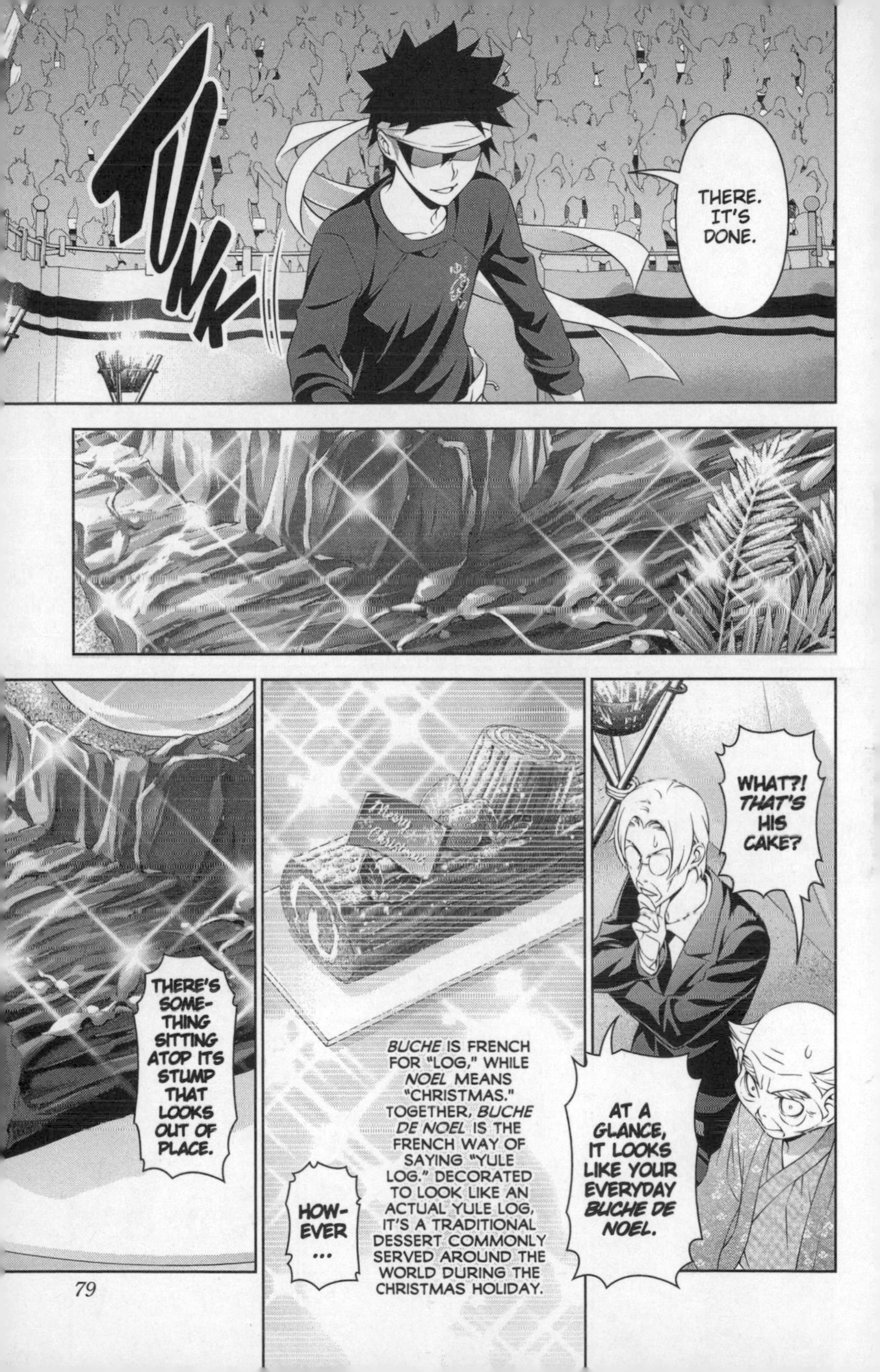
TONK
THERE. IT'S DONE.
WHAT?! *THAT'S* HIS CAKE?
AT A GLANCE, IT LOOKS LIKE YOUR EVERYDAY *BUCHE DE NOEL*.
Merry Christmas
BUCHE IS FRENCH FOR "LOG," WHILE *NOEL* MEANS "CHRISTMAS." TOGETHER, *BUCHE DE NOEL* IS THE FRENCH WAY OF SAYING "YULE LOG." DECORATED TO LOOK LIKE AN ACTUAL YULE LOG, IT'S A TRADITIONAL DESSERT COMMONLY SERVED AROUND THE WORLD DURING THE CHRISTMAS HOLIDAY.
HOW-EVER...
THERE'S SOME-THING SITTING ATOP ITS STUMP THAT LOOKS OUT OF PLACE.

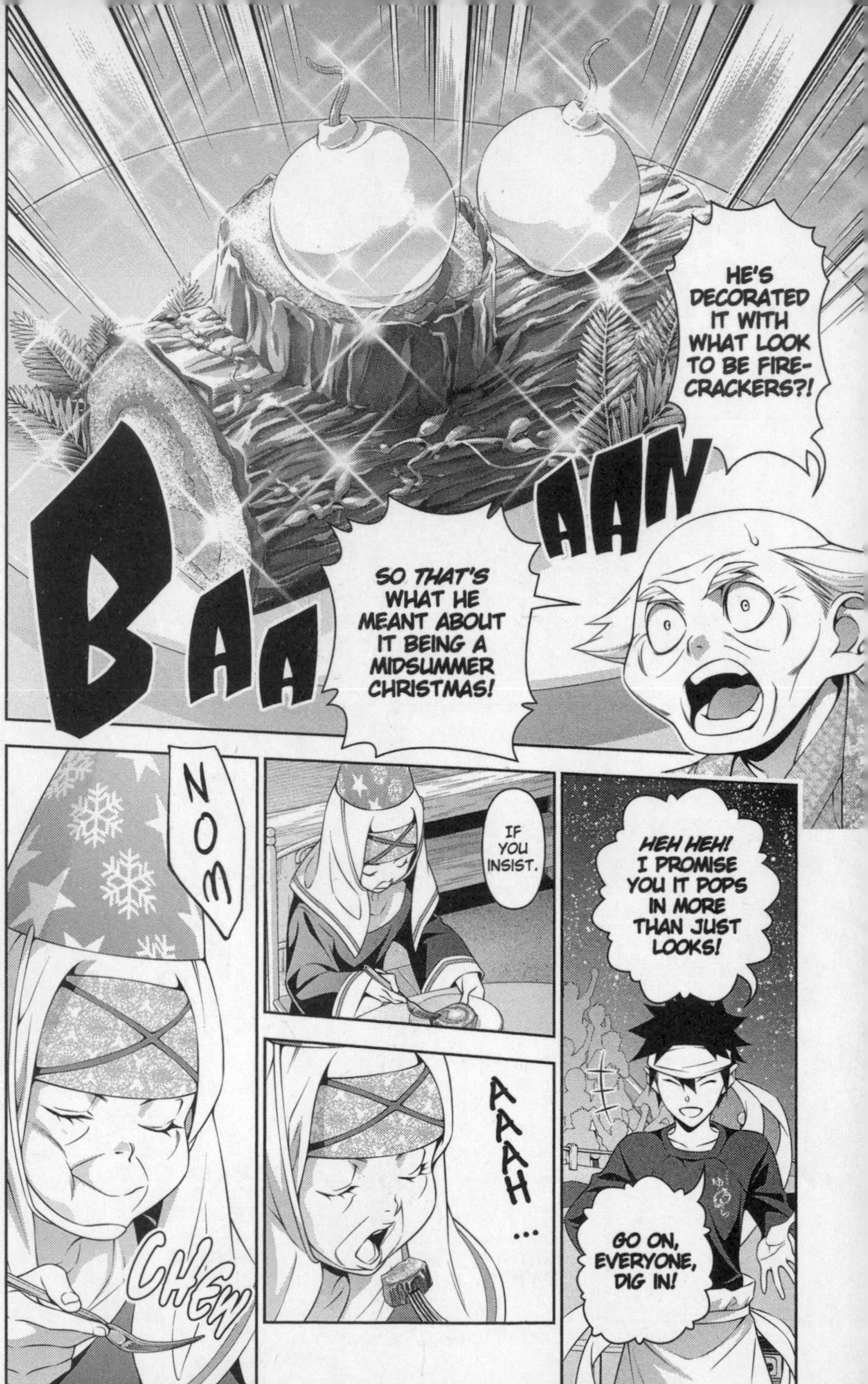
HE'S DECORATED IT WITH WHAT LOOK TO BE FIRE-CRACKERS?!
BAAAAAN
SO *THAT'S* WHAT HE MEANT ABOUT IT BEING A MIDSUMMER CHRISTMAS!
HEH HEH! I PROMISE YOU IT POPS IN MORE THAN JUST LOOKS!
GO ON, EVERYONE, DIG IN!
IF YOU INSIST.
AAAH...
NOM
CHEW

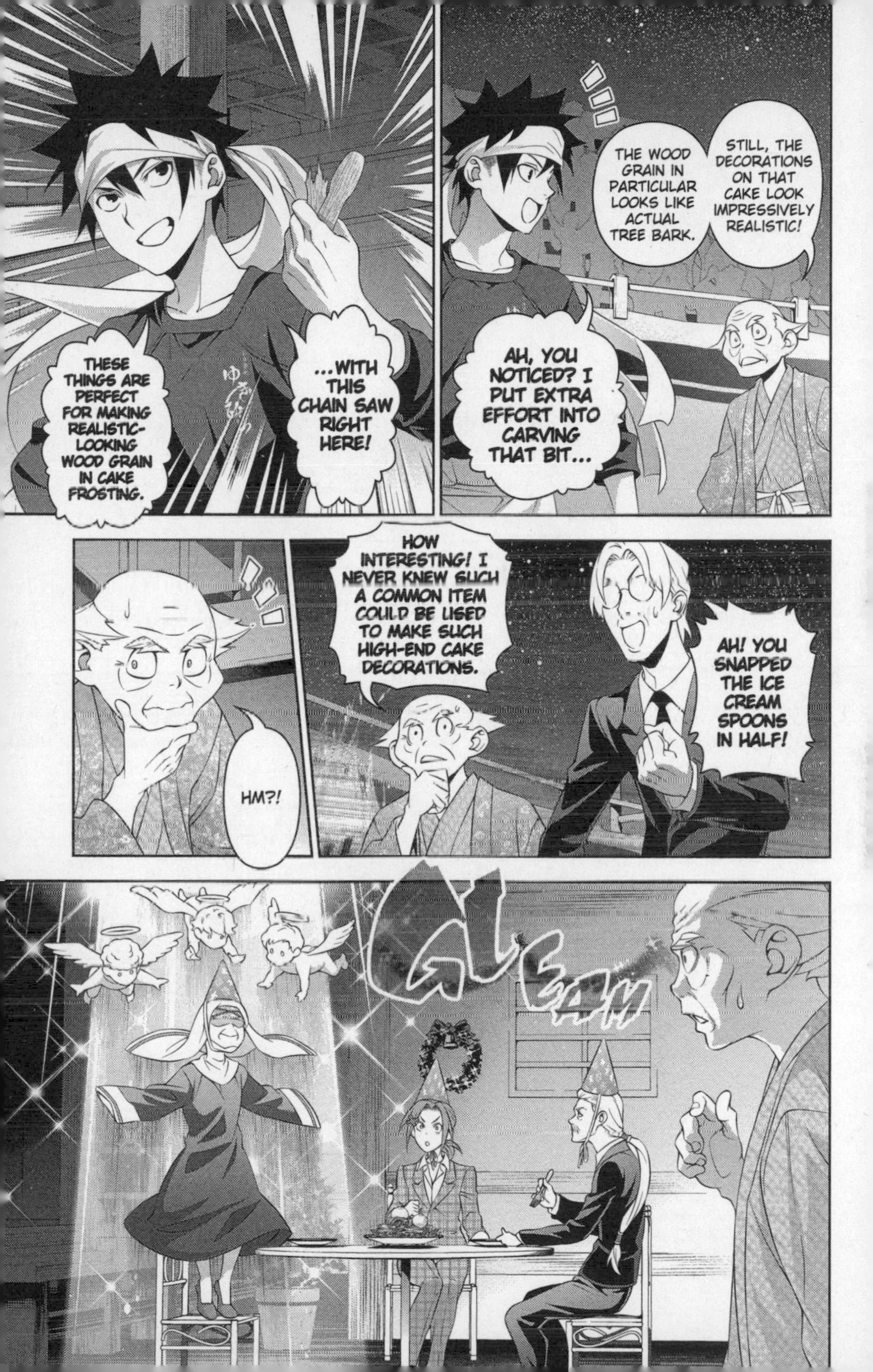
STILL, THE DECORATIONS ON THAT CAKE LOOK IMPRESSIVELY REALISTIC!
THE WOOD GRAIN IN PARTICULAR LOOKS LIKE ACTUAL TREE BARK.
AH, YOU NOTICED? I PUT EXTRA EFFORT INTO CARVING THAT BIT...
...WITH THIS CHAIN SAW RIGHT HERE!
THESE THINGS ARE PERFECT FOR MAKING REALISTIC-LOOKING WOOD GRAIN IN CAKE FROSTING.
AH! YOU SNAPPED THE ICE CREAM SPOONS IN HALF!
HOW INTERESTING! I NEVER KNEW SUCH A COMMON ITEM COULD BE USED TO MAKE SUCH HIGH-END CAKE DECORATIONS.
HM?!
GLEAM

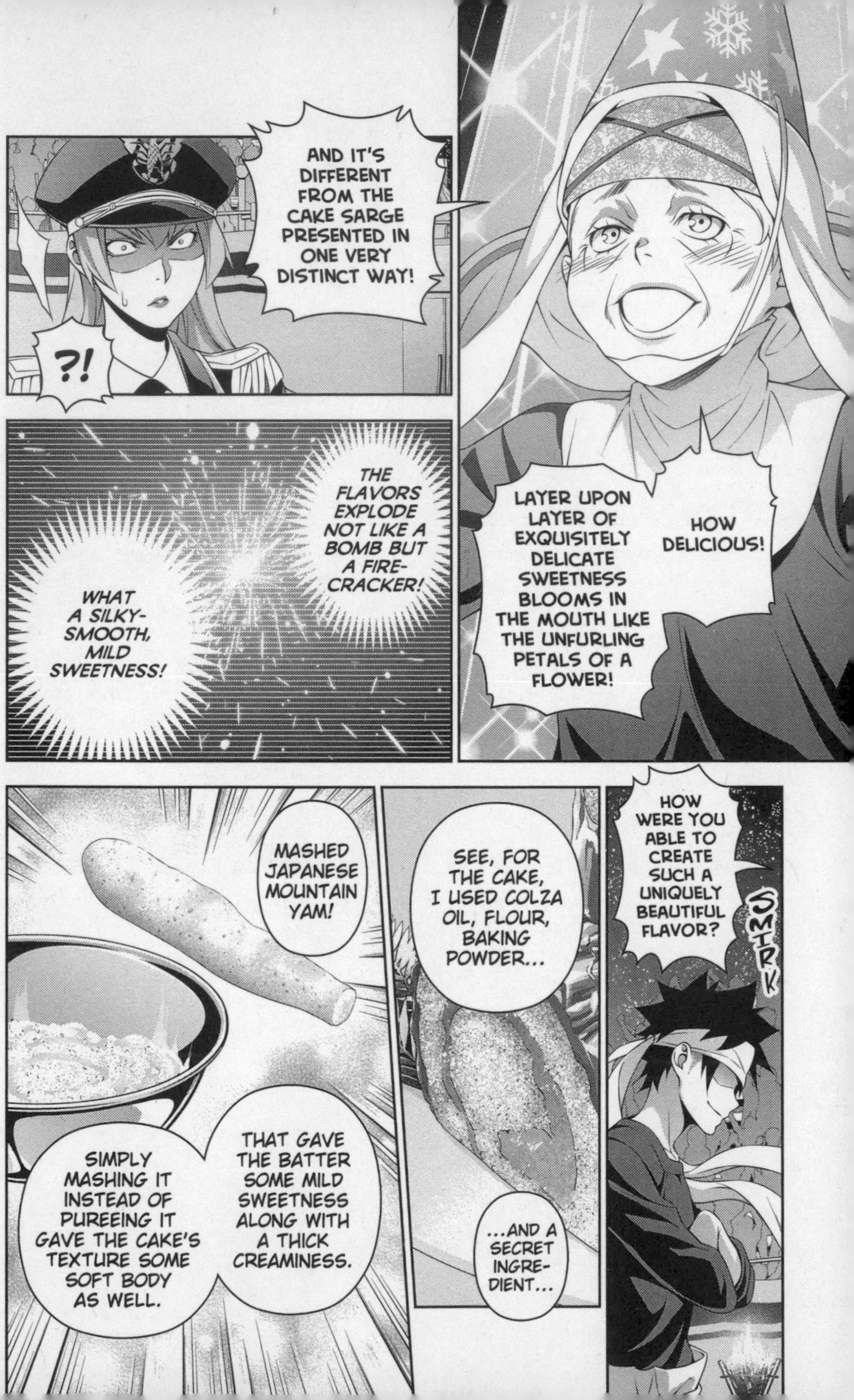
HOW DELICIOUS!
LAYER UPON LAYER OF EXQUISITELY DELICATE SWEETNESS BLOOMS IN THE MOUTH LIKE THE UNFURLING PETALS OF A FLOWER!
AND IT'S DIFFERENT FROM THE CAKE SARGE PRESENTED IN ONE VERY DISTINCT WAY!
?!
THE FLAVORS EXPLODE NOT LIKE A BOMB BUT A FIRE-CRACKER!
WHAT A SILKY-SMOOTH, MILD SWEETNESS!
HOW WERE YOU ABLE TO CREATE SUCH A UNIQUELY BEAUTIFUL FLAVOR?
SMIRK
SEE, FOR THE CAKE, I USED COLZA OIL, FLOUR, BAKING POWDER...
...AND A SECRET INGRE-DIENT...
MASHED JAPANESE MOUNTAIN YAM!
THAT GAVE THE BATTER SOME MILD SWEETNESS ALONG WITH A THICK CREAMINESS.
SIMPLY MASHING IT INSTEAD OF PUREEING IT GAVE THE CAKE'S TEXTURE SOME SOFT BODY AS WELL.

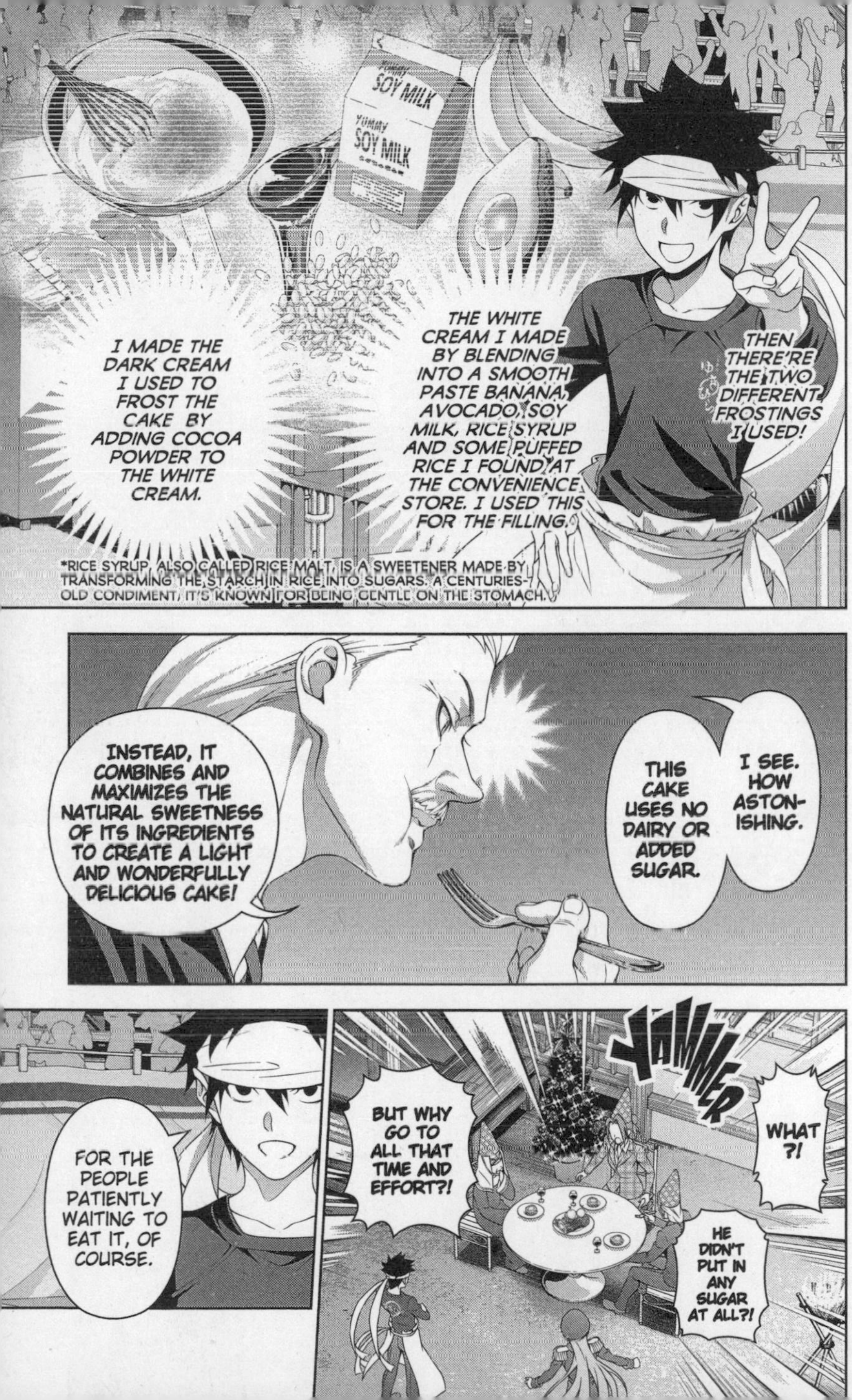
SOY MILK
YUMMY SOY MILK
THEN THERE'RE THE TWO DIFFERENT FROSTINGS I USED!
THE WHITE CREAM I MADE BY BLENDING INTO A SMOOTH PASTE BANANA, AVOCADO, SOY MILK, RICE SYRUP AND SOME PUFFED RICE I FOUND AT THE CONVENIENCE STORE. I USED THIS FOR THE FILLING.
I MADE THE DARK CREAM I USED TO FROST THE CAKE BY ADDING COCOA POWDER TO THE WHITE CREAM.
*RICE SYRUP, ALSO CALLED RICE MALT, IS A SWEETENER MADE BY TRANSFORMING THE STARCH IN RICE INTO SUGARS. A CENTURIES-OLD CONDIMENT, IT'S KNOWN FOR BEING GENTLE ON THE STOMACH.
I SEE. HOW ASTON-ISHING.
THIS CAKE USES NO DAIRY OR ADDED SUGAR.
INSTEAD, IT COMBINES AND MAXIMIZES THE NATURAL SWEETNESS OF ITS INGREDIENTS TO CREATE A LIGHT AND WONDERFULLY DELICIOUS CAKE!
YAMMER
WHAT?!
HE DIDN'T PUT IN ANY SUGAR AT ALL?!
BUT WHY GO TO ALL THAT TIME AND EFFORT?!
FOR THE PEOPLE PATIENTLY WAITING TO EAT IT, OF COURSE.

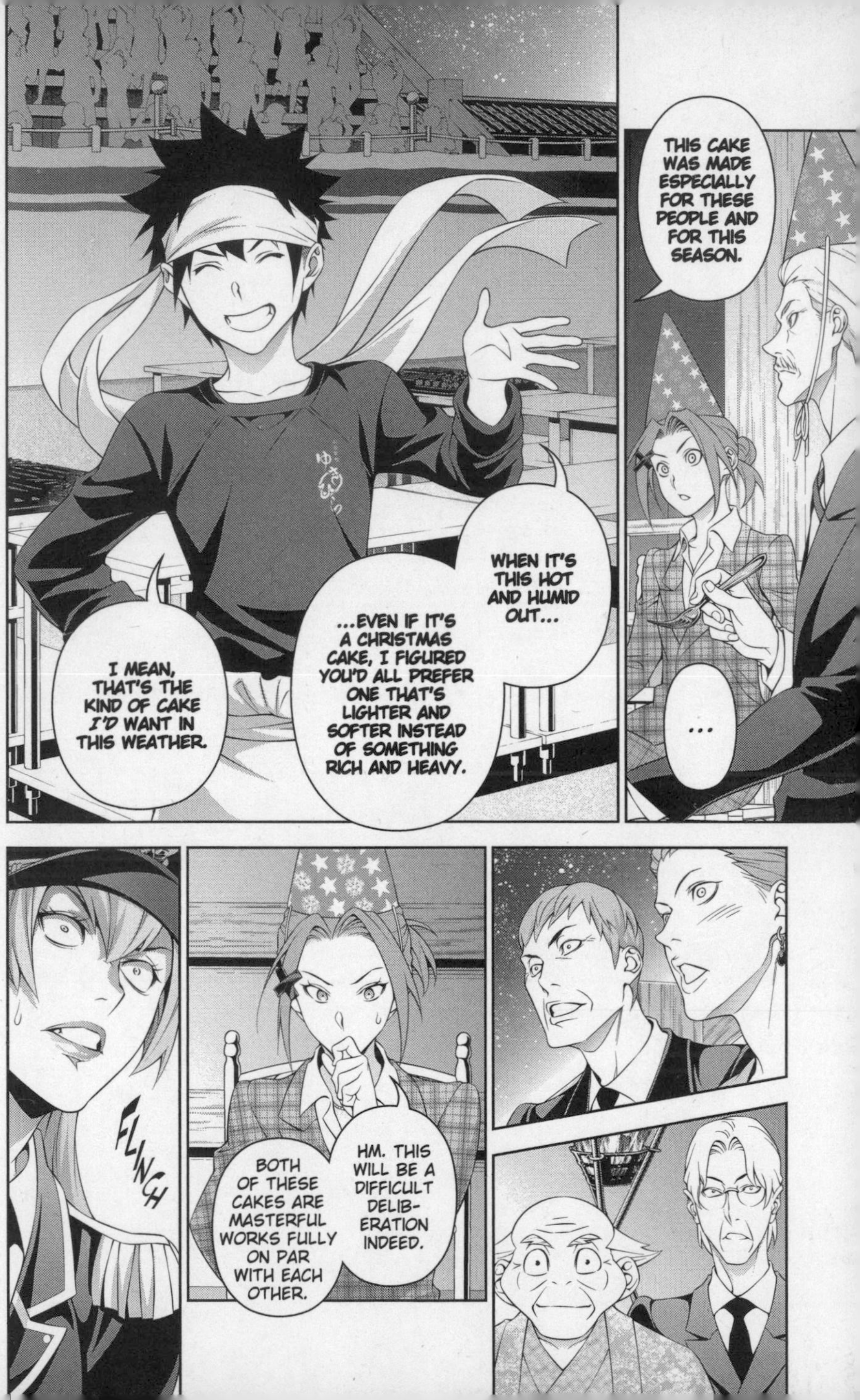
THIS CAKE WAS MADE ESPECIALLY FOR THESE PEOPLE AND FOR THIS SEASON.
...
WHEN IT'S THIS HOT AND HUMID OUT...
...EVEN IF IT'S A CHRISTMAS CAKE, I FIGURED YOU'D ALL PREFER ONE THAT'S LIGHTER AND SOFTER INSTEAD OF SOMETHING RICH AND HEAVY.
I MEAN, THAT'S THE KIND OF CAKE *I'D* WANT IN THIS WEATHER.
HM. THIS WILL BE A DIFFICULT DELIB-ERATION INDEED.
BOTH OF THESE CAKES ARE MASTERFUL WORKS FULLY ON PAR WITH EACH OTHER.
FLINCH

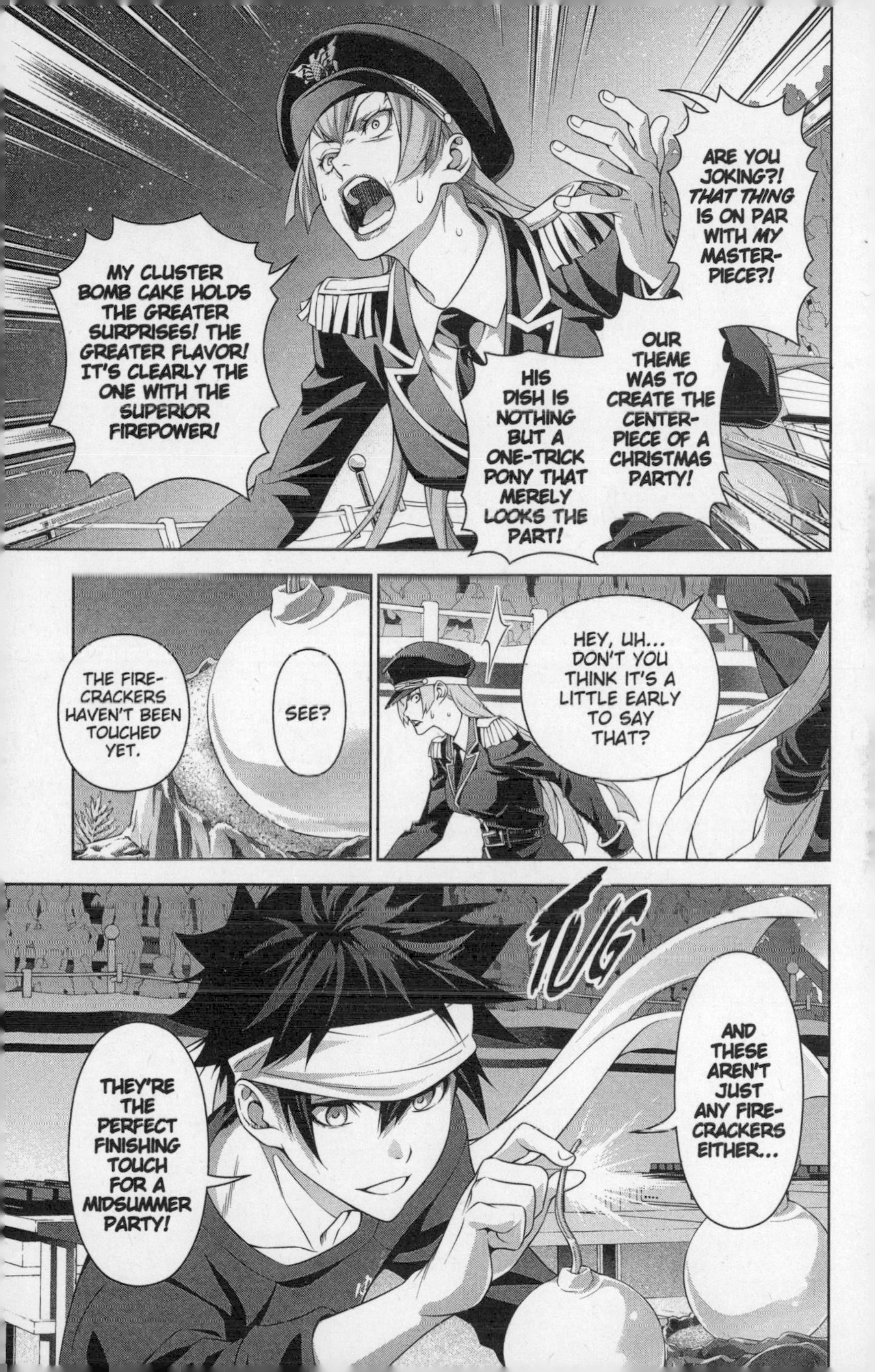
ARE YOU JOKING?! *THAT THING* IS ON PAR WITH *MY* MASTER-PIECE?!
OUR THEME WAS TO CREATE THE CENTER-PIECE OF A CHRISTMAS PARTY!
HIS DISH IS NOTHING BUT A ONE-TRICK PONY THAT MERELY LOOKS THE PART!
MY CLUSTER BOMB CAKE HOLDS THE GREATER SURPRISES! THE GREATER FLAVOR! IT'S CLEARLY THE ONE WITH THE SUPERIOR FIREPOWER!
HEY, UH... DON'T YOU THINK IT'S A LITTLE EARLY TO SAY THAT?
SEE?
THE FIRE-CRACKERS HAVEN'T BEEN TOUCHED YET.
TUG
AND THESE AREN'T JUST ANY FIRE-CRACKERS EITHER...
THEY'RE THE PERFECT FINISHING TOUCH FOR A MIDSUMMER PARTY!

THIS BOOKER'S
SPECIAL TRAIT

WHEN SHE
TASTES A
PARTICULARLY
DELICIOUS
DISH, IT NEARLY
TAKES HER TO
HEAVEN.

*NOTE,
ONLY
NEARLY.
SHE IS
FINE.

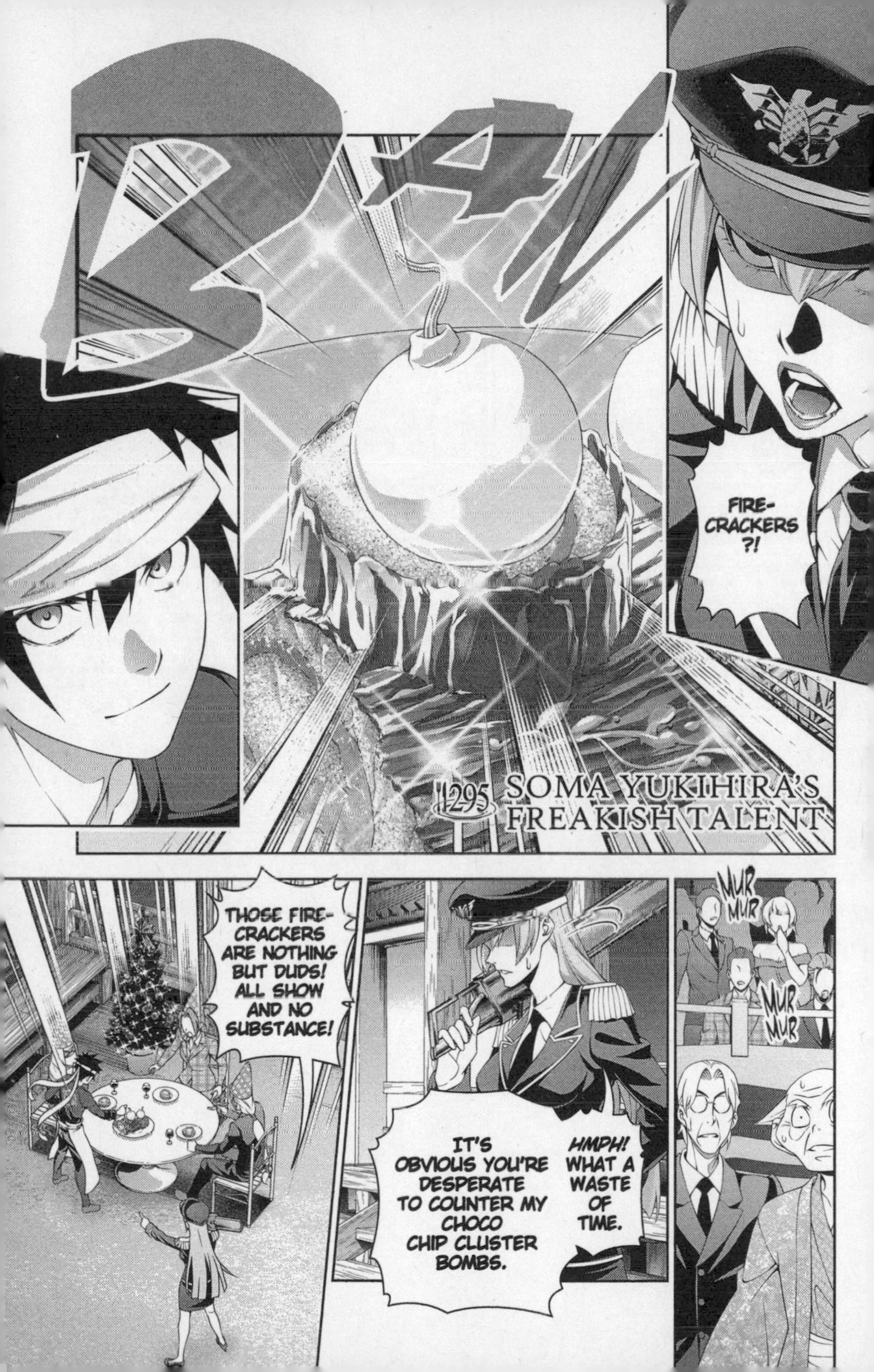
FIRE-CRACKERS ?!
295 SOMA YUKIHIRA'S FREAKISH TALENT
MUR MUR
MUR MUR
HMPH! WHAT A WASTE OF TIME.
IT'S OBVIOUS YOU'RE DESPERATE TO COUNTER MY CHOCO CHIP CLUSTER BOMBS.
THOSE FIRE-CRACKERS ARE NOTHING BUT DUDS! ALL SHOW AND NO SUBSTANCE!

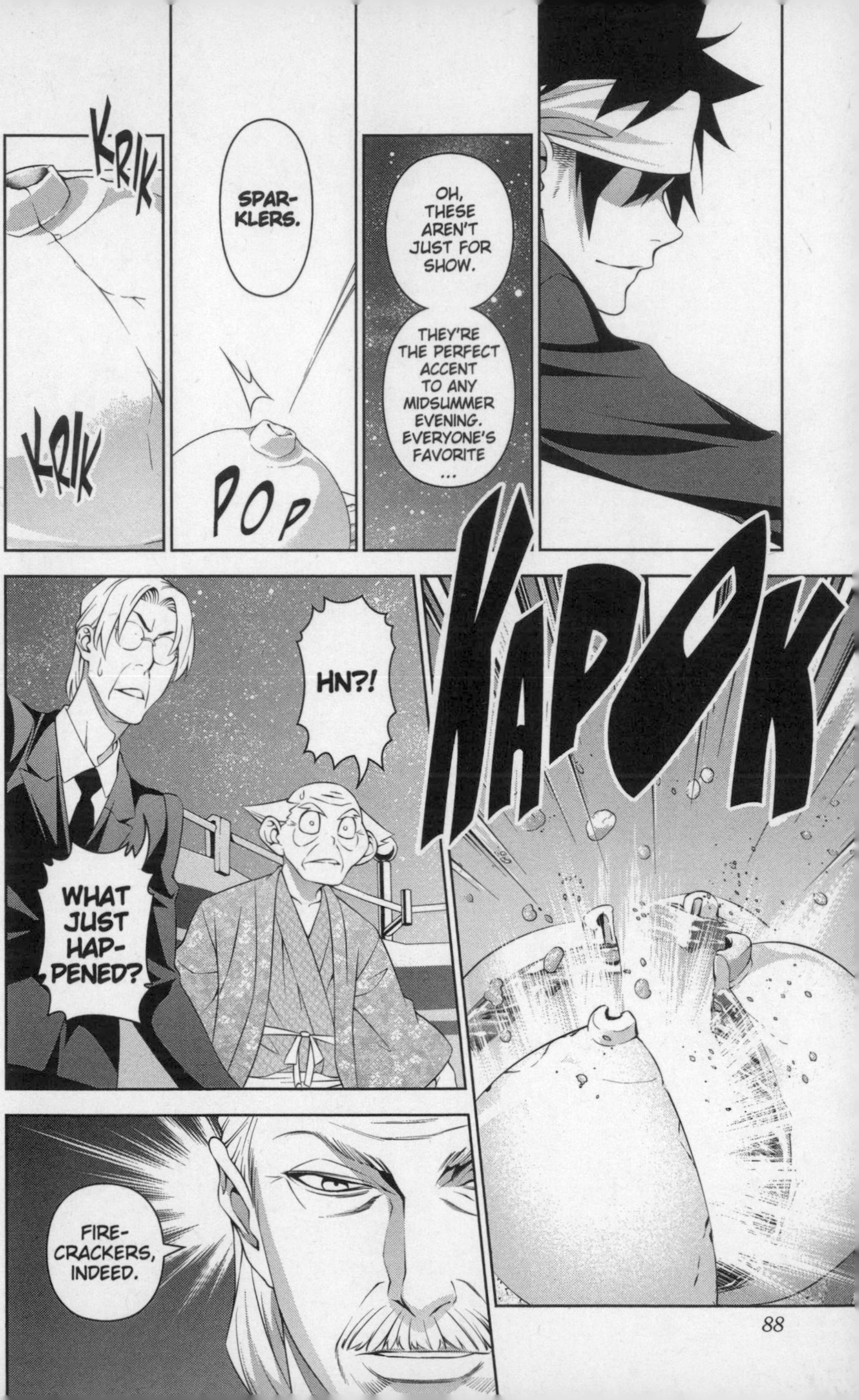
OH, THESE AREN'T JUST FOR SHOW.
THEY'RE THE PERFECT ACCENT TO ANY MIDSUMMER EVENING. EVERYONE'S FAVORITE ...
SPAR-KLERS.
POP
KRIK
KRIK
KAPOK
HN?!
WHAT JUST HAP-PENED?
FIRE-CRACKERS, INDEED.

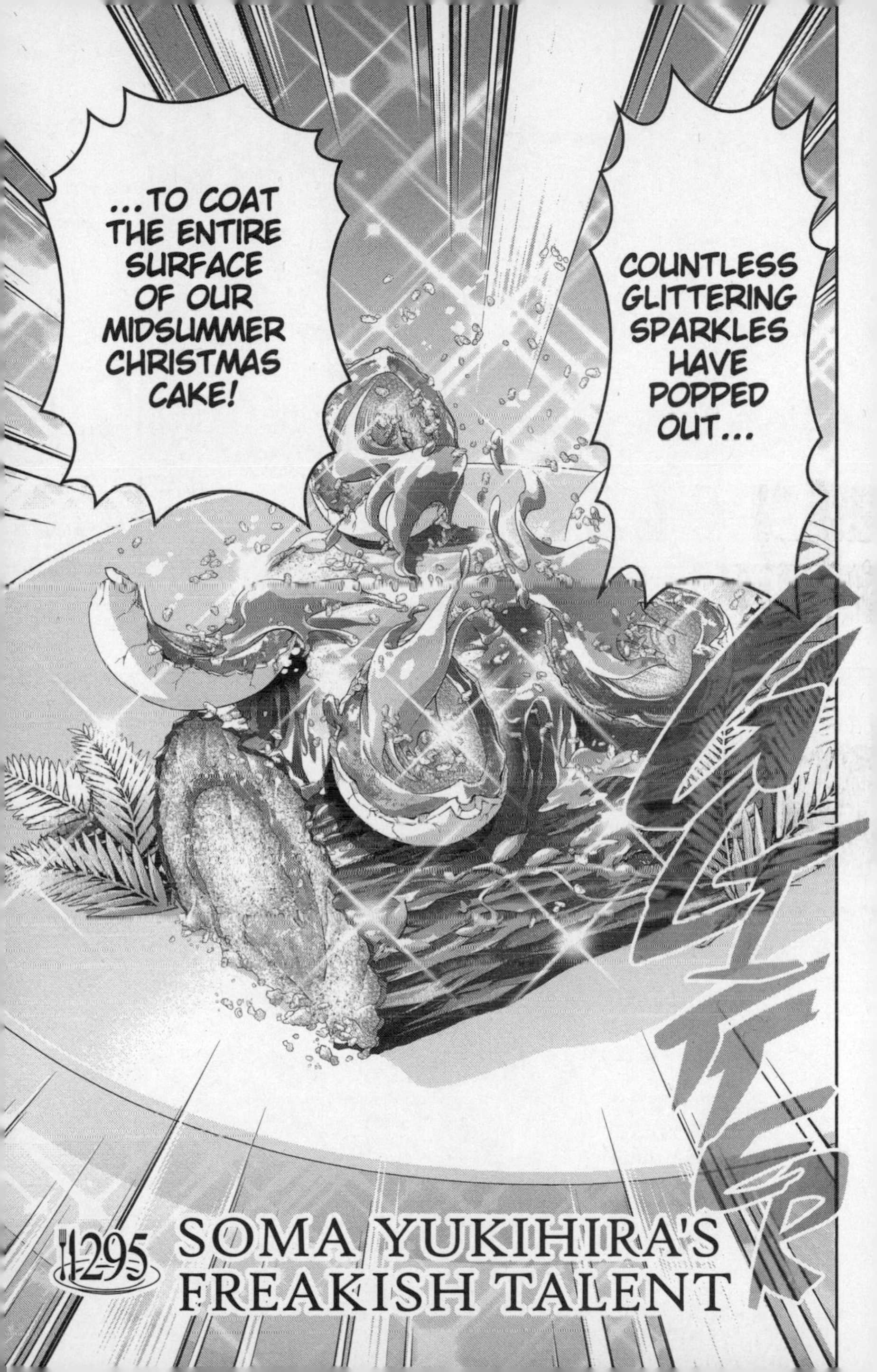
COUNTLESS GLITTERING SPARKLES HAVE POPPED OUT...
...TO COAT THE ENTIRE SURFACE OF OUR MIDSUMMER CHRISTMAS CAKE!
295
SOMA YUKIHIRA'S FREAKISH TALENT

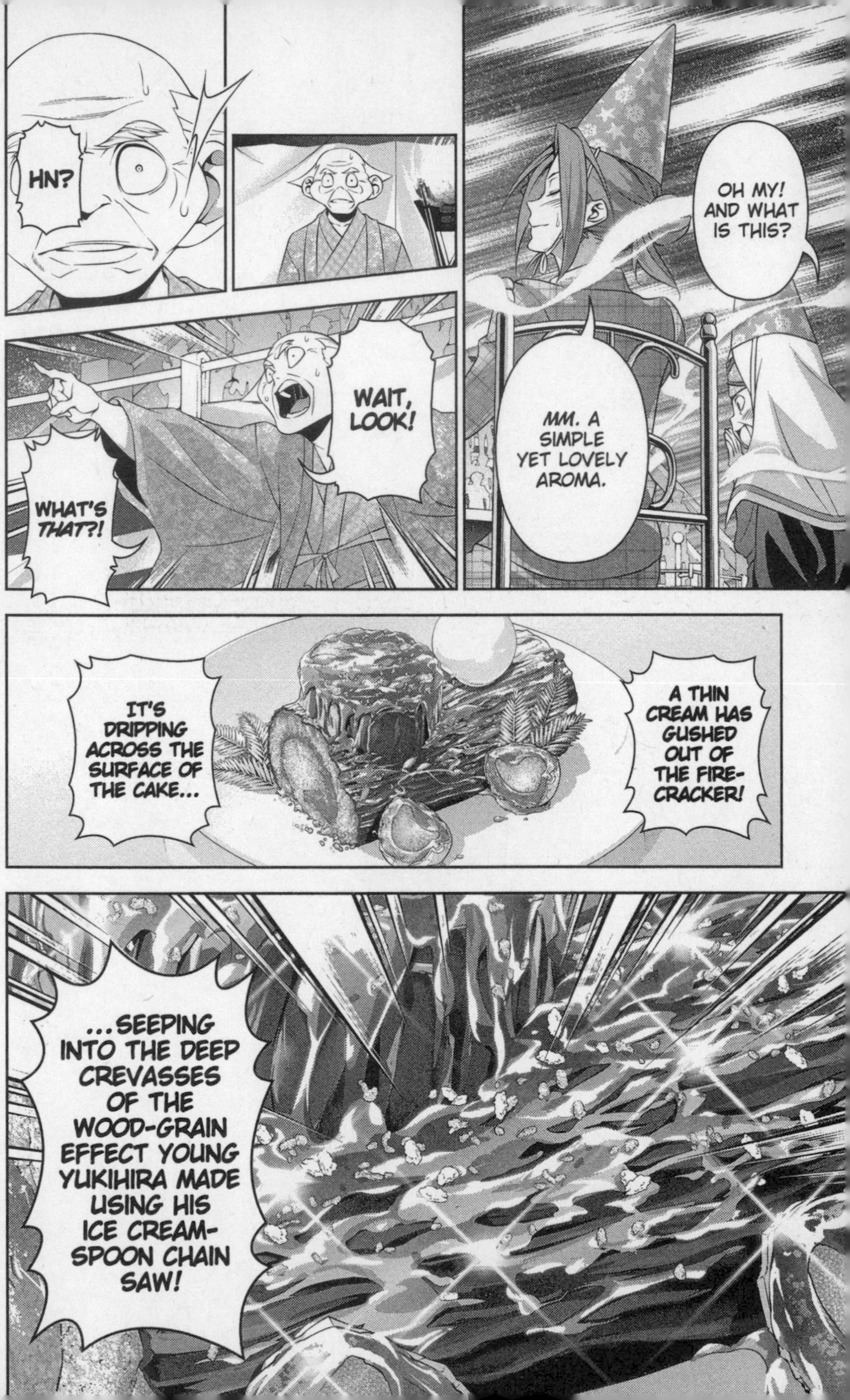
OH MY! AND WHAT IS THIS?
MM. A SIMPLE YET LOVELY AROMA.
HN?
WAIT, LOOK!
WHAT'S *THAT?!*
A THIN CREAM HAS GUSHED OUT OF THE FIRE-CRACKER!
IT'S DRIPPING ACROSS THE SURFACE OF THE CAKE...
...SEEPING INTO THE DEEP CREVASSES OF THE WOOD-GRAIN EFFECT YOUNG YUKIHIRA MADE USING HIS ICE CREAM-SPOON CHAIN SAW!

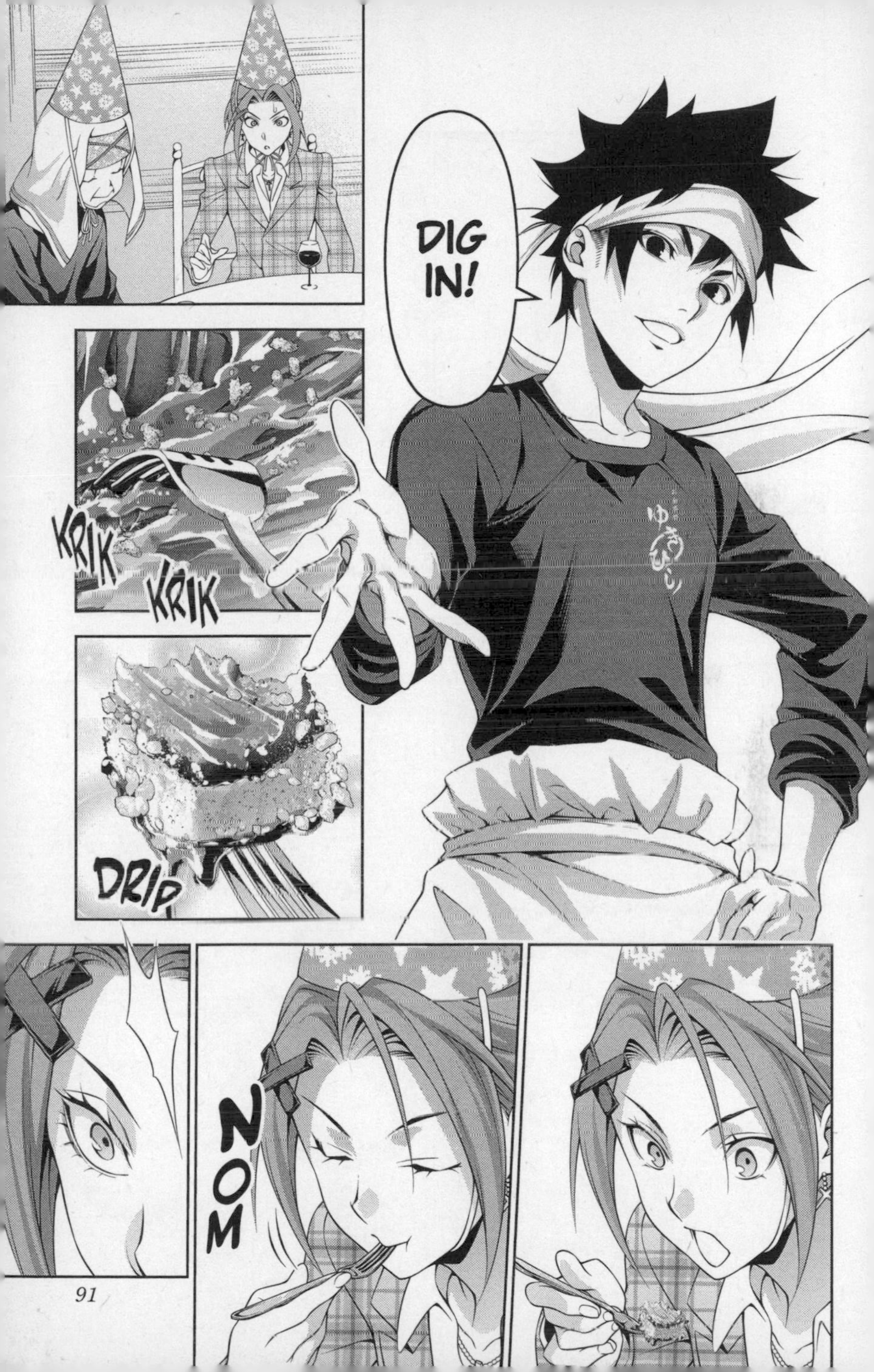
DIG IN!
KRIK KRIK
DRIP
NOM NOM

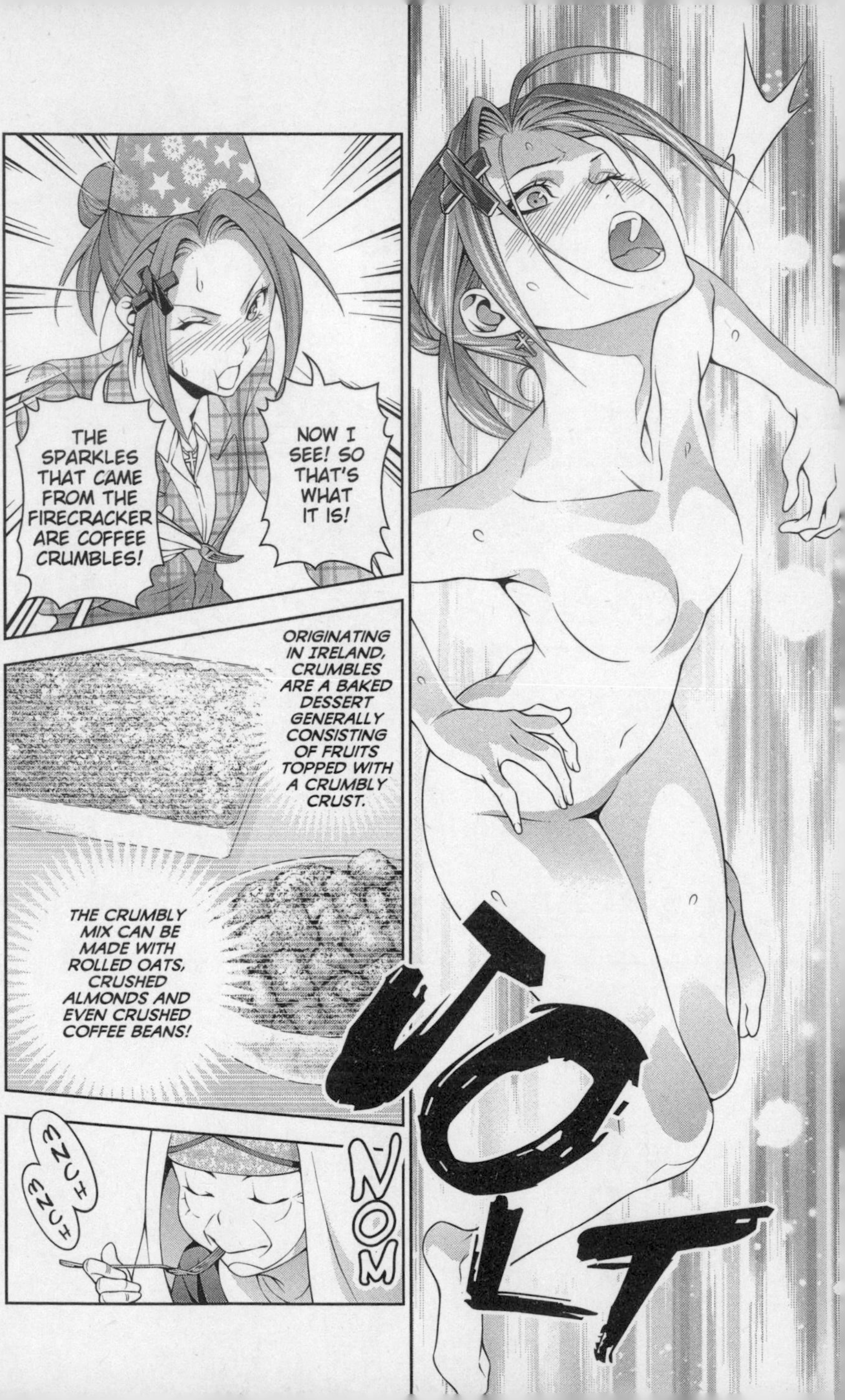
JOLT
NOW I SEE! SO THAT'S WHAT IT IS!
THE SPARKLES THAT CAME FROM THE FIRECRACKER ARE COFFEE CRUMBLES!
ORIGINATING IN IRELAND, CRUMBLES ARE A BAKED DESSERT GENERALLY CONSISTING OF FRUITS TOPPED WITH A CRUMBLY CRUST.
THE CRUMBLY MIX CAN BE MADE WITH ROLLED OATS, CRUSHED ALMONDS AND EVEN CRUSHED COFFEE BEANS!
NOM
MNCH MNCH

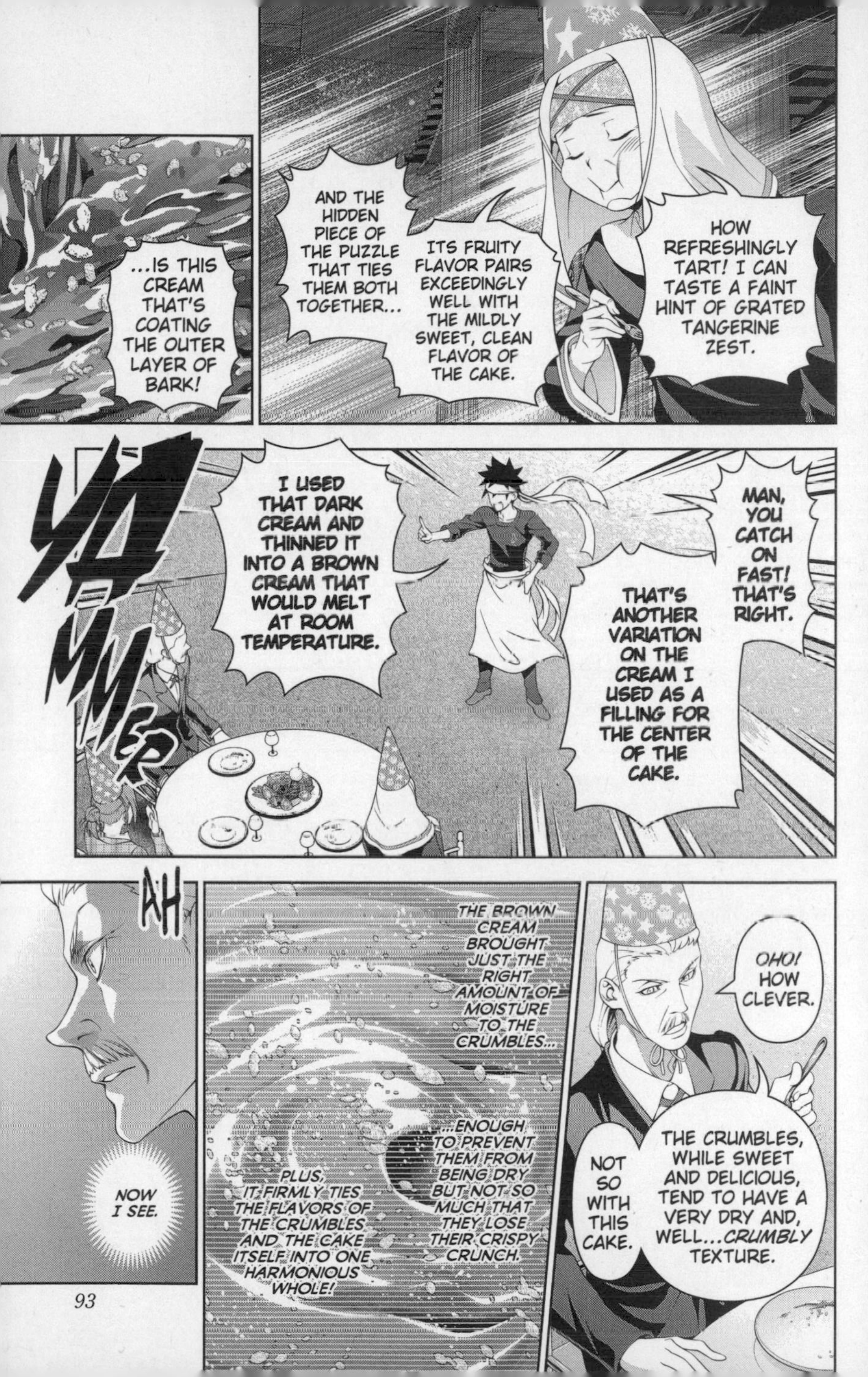
HOW REFRESHINGLY TART! I CAN TASTE A FAINT HINT OF GRATED TANGERINE ZEST.
ITS FRUITY FLAVOR PAIRS EXCEEDINGLY WELL WITH THE MILDLY SWEET, CLEAN FLAVOR OF THE CAKE.
AND THE HIDDEN PIECE OF THE PUZZLE THAT TIES THEM BOTH TOGETHER...
...IS THIS CREAM THAT'S COATING THE OUTER LAYER OF BARK!
MAN, YOU CATCH ON FAST! THAT'S RIGHT.
THAT'S ANOTHER VARIATION ON THE CREAM I USED AS A FILLING FOR THE CENTER OF THE CAKE.
I USED THAT DARK CREAM AND THINNED IT INTO A BROWN CREAM THAT WOULD MELT AT ROOM TEMPERATURE.
OHO! HOW CLEVER.
THE CRUMBLES, WHILE SWEET AND DELICIOUS, TEND TO HAVE A VERY DRY AND, WELL...*CRUMBLY* TEXTURE.
NOT SO WITH THIS CAKE.
THE BROWN CREAM BROUGHT JUST THE RIGHT AMOUNT OF MOISTURE TO THE CRUMBLES...
...ENOUGH TO PREVENT THEM FROM BEING DRY BUT NOT SO MUCH THAT THEY LOSE THEIR CRISPY CRUNCH.
PLUS, IT FIRMLY TIES THE FLAVORS OF THE CRUMBLES AND THE CAKE ITSELF INTO ONE HARMONIOUS WHOLE!
AH
NOW I SEE.

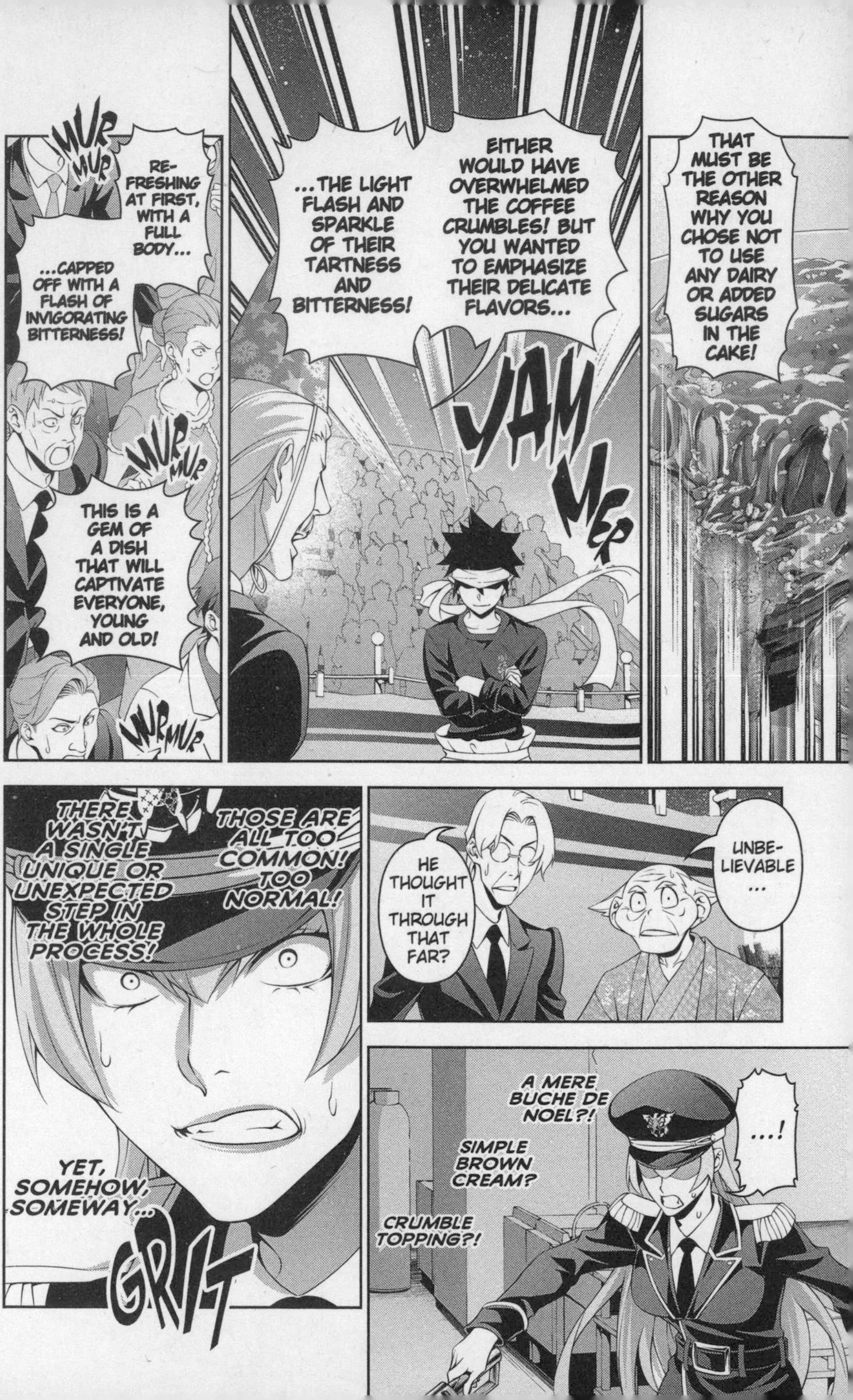
THAT MUST BE THE OTHER REASON WHY YOU CHOSE NOT TO USE ANY DAIRY OR ADDED SUGARS IN THE CAKE!
EITHER WOULD HAVE OVERWHELMED THE COFFEE CRUMBLES! BUT YOU WANTED TO EMPHASIZE THEIR DELICATE FLAVORS...
...THE LIGHT FLASH AND SPARKLE OF THEIR TARTNESS AND BITTERNESS!
JAM
MER
MUR MUR
RE-FRESHING AT FIRST, WITH A FULL BODY...
...CAPPED OFF WITH A FLASH OF INVIGORATING BITTERNESS!
MUR MUR
THIS IS A GEM OF A DISH THAT WILL CAPTIVATE EVERYONE, YOUNG AND OLD!
MUR MUR
UNBE-LIEVABLE ...
HE THOUGHT IT THROUGH THAT FAR?
...!
A MERE BUCHE DE NOEL?!
SIMPLE BROWN CREAM?
CRUMBLE TOPPING?!
THOSE ARE ALL TOO COMMON! TOO NORMAL!
THERE WASN'T A SINGLE UNIQUE OR UNEXPECTED STEP IN THE WHOLE PROCESS!
YET, SOMEHOW, SOMEWAY...
GRIT

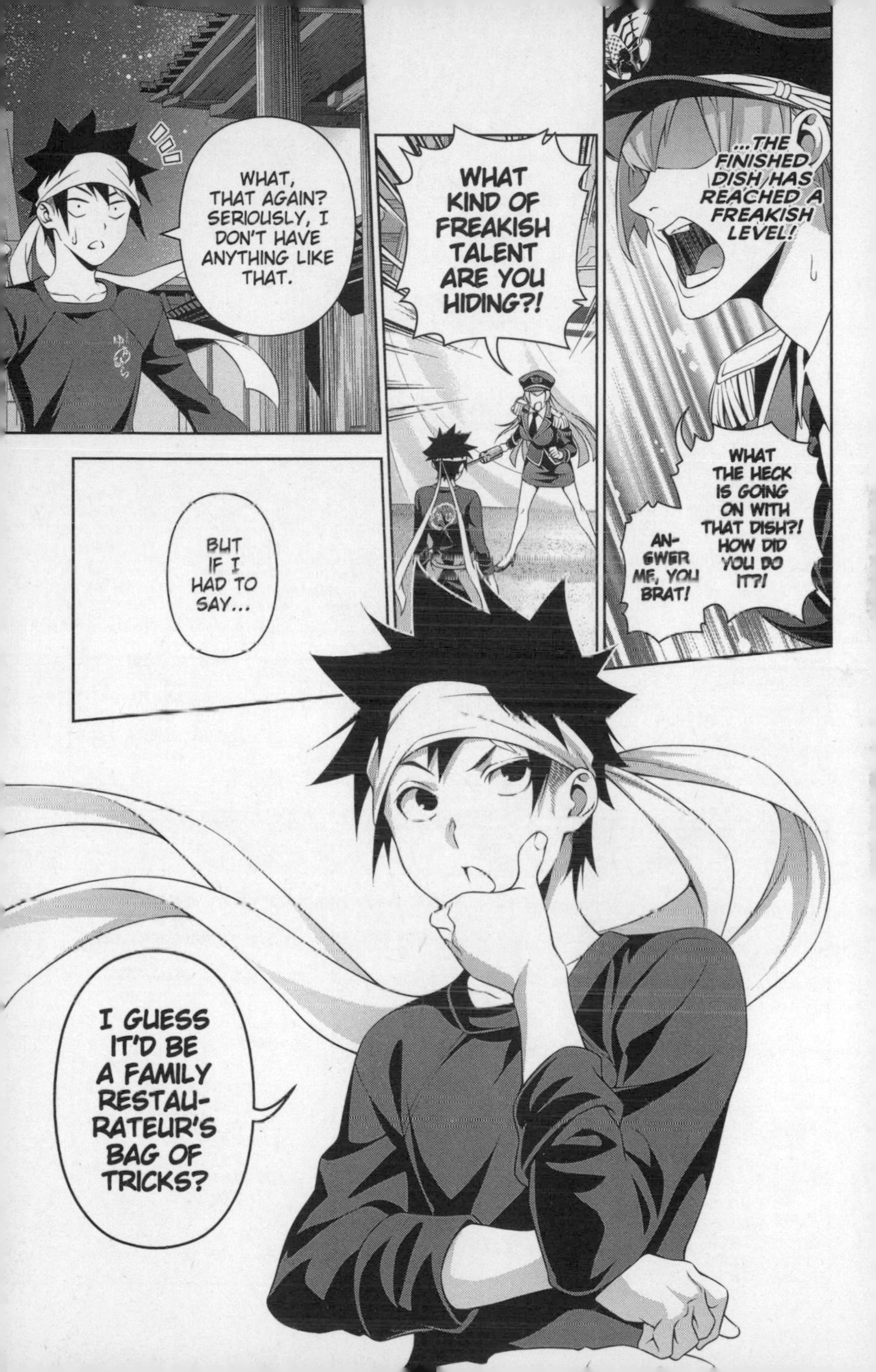
...THE FINISHED DISH HAS REACHED A FREAKISH LEVEL!
WHAT THE HECK IS GOING ON WITH THAT DISH?! HOW DID YOU DO IT?!
AN-SWER ME, YOU BRAT!
WHAT KIND OF FREAKISH TALENT ARE YOU HIDING?!
WHAT, THAT AGAIN? SERIOUSLY, I DON'T HAVE ANYTHING LIKE THAT.
BUT IF I HAD TO SAY...
I GUESS IT'D BE A FAMILY RESTAU-RATEUR'S BAG OF TRICKS?

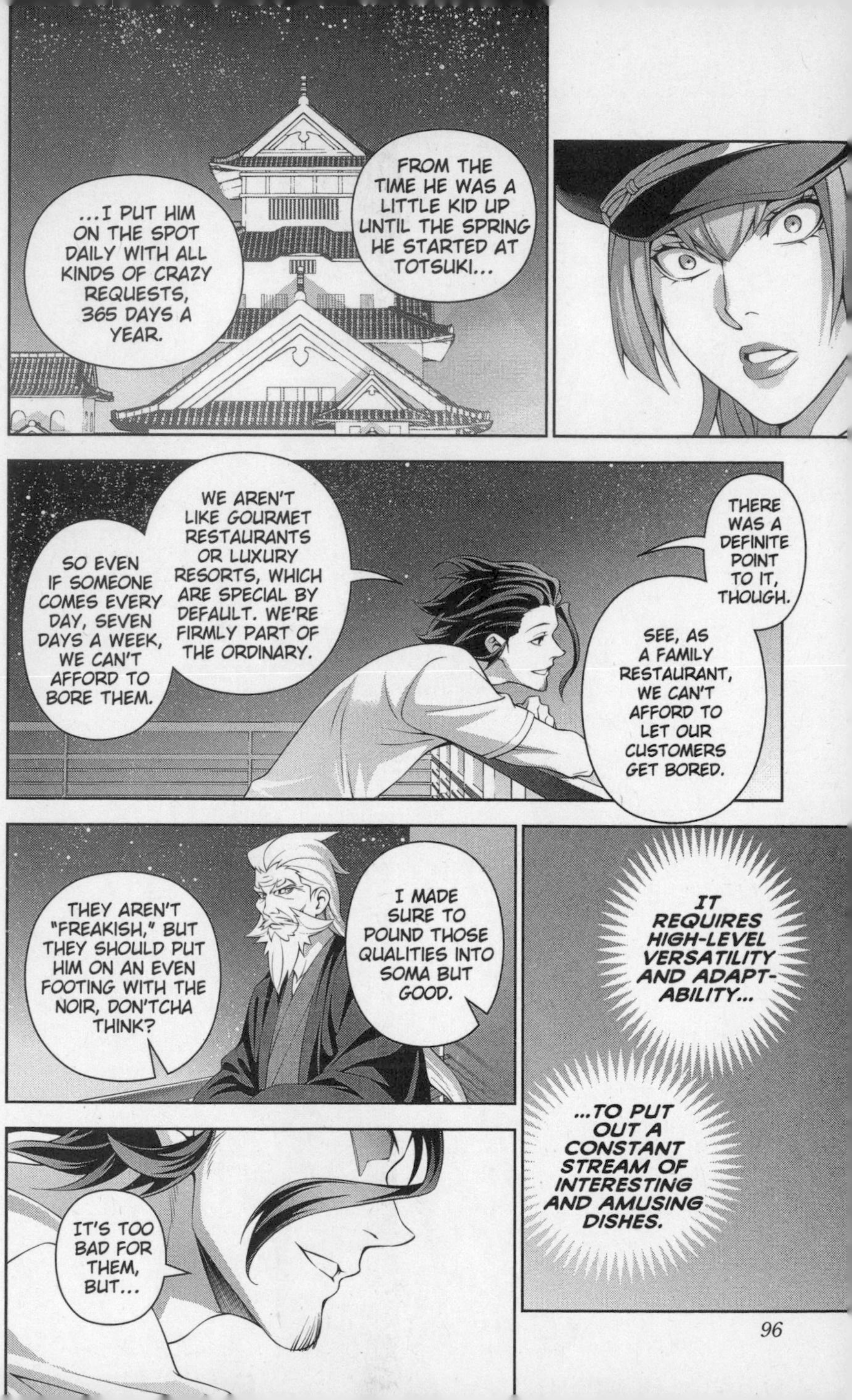
FROM THE TIME HE WAS A LITTLE KID UP UNTIL THE SPRING HE STARTED AT TOTSUKI...
...I PUT HIM ON THE SPOT DAILY WITH ALL KINDS OF CRAZY REQUESTS, 365 DAYS A YEAR.
THERE WAS A DEFINITE POINT TO IT, THOUGH.
SEE, AS A FAMILY RESTAURANT, WE CAN'T AFFORD TO LET OUR CUSTOMERS GET BORED.
WE AREN'T LIKE GOURMET RESTAURANTS OR LUXURY RESORTS, WHICH ARE SPECIAL BY DEFAULT. WE'RE FIRMLY PART OF THE ORDINARY.
SO EVEN IF SOMEONE COMES EVERY DAY, SEVEN DAYS A WEEK, WE CAN'T AFFORD TO BORE THEM.
IT REQUIRES HIGH-LEVEL VERSATILITY AND ADAPT-ABILITY...
...TO PUT OUT A CONSTANT STREAM OF INTERESTING AND AMUSING DISHES.
I MADE SURE TO POUND THOSE QUALITIES INTO SOMA BUT GOOD.
THEY AREN'T "FREAKISH," BUT THEY SHOULD PUT HIM ON AN EVEN FOOTING WITH THE NOIR, DON'TCHA THINK?
IT'S TOO BAD FOR THEM, BUT...

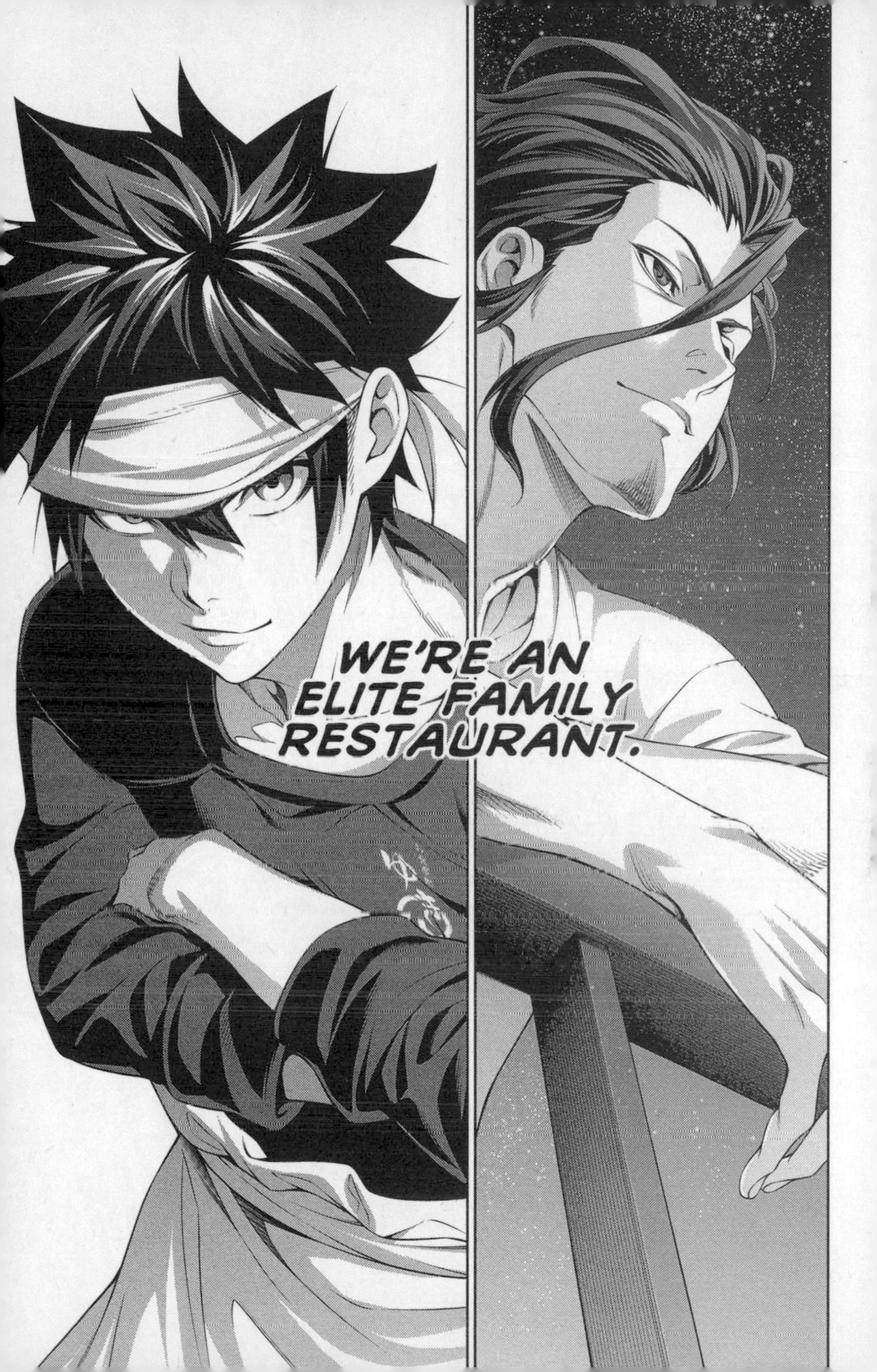
WE'RE AN ELITE FAMILY RESTAURANT.

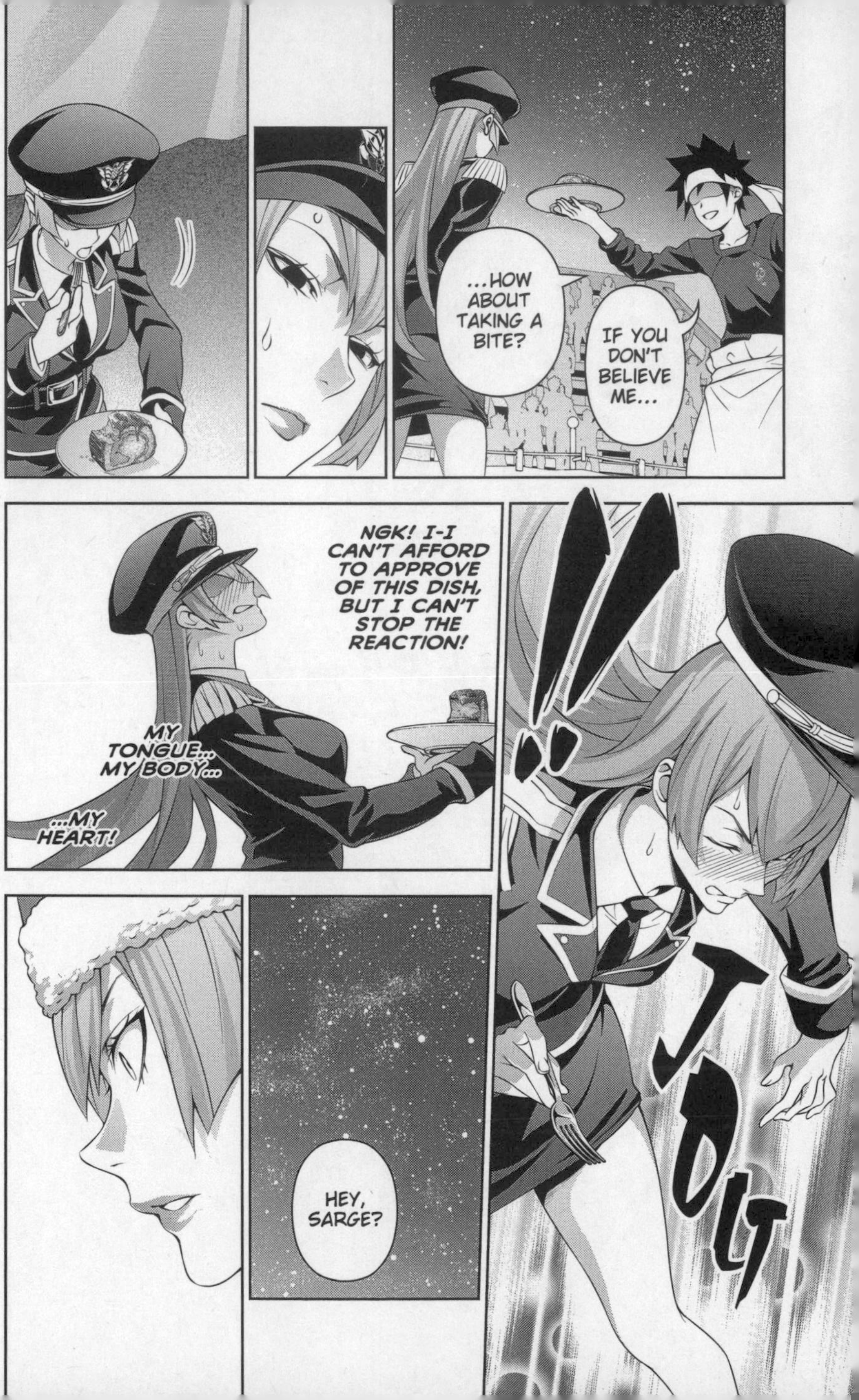
IF YOU DON'T BELIEVE ME...
...HOW ABOUT TAKING A BITE?
NGK! I-I CAN'T AFFORD TO APPROVE OF THIS DISH, BUT I CAN'T STOP THE REACTION!
MY TONGUE... MY BODY...
...MY HEART!
HEY, SARGE?

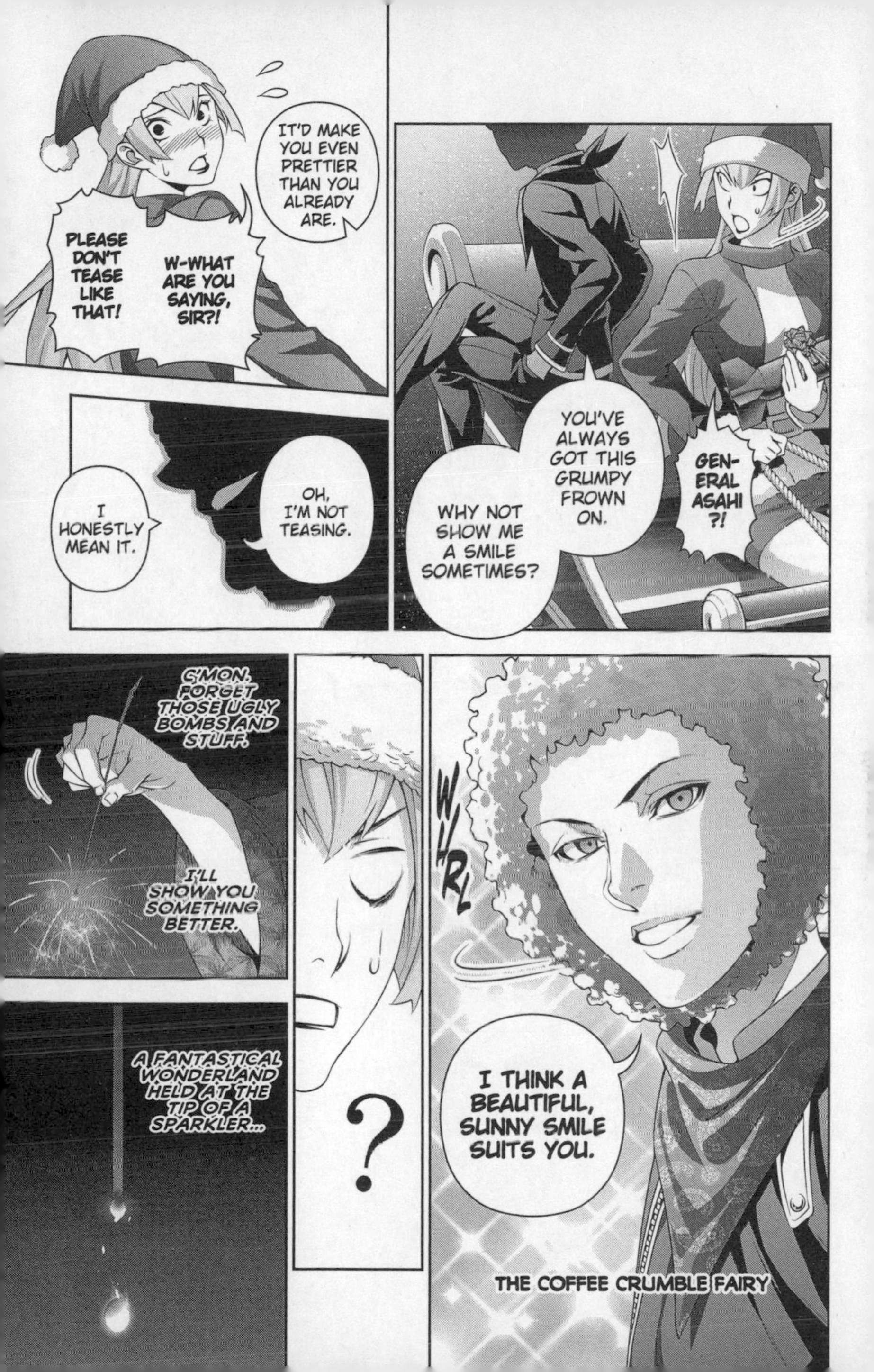
GEN-ERAL ASAHI?!
YOU'VE ALWAYS GOT THIS GRUMPY FROWN ON.
WHY NOT SHOW ME A SMILE SOMETIMES?
IT'D MAKE YOU EVEN PRETTIER THAN YOU ALREADY ARE.
W-WHAT ARE YOU SAYING, SIR?!
PLEASE DON'T TEASE LIKE THAT!
OH, I'M NOT TEASING.
I HONESTLY MEAN IT.
WHRL
I THINK A BEAUTIFUL, SUNNY SMILE SUITS YOU.
THE COFFEE CRUMBLE FAIRY
?
C'MON. FORGET THOSE UGLY BOMBS AND STUFF.
I'LL SHOW YOU SOMETHING BETTER.
A FANTASTICAL WONDERLAND HELD AT THE TIP OF A SPARKLER...

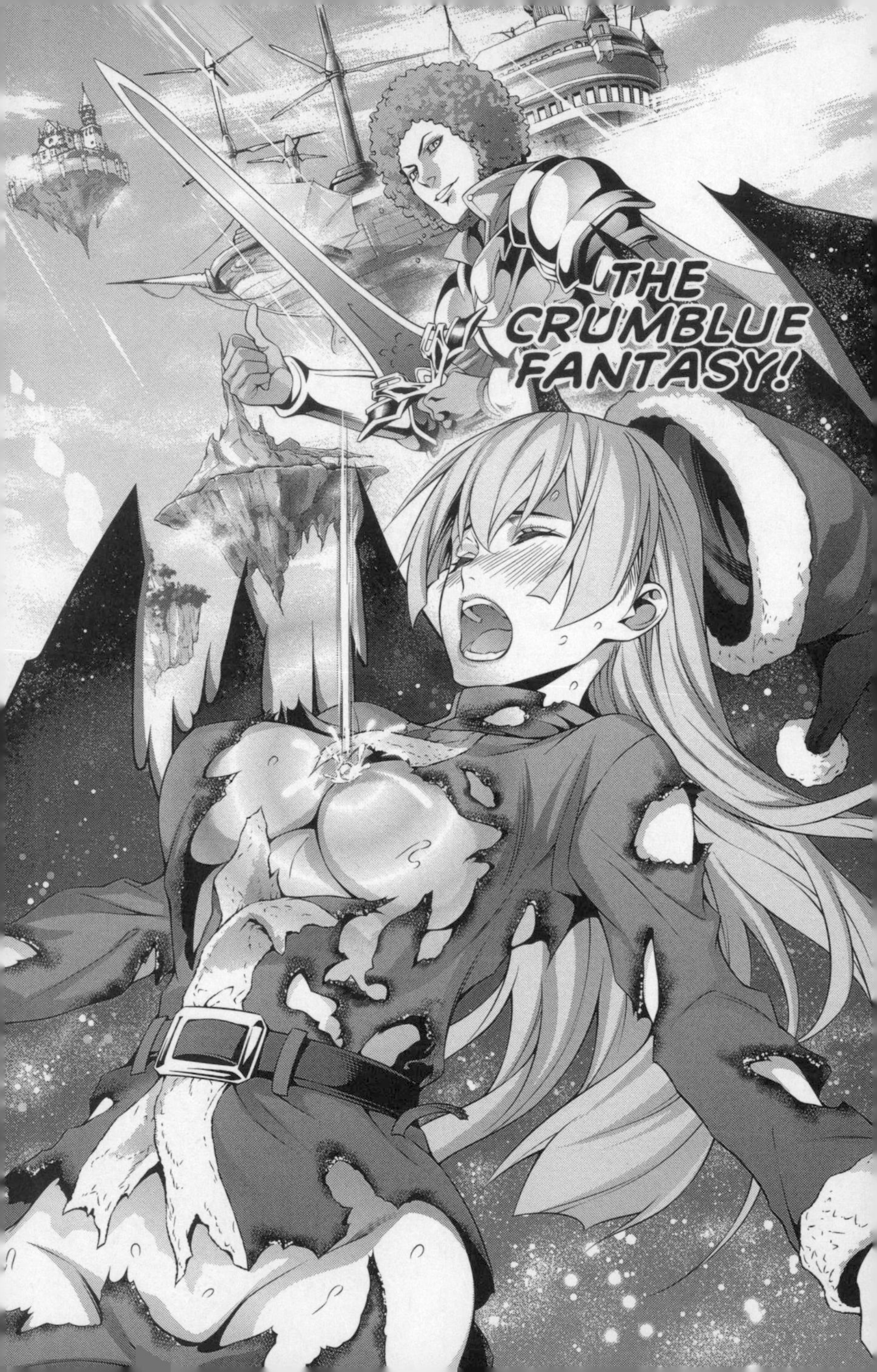
THE CRUMBLUE FANTASY!

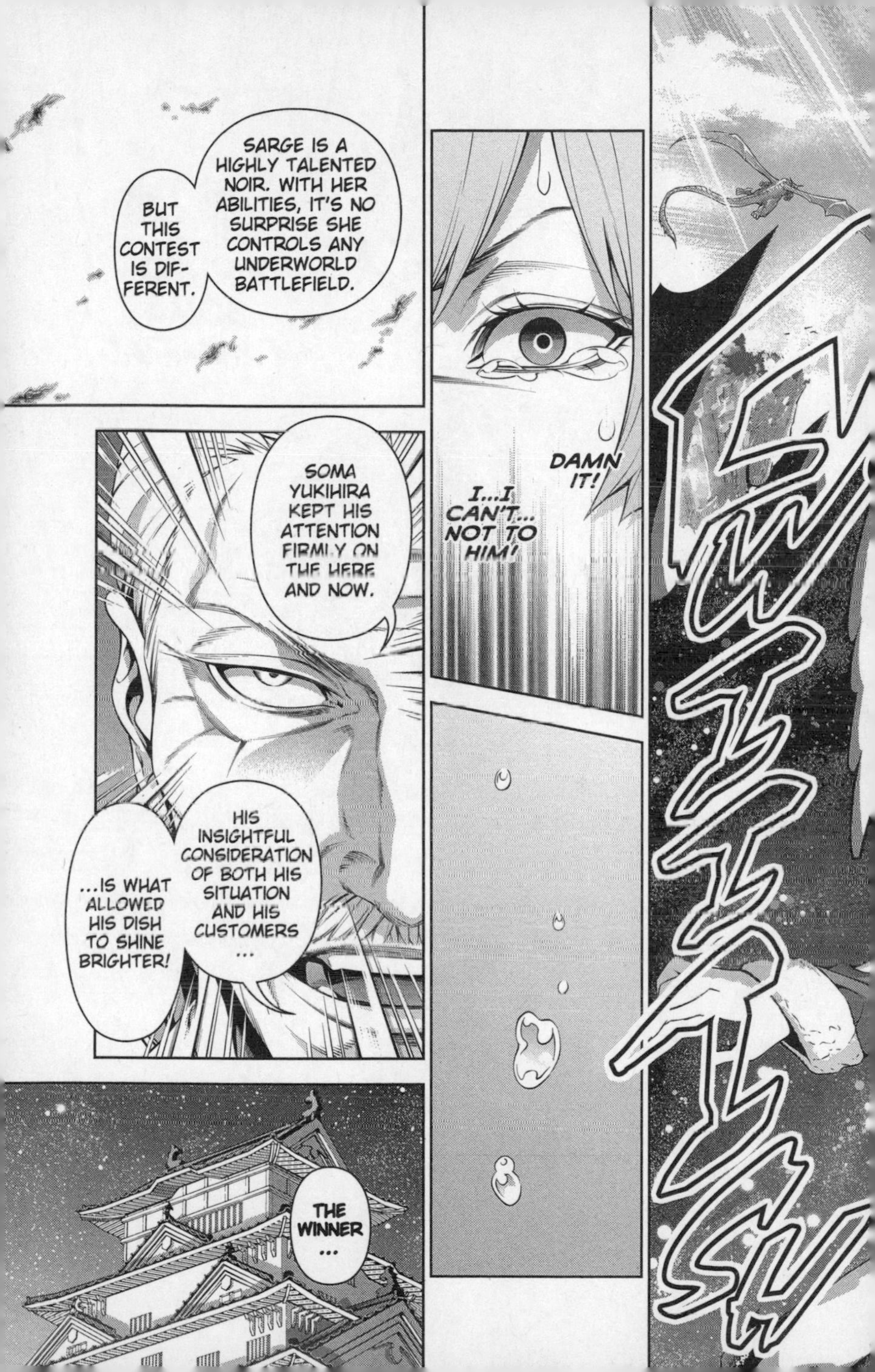
DAMN IT!
I...I CAN'T... NOT TO HIM!
SARGE IS A HIGHLY TALENTED NOIR. WITH HER ABILITIES, IT'S NO SURPRISE SHE CONTROLS ANY UNDERWORLD BATTLEFIELD.
BUT THIS CONTEST IS DIF-FERENT.
SOMA YUKIHIRA KEPT HIS ATTENTION FIRMLY ON THE HERE AND NOW.
HIS INSIGHTFUL CONSIDERATION OF BOTH HIS SITUATION AND HIS CUSTOMERS ...
...IS WHAT ALLOWED HIS DISH TO SHINE BRIGHTER!
THE WINNER ...

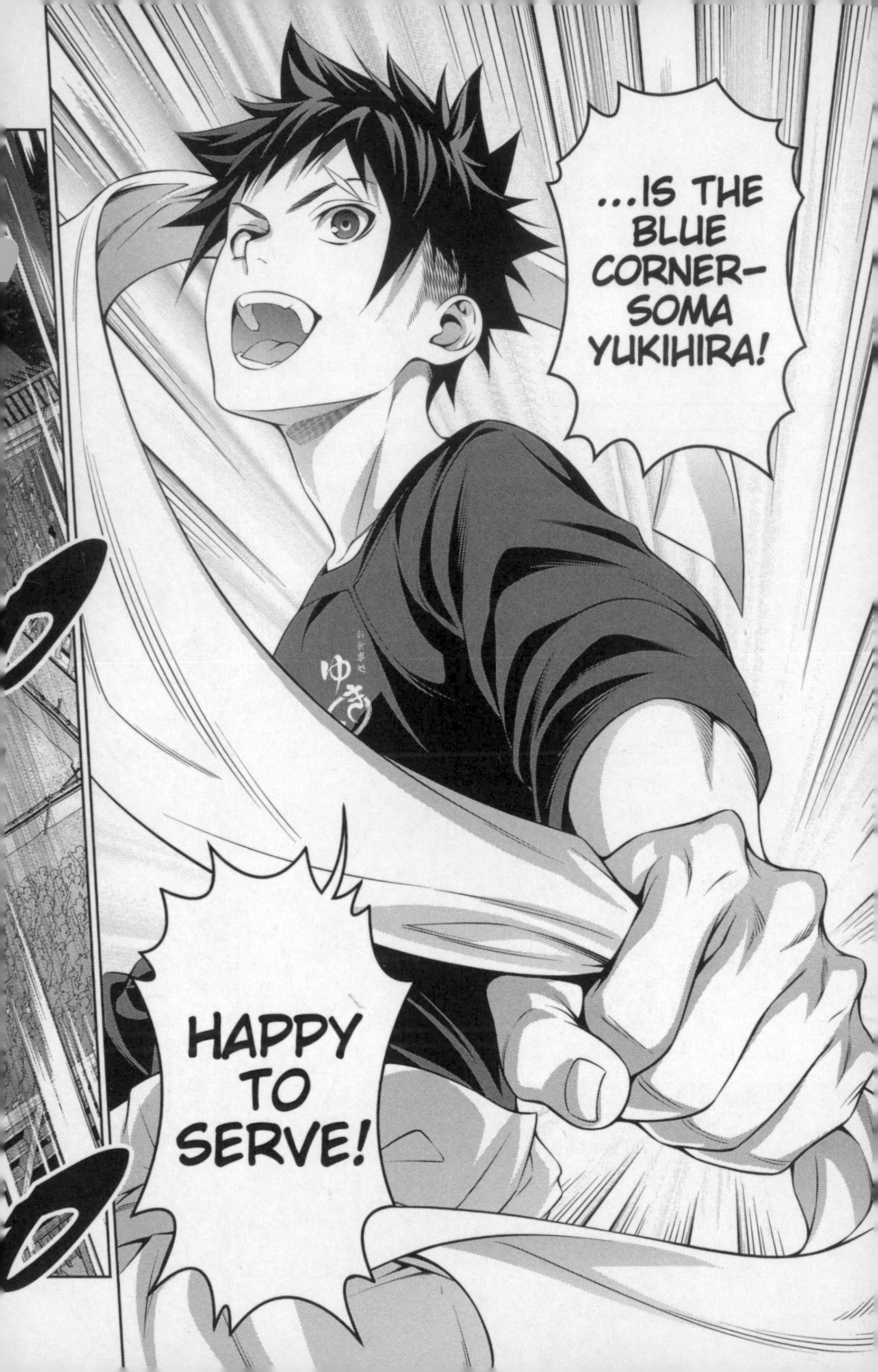
...IS THE BLUE CORNER-SOMA YUKIHIRA!
HAPPY TO SERVE!

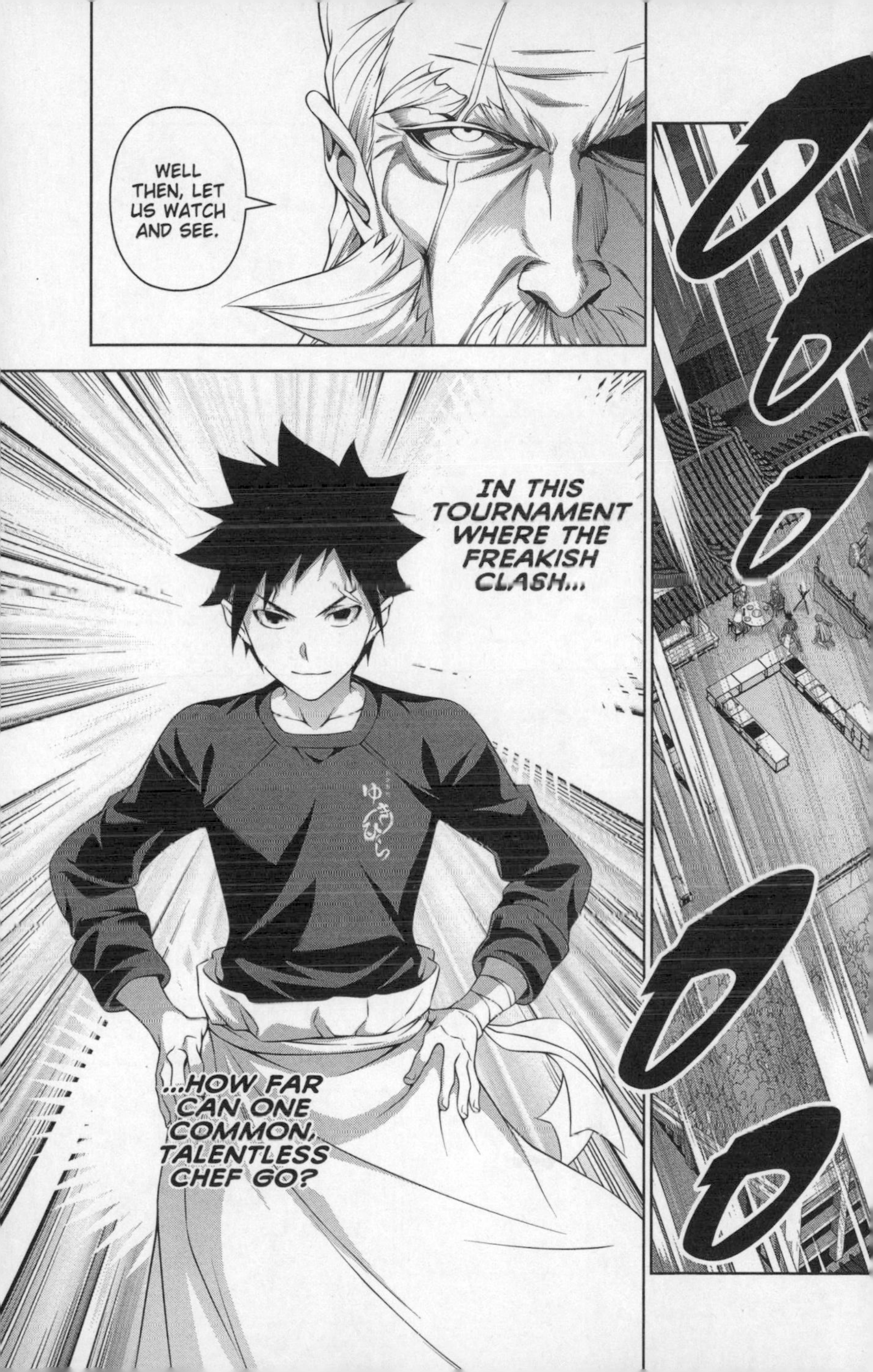
WELL THEN, LET US WATCH AND SEE.
IN THIS TOURNAMENT WHERE THE FREAKISH CLASH...
...HOW FAR CAN ONE COMMON, TALENTLESS CHEF GO?

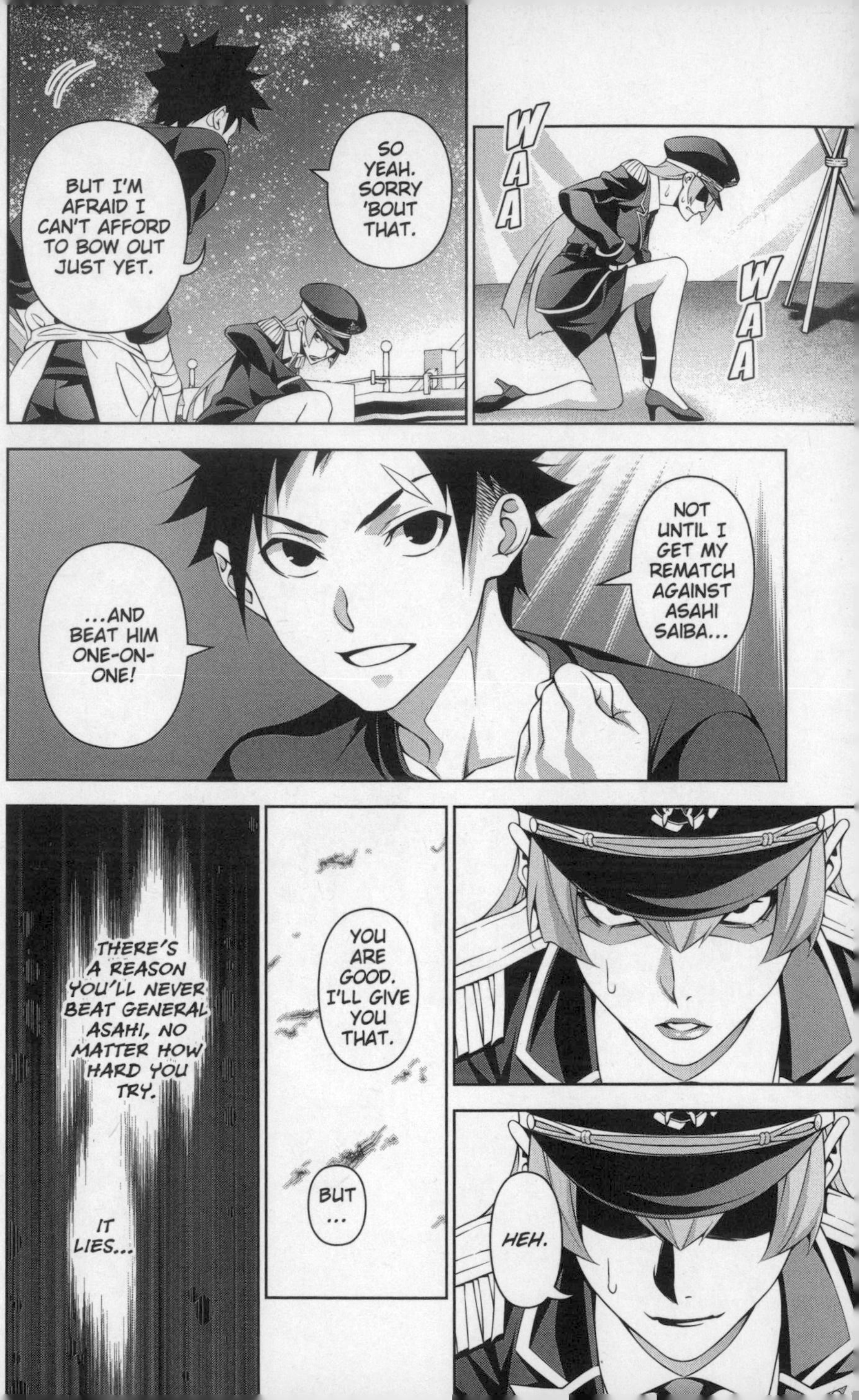
WAA
WAA
SO YEAH. SORRY 'BOUT THAT.
BUT I'M AFRAID I CAN'T AFFORD TO BOW OUT JUST YET.
NOT UNTIL I GET MY REMATCH AGAINST ASAHI SAIBA...
...AND BEAT HIM ONE-ON-ONE!
HEH.
YOU ARE GOOD. I'LL GIVE YOU THAT.
BUT...
THERE'S A REASON YOU'LL NEVER BEAT GENERAL ASAHI, NO MATTER HOW HARD YOU TRY.
IT LIES...

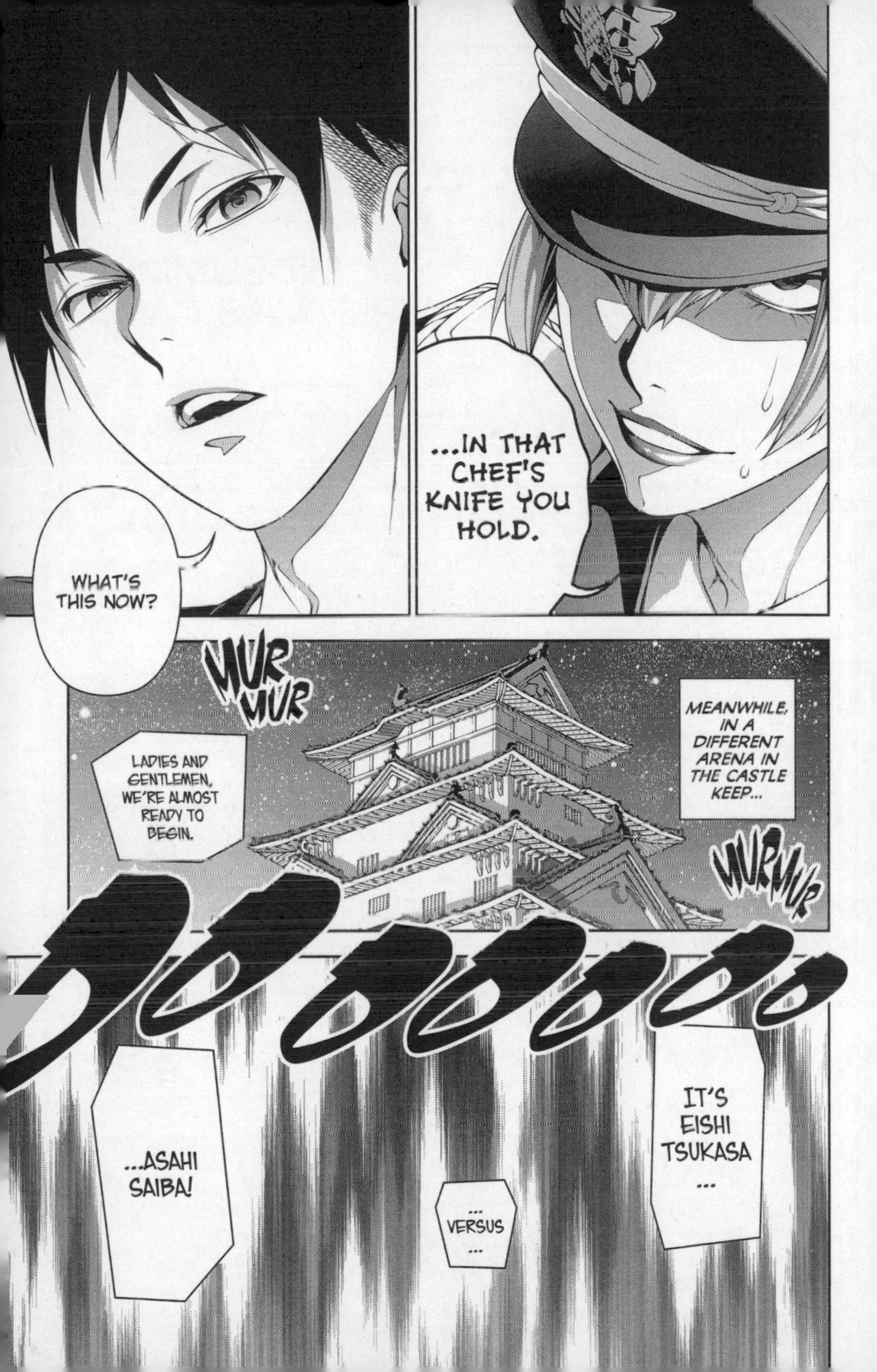
...IN THAT CHEF'S KNIFE YOU HOLD.
WHAT'S THIS NOW?
MEANWHILE, IN A DIFFERENT ARENA IN THE CASTLE KEEP...
MUR MUR
LADIES AND GENTLEMEN, WE'RE ALMOST READY TO BEGIN.
MURMUR
IT'S EISHI TSUKASA...
...VERSUS...
...ASAHI SAIBA!

ARTIST: YUTO TSUKUDA RECIPE BY: YUKI MORISAKI

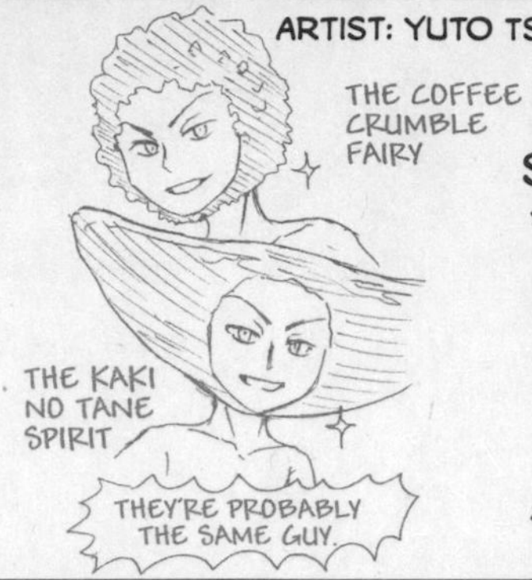
THE COFFEE CRUMBLE FAIRY
THE KAKI NO TANE SPIRIT
THEY'RE PROBABLY THE SAME GUY.

VOLUME 34 SPECIAL SUPPLEMENT!

PRACTICAL RECIPE #2

SOMA'S SPECIAL HOME VERSION

MIDSUMMER CHRISTMAS CAKE

INGREDIENTS
(MAKES 1 8" ROLL CAKE)

★COFFEE CRUMBLES

[A] 50 GRAMS EACH FLOUR, ALMOND FLOUR
1 TABLESPOON INSTANT COFFEE

2 TABLESPOONS RAPESEED OIL/30 GRAMS RICE BRAN

★MOUNTAIN YAM BATTER

80 GRAMS JAPANESE MOUNTAIN YAM

[B] 200 GRAMS FLOUR
1 TABLESPOON BAKING POWDER

[C] 4 TABLESPOONS EACH RAPESEED OIL, RICE BRAN
150 CC SOY MILK

★AVOCADO BANANA CHOCOLATE CREAM

[D] 1 AVOCADO/1 BANANA
2 TABLESPOONS EACH COCOA POWDER, RICE BRAN

★TOFU CHOCOLATE CREAM

300 GRAMS MEDIUM TOFU

[E] 100 CC WATER/70 GRAMS RICE BRAN
2 GRAMS POWDERED AGAR

1 TABLESPOON RAPESEED OIL
COCOA POWDER

[GARNISHES] VARIOUS NUTS AND DECORATIONS AS DESIRED

1. ★MAKE THE COFFEE CRUMBLES★ POUR (A) INTO A BOWL AND WHISK TOGETHER.

2. ADD THE RAPESEED OIL AND RICE BRAN. MIX TOGETHER WITH YOUR HANDS UNTIL CRUMBLES ARE FORMED.

3. LINE A BAKING SHEET WITH PARCHMENT PAPER, THEN SPREAD THE CRUMBLES FROM (2) OVER IT. PLACE IN A 335°F OVEN AND BAKE FOR 20 MINUTES OR UNTIL DONE. REMOVE FROM THE OVEN AND ALLOW TO COOL.

4. ★MAKE THE MOUNTAIN YAM BATTER★ GRATE THE MOUNTAIN YAM INTO A BOWL AND STIR IN (C) UNTIL COMBINED.

5. SIFT (B) INTO A BOWL. POUR IN (4) AND MIX UNTIL COMBINED.

6. LINE A JELLY ROLL PAN WITH PARCHMENT PAPER. POUR THE BATTER IN AND BAKE IN A 320°F OVEN FOR 15 MINUTES OR UNTIL GOLDEN BROWN. SET ASIDE AND ALLOW TO COOL.

7. ★MAKE THE AVOCADO BANANA CHOCOLATE CREAM★ PUT (D) IN A FOOD PROCESSOR AND BLEND UNTIL SMOOTH.

8. ★MAKE THE TOFU CHOCOLATE CREAM★ WRAP THE TOFU IN PAPER TOWEL AND HEAT IN THE MICROWAVE FOR 2.5 MINUTES. ALLOW TO COOL, THEN REMOVE ANY EXCESS MOISTURE. PUT (E) IN A SAUCE PAN AND STIR OVER MEDIUM HEAT UNTIL ALL THE SOLIDS ARE DISSOLVED. POUR IN THE RAPESEED OIL AND STIR.

9. POUR (8) INTO A FOOD PROCESSOR, ADD THE COCOA POWDER AND BLEND UNTIL SMOOTH. POUR INTO A BOWL AND PUT IN THE REFRIGERATOR TO CHILL.

10. PUT THE COOLED CAKE FROM (6) ON A SHEET OF PLASTIC WRAP AND SPREAD (7) EVENLY OVER THE TOP. SPRINKLE (3) OVER THE CAKE AS DESIRED. USE THE PLASTIC WRAP TO FIRMLY ROLL THE CAKE INTO A LOG. PLACE WRAPPED LOG IN THE REFRIGERATOR TO CHILL FOR AT LEAST ONE HOUR.

11. CUT ABOUT 1 INCH OFF THE END OF THE ROLL CAKE TO USE AS THE STUMP AND SET TO THE SIDE. SPREAD (9) EVENLY OVER THE ENTIRE ROLL CAKE. PLACE THE STUMP ON TOP OF THE CAKE, THEN SPREAD WITH MORE OF (9). USE A FORK OR OTHER SERRATED EDGE TO MAKE A BARK PATTERN ON THE OUTSIDE OF THE CAKE AS DESIRED. DECORATE WITH THE REMAINDER OF (3) AND WHATEVER NUTS OR DECORATIONS YOU LIKE, AND DONE!

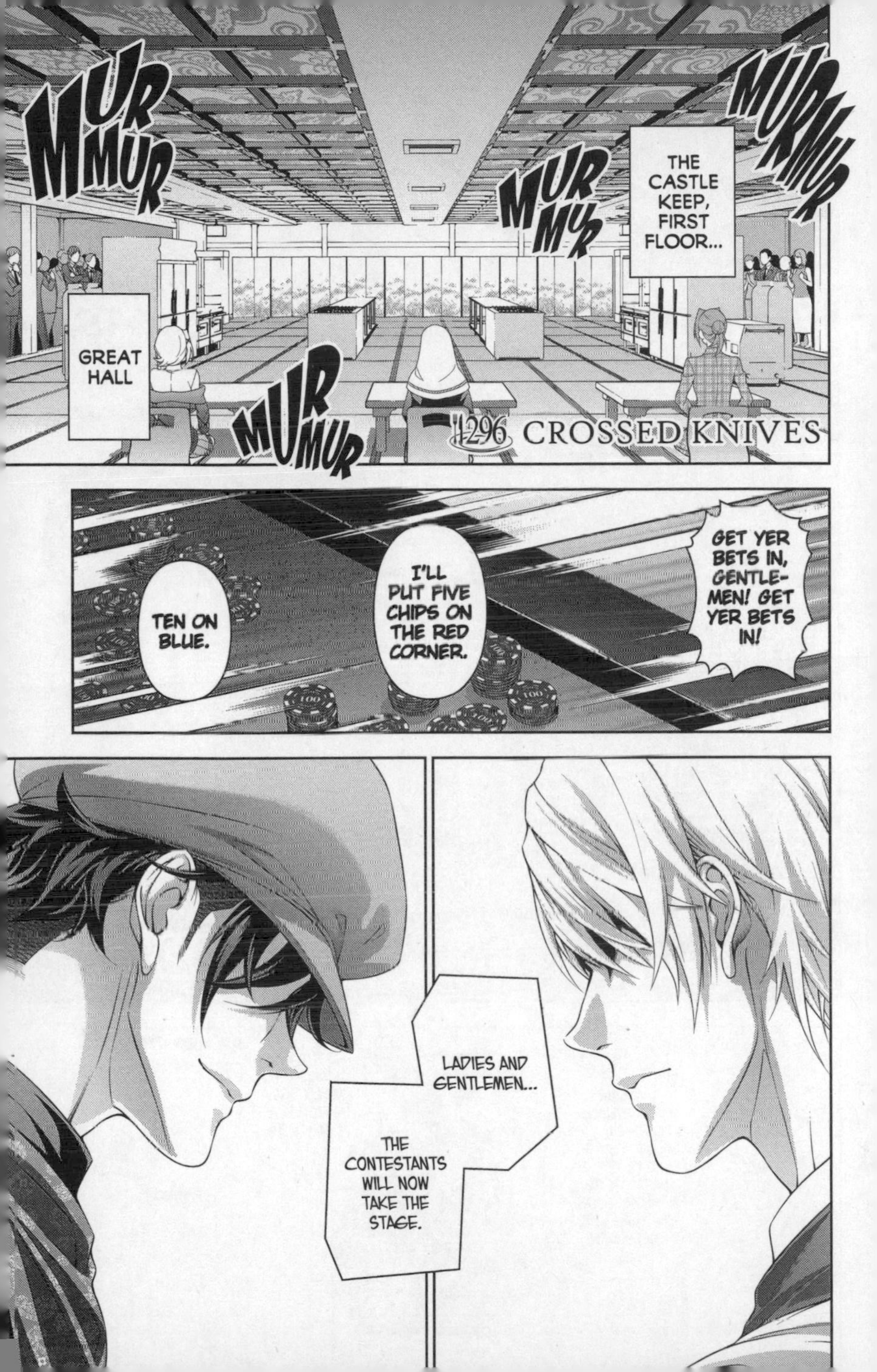
MURMUR
THE CASTLE KEEP, FIRST FLOOR...
MUR MUR
MUR MUR
GREAT HALL
MUR MUR
#296 CROSSED KNIVES
GET YER BETS IN, GENTLEMEN! GET YER BETS IN!
I'LL PUT FIVE CHIPS ON THE RED CORNER.
TEN ON BLUE.
LADIES AND GENTLEMEN...
THE CONTESTANTS WILL NOW TAKE THE STAGE.

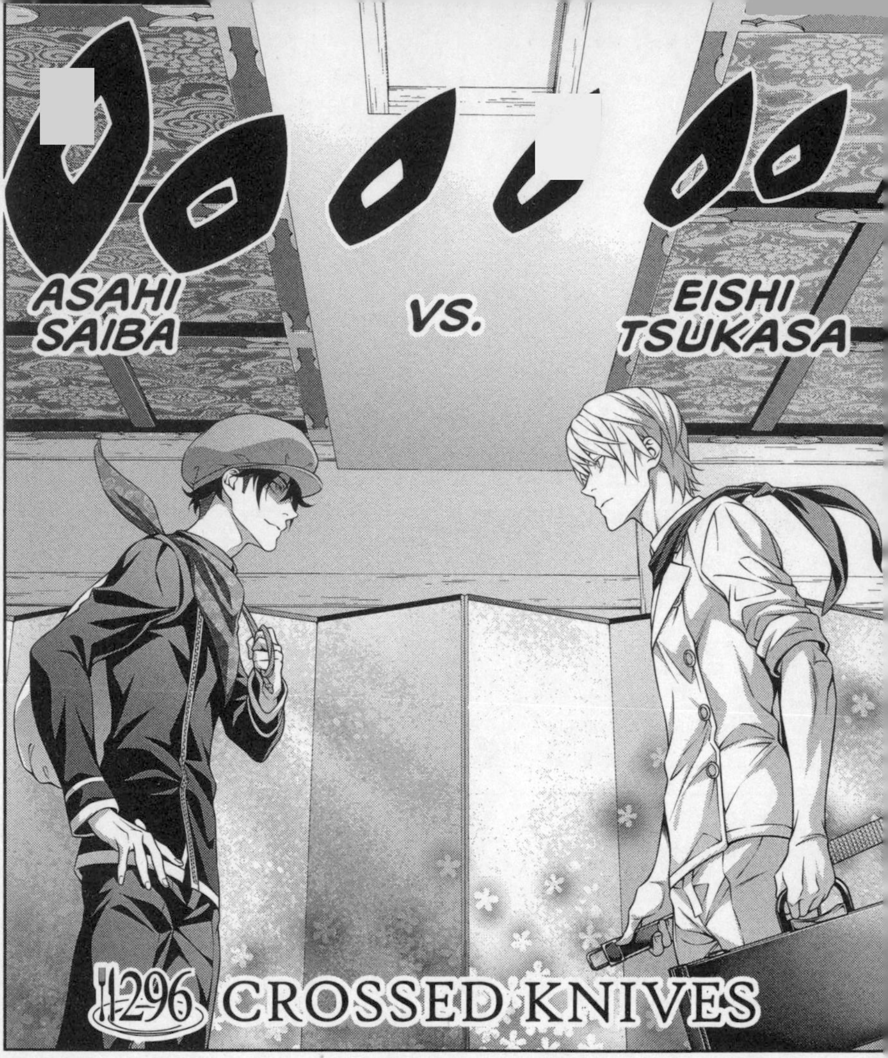
EISHI TSUKASA
VS.
ASAHI SAIBA
296 CROSSED KNIVES
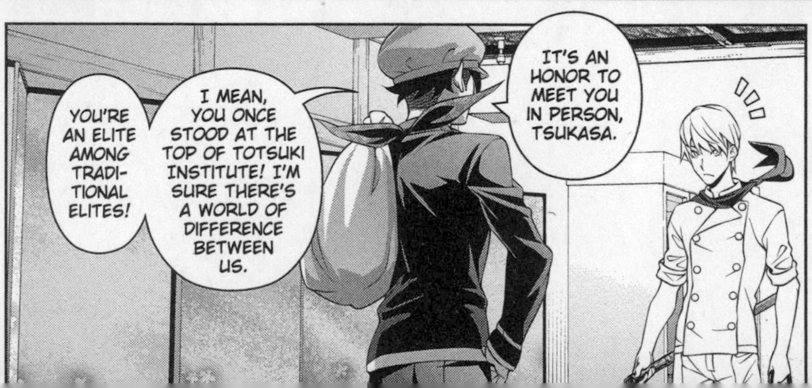
IT'S AN HONOR TO MEET YOU IN PERSON, TSUKASA.
I MEAN, YOU ONCE STOOD AT THE TOP OF TOTSUKI INSTITUTE! I'M SURE THERE'S A WORLD OF DIFFERENCE BETWEEN US.
YOU'RE AN ELITE AMONG TRADI-TIONAL ELITES!

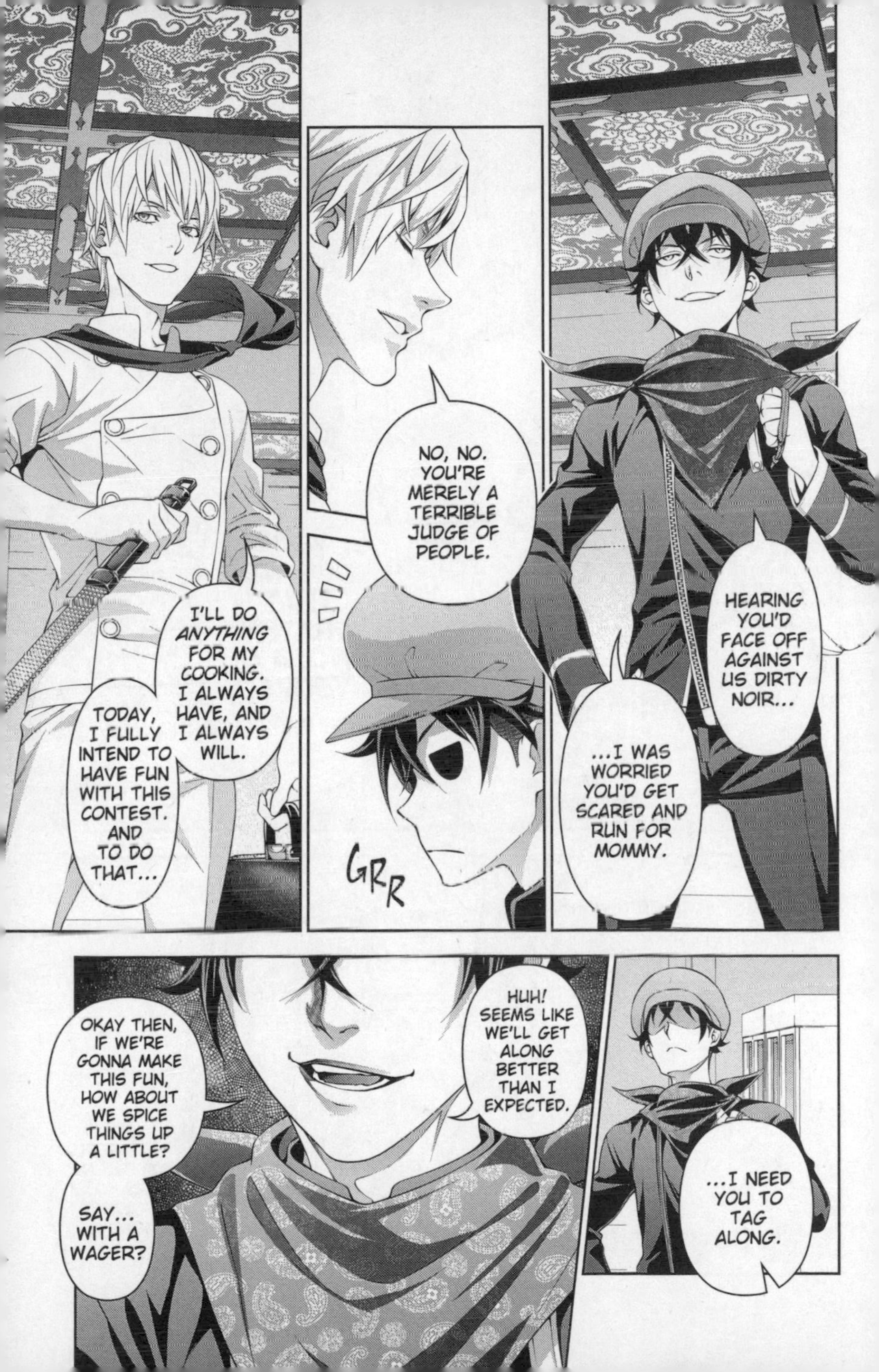
HEARING YOU'D FACE OFF AGAINST US DIRTY NOIR...
...I WAS WORRIED YOU'D GET SCARED AND RUN FOR MOMMY.
NO, NO. YOU'RE MERELY A TERRIBLE JUDGE OF PEOPLE.
GRR
I'LL DO *ANYTHING* FOR MY COOKING. I ALWAYS HAVE, AND I ALWAYS WILL.
TODAY, I FULLY INTEND TO HAVE FUN WITH THIS CONTEST. AND TO DO THAT...
...I NEED YOU TO TAG ALONG.
HUH! SEEMS LIKE WE'LL GET ALONG BETTER THAN I EXPECTED.
OKAY THEN, IF WE'RE GONNA MAKE THIS FUN, HOW ABOUT WE SPICE THINGS UP A LITTLE?
SAY... WITH A WAGER?

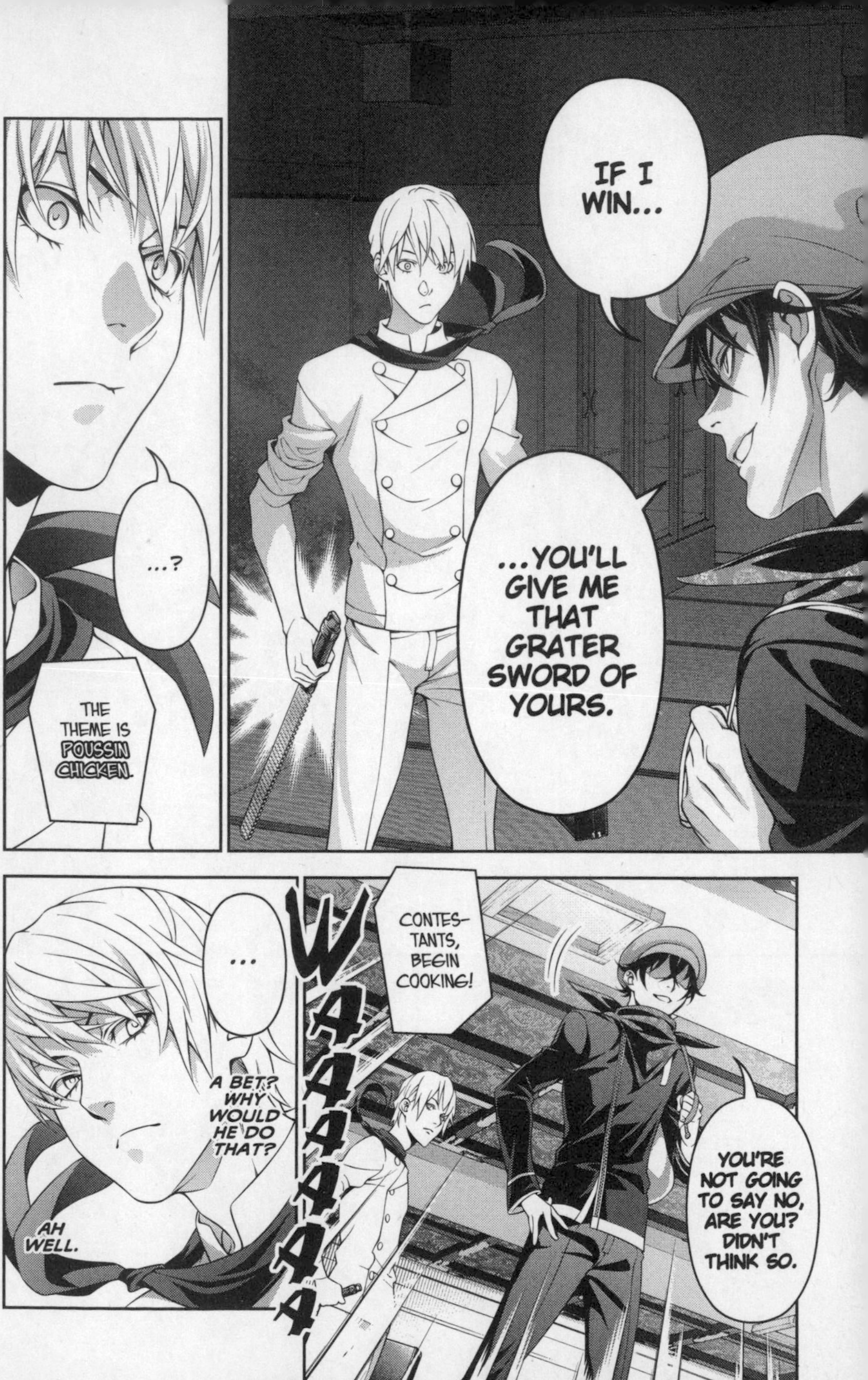
IF I WIN...
...YOU'LL GIVE ME THAT GRATER SWORD OF YOURS.
...?
THE THEME IS POUSSIN CHICKEN.
CONTES-TANTS, BEGIN COOKING!
YOU'RE NOT GOING TO SAY NO, ARE YOU? DIDN'T THINK SO.
WAAAAAAA
...
A BET? WHY WOULD HE DO THAT?
AH WELL.

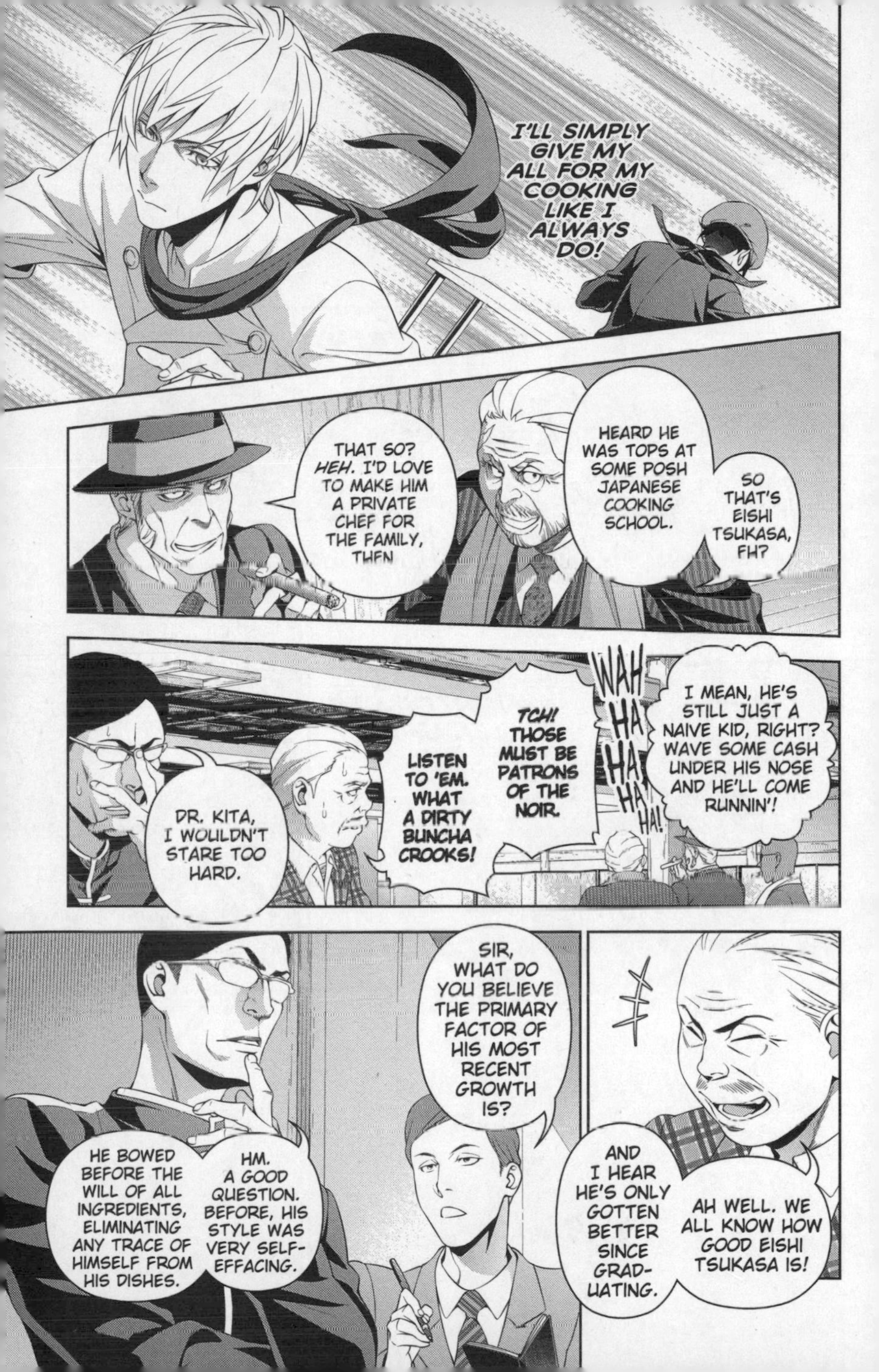
I'LL SIMPLY GIVE MY ALL FOR MY COOKING LIKE I ALWAYS DO!
SO THAT'S EISHI TSUKASA, EH?
HEARD HE WAS TOPS AT SOME POSH JAPANESE COOKING SCHOOL.
THAT SO? HEH. I'D LOVE TO MAKE HIM A PRIVATE CHEF FOR THE FAMILY, THEN
I MEAN, HE'S STILL JUST A NAIVE KID, RIGHT? WAVE SOME CASH UNDER HIS NOSE AND HE'LL COME RUNNIN'!
WAH HA HA HA HA HA!
TCH! THOSE MUST BE PATRONS OF THE NOIR.
LISTEN TO 'EM. WHAT A DIRTY BUNCHA CROOKS!
DR. KITA, I WOULDN'T STARE TOO HARD.
AH WELL. WE ALL KNOW HOW GOOD EISHI TSUKASA IS!
AND I HEAR HE'S ONLY GOTTEN BETTER SINCE GRAD-UATING.
SIR, WHAT DO YOU BELIEVE THE PRIMARY FACTOR OF HIS MOST RECENT GROWTH IS?
HM. A GOOD QUESTION. BEFORE, HIS STYLE WAS VERY SELF-EFFACING.
HE BOWED BEFORE THE WILL OF ALL INGREDIENTS, ELIMINATING ANY TRACE OF HIMSELF FROM HIS DISHES.

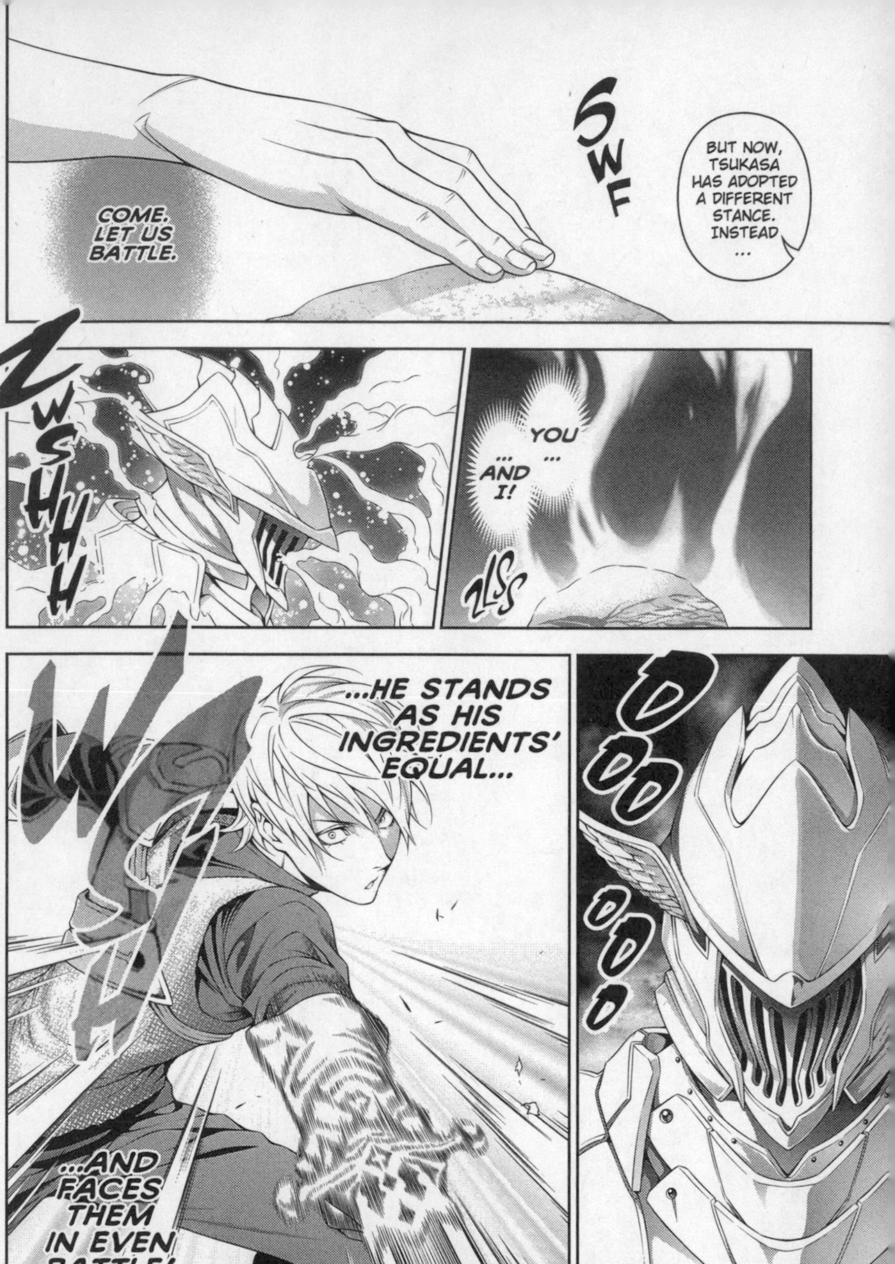
BUT NOW, TSUKASA HAS ADOPTED A DIFFERENT STANCE. INSTEAD ...
SWF
COME. LET US BATTLE.
YOU ... ... AND I!
ZLSS
ZWSHHHH
DDDDDDDD
...HE STANDS AS HIS INGREDIENTS' EQUAL...
...AND FACES THEM IN EVEN BATTLE!

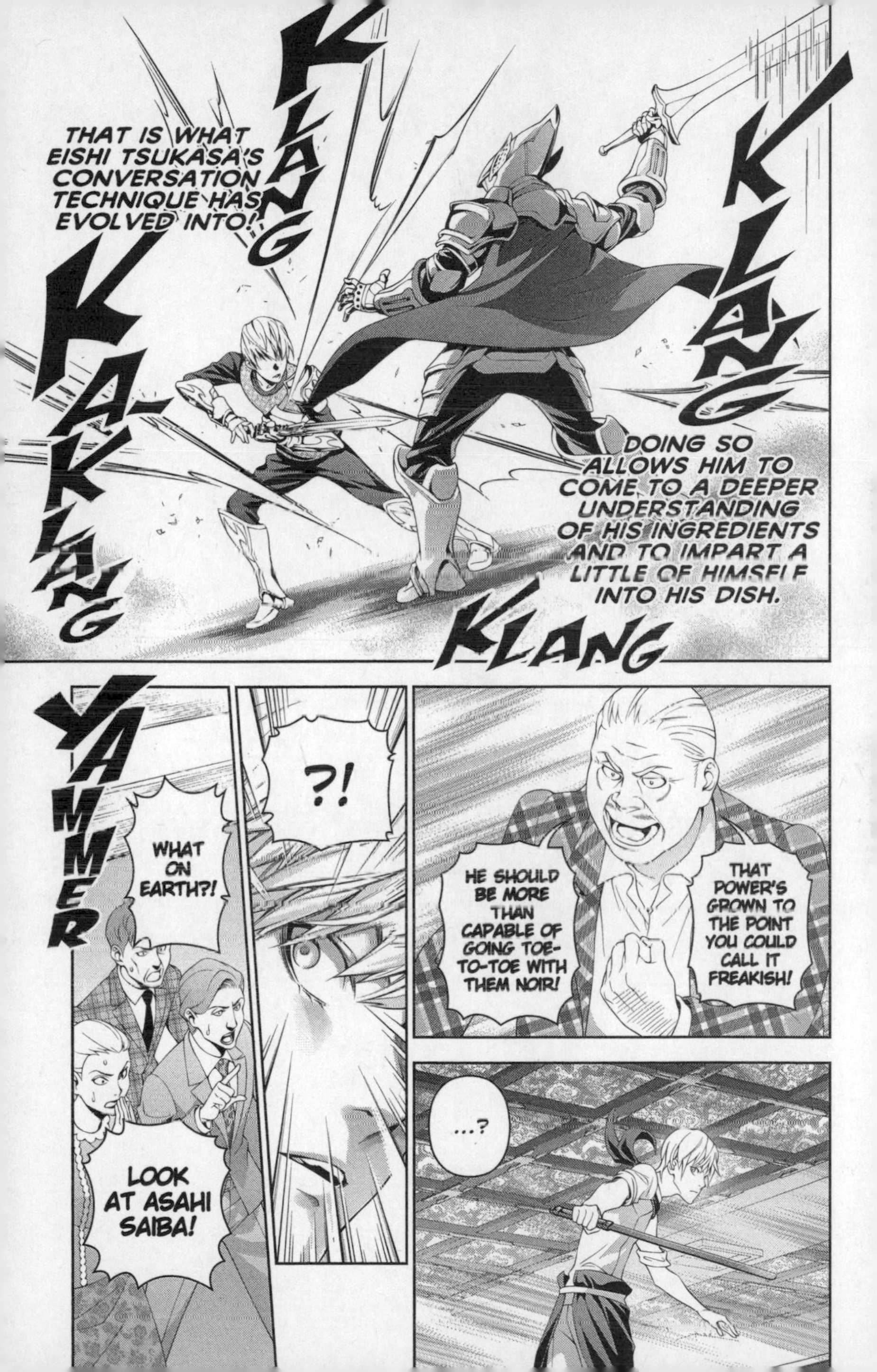

KLANG
KLANG
THAT IS WHAT EISHI TSUKASA'S CONVERSATION TECHNIQUE HAS EVOLVED INTO!
DOING SO ALLOWS HIM TO COME TO A DEEPER UNDERSTANDING OF HIS INGREDIENTS AND TO IMPART A LITTLE OF HIMSELF INTO HIS DISH.
KA-KLANG
KLANG
THAT POWER'S GROWN TO THE POINT YOU COULD CALL IT FREAKISH!
HE SHOULD BE MORE THAN CAPABLE OF GOING TOE-TO-TOE WITH THEM NOIR!
...?
?!
YAMMER
WHAT ON EARTH?!
LOOK AT ASAHI SAIBA!

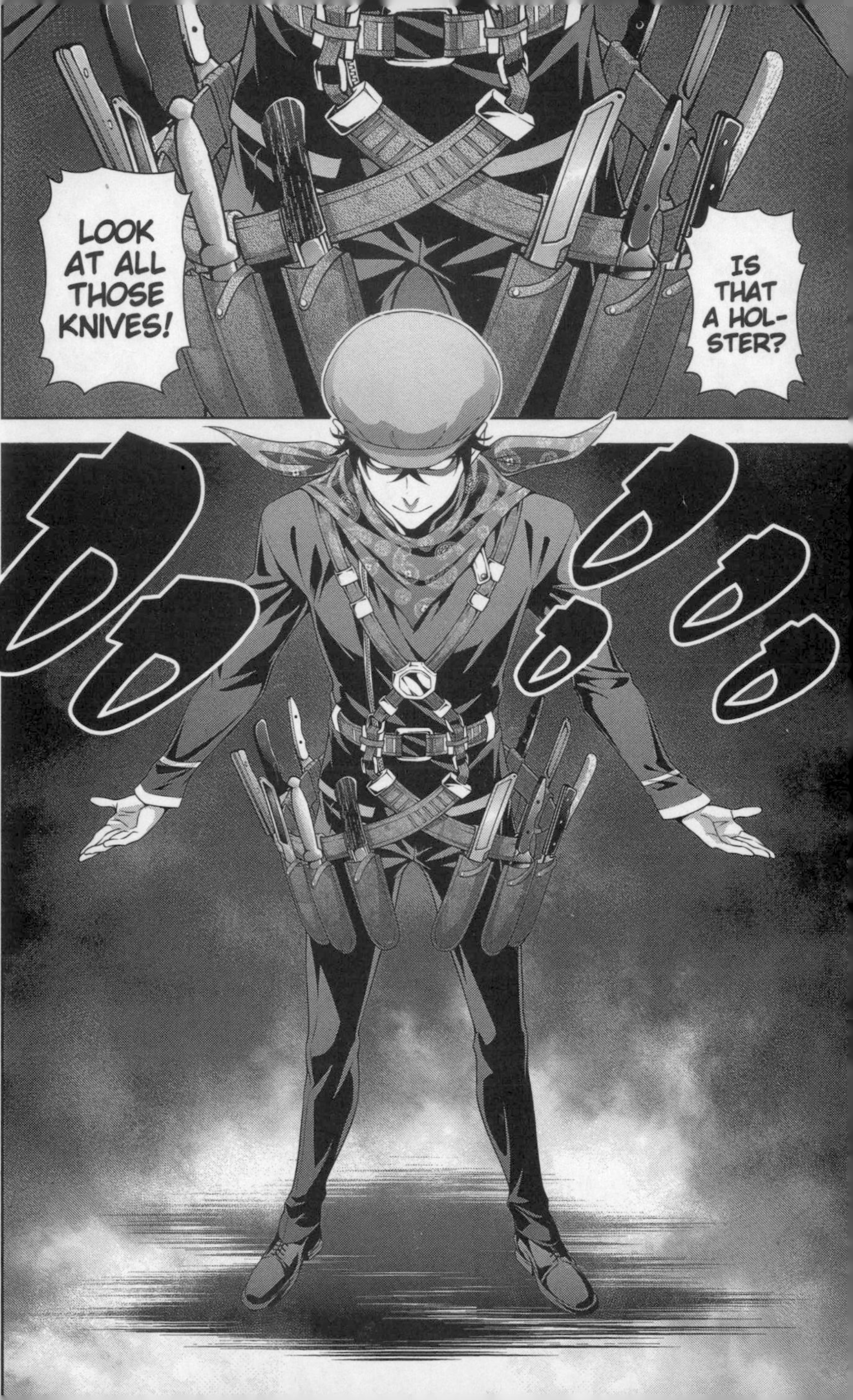
IS THAT A HOL- STER?
LOOK AT ALL THOSE KNIVES!

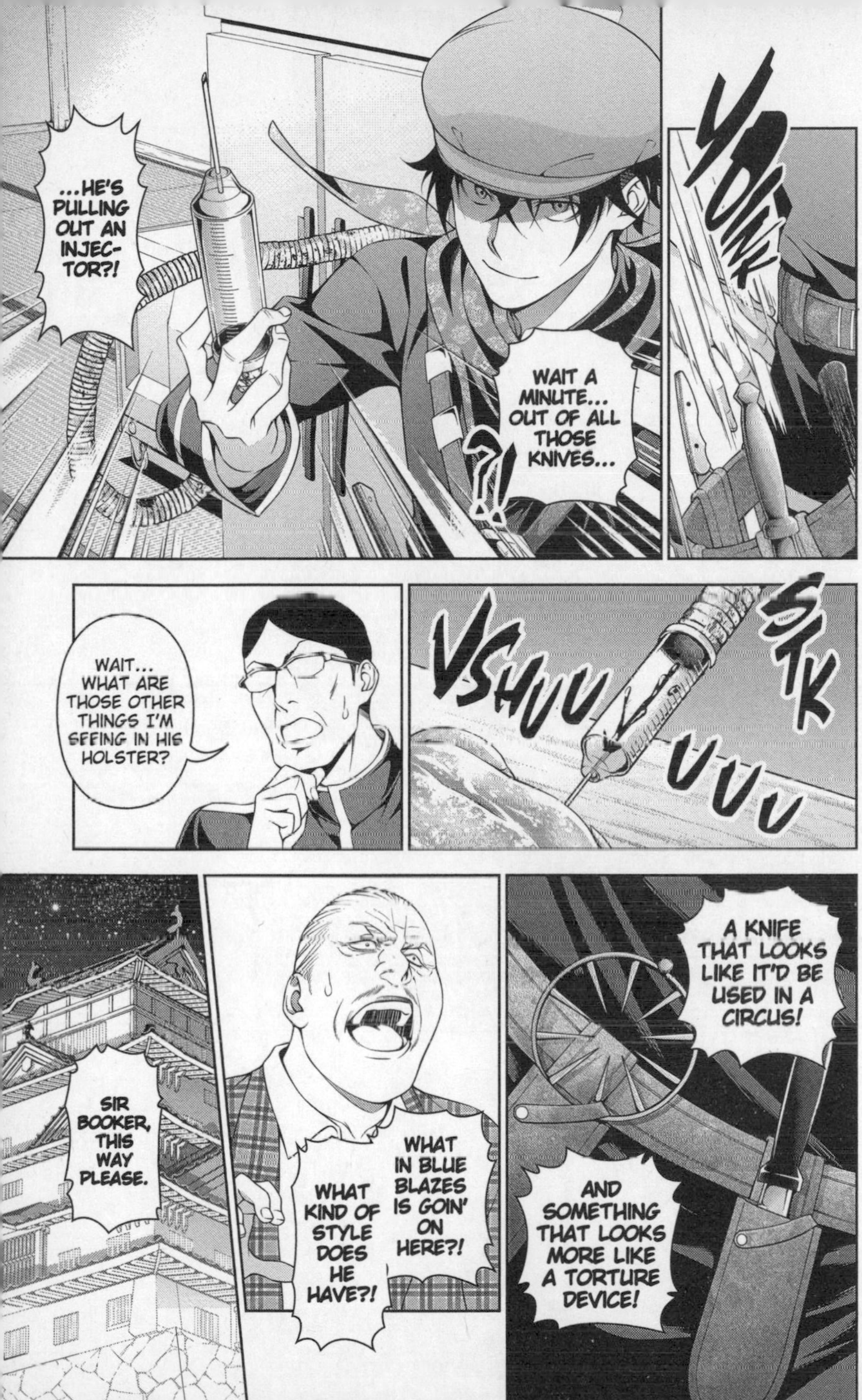
YOINK
WAIT A MINUTE... OUT OF ALL THOSE KNIVES...
?!
...HE'S PULLING OUT AN INJECTOR?!
STK
VSHUUUUUU
WAIT... WHAT ARE THOSE OTHER THINGS I'M SEEING IN HIS HOLSTER?
A KNIFE THAT LOOKS LIKE IT'D BE USED IN A CIRCUS!
AND SOMETHING THAT LOOKS MORE LIKE A TORTURE DEVICE!
WHAT IN BLUE BLAZES IS GOIN' ON HERE?!
WHAT KIND OF STYLE DOES HE HAVE?!
SIR BOOKER, THIS WAY PLEASE.

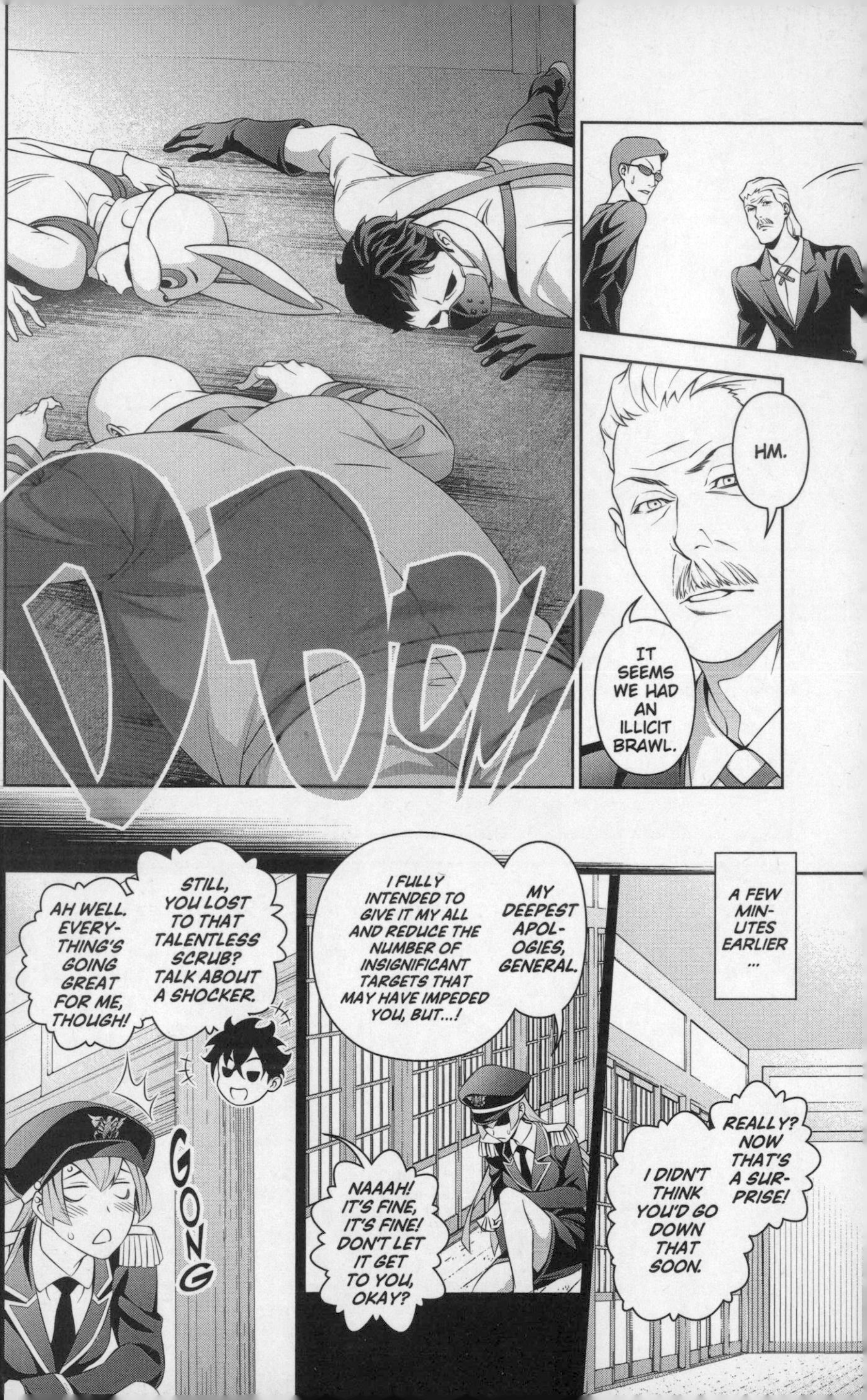
HM.
IT SEEMS WE HAD AN ILLICIT BRAWL.
A FEW MIN-UTES EARLIER ...
REALLY? NOW THAT'S A SUR-PRISE!
I DIDN'T THINK YOU'D GO DOWN THAT SOON.
MY DEEPEST APOL-OGIES, GENERAL.
I FULLY INTENDED TO GIVE IT MY ALL AND REDUCE THE NUMBER OF INSIGNIFICANT TARGETS THAT MAY HAVE IMPEDED YOU, BUT...!
NAAAH! IT'S FINE, IT'S FINE! DON'T LET IT GET TO YOU, OKAY?
STILL, YOU LOST TO THAT TALENTLESS SCRUB? TALK ABOUT A SHOCKER.
AH WELL. EVERY-THING'S GOING GREAT FOR ME, THOUGH!
GONG

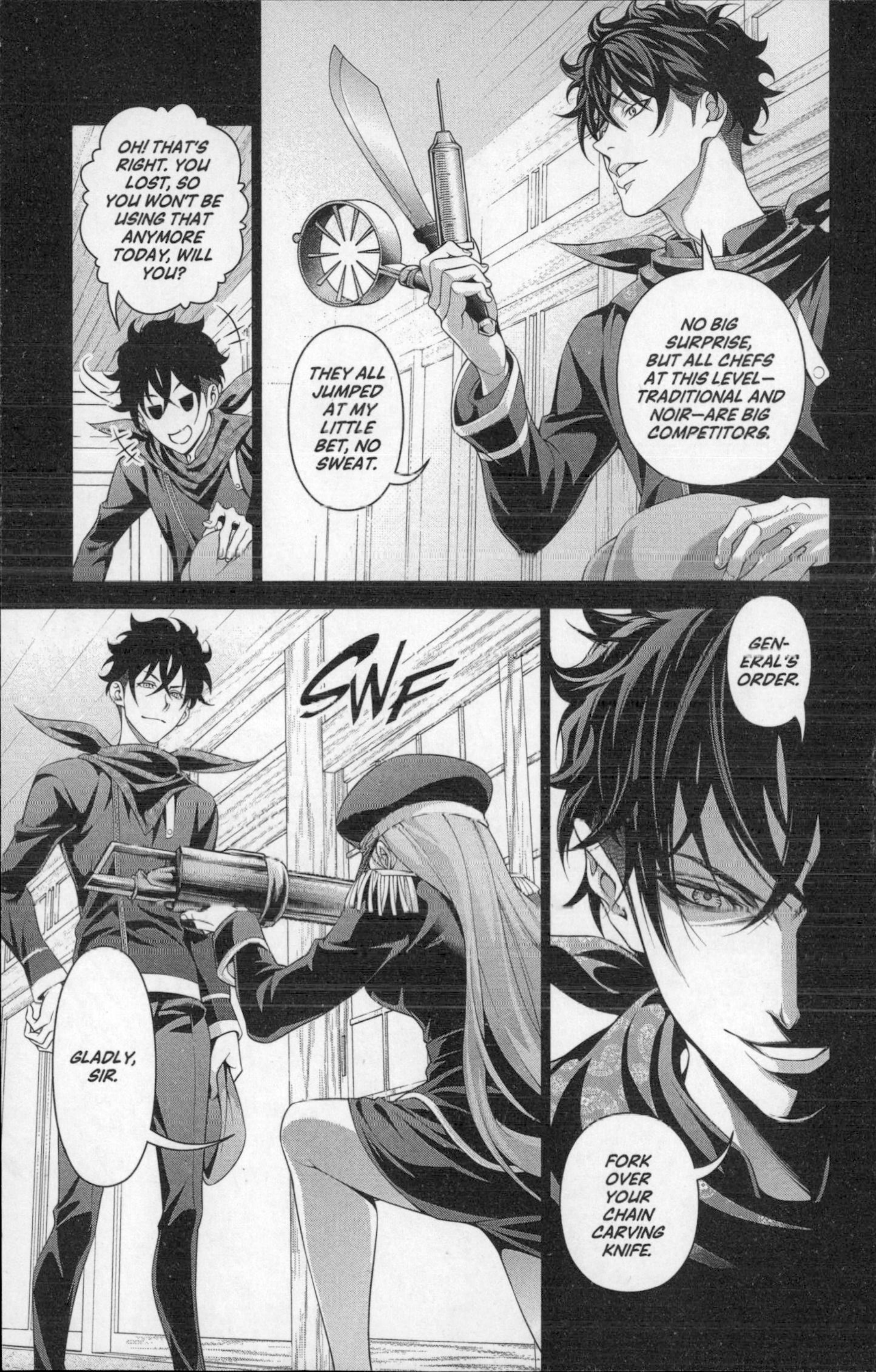
NO BIG SURPRISE, BUT ALL CHEFS AT THIS LEVEL—TRADITIONAL AND NOIR—ARE BIG COMPETITORS.
THEY ALL JUMPED AT MY LITTLE BET, NO SWEAT.
OH! THAT'S RIGHT. YOU LOST, SO YOU WON'T BE USING THAT ANYMORE TODAY, WILL YOU?
GEN-ERAL'S ORDER.
FORK OVER YOUR CHAIN CARVING KNIFE.
SWF
GLADLY, SIR.

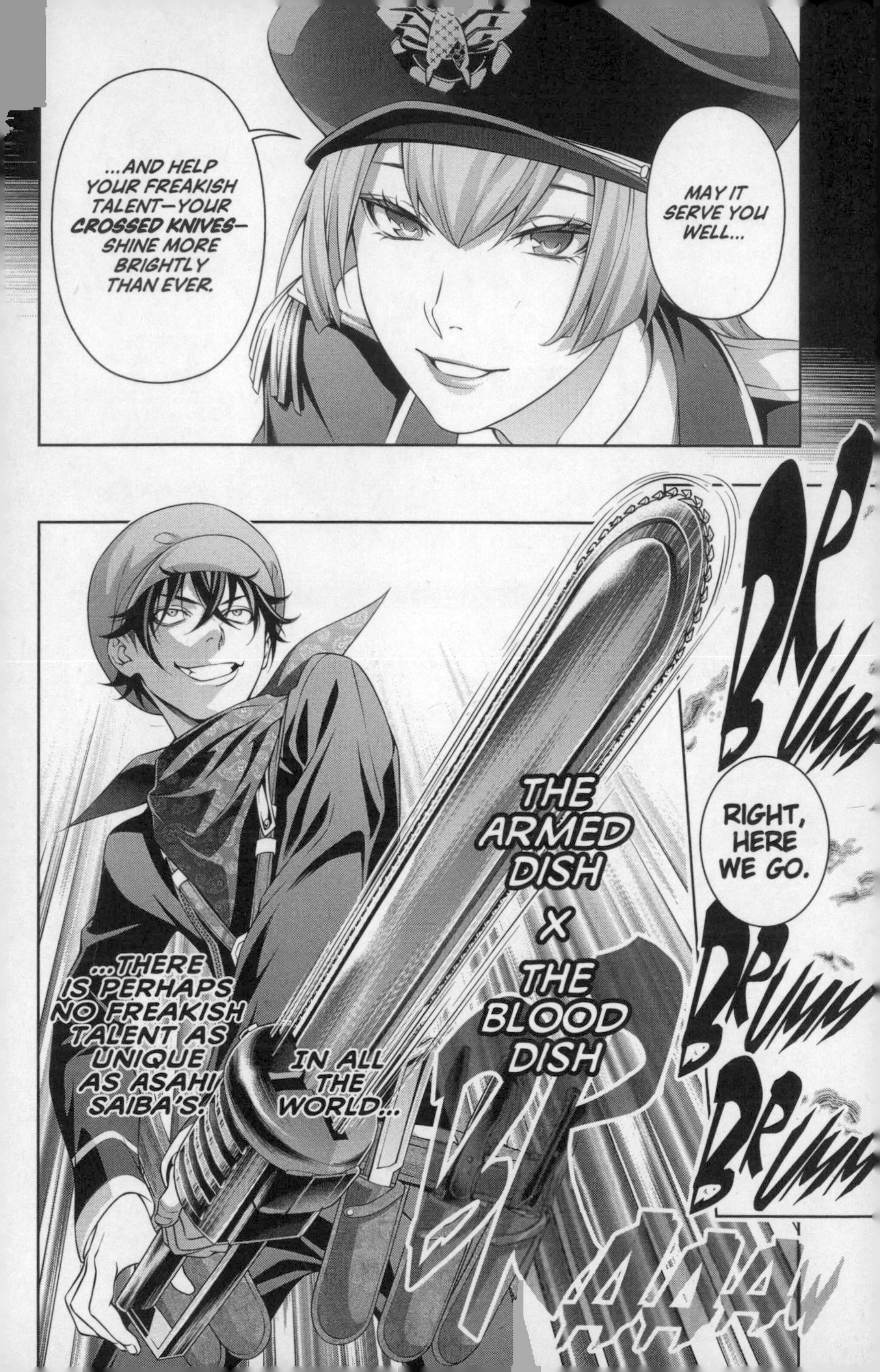
MAY IT SERVE YOU WELL...
...AND HELP YOUR FREAKISH TALENT—YOUR CROSSED KNIVES—SHINE MORE BRIGHTLY THAN EVER.
RIGHT, HERE WE GO.
THE ARMED DISH x THE BLOOD DISH
IN ALL THE WORLD...
...THERE IS PERHAPS NO FREAKISH TALENT AS UNIQUE AS ASAHI SAIBA'S!

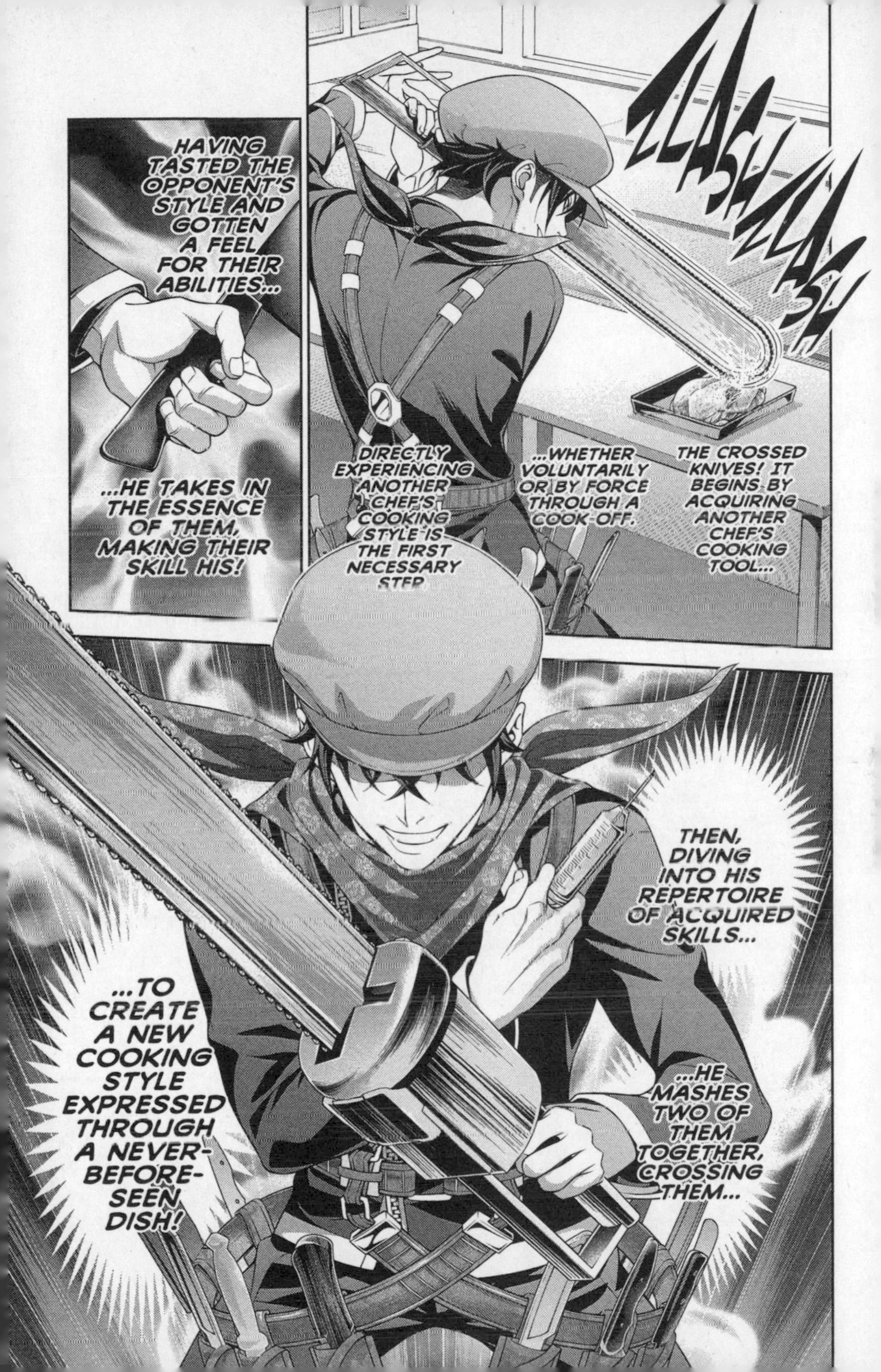
ZLASH ZLASH ZLASH
THE CROSSED KNIVES! IT BEGINS BY ACQUIRING ANOTHER CHEF'S COOKING TOOL...
...WHETHER VOLUNTARILY OR BY FORCE THROUGH A COOK-OFF.
DIRECTLY EXPERIENCING ANOTHER CHEF'S COOKING STYLE IS THE FIRST NECESSARY STEP.
HAVING TASTED THE OPPONENT'S STYLE AND GOTTEN A FEEL FOR THEIR ABILITIES...
...HE TAKES IN THE ESSENCE OF THEM, MAKING THEIR SKILL HIS!
THEN, DIVING INTO HIS REPERTOIRE OF ACQUIRED SKILLS...
...HE MASHES TWO OF THEM TOGETHER, CROSSING THEM...
...TO CREATE A NEW COOKING STYLE EXPRESSED THROUGH A NEVER-BEFORE-SEEN DISH!

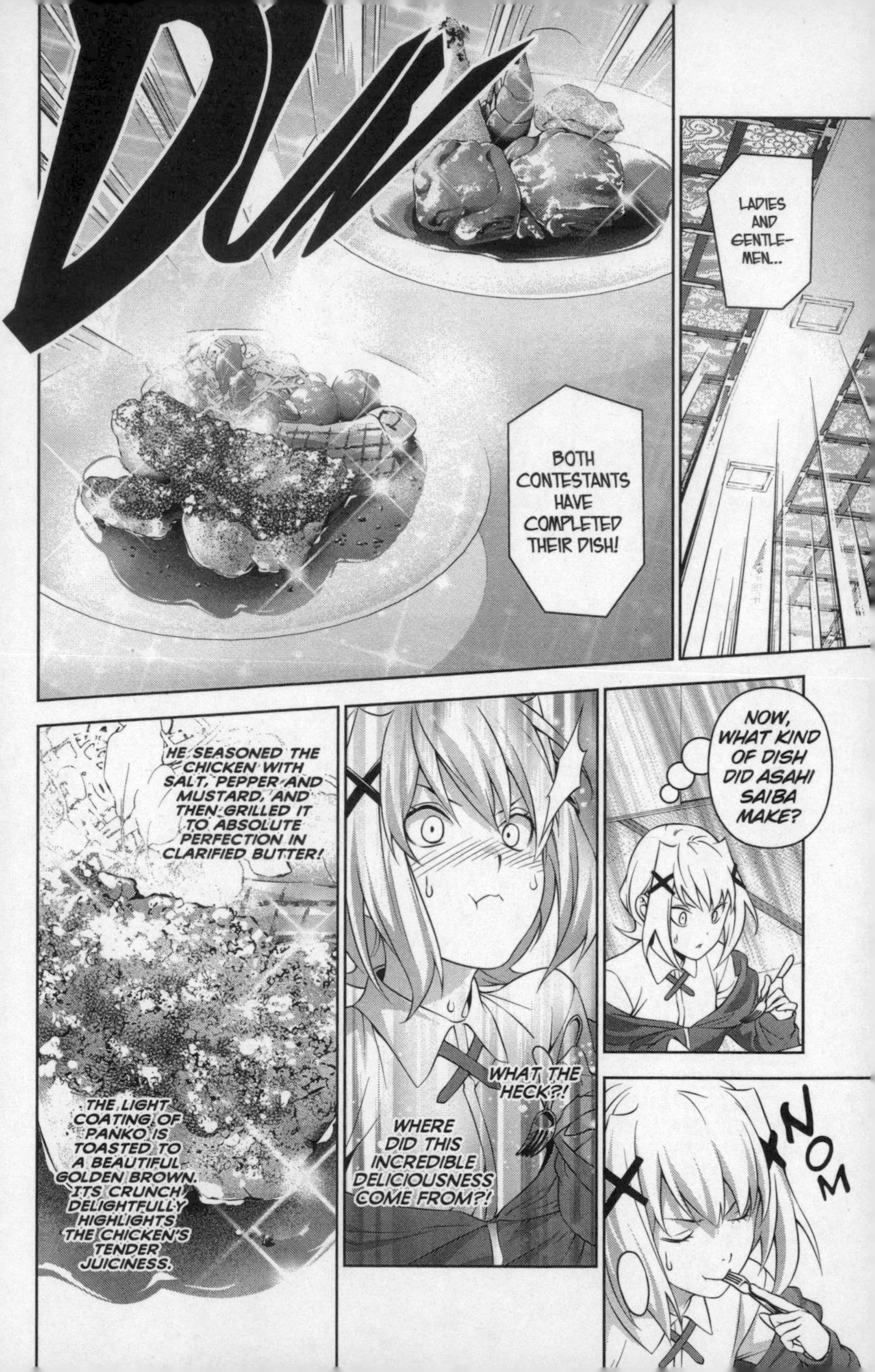
LADIES AND GENTLE-MEN...
DUN
BOTH CONTESTANTS HAVE COMPLETED THEIR DISH!
NOW, WHAT KIND OF DISH DID ASAHI SAIBA MAKE?
NOM NOM
WHAT THE HECK?!
WHERE DID THIS INCREDIBLE DELICIOUSNESS COME FROM?!
HE SEASONED THE CHICKEN WITH SALT, PEPPER AND MUSTARD, AND THEN GRILLED IT TO ABSOLUTE PERFECTION IN CLARIFIED BUTTER!
THE LIGHT COATING OF PANKO IS TOASTED TO A BEAUTIFUL GOLDEN BROWN. ITS CRUNCH DELIGHTFULLY HIGHLIGHTS THE CHICKEN'S TENDER JUICINESS.

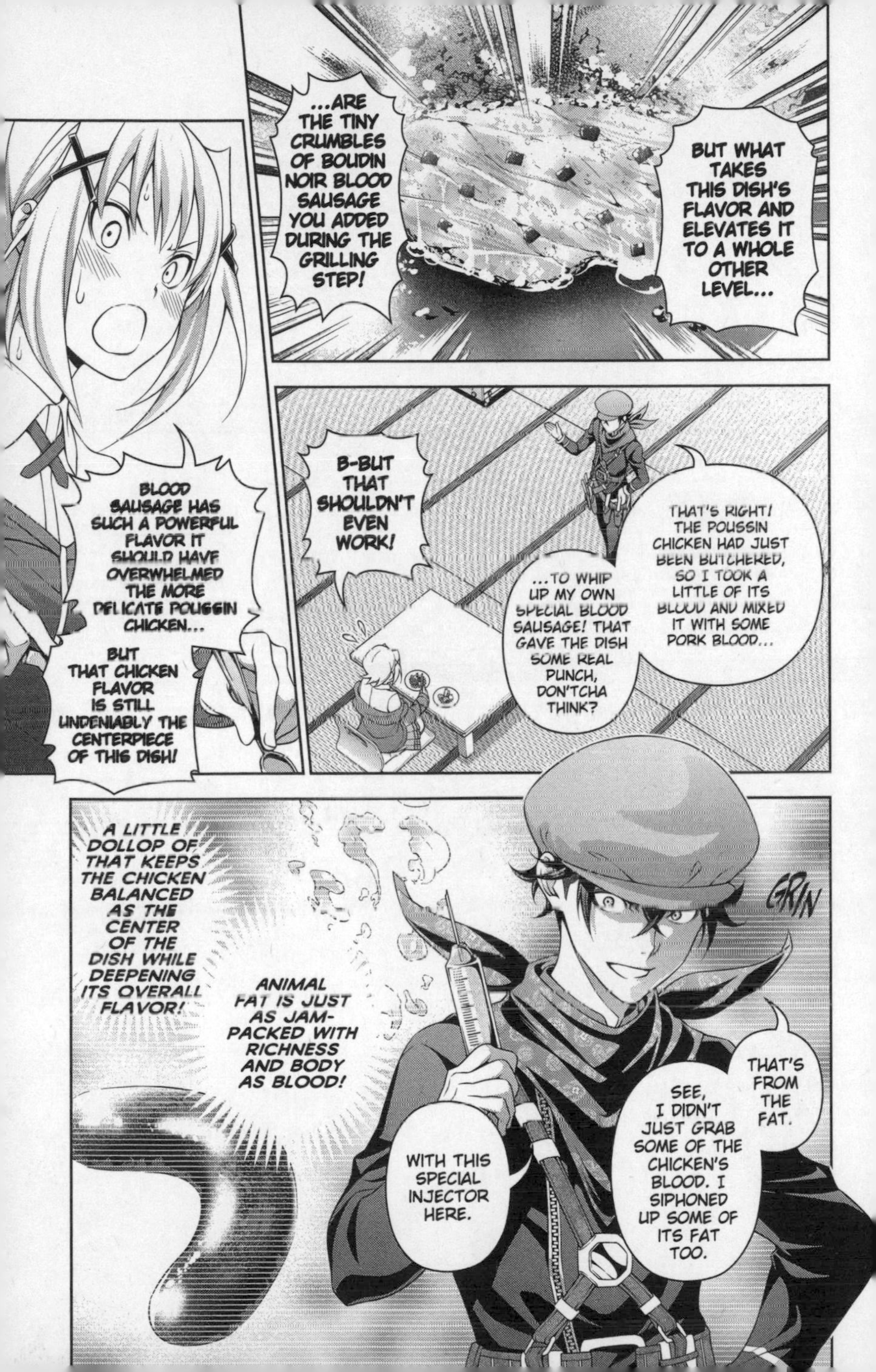
BUT WHAT TAKES THIS DISH'S FLAVOR AND ELEVATES IT TO A WHOLE OTHER LEVEL...
...ARE THE TINY CRUMBLES OF BOUDIN NOIR BLOOD SAUSAGE YOU ADDED DURING THE GRILLING STEP!
THAT'S RIGHT! THE POUSSIN CHICKEN HAD JUST BEEN BUTCHERED, SO I TOOK A LITTLE OF ITS BLOOD AND MIXED IT WITH SOME PORK BLOOD...
...TO WHIP UP MY OWN SPECIAL BLOOD SAUSAGE! THAT GAVE THE DISH SOME REAL PUNCH, DON'TCHA THINK?
B-BUT THAT SHOULDN'T EVEN WORK!
BLOOD SAUSAGE HAS SUCH A POWERFUL FLAVOR IT SHOULD HAVE OVERWHELMED THE MORE DELICATE POUSSIN CHICKEN...
BUT THAT CHICKEN FLAVOR IS STILL UNDENIABLY THE CENTERPIECE OF THIS DISH!
GRIN
THAT'S FROM THE FAT.
SEE, I DIDN'T JUST GRAB SOME OF THE CHICKEN'S BLOOD. I SIPHONED UP SOME OF ITS FAT TOO.
WITH THIS SPECIAL INJECTOR HERE.
ANIMAL FAT IS JUST AS JAM-PACKED WITH RICHNESS AND BODY AS BLOOD!
A LITTLE DOLLOP OF THAT KEEPS THE CHICKEN BALANCED AS THE CENTER OF THE DISH WHILE DEEPENING ITS OVERALL FLAVOR!

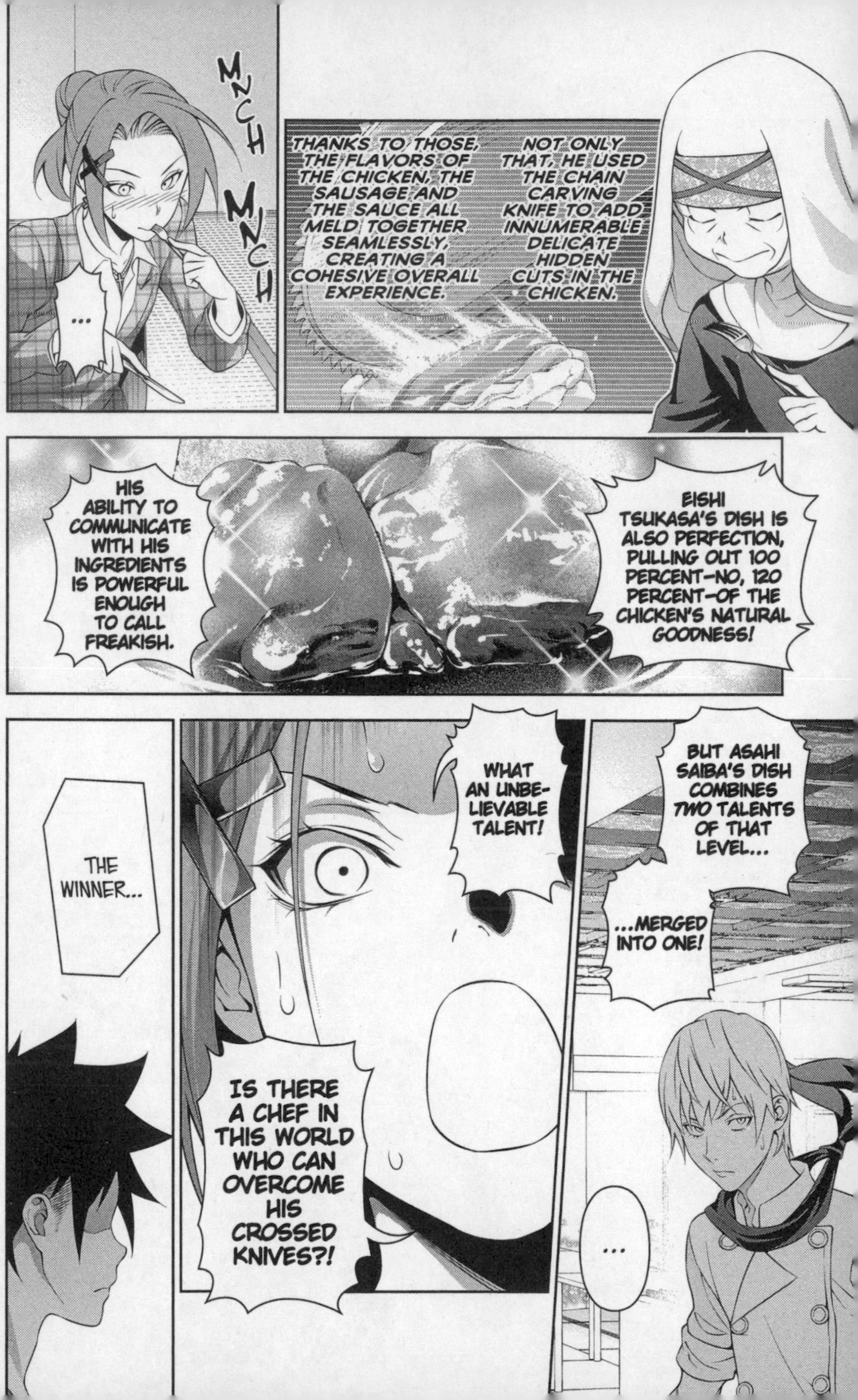
NOT ONLY THAT, HE USED THE CHAIN CARVING KNIFE TO ADD INNUMERABLE DELICATE HIDDEN CUTS IN THE CHICKEN.
THANKS TO THOSE, THE FLAVORS OF THE CHICKEN, THE SAUSAGE AND THE SAUCE ALL MELD TOGETHER SEAMLESSLY, CREATING A COHESIVE OVERALL EXPERIENCE.
MNCH MNCH
...
EISHI TSUKASA'S DISH IS ALSO PERFECTION, PULLING OUT 100 PERCENT—NO, 120 PERCENT—OF THE CHICKEN'S NATURAL GOODNESS!
HIS ABILITY TO COMMUNICATE WITH HIS INGREDIENTS IS POWERFUL ENOUGH TO CALL FREAKISH.
BUT ASAHI SAIBA'S DISH COMBINES *TWO* TALENTS OF THAT LEVEL...
...MERGED INTO ONE!
...
WHAT AN UNBE-LIEVABLE TALENT!
IS THERE A CHEF IN THIS WORLD WHO CAN OVERCOME HIS CROSSED KNIVES?!
THE WINNER...

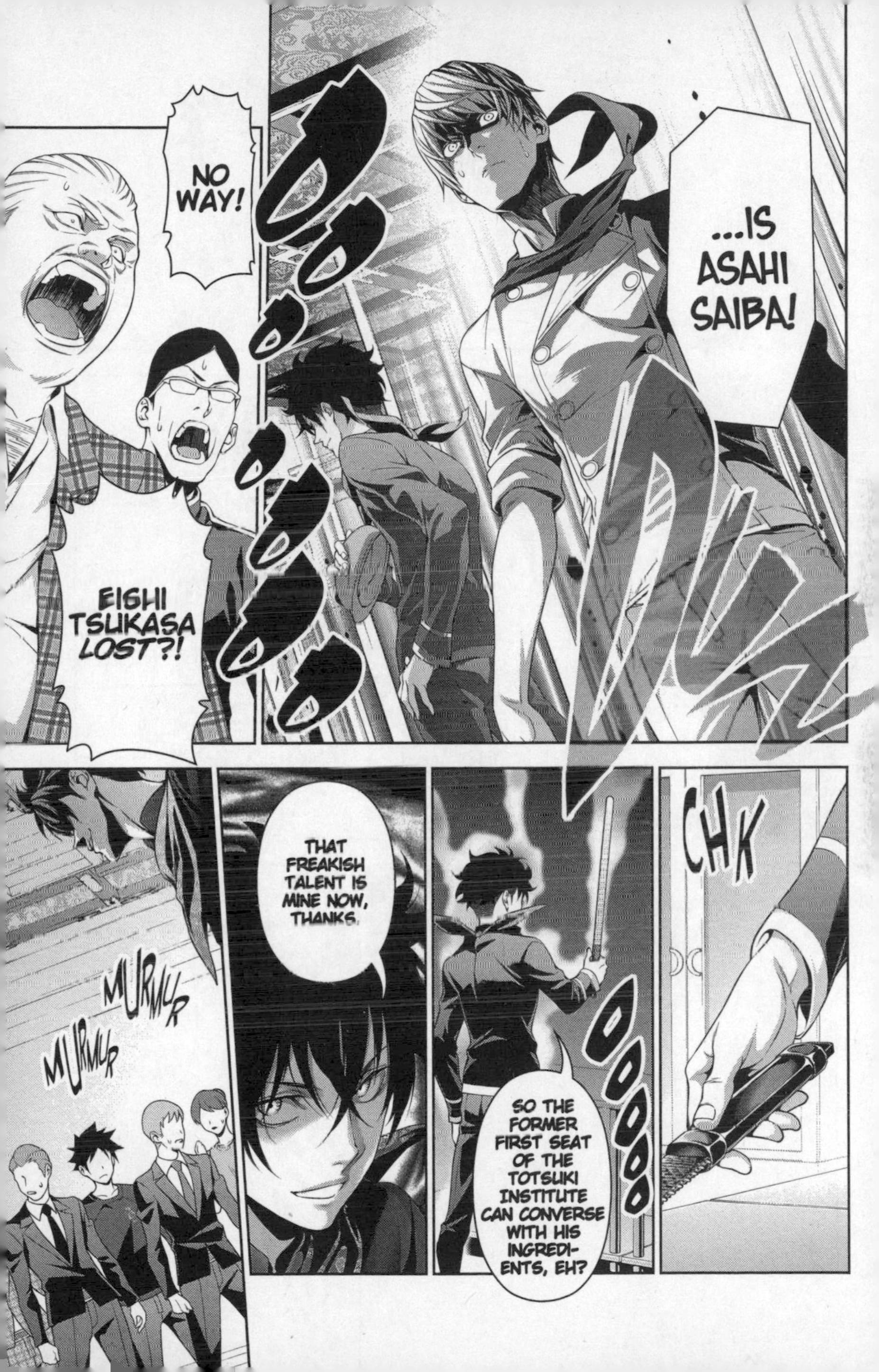
...IS ASAHI SAIBA!
NO WAY!
EISHI TSUKASA LOST?!
CHK
SO THE FORMER FIRST SEAT OF THE TOTSUKI INSTITUTE CAN CONVERSE WITH HIS INGREDI- ENTS, EH?
THAT FREAKISH TALENT IS MINE NOW, THANKS.
MURMUR
MURMUR

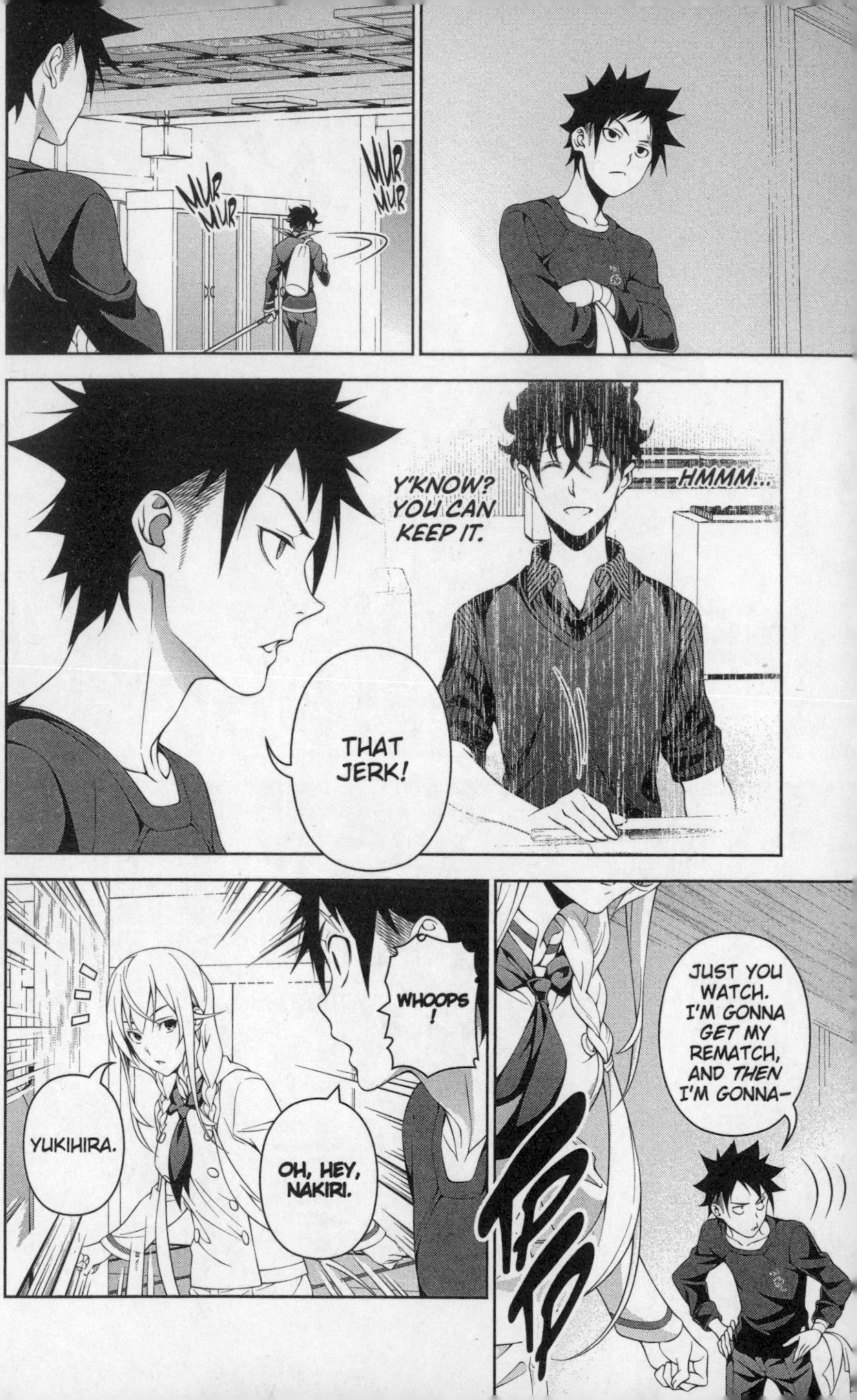
MUR MUR
MUR MUR
HMMM...
Y'KNOW? YOU CAN KEEP IT.
THAT JERK!
JUST YOU WATCH. I'M GONNA GET MY REMATCH, AND THEN I'M GONNA-
WHOOPS!
YUKIHIRA.
OH, HEY, NAKIRI.

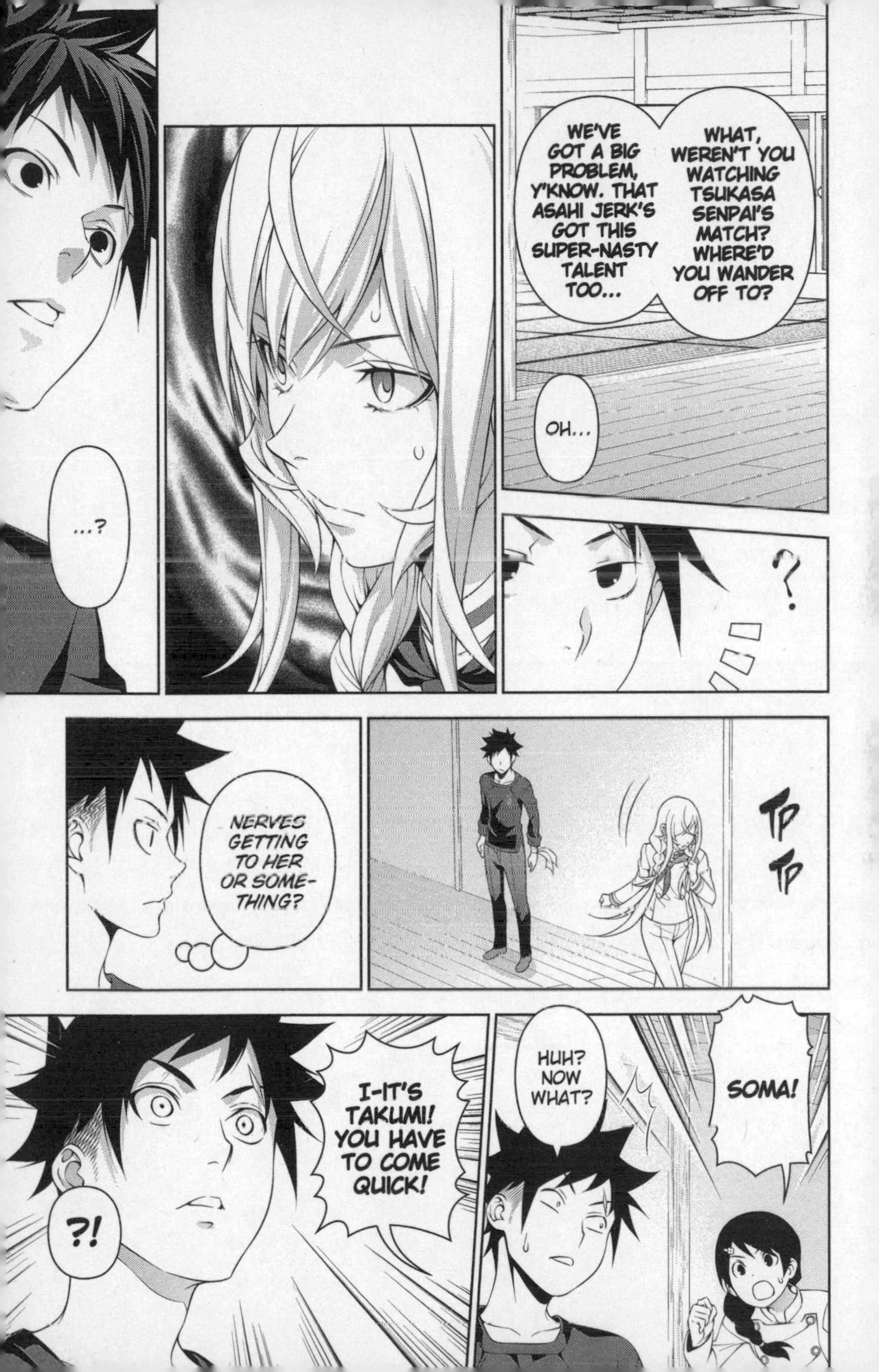
WHAT, WEREN'T YOU WATCHING TSUKASA SENPAI'S MATCH? WHERE'D YOU WANDER OFF TO?
WE'VE GOT A BIG PROBLEM, Y'KNOW. THAT ASAHI JERK'S GOT THIS SUPER-NASTY TALENT TOO...
OH...
?
...?
TP TP
NERVES GETTING TO HER OR SOME-THING?
SOMA!
HUH? NOW WHAT?
I-IT'S TAKUMI! YOU HAVE TO COME QUICK!
?!

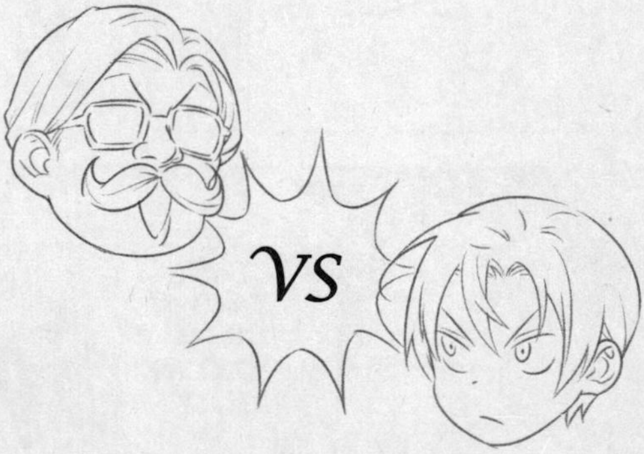
VS

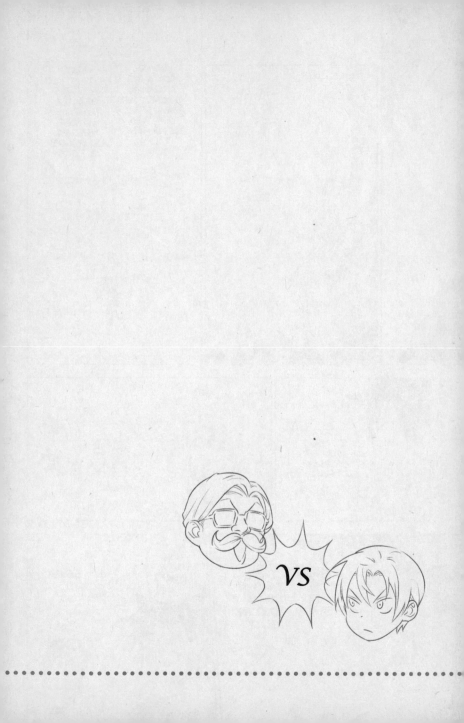

297 THE MISSING HALF OF THE MOON

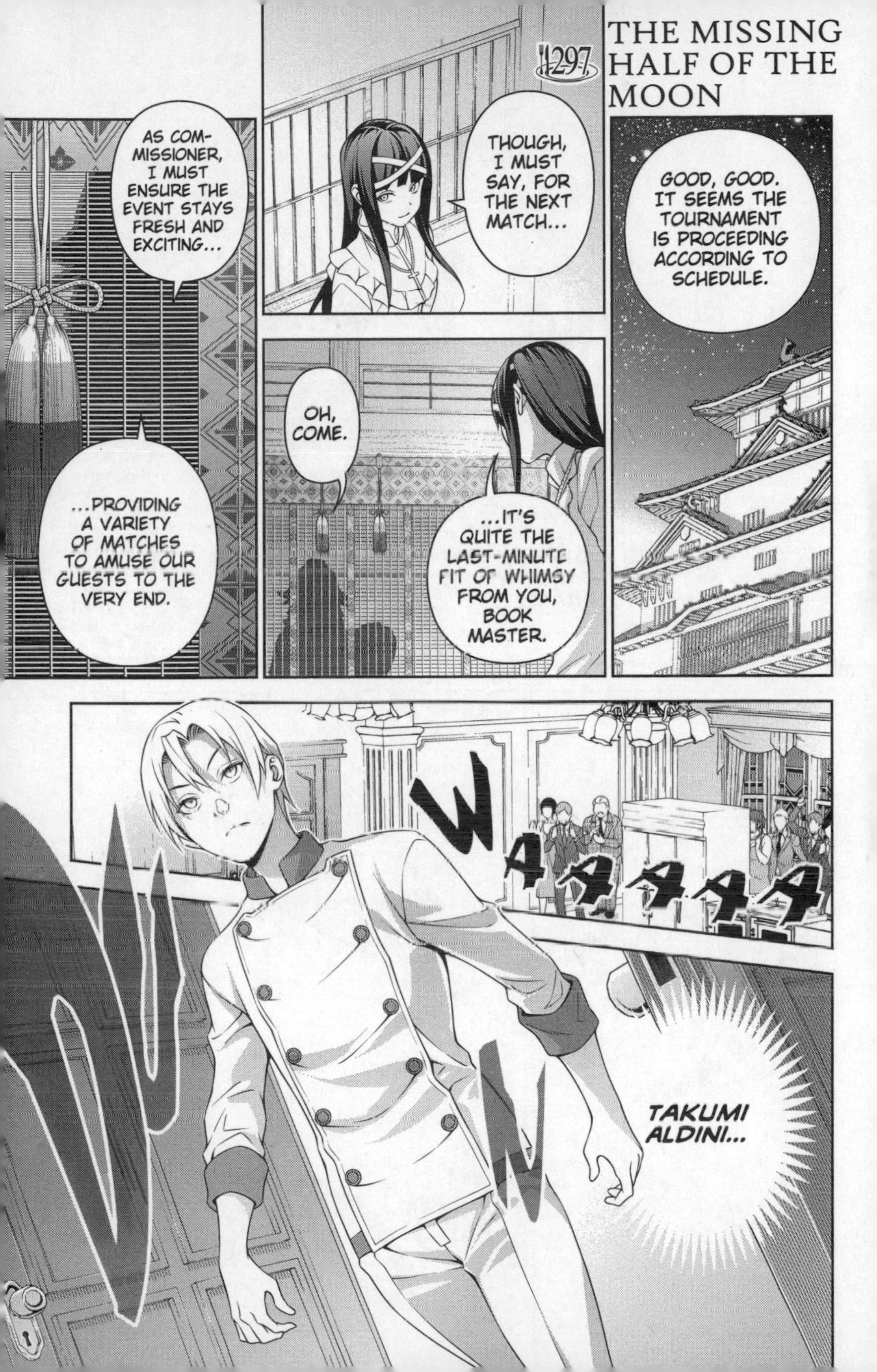

GOOD, GOOD. IT SEEMS THE TOURNAMENT IS PROCEEDING ACCORDING TO SCHEDULE.
THOUGH, I MUST SAY, FOR THE NEXT MATCH...
...IT'S QUITE THE LAST-MINUTE FIT OF WHIMSY FROM YOU, BOOK MASTER.
OH, COME.
AS COM-MISSIONER, I MUST ENSURE THE EVENT STAYS FRESH AND EXCITING...
...PROVIDING A VARIETY OF MATCHES TO AMUSE OUR GUESTS TO THE VERY END.
WAAAAA
TAKUMI ALDINI...

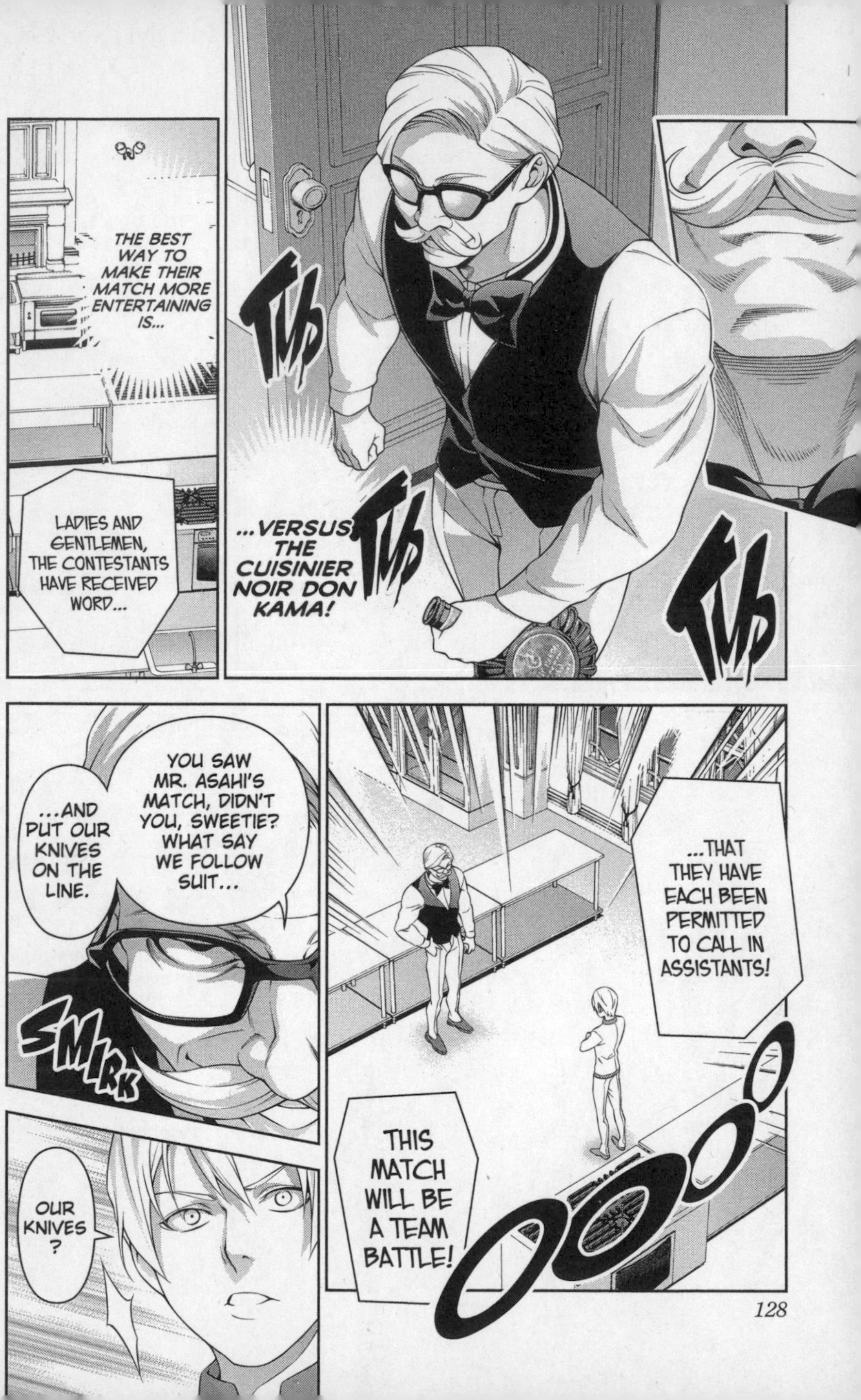
TUP
...VERSUS THE CUISINIER NOIR DON KAMA!
TUP
TUP
THE BEST WAY TO MAKE THEIR MATCH MORE ENTERTAINING IS...
LADIES AND GENTLEMEN, THE CONTESTANTS HAVE RECEIVED WORD...
...THAT THEY HAVE EACH BEEN PERMITTED TO CALL IN ASSISTANTS!
THIS MATCH WILL BE A TEAM BATTLE!
OOOOO
YOU SAW MR. ASAHI'S MATCH, DIDN'T YOU, SWEETIE? WHAT SAY WE FOLLOW SUIT...
...AND PUT OUR KNIVES ON THE LINE.
SMIRK
OUR KNIVES?

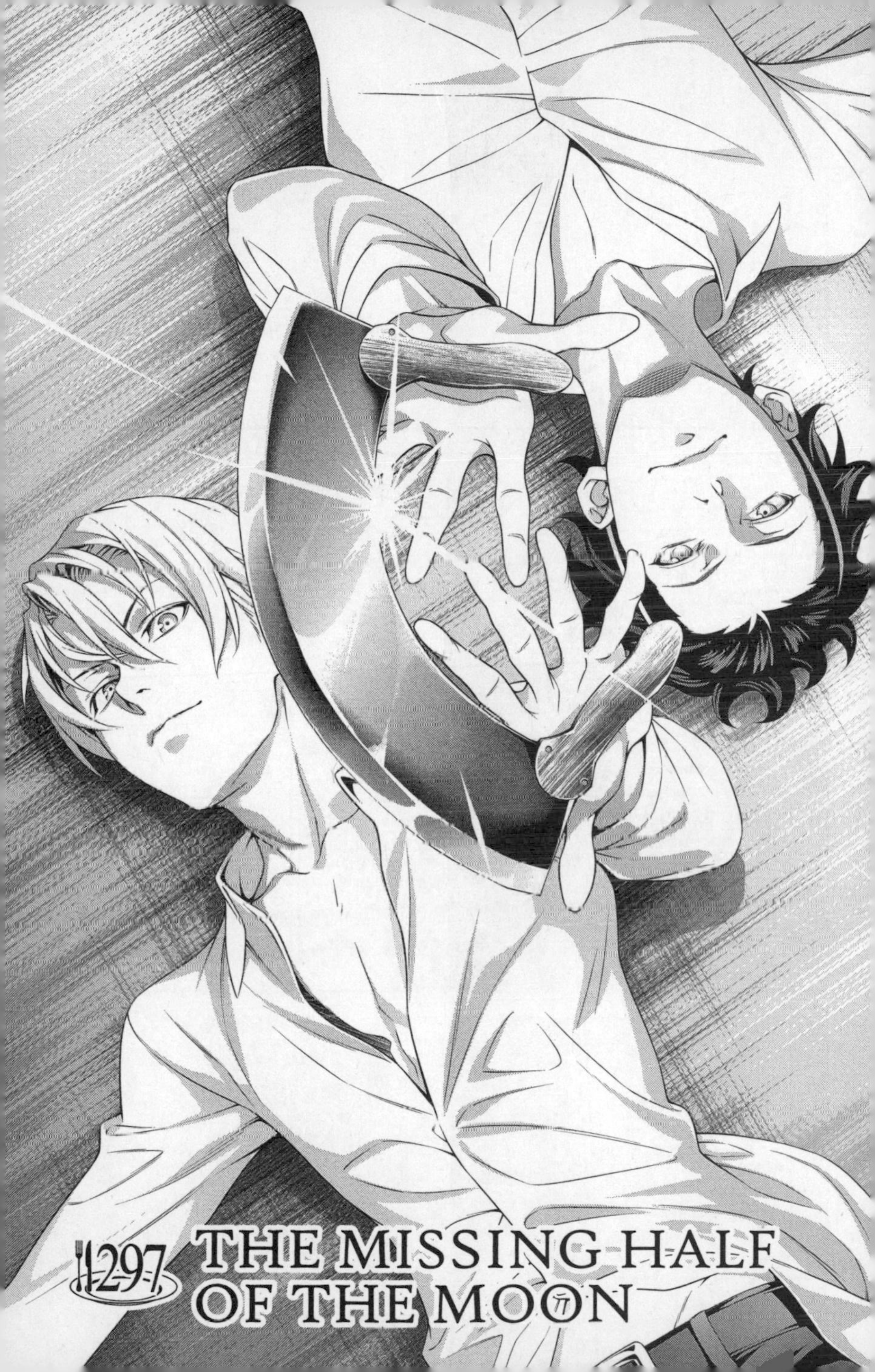

297 THE MISSING HALF OF THE MOON

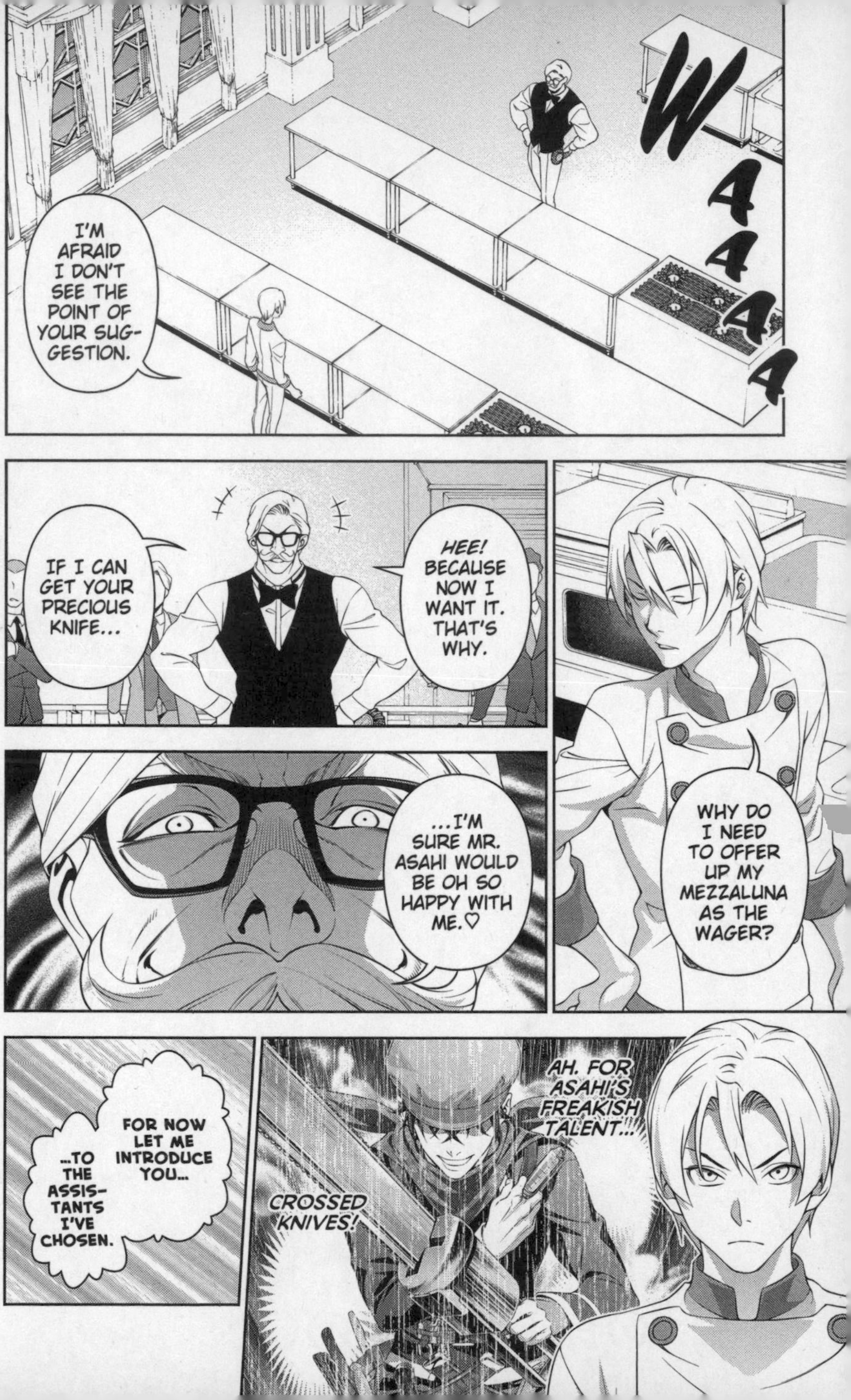
WAAAA
I'M AFRAID I DON'T SEE THE POINT OF YOUR SUG-GESTION.
WHY DO I NEED TO OFFER UP MY MEZZALUNA AS THE WAGER?
HEE! BECAUSE NOW I WANT IT. THAT'S WHY.
IF I CAN GET YOUR PRECIOUS KNIFE...
...I'M SURE MR. ASAHI WOULD BE OH SO HAPPY WITH ME.♡
AH. FOR ASAHI'S FREAKISH TALENT...
CROSSED KNIVES!
FOR NOW LET ME INTRODUCE YOU...
...TO THE ASSISTANTS I'VE CHOSEN.

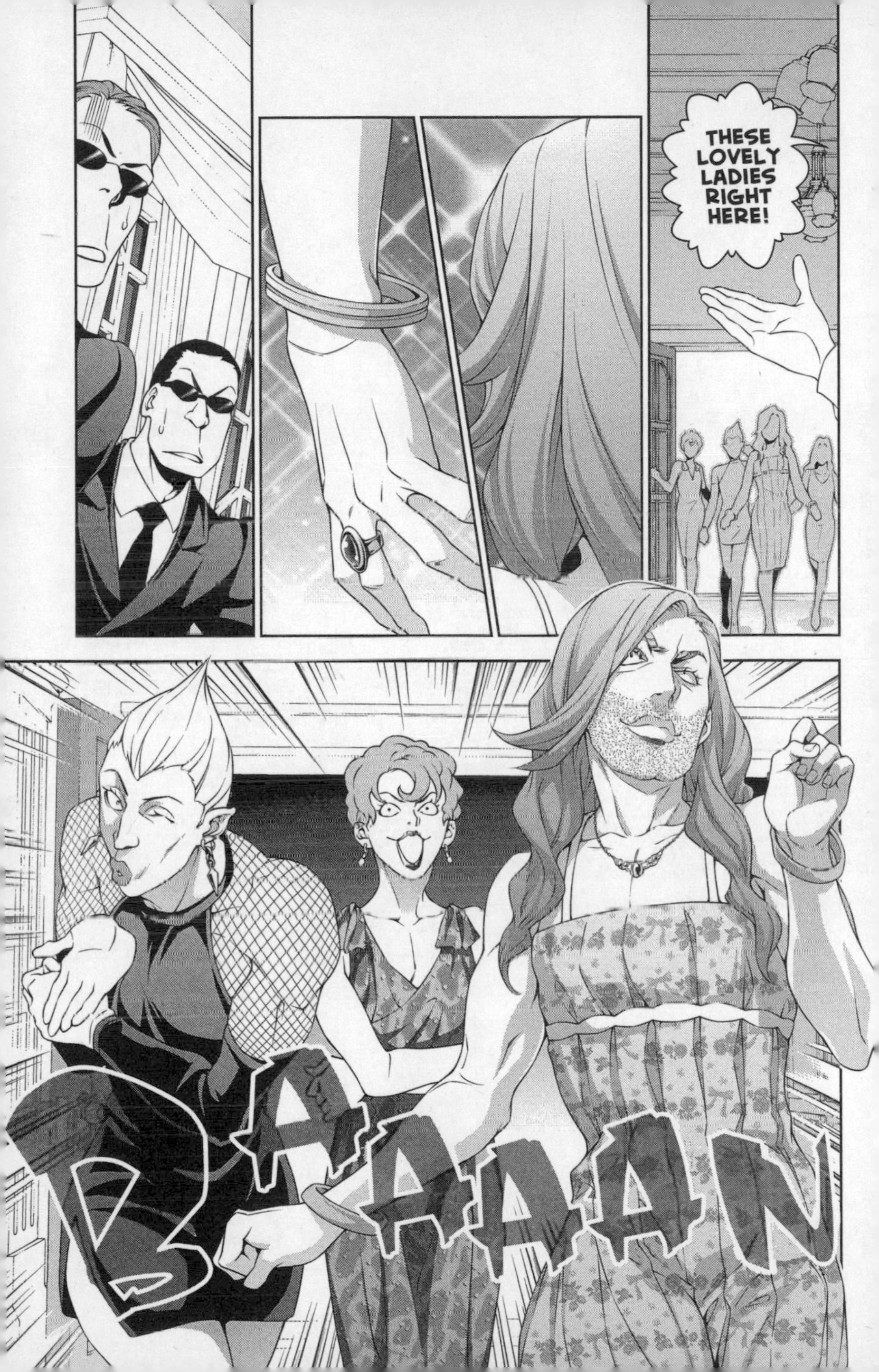
THESE LOVELY LADIES RIGHT HERE!
DAAAN

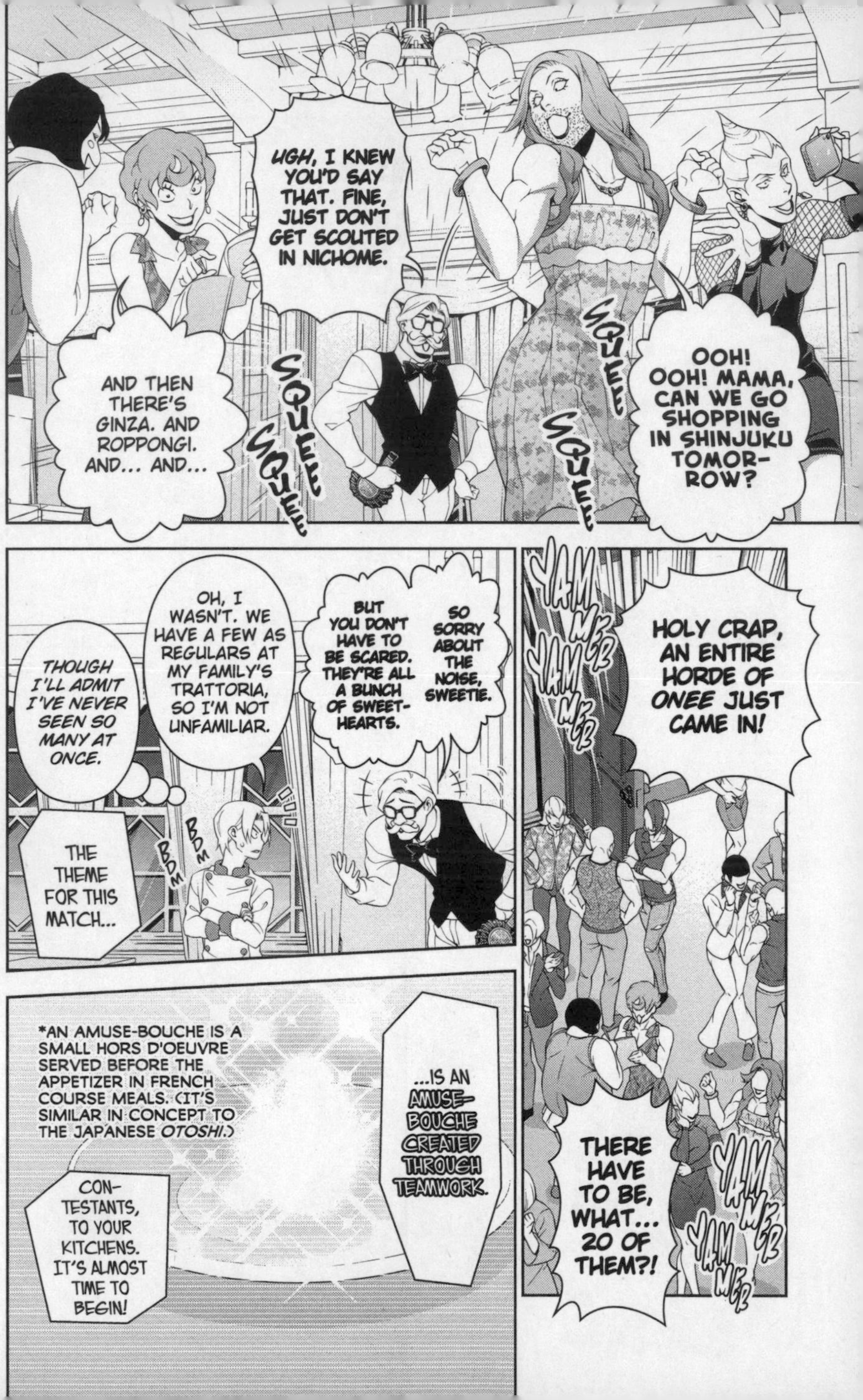
OOH! OOH! MAMA, CAN WE GO SHOPPING IN SHINJUKU TOMORROW?
SQUEE
SQUEE
UGH, I KNEW YOU'D SAY THAT. FINE, JUST DON'T GET SCOUTED IN NICHOME.
SQUEE
SQUEE
AND THEN THERE'S GINZA. AND ROPPONGI. AND... AND...
HOLY CRAP, AN ENTIRE HORDE OF *ONEE* JUST CAME IN!
YAMMER YAMMER
THERE HAVE TO BE, WHAT... 20 OF THEM?!
YAMMER YAMMER
SO SORRY ABOUT THE NOISE, SWEETIE.
BUT YOU DON'T HAVE TO BE SCARED. THEY'RE ALL A BUNCH OF SWEET-HEARTS.
OH, I WASN'T. WE HAVE A FEW AS REGULARS AT MY FAMILY'S TRATTORIA, SO I'M NOT UNFAMILIAR.
THOUGH I'LL ADMIT I'VE NEVER SEEN SO MANY AT ONCE.
BDM BDM
THE THEME FOR THIS MATCH...
...IS AN AMUSE-BOUCHE CREATED THROUGH TEAMWORK.
*AN AMUSE-BOUCHE IS A SMALL HORS D'OEUVRE SERVED BEFORE THE APPETIZER IN FRENCH COURSE MEALS. (IT'S SIMILAR IN CONCEPT TO THE JAPANESE *OTOSHI*.)
CON-TESTANTS, TO YOUR KITCHENS. IT'S ALMOST TIME TO BEGIN!

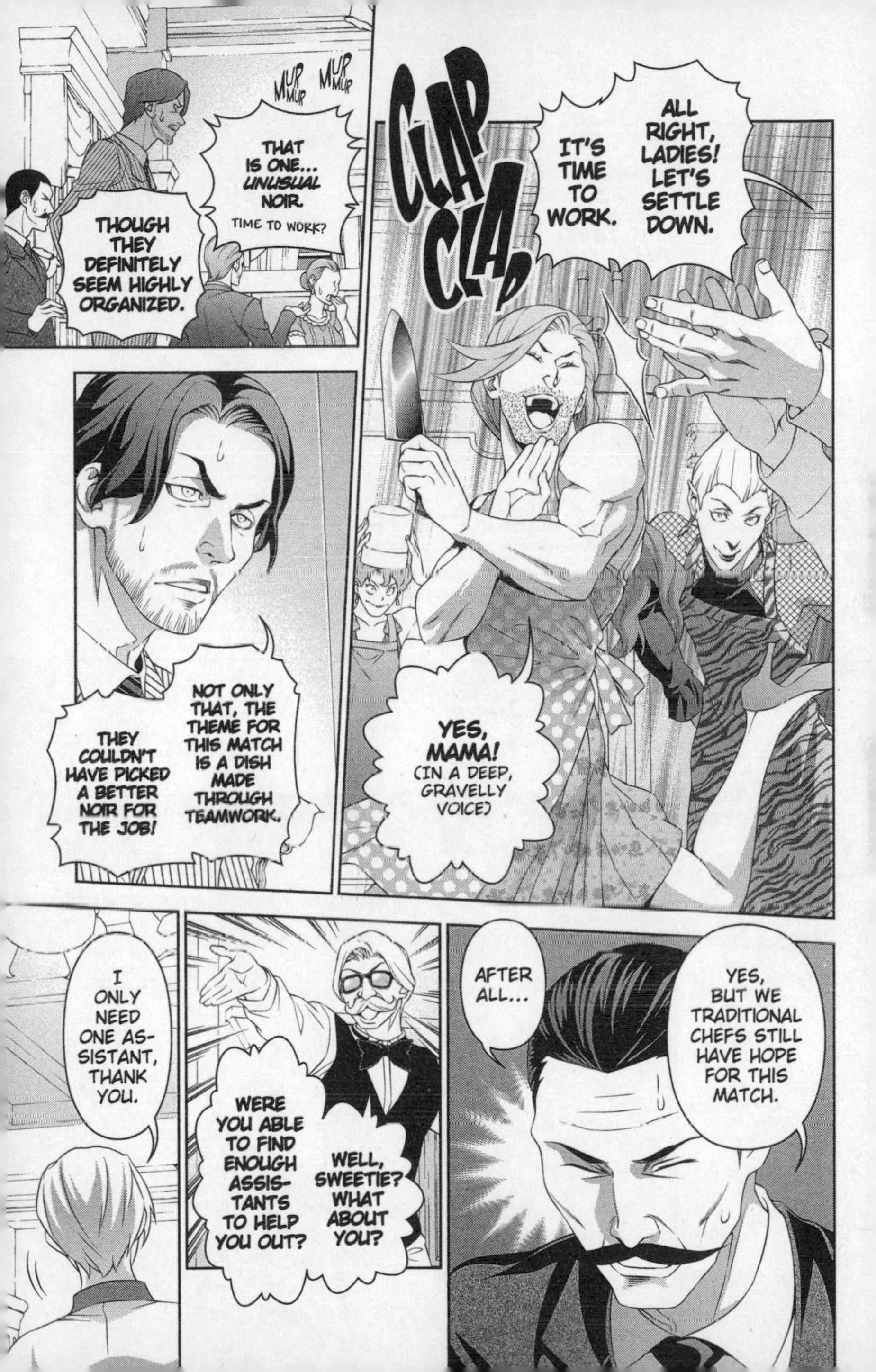
ALL RIGHT, LADIES! LET'S SETTLE DOWN.
IT'S TIME TO WORK.
CLAP CLAP
YES, MAMA! (IN A DEEP, GRAVELLY VOICE)
MUR MUR MUR MUR
THAT IS ONE... UNUSUAL NOIR.
TIME TO WORK?
THOUGH THEY DEFINITELY SEEM HIGHLY ORGANIZED.
NOT ONLY THAT, THE THEME FOR THIS MATCH IS A DISH MADE THROUGH TEAMWORK.
THEY COULDN'T HAVE PICKED A BETTER NOIR FOR THE JOB!
YES, BUT WE TRADITIONAL CHEFS STILL HAVE HOPE FOR THIS MATCH.
AFTER ALL...
WERE YOU ABLE TO FIND ENOUGH ASSIS-TANTS TO HELP YOU OUT?
WELL, SWEETIE? WHAT ABOUT YOU?
I ONLY NEED ONE AS-SISTANT, THANK YOU.

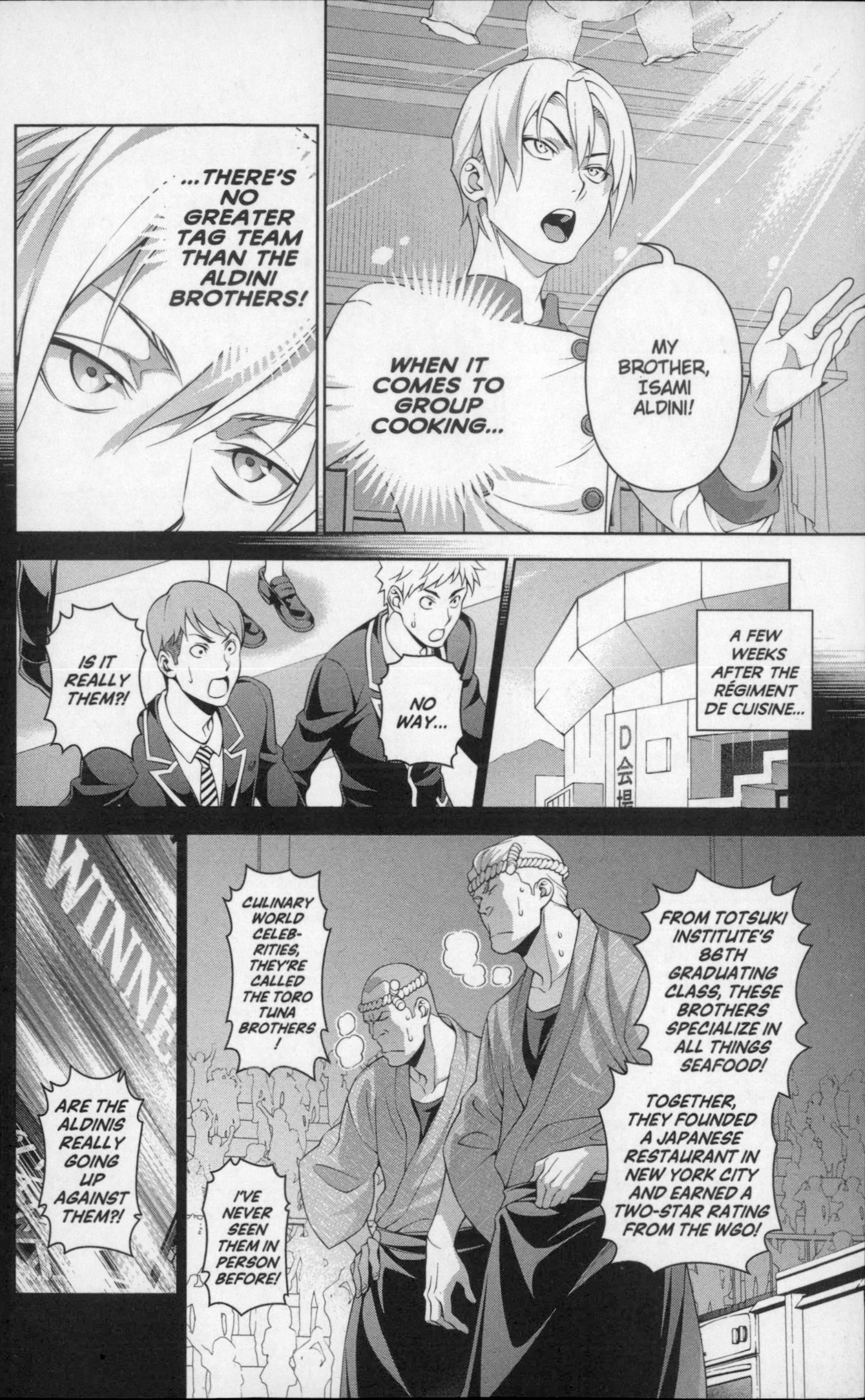
MY BROTHER, ISAMI ALDINI!
WHEN IT COMES TO GROUP COOKING...
...THERE'S NO GREATER TAG TEAM THAN THE ALDINI BROTHERS!
A FEW WEEKS AFTER THE RÉGIMENT DE CUISINE...
NO WAY...
IS IT REALLY THEM?!
FROM TOTSUKI INSTITUTE'S 86TH GRADUATING CLASS, THESE BROTHERS SPECIALIZE IN ALL THINGS SEAFOOD!
TOGETHER, THEY FOUNDED A JAPANESE RESTAURANT IN NEW YORK CITY AND EARNED A TWO-STAR RATING FROM THE WGO!
CULINARY WORLD CELEBRITIES, THEY'RE CALLED THE TORO TUNA BROTHERS!
I'VE NEVER SEEN THEM IN PERSON BEFORE!
ARE THE ALDINIS REALLY GOING UP AGAINST THEM?!

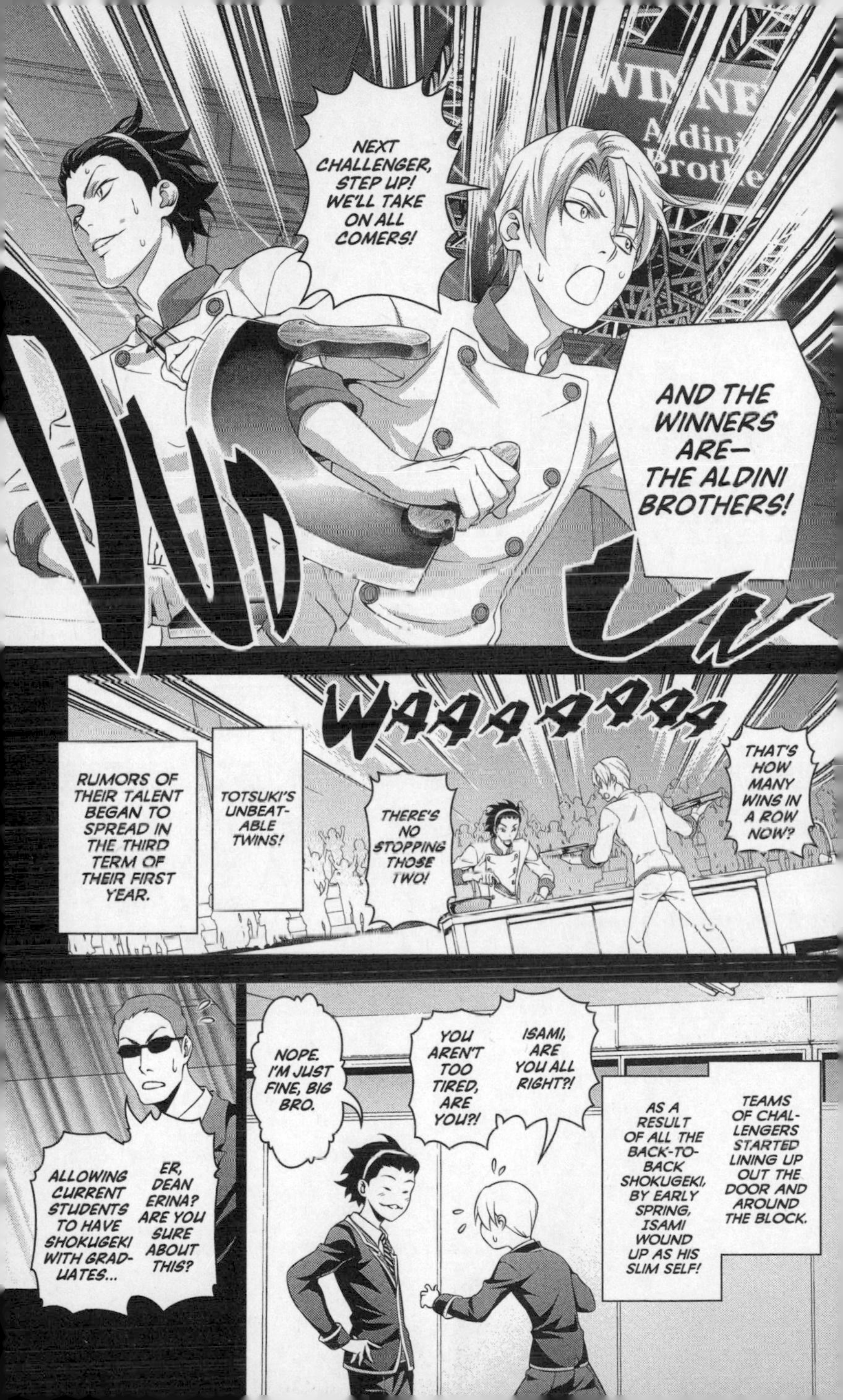
AND THE WINNERS ARE— THE ALDINI BROTHERS!
NEXT CHALLENGER, STEP UP! WE'LL TAKE ON ALL COMERS!
WAAAAAAA
THAT'S HOW MANY WINS IN A ROW NOW?
THERE'S NO STOPPING THOSE TWO!
TOTSUKI'S UNBEAT-ABLE TWINS!
RUMORS OF THEIR TALENT BEGAN TO SPREAD IN THE THIRD TERM OF THEIR FIRST YEAR.
TEAMS OF CHAL-LENGERS STARTED LINING UP OUT THE DOOR AND AROUND THE BLOCK.
AS A RESULT OF ALL THE BACK-TO-BACK SHOKUGEKI, BY EARLY SPRING, ISAMI WOUND UP AS HIS SLIM SELF!
ISAMI, ARE YOU ALL RIGHT?!
YOU AREN'T TOO TIRED, ARE YOU?!
NOPE. I'M JUST FINE, BIG BRO.
ER, DEAN ERINA? ARE YOU SURE ABOUT THIS?
ALLOWING CURRENT STUDENTS TO HAVE SHOKUGEKI WITH GRAD-UATES...

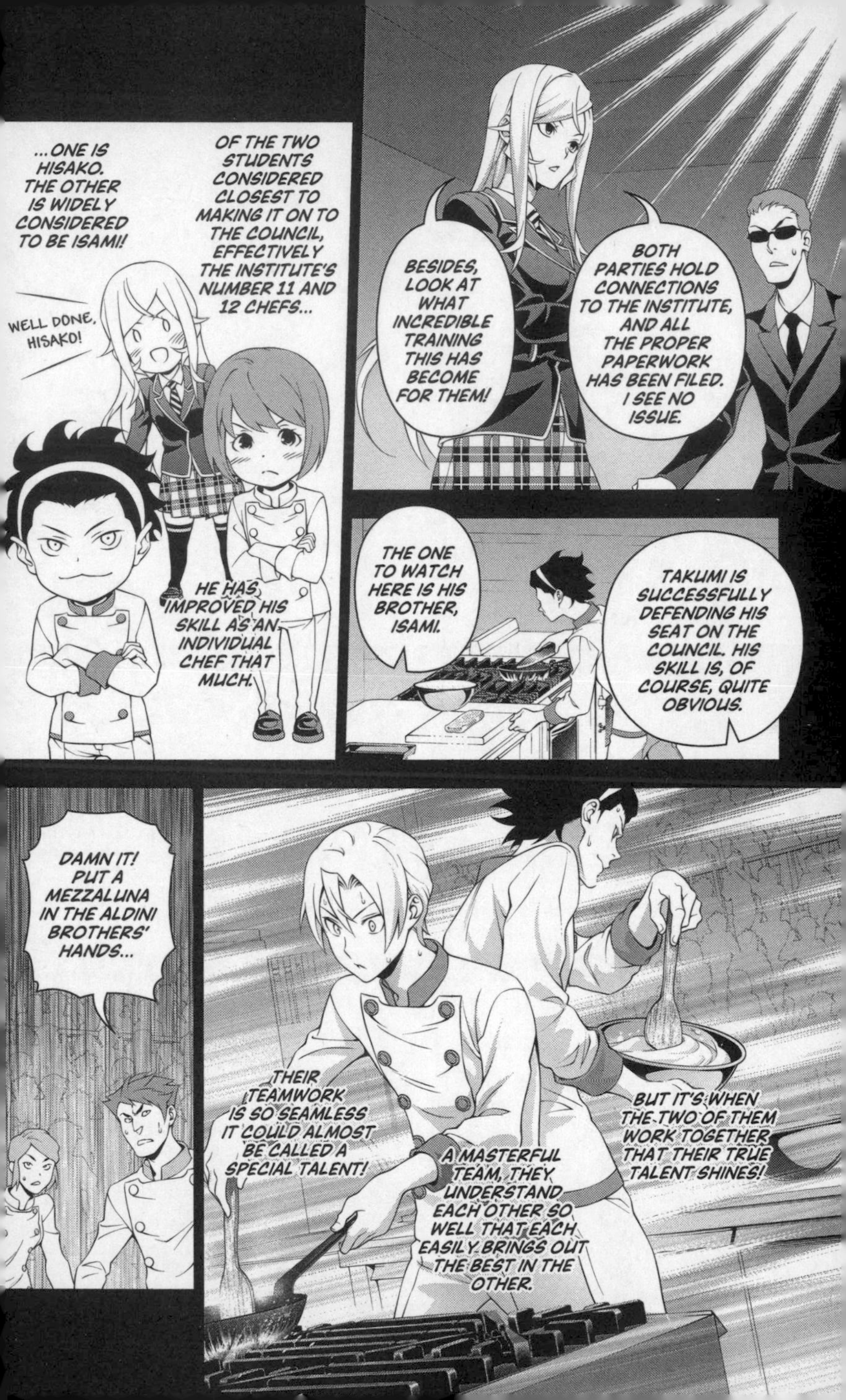
BOTH PARTIES HOLD CONNECTIONS TO THE INSTITUTE, AND ALL THE PROPER PAPERWORK HAS BEEN FILED. I SEE NO ISSUE.
BESIDES, LOOK AT WHAT INCREDIBLE TRAINING THIS HAS BECOME FOR THEM!
TAKUMI IS SUCCESSFULLY DEFENDING HIS SEAT ON THE COUNCIL. HIS SKILL IS, OF COURSE, QUITE OBVIOUS.
THE ONE TO WATCH HERE IS HIS BROTHER, ISAMI.
OF THE TWO STUDENTS CONSIDERED CLOSEST TO MAKING IT ON TO THE COUNCIL, EFFECTIVELY THE INSTITUTE'S NUMBER 11 AND 12 CHEFS...
...ONE IS HISAKO. THE OTHER IS WIDELY CONSIDERED TO BE ISAMI!
WELL DONE, HISAKO!
HE HAS IMPROVED HIS SKILL AS AN INDIVIDUAL CHEF THAT MUCH.
BUT IT'S WHEN THE TWO OF THEM WORK TOGETHER THAT THEIR TRUE TALENT SHINES!
THEIR TEAMWORK IS SO SEAMLESS IT COULD ALMOST BE CALLED A SPECIAL TALENT!
A MASTERFUL TEAM, THEY UNDERSTAND EACH OTHER SO WELL THAT EACH EASILY BRINGS OUT THE BEST IN THE OTHER.
DAMN IT! PUT A MEZZALUNA IN THE ALDINI BROTHERS' HANDS...

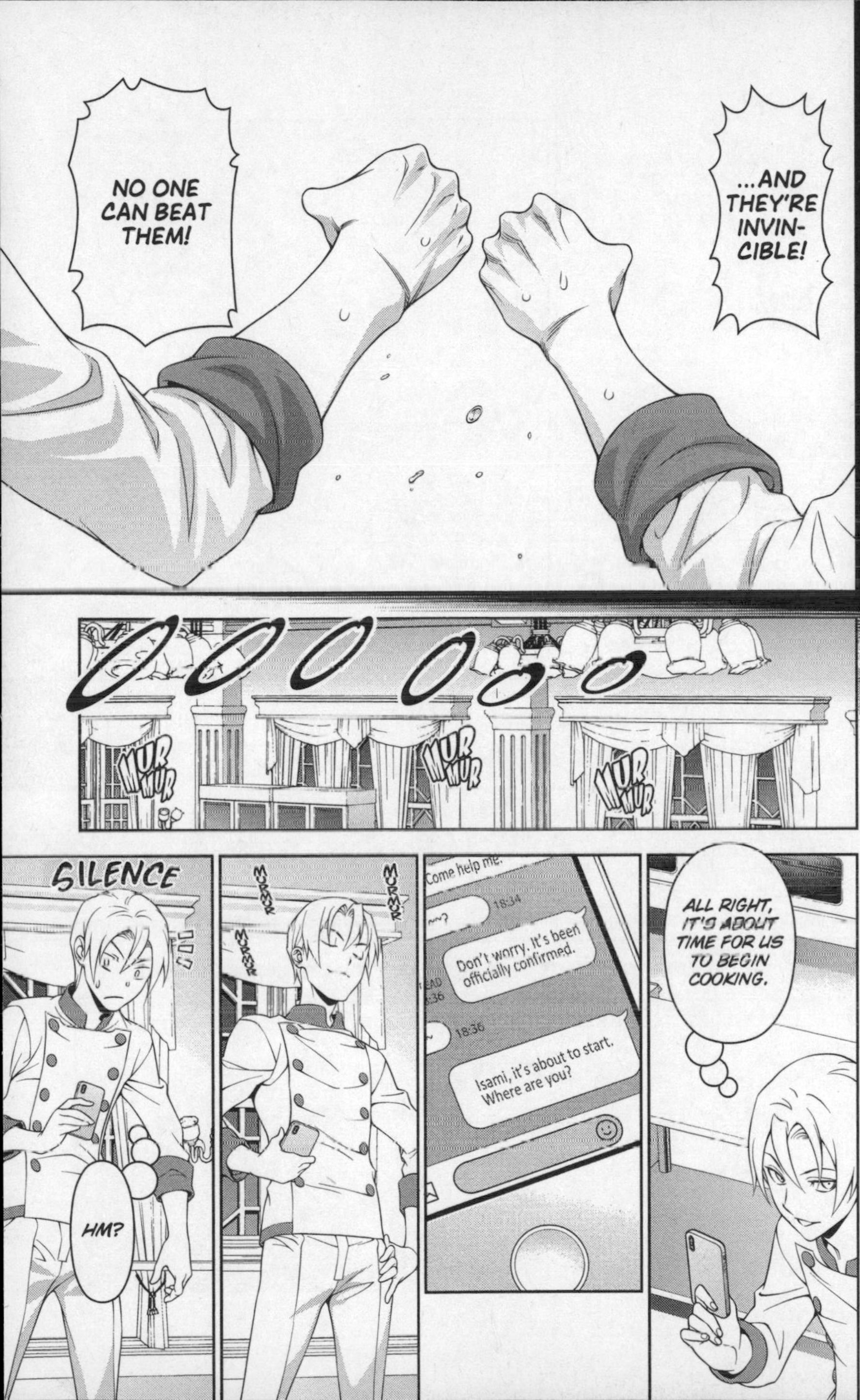
...AND THEY'RE INVINCIBLE!
NO ONE CAN BEAT THEM!
MURMUR
MURMUR
MURMUR
ALL RIGHT, IT'S ABOUT TIME FOR US TO BEGIN COOKING.
Come help me.
18:34
Don't worry. It's been officially confirmed.
18:36
Isami, it's about to start. Where are you?
MURMUR
MURMUR
MURMUR
SILENCE
HM?

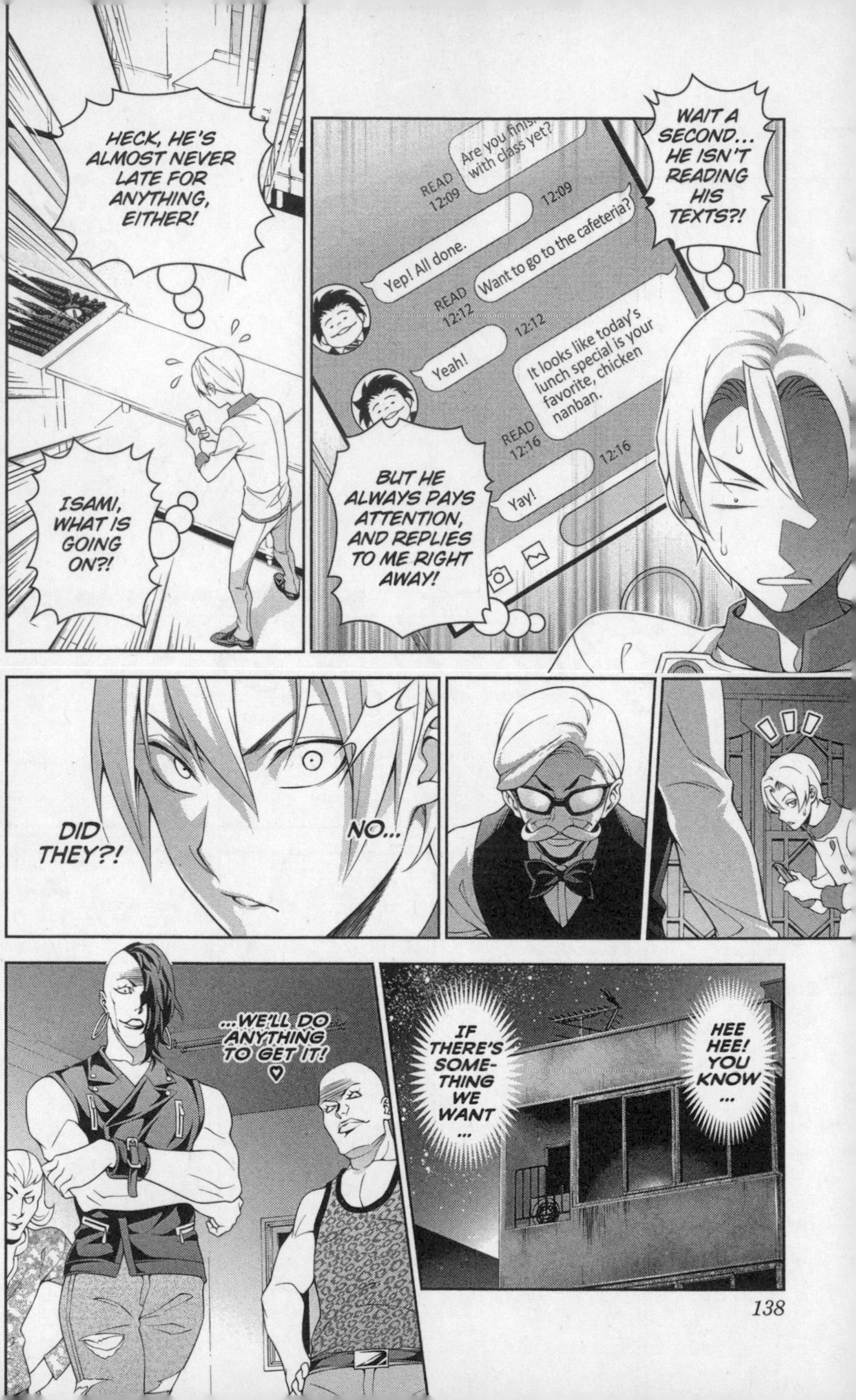
WAIT A SECOND... HE ISN'T READING HIS TEXTS?!
Are you finis
with class yet?
READ 12:09
12:09
Yep! All done.
Want to go to the cafeteria?
READ 12:12
12:12
Yeah!
It looks like today's lunch special is your favorite, chicken nanban.
READ 12:16
12:16
Yay!
BUT HE ALWAYS PAYS ATTENTION, AND REPLIES TO ME RIGHT AWAY!
HECK, HE'S ALMOST NEVER LATE FOR ANYTHING, EITHER!
ISAMI, WHAT IS GOING ON?!
NO...
DID THEY?!
HEE HEE! YOU KNOW...
IF THERE'S SOME-THING WE WANT...
...WE'LL DO ANYTHING TO GET IT! ♥

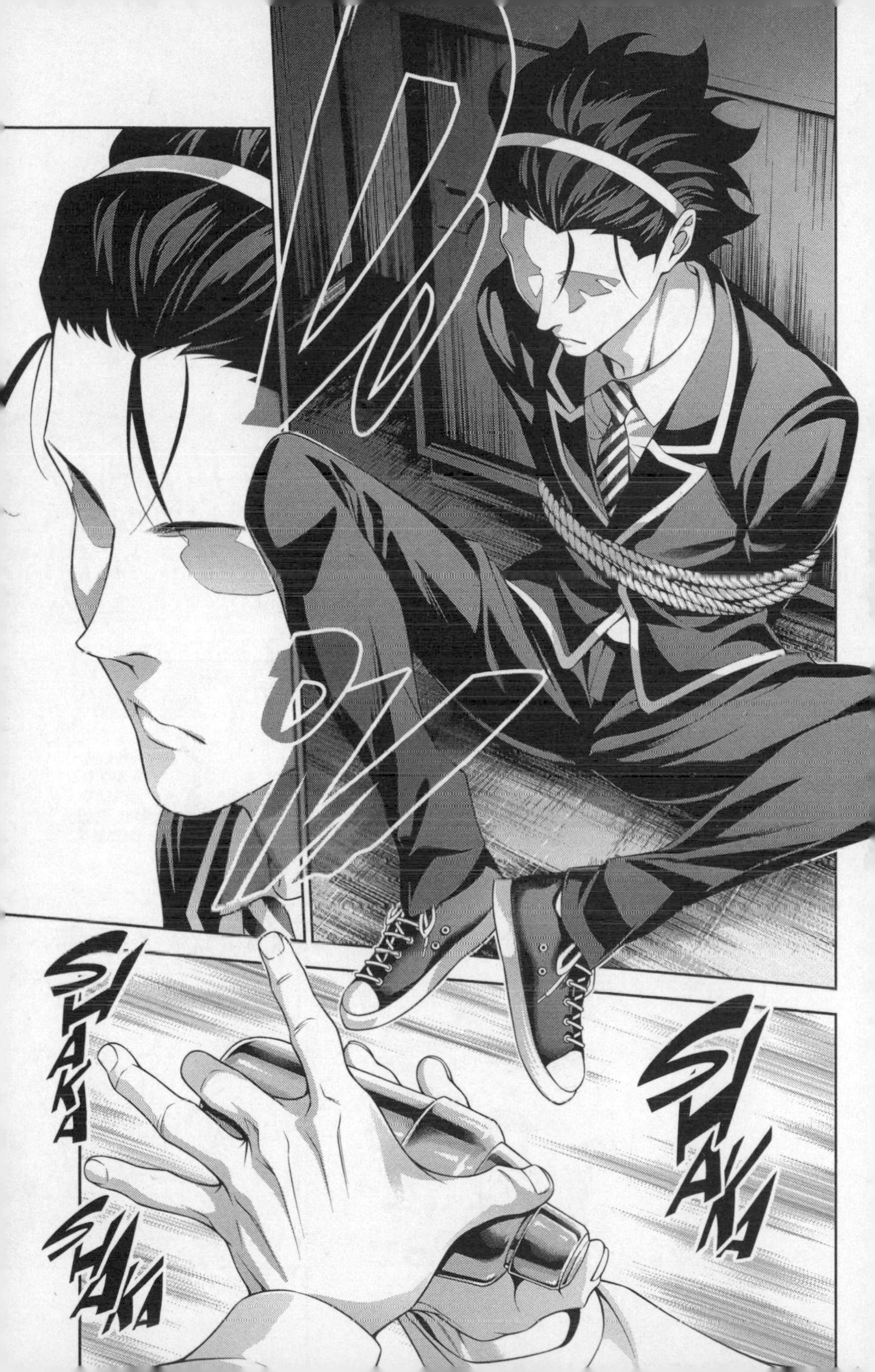
SHAKA
SHAKA
SHAKA

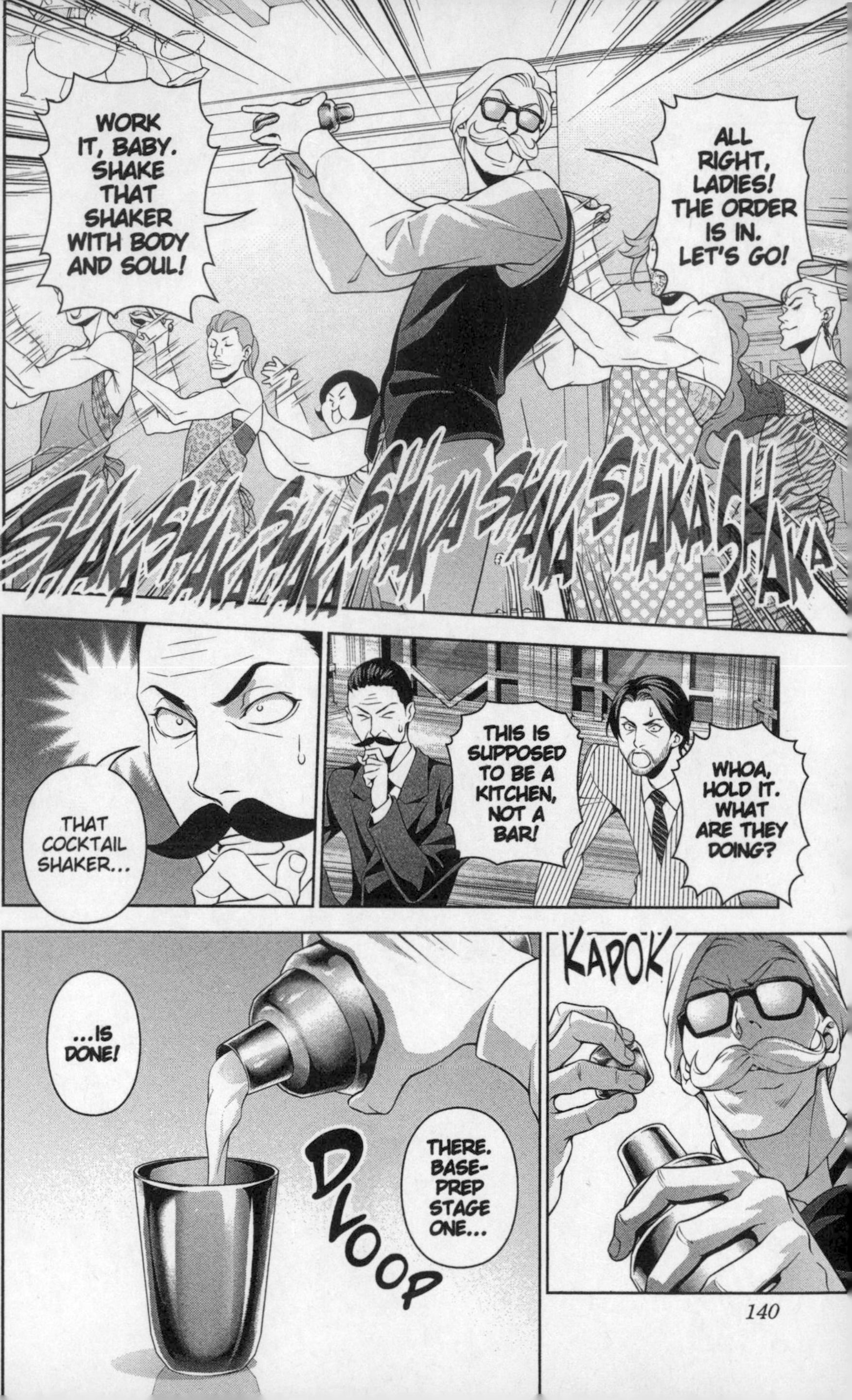
ALL RIGHT, LADIES! THE ORDER IS IN. LET'S GO!
WORK IT, BABY. SHAKE THAT SHAKER WITH BODY AND SOUL!
SHAKA SHAKA SHAKA SHAKA SHAKA SHAKA SHAKA SHAKA
WHOA, HOLD IT. WHAT ARE THEY DOING?
THIS IS SUPPOSED TO BE A KITCHEN, NOT A BAR!
THAT COCKTAIL SHAKER...
KAPOK
THERE. BASE-PREP STAGE ONE...
...IS DONE!
DVOOP

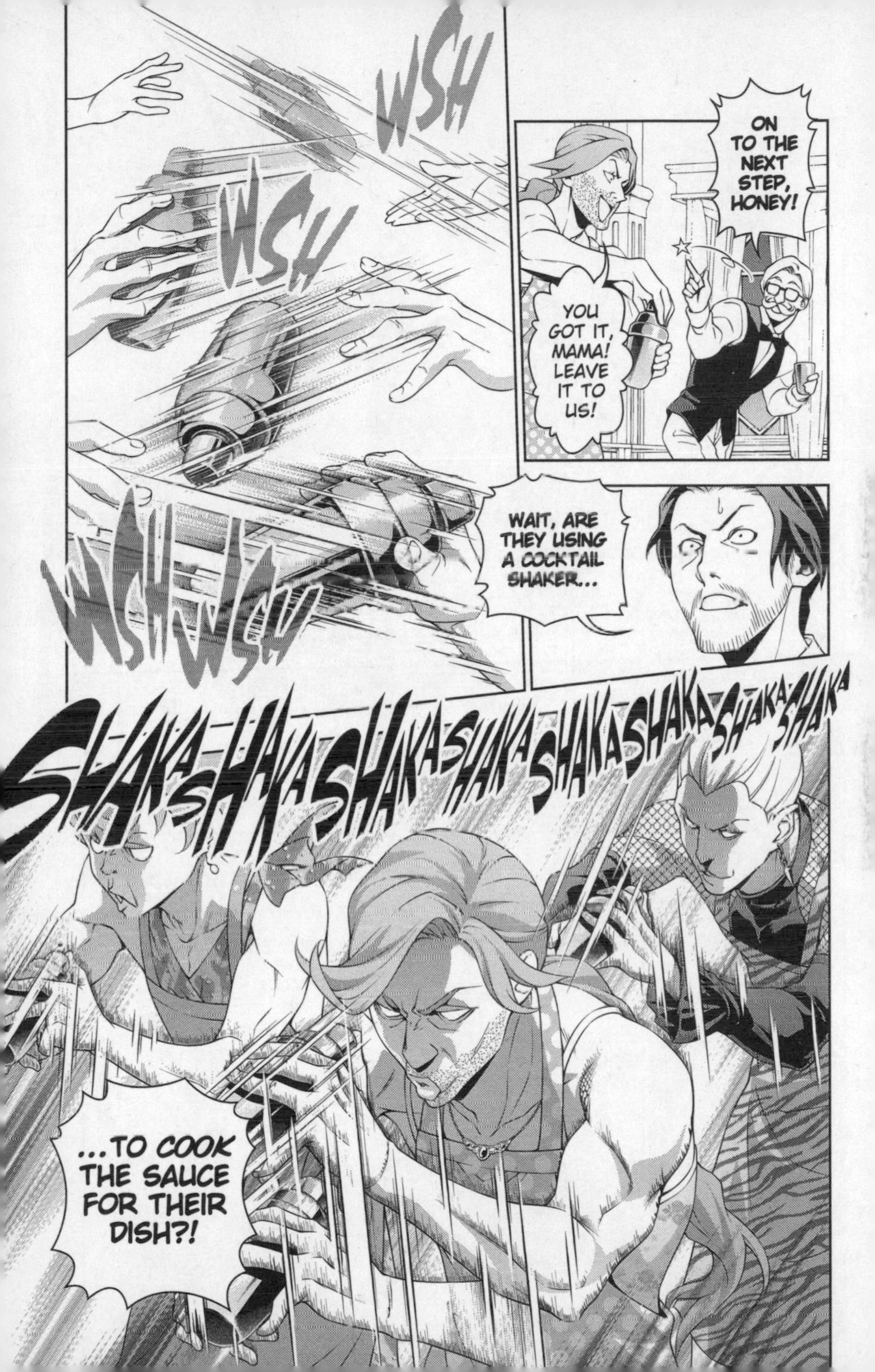

ON TO THE NEXT STEP, HONEY!
YOU GOT IT, MAMA! LEAVE IT TO US!
WAIT, ARE THEY USING A COCKTAIL SHAKER...
WSH
WSH
WSH WSH
SHAKA SHAKA SHAKA SHAKA SHAKA
...TO COOK THE SAUCE FOR THEIR DISH?!

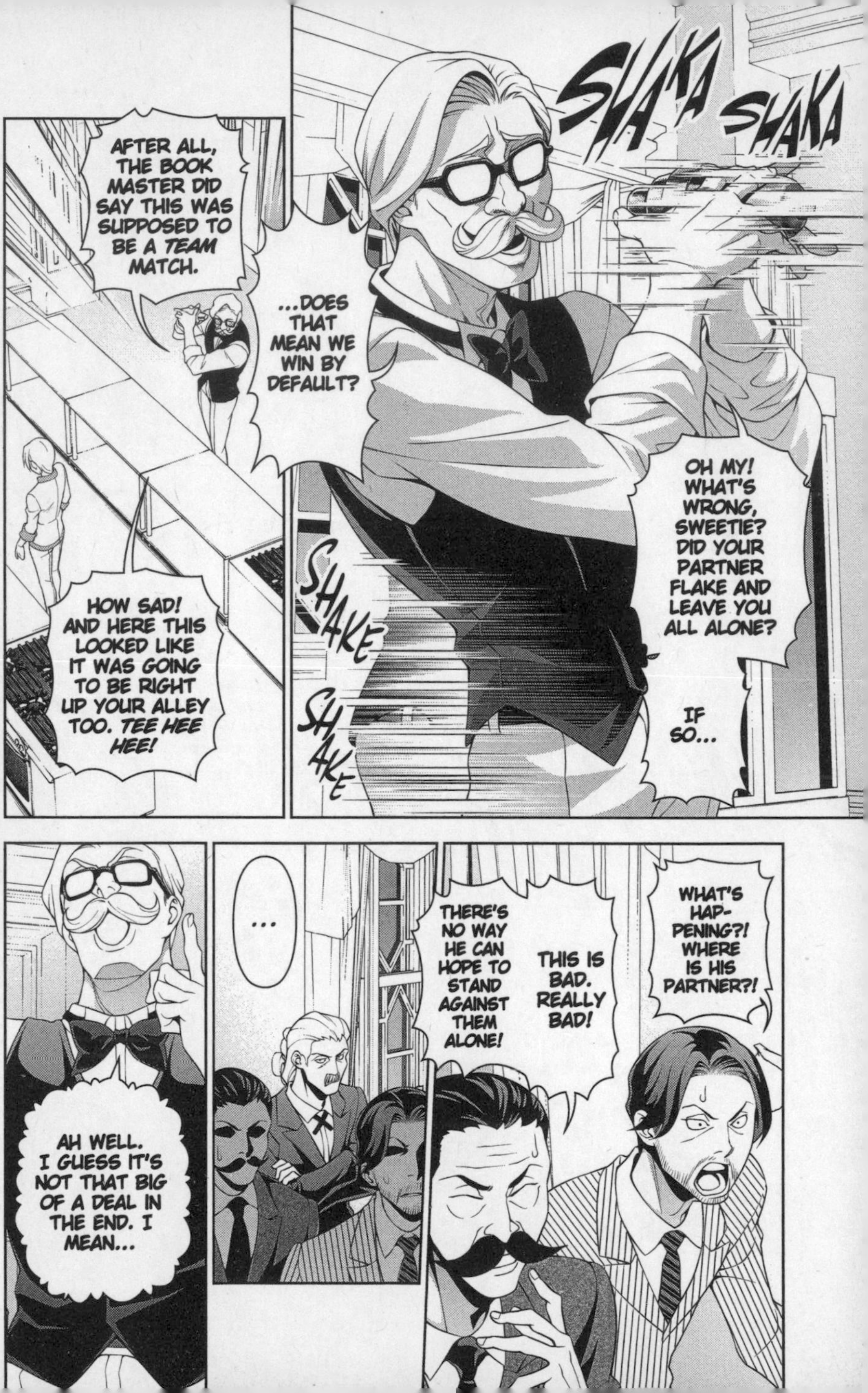
SHAKA SHAKA
OH MY! WHAT'S WRONG, SWEETIE? DID YOUR PARTNER FLAKE AND LEAVE YOU ALL ALONE?
IF SO...
...DOES THAT MEAN WE WIN BY DEFAULT?
SHAKE SHAKE
AFTER ALL, THE BOOK MASTER DID SAY THIS WAS SUPPOSED TO BE A *TEAM* MATCH.
HOW SAD! AND HERE THIS LOOKED LIKE IT WAS GOING TO BE RIGHT UP YOUR ALLEY TOO. *TEE HEE HEE!*
WHAT'S HAP-PENING?! WHERE IS HIS PARTNER?!
THIS IS BAD. REALLY BAD!
THERE'S NO WAY HE CAN HOPE TO STAND AGAINST THEM ALONE!
...
AH WELL. I GUESS IT'S NOT THAT BIG OF A DEAL IN THE END. I MEAN...

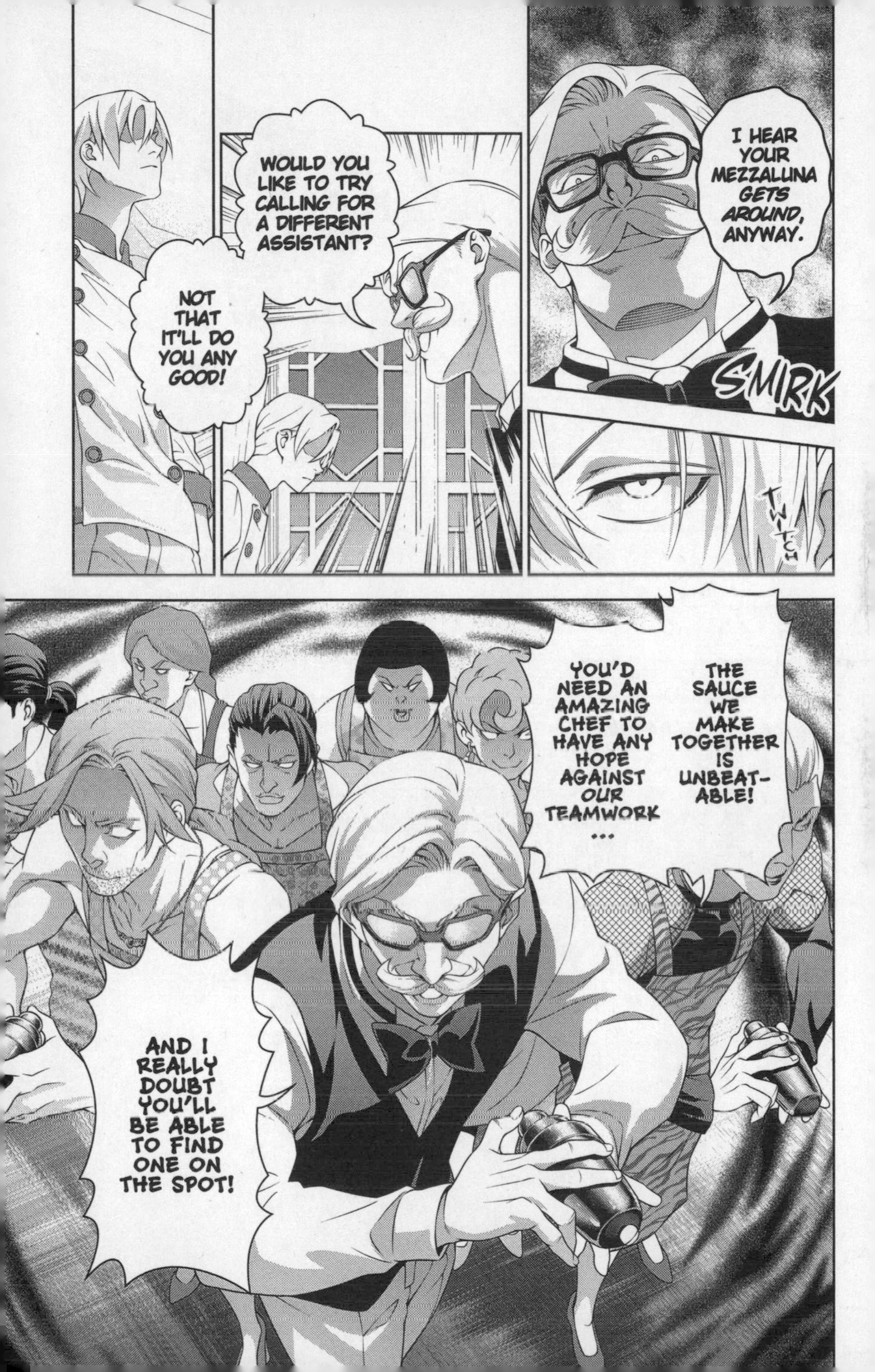
I HEAR YOUR MEZZALUNA GETS AROUND, ANYWAY.
SMIRK
TWITCH
WOULD YOU LIKE TO TRY CALLING FOR A DIFFERENT ASSISTANT?
NOT THAT IT'LL DO YOU ANY GOOD!
THE SAUCE WE MAKE TOGETHER IS UNBEAT-ABLE!
YOU'D NEED AN AMAZING CHEF TO HAVE ANY HOPE AGAINST OUR TEAMWORK ...
AND I REALLY DOUBT YOU'LL BE ABLE TO FIND ONE ON THE SPOT!

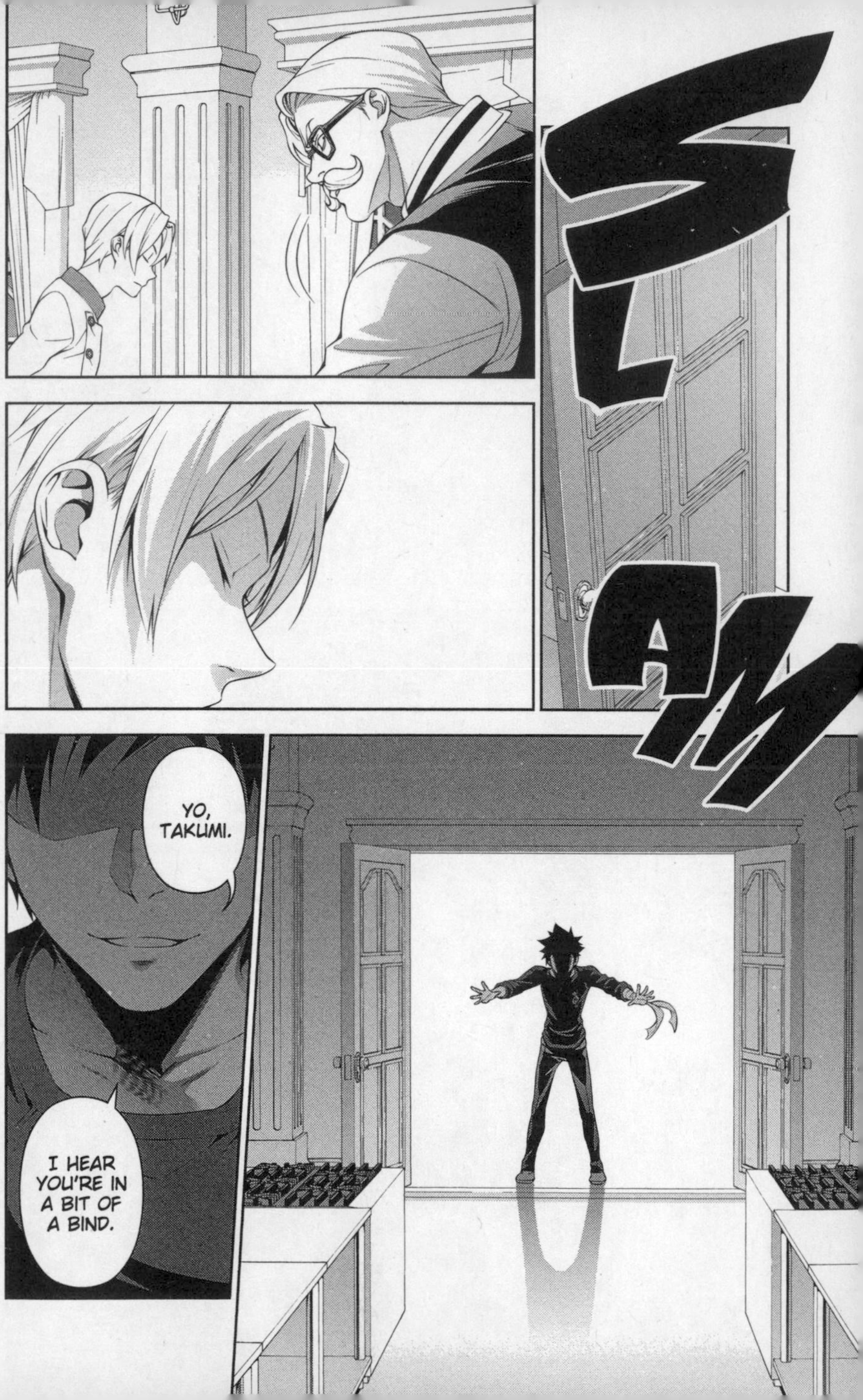
SLAM
YO, TAKUMI.
I HEAR YOU'RE IN A BIT OF A BIND.

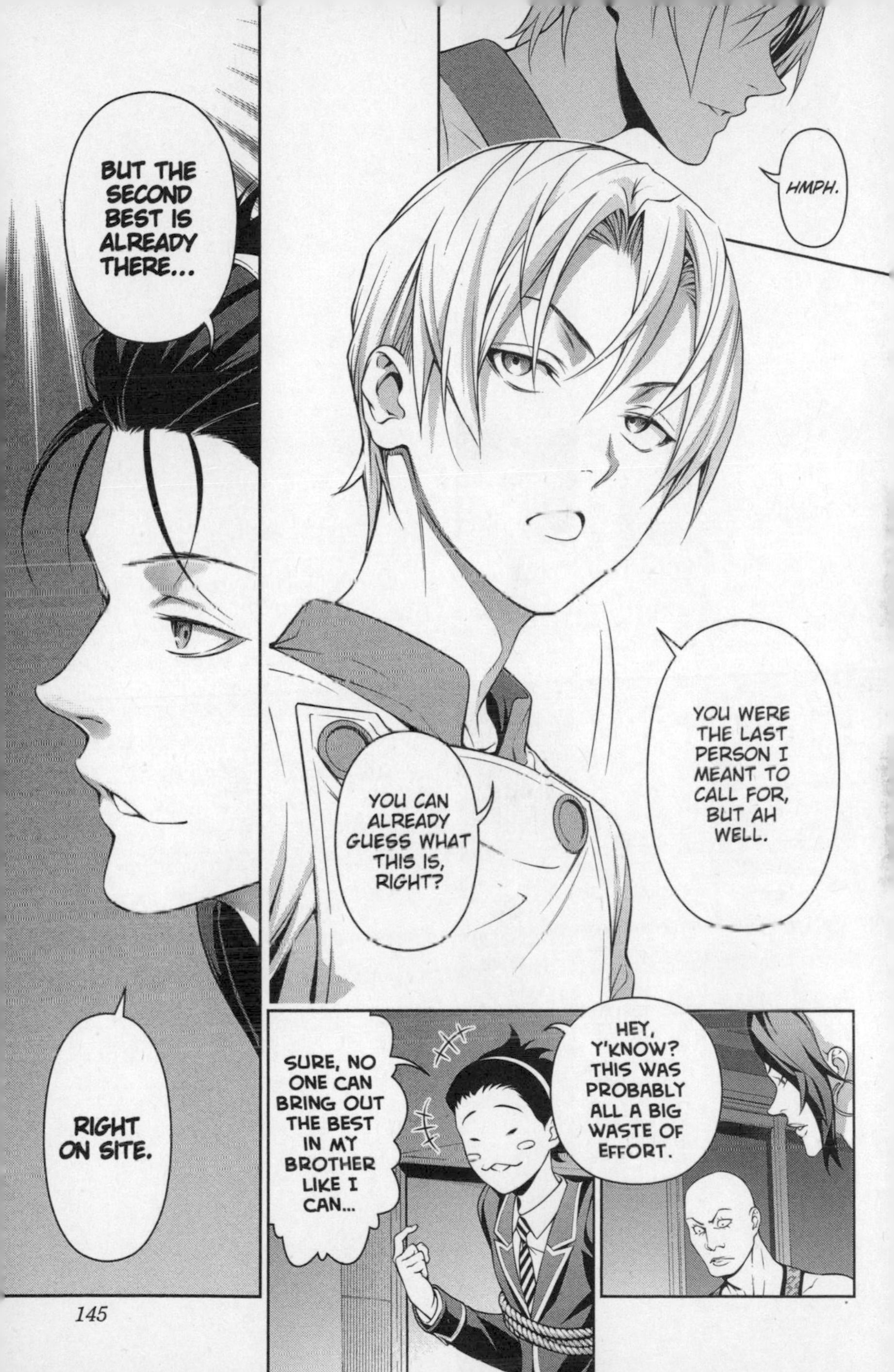
HMPH.
YOU WERE THE LAST PERSON I MEANT TO CALL FOR, BUT AH WELL.
YOU CAN ALREADY GUESS WHAT THIS IS, RIGHT?
HEY, Y'KNOW? THIS WAS PROBABLY ALL A BIG WASTE OF EFFORT.
SURE, NO ONE CAN BRING OUT THE BEST IN MY BROTHER LIKE I CAN...
BUT THE SECOND BEST IS ALREADY THERE...
RIGHT ON SITE.

FRIENDS?
COLLEAGUES?

NO.
WE'RE
NOTHING
LIKE
THAT.

WHEN
CHAPTER 298
RAN IN THE
MAGAZINE,
THE EDITOR'S
COMMENT
FOR IT WAS
SO COOL I
DECIDED TO
ADD IT HERE.

298 WHAT THEY HAVE

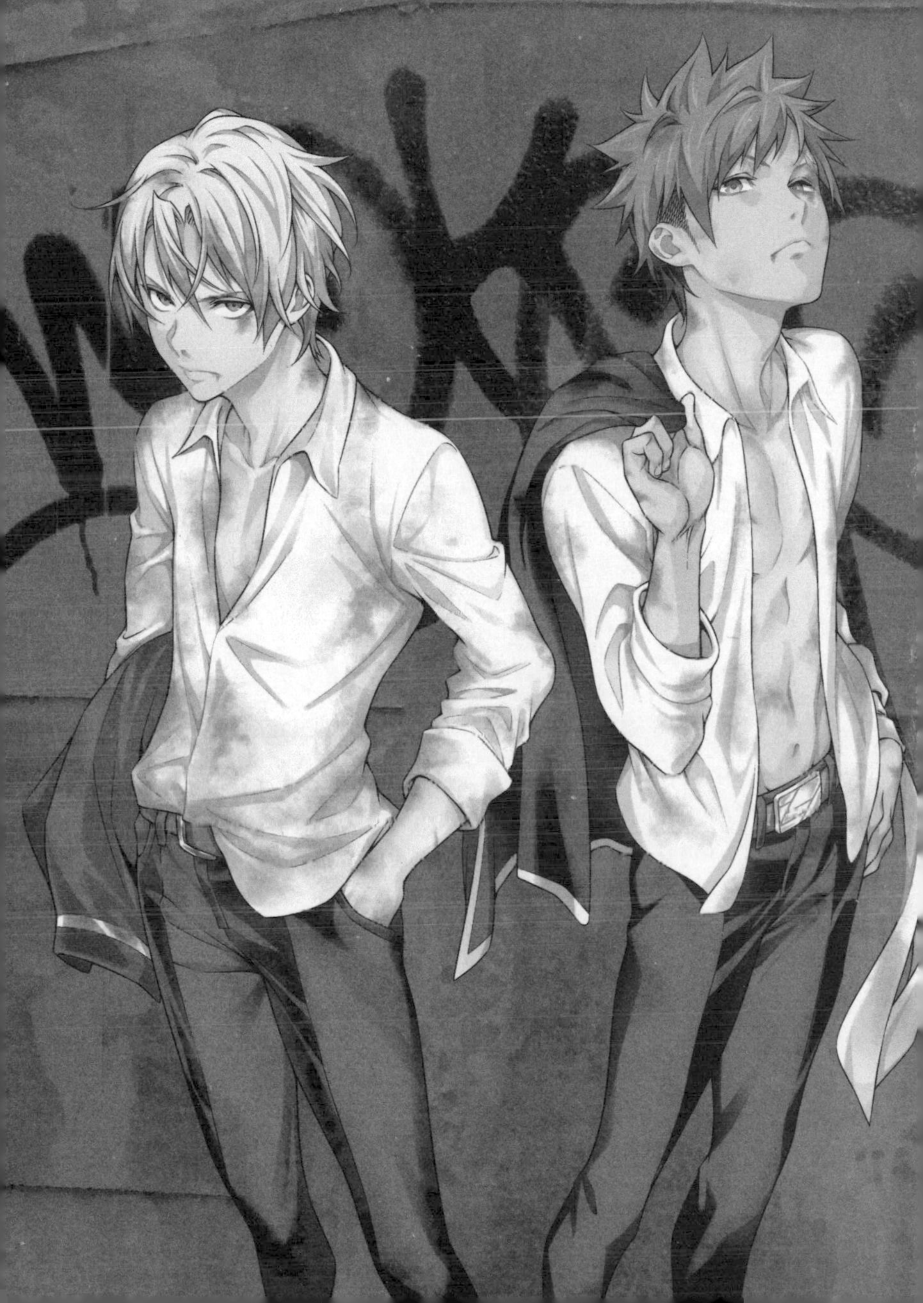

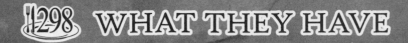

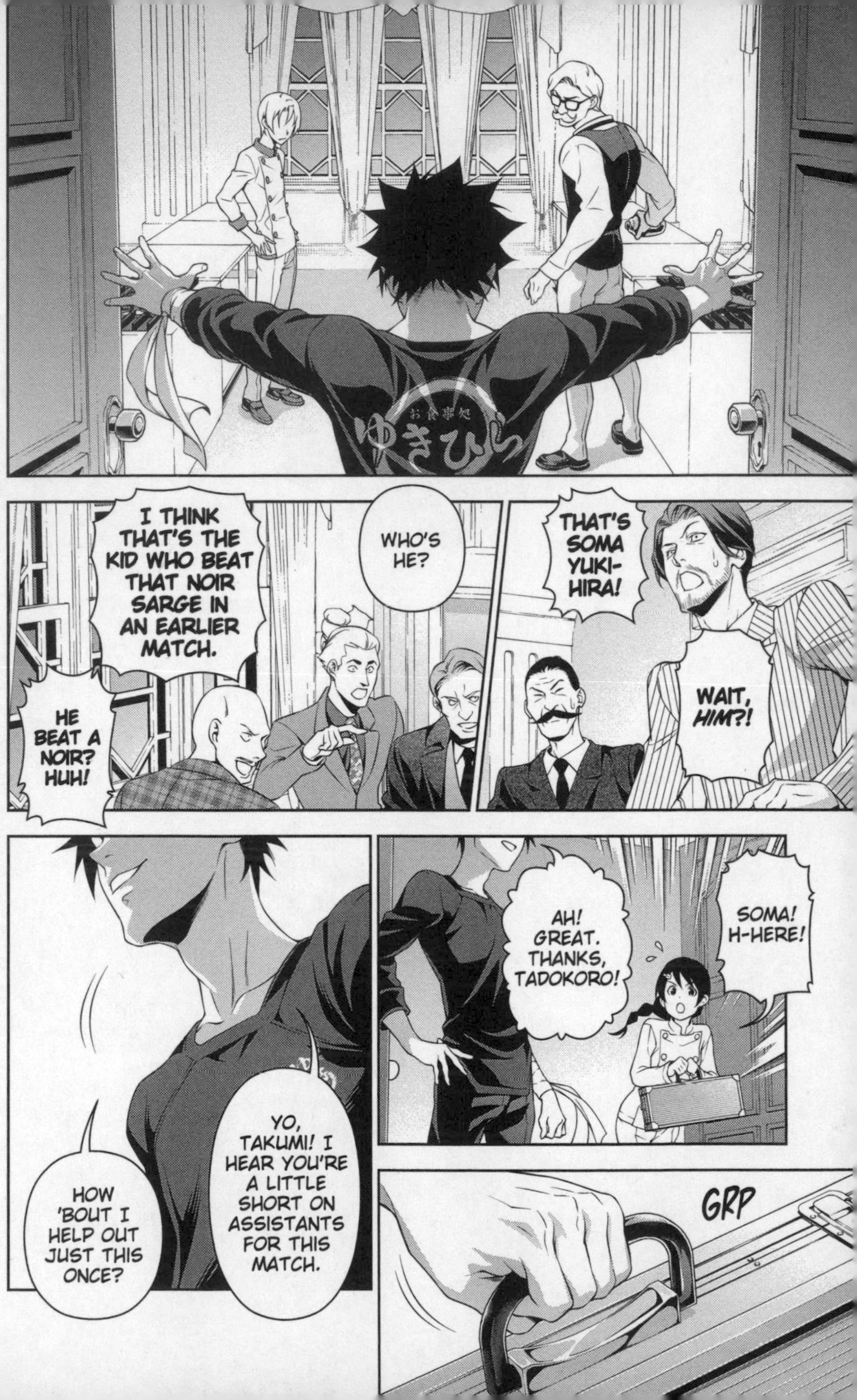
お食事処
ゆきひら
THAT'S SOMA YUKI-HIRA!
WAIT, *HIM*?!
WHO'S HE?
I THINK THAT'S THE KID WHO BEAT THAT NOIR SARGE IN AN EARLIER MATCH.
HE BEAT A NOIR? HUH!
SOMA! H-HERE!
AH! GREAT. THANKS, TADOKORO!
GRP
YO, TAKUMI! I HEAR YOU'RE A LITTLE SHORT ON ASSISTANTS FOR THIS MATCH.
HOW 'BOUT I HELP OUT JUST THIS ONCE?

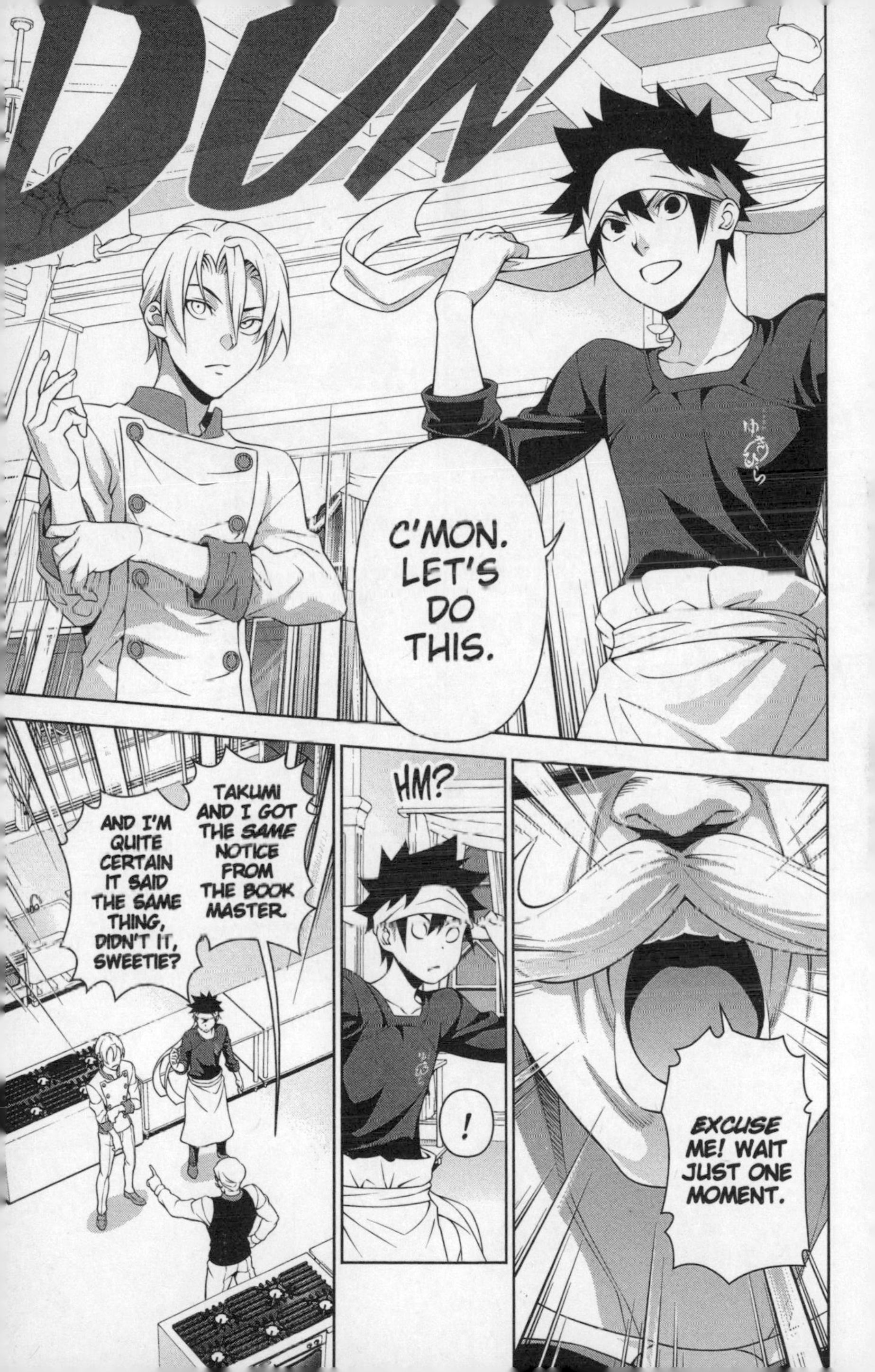
DUN
C'MON. LET'S DO THIS.
EXCUSE ME! WAIT JUST ONE MOMENT.
HM?
!
TAKUMI AND I GOT THE *SAME* NOTICE FROM THE BOOK MASTER.
AND I'M QUITE CERTAIN IT SAID THE SAME THING, DIDN'T IT, SWEETIE?

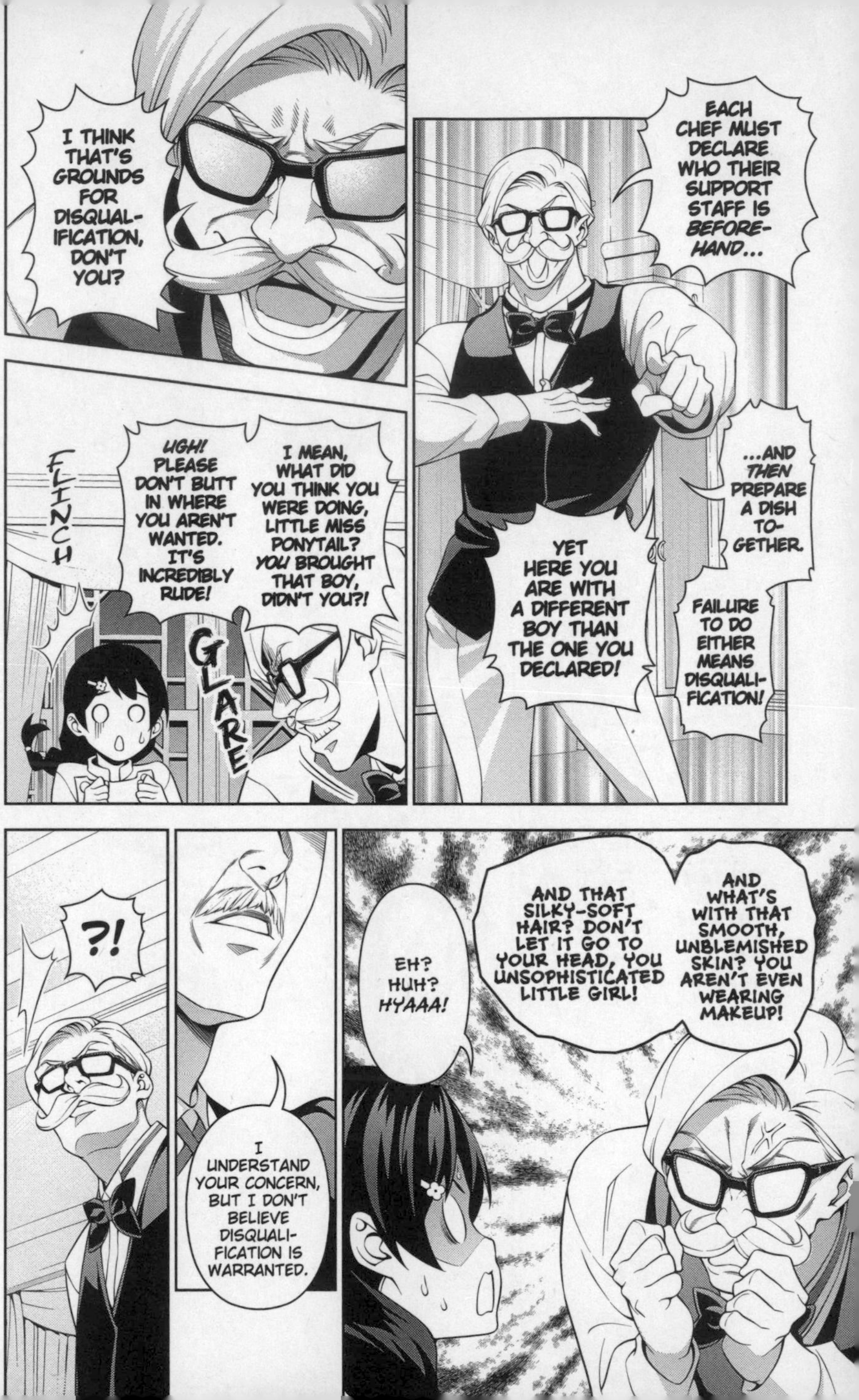
EACH CHEF MUST DECLARE WHO THEIR SUPPORT STAFF IS *BEFORE-HAND*...
...AND *THEN* PREPARE A DISH TO-GETHER.
FAILURE TO DO EITHER MEANS DISQUALI-FICATION!
YET HERE YOU ARE WITH A DIFFERENT BOY THAN THE ONE YOU DECLARED!
I THINK THAT'S GROUNDS FOR DISQUAL-IFICATION, DON'T YOU?
I MEAN, WHAT DID YOU THINK YOU WERE DOING, LITTLE MISS PONYTAIL? *YOU* BROUGHT THAT BOY, DIDN'T YOU?!
GLARE
UGH! PLEASE DON'T BUTT IN WHERE YOU AREN'T WANTED. IT'S INCREDIBLY RUDE!
FLINCH
AND WHAT'S WITH THAT SMOOTH, UNBLEMISHED SKIN? YOU AREN'T EVEN WEARING MAKEUP!
AND THAT SILKY-SOFT HAIR? DON'T LET IT GO TO YOUR HEAD, YOU UNSOPHISTICATED LITTLE GIRL!
EH? HUH? *HYAAA!*
I UNDERSTAND YOUR CONCERN, BUT I DON'T BELIEVE DISQUALI-FICATION IS WARRANTED.
?!

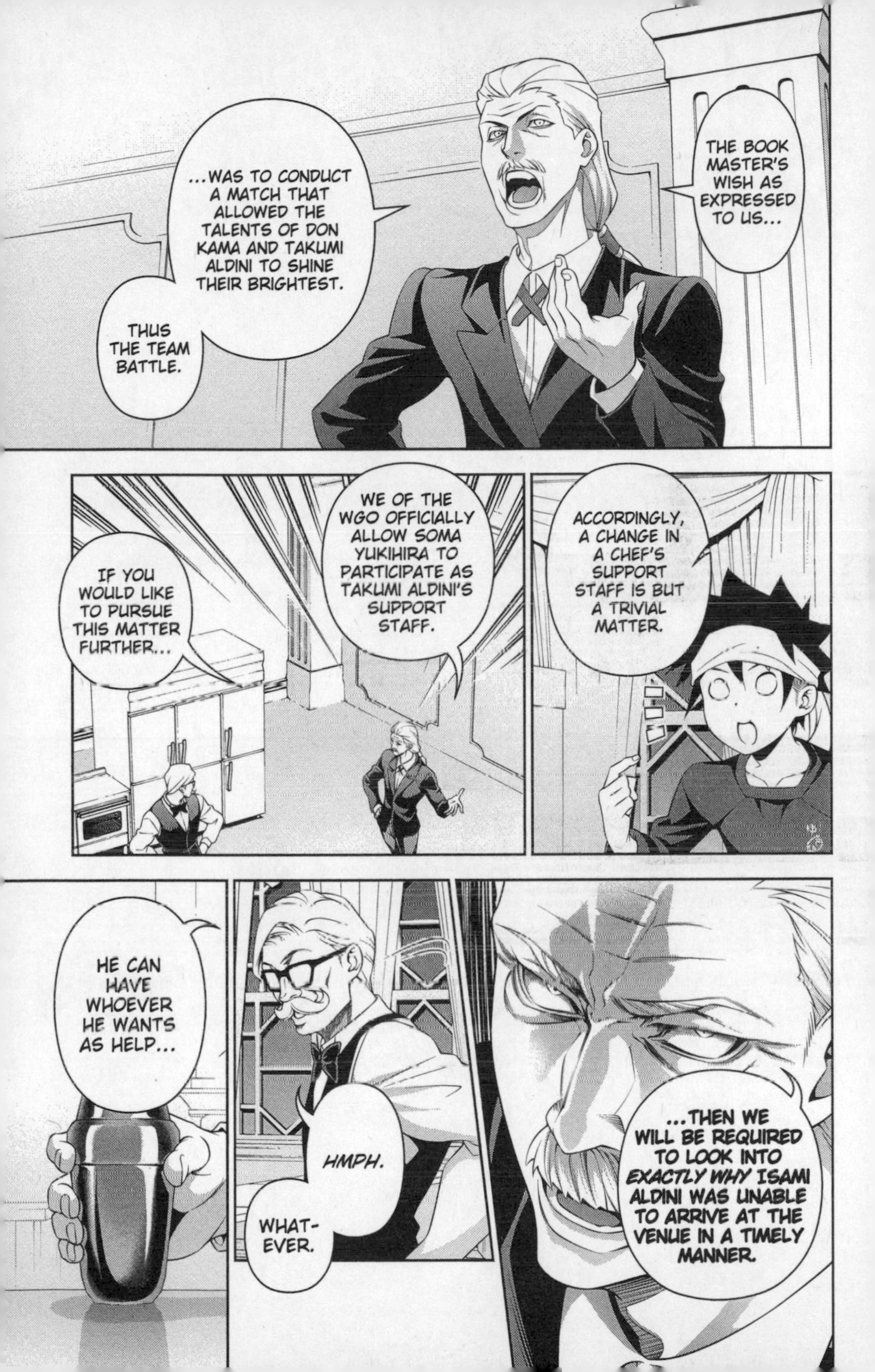
THE BOOK MASTER'S WISH AS EXPRESSED TO US...
...WAS TO CONDUCT A MATCH THAT ALLOWED THE TALENTS OF DON KAMA AND TAKUMI ALDINI TO SHINE THEIR BRIGHTEST.
THUS THE TEAM BATTLE.
ACCORDINGLY, A CHANGE IN A CHEF'S SUPPORT STAFF IS BUT A TRIVIAL MATTER.
WE OF THE WGO OFFICIALLY ALLOW SOMA YUKIHIRA TO PARTICIPATE AS TAKUMI ALDINI'S SUPPORT STAFF.
IF YOU WOULD LIKE TO PURSUE THIS MATTER FURTHER...
...THEN WE WILL BE REQUIRED TO LOOK INTO *EXACTLY WHY* ISAMI ALDINI WAS UNABLE TO ARRIVE AT THE VENUE IN A TIMELY MANNER.
HMPH.
WHAT-EVER.
HE CAN HAVE WHOEVER HE WANTS AS HELP...

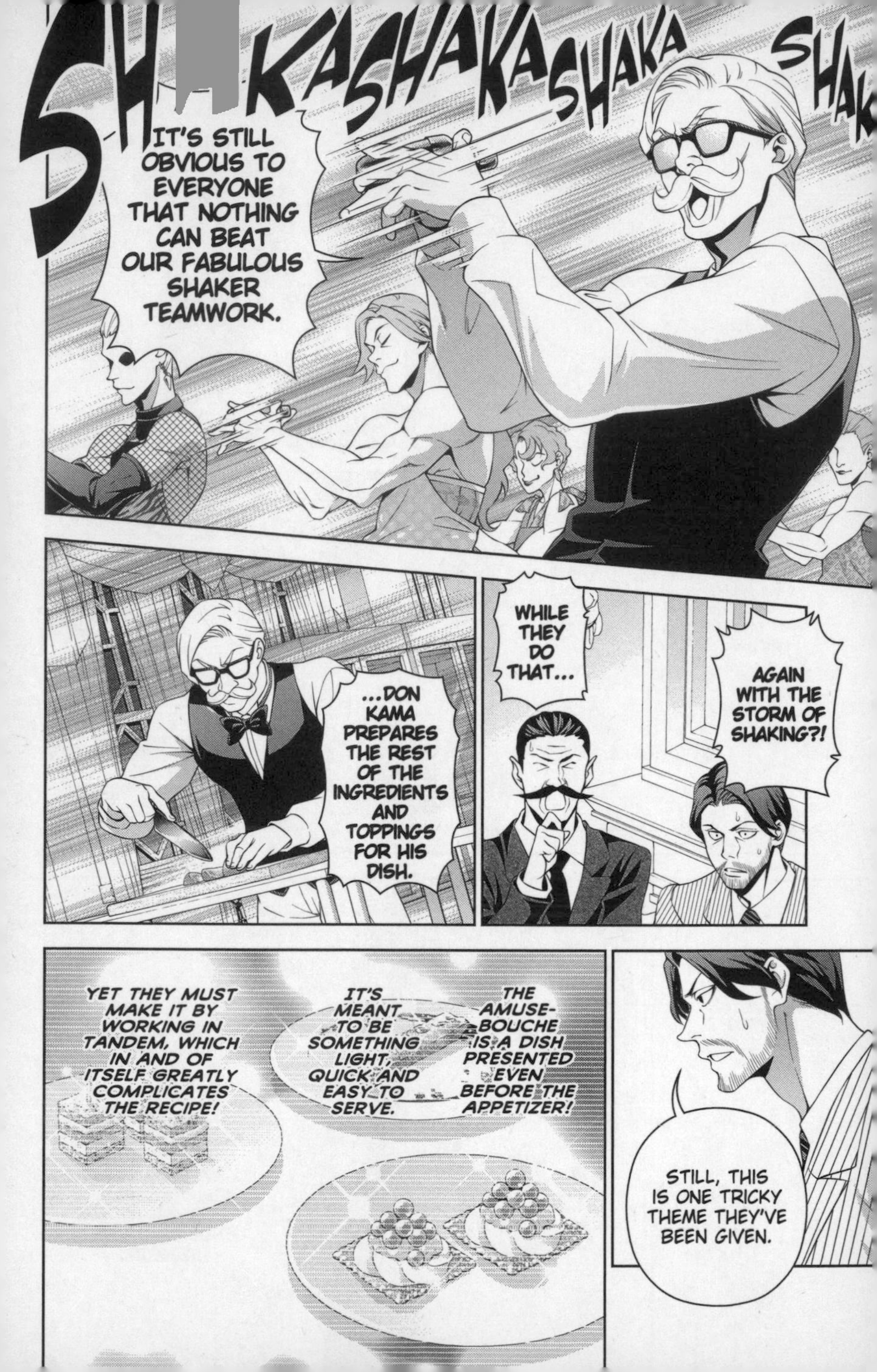
SH KASHAKA SHAKA SHAK
IT'S STILL OBVIOUS TO EVERYONE THAT NOTHING CAN BEAT OUR FABULOUS SHAKER TEAMWORK.
AGAIN WITH THE STORM OF SHAKING?!
WHILE THEY DO THAT...
...DON KAMA PREPARES THE REST OF THE INGREDIENTS AND TOPPINGS FOR HIS DISH.
STILL, THIS IS ONE TRICKY THEME THEY'VE BEEN GIVEN.
THE AMUSE-BOUCHE IS A DISH PRESENTED EVEN BEFORE THE APPETIZER!
IT'S MEANT TO BE SOMETHING LIGHT, QUICK AND EASY TO SERVE.
YET THEY MUST MAKE IT BY WORKING IN TANDEM, WHICH IN AND OF ITSELF GREATLY COMPLICATES THE RECIPE!

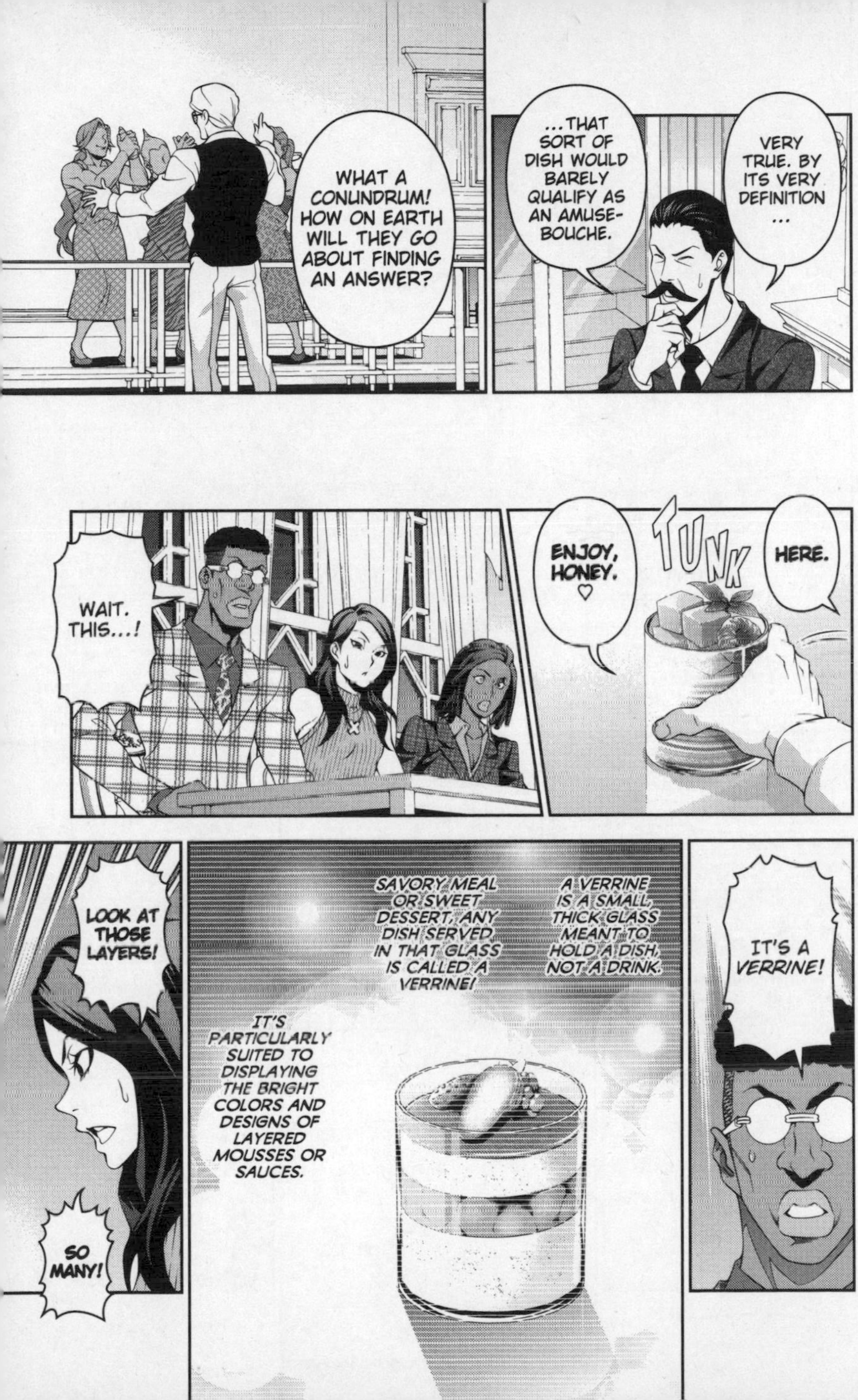
VERY TRUE. BY ITS VERY DEFINITION ...
...THAT SORT OF DISH WOULD BARELY QUALIFY AS AN AMUSE-BOUCHE.
WHAT A CONUNDRUM! HOW ON EARTH WILL THEY GO ABOUT FINDING AN ANSWER?
HERE.
TUNK
ENJOY, HONEY. ♡
WAIT. THIS...!
IT'S A VERRINE!
A VERRINE IS A SMALL, THICK GLASS MEANT TO HOLD A DISH, NOT A DRINK.
SAVORY MEAL OR SWEET DESSERT, ANY DISH SERVED IN THAT GLASS IS CALLED A VERRINE!
IT'S PARTICULARLY SUITED TO DISPLAYING THE BRIGHT COLORS AND DESIGNS OF LAYERED MOUSSES OR SAUCES.
LOOK AT THOSE LAYERS!
SO MANY!

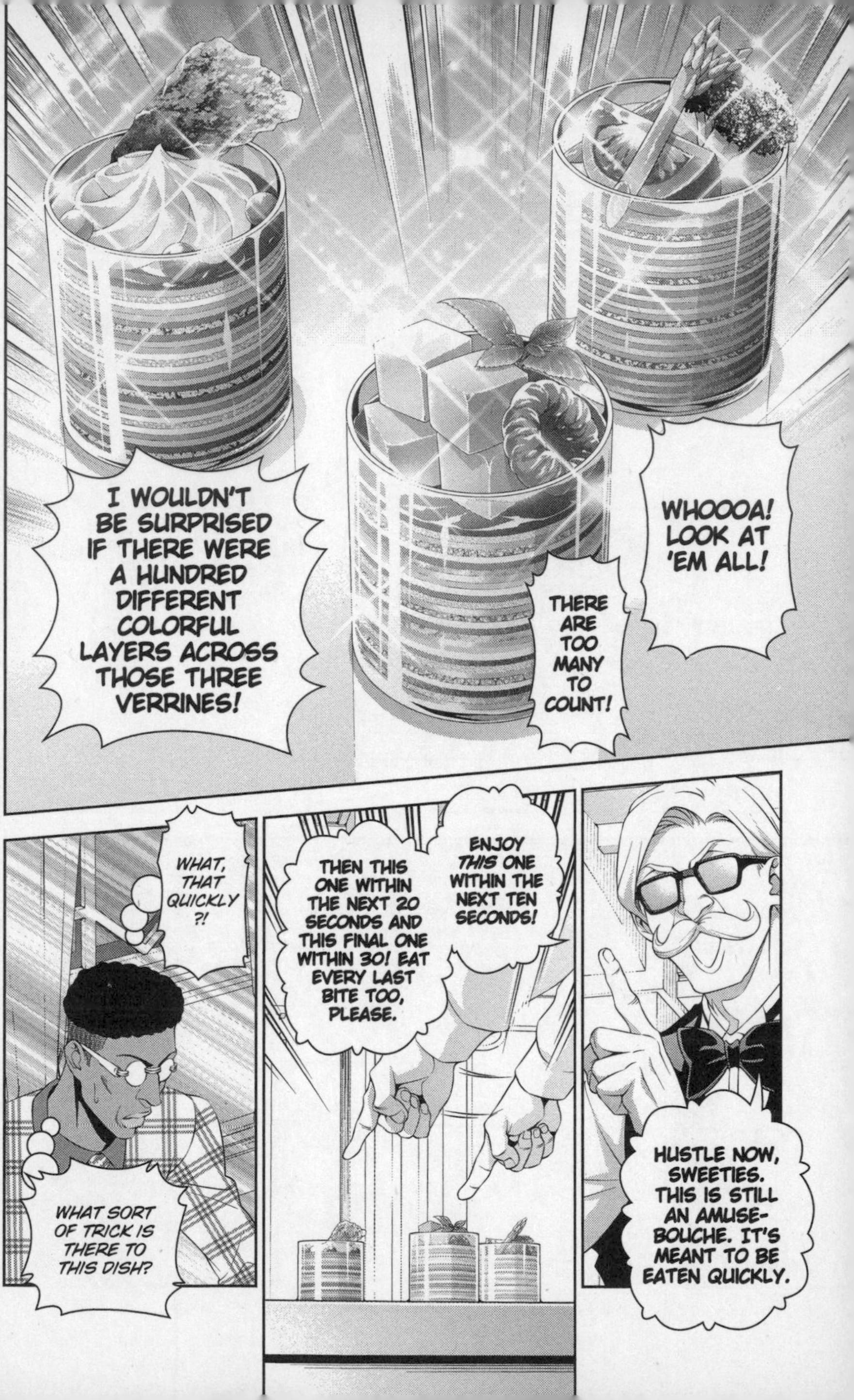
WHOOOA! LOOK AT 'EM ALL!
THERE ARE TOO MANY TO COUNT!
I WOULDN'T BE SURPRISED IF THERE WERE A HUNDRED DIFFERENT COLORFUL LAYERS ACROSS THOSE THREE VERRINES!
HUSTLE NOW, SWEETIES. THIS IS STILL AN AMUSE-BOUCHE. IT'S MEANT TO BE EATEN QUICKLY.
ENJOY *THIS* ONE WITHIN THE NEXT TEN SECONDS!
THEN THIS ONE WITHIN THE NEXT 20 SECONDS AND THIS FINAL ONE WITHIN 30! EAT EVERY LAST BITE TOO, PLEASE.
WHAT, THAT QUICKLY?!
WHAT SORT OF TRICK IS THERE TO THIS DISH?

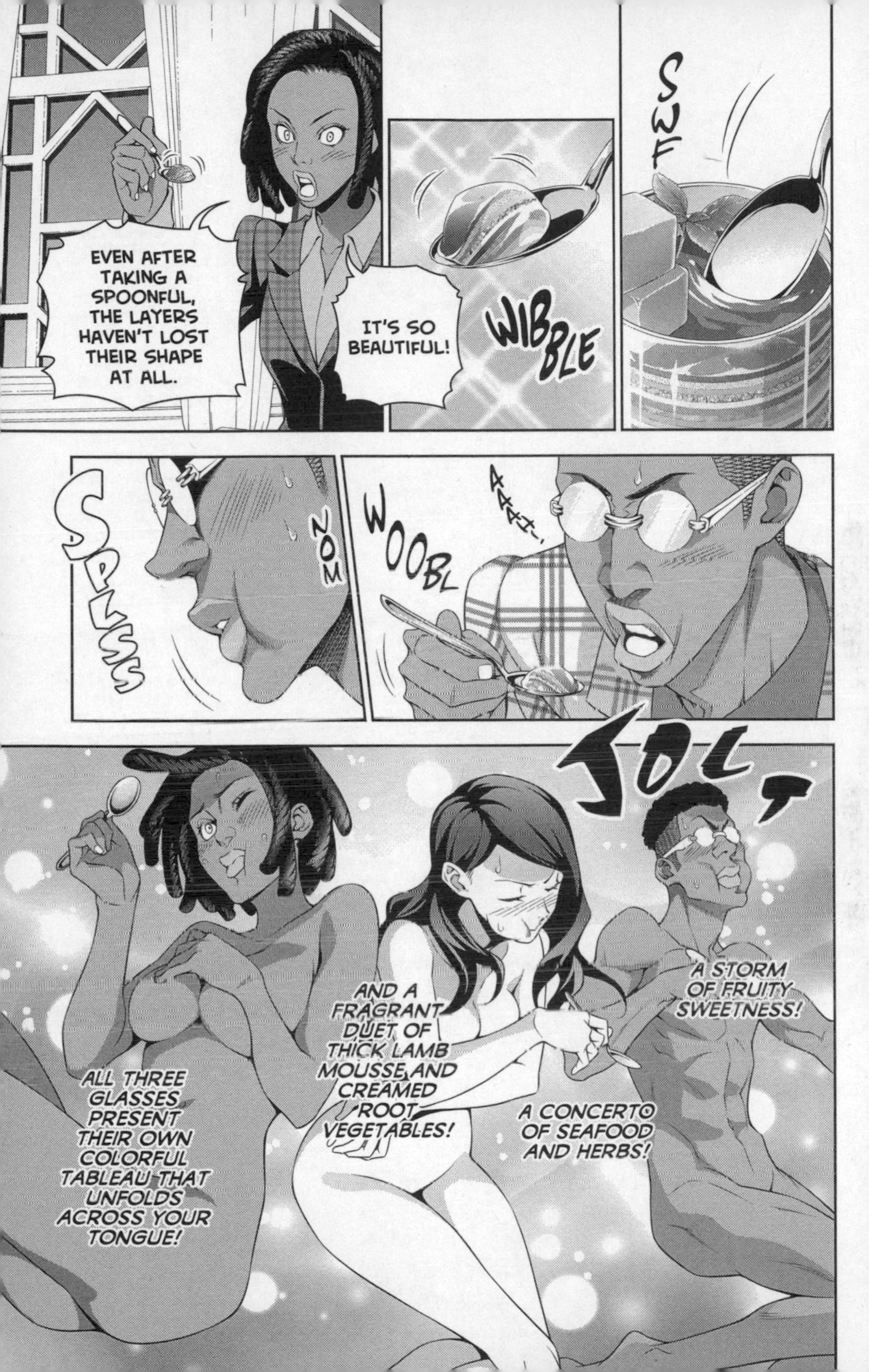
SWF
WIBBLE
IT'S SO BEAUTIFUL!
EVEN AFTER TAKING A SPOONFUL, THE LAYERS HAVEN'T LOST THEIR SHAPE AT ALL.
WOOBL
NOM
SPLSS
JOLT
A STORM OF FRUITY SWEETNESS!
A CONCERTO OF SEAFOOD AND HERBS!
AND A FRAGRANT DUET OF THICK LAMB MOUSSE AND CREAMED ROOT VEGETABLES!
ALL THREE GLASSES PRESENT THEIR OWN COLORFUL TABLEAU THAT UNFOLDS ACROSS YOUR TONGUE!

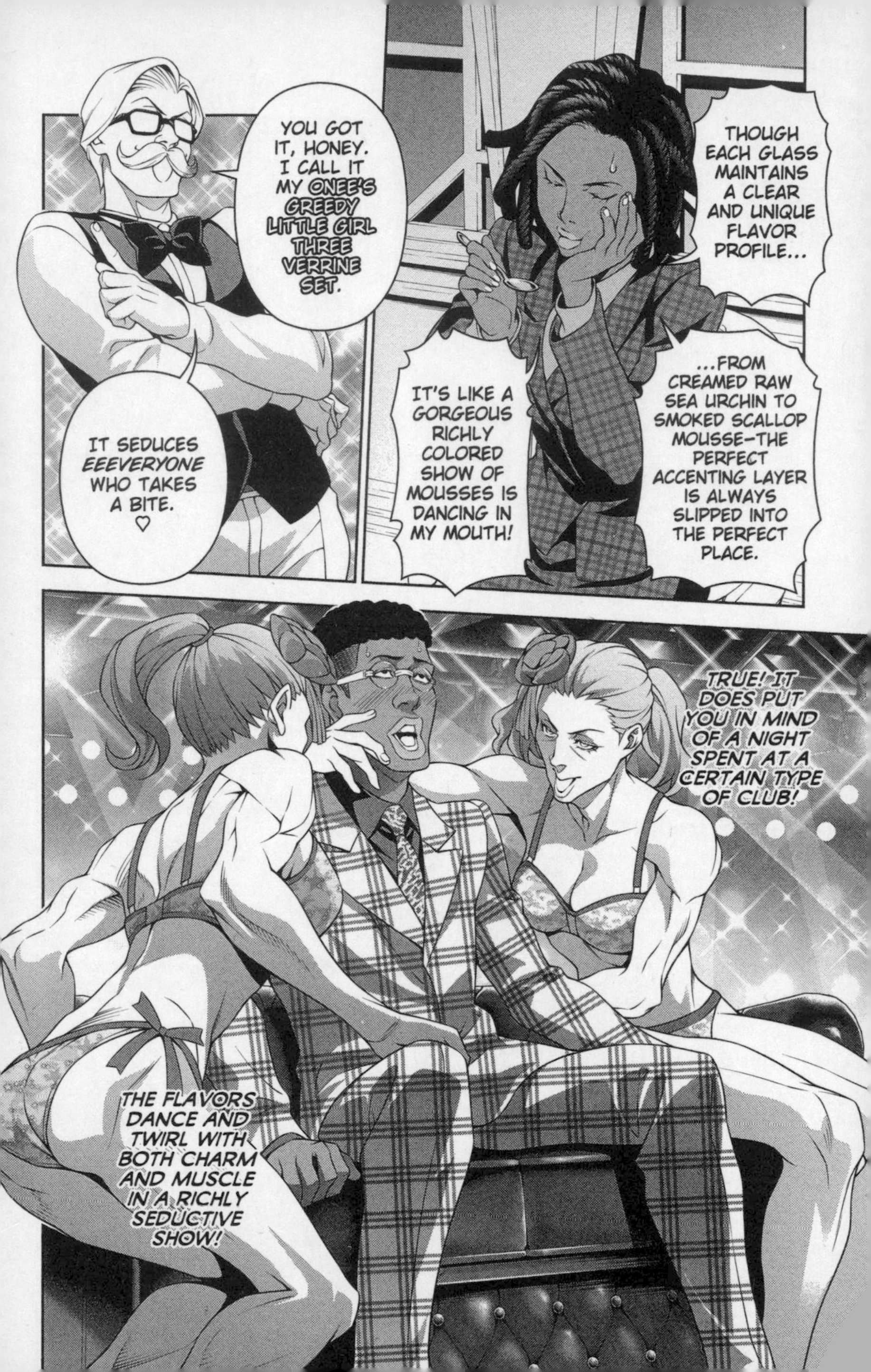
THOUGH EACH GLASS MAINTAINS A CLEAR AND UNIQUE FLAVOR PROFILE...
...FROM CREAMED RAW SEA URCHIN TO SMOKED SCALLOP MOUSSE—THE PERFECT ACCENTING LAYER IS ALWAYS SLIPPED INTO THE PERFECT PLACE.
IT'S LIKE A GORGEOUS RICHLY COLORED SHOW OF MOUSSES IS DANCING IN MY MOUTH!
YOU GOT IT, HONEY. I CALL IT MY ONEE'S GREEDY LITTLE GIRL THREE VERRINE SET.
IT SEDUCES EEEVERYONE WHO TAKES A BITE. ♡
TRUE! IT DOES PUT YOU IN MIND OF A NIGHT SPENT AT A CERTAIN TYPE OF CLUB!
THE FLAVORS DANCE AND TWIRL WITH BOTH CHARM AND MUSCLE IN A RICHLY SEDUCTIVE SHOW!

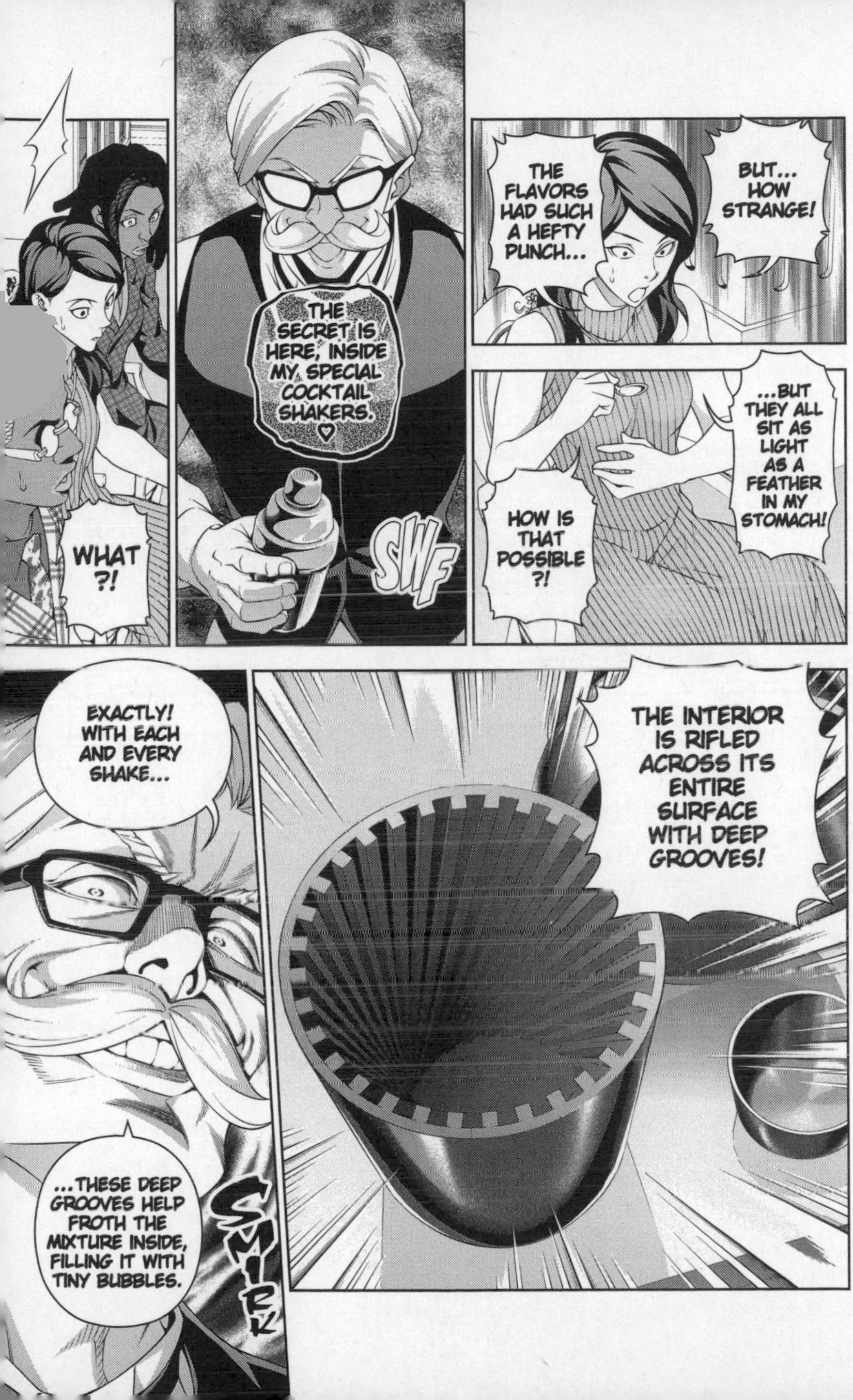
BUT... HOW STRANGE!
THE FLAVORS HAD SUCH A HEFTY PUNCH...
...BUT THEY ALL SIT AS LIGHT AS A FEATHER IN MY STOMACH!
HOW IS THAT POSSIBLE ?!
THE SECRET IS HERE, INSIDE MY SPECIAL COCKTAIL SHAKERS. ♡
SWF
WHAT ?!
THE INTERIOR IS RIFLED ACROSS ITS ENTIRE SURFACE WITH DEEP GROOVES!
EXACTLY! WITH EACH AND EVERY SHAKE...
...THESE DEEP GROOVES HELP FROTH THE MIXTURE INSIDE, FILLING IT WITH TINY BUBBLES.
SMIRK

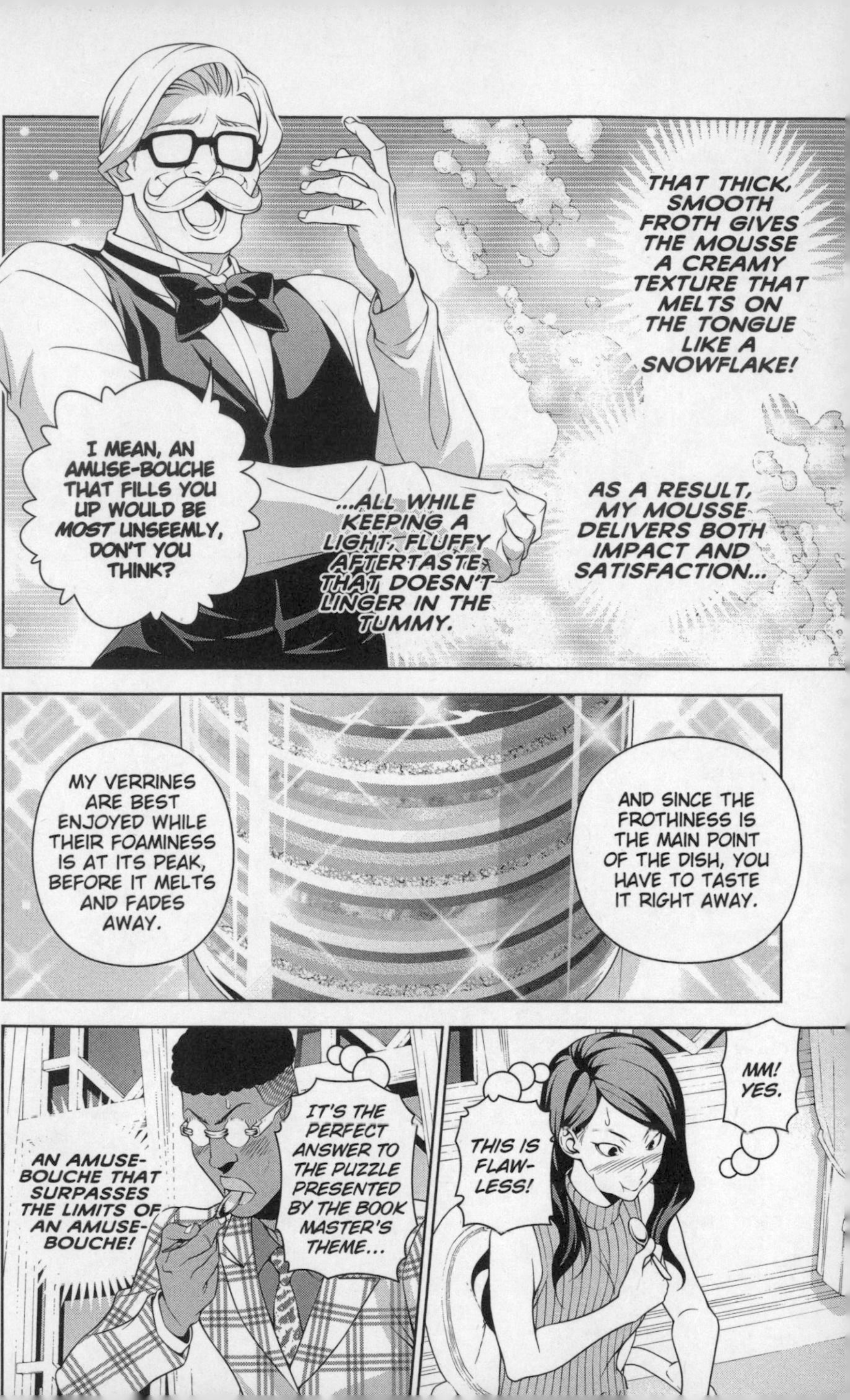
THAT THICK, SMOOTH FROTH GIVES THE MOUSSE A CREAMY TEXTURE THAT MELTS ON THE TONGUE LIKE A SNOWFLAKE!
AS A RESULT, MY MOUSSE DELIVERS BOTH IMPACT AND SATISFACTION...
...ALL WHILE KEEPING A LIGHT, FLUFFY AFTERTASTE THAT DOESN'T LINGER IN THE TUMMY.
I MEAN, AN AMUSE-BOUCHE THAT FILLS YOU UP WOULD BE MOST UNSEEMLY, DON'T YOU THINK?
MY VERRINES ARE BEST ENJOYED WHILE THEIR FOAMINESS IS AT ITS PEAK, BEFORE IT MELTS AND FADES AWAY.
AND SINCE THE FROTHINESS IS THE MAIN POINT OF THE DISH, YOU HAVE TO TASTE IT RIGHT AWAY.
MM! YES.
THIS IS FLAW-LESS!
IT'S THE PERFECT ANSWER TO THE PUZZLE PRESENTED BY THE BOOK MASTER'S THEME...
AN AMUSE-BOUCHE THAT SURPASSES THE LIMITS OF AN AMUSE-BOUCHE!

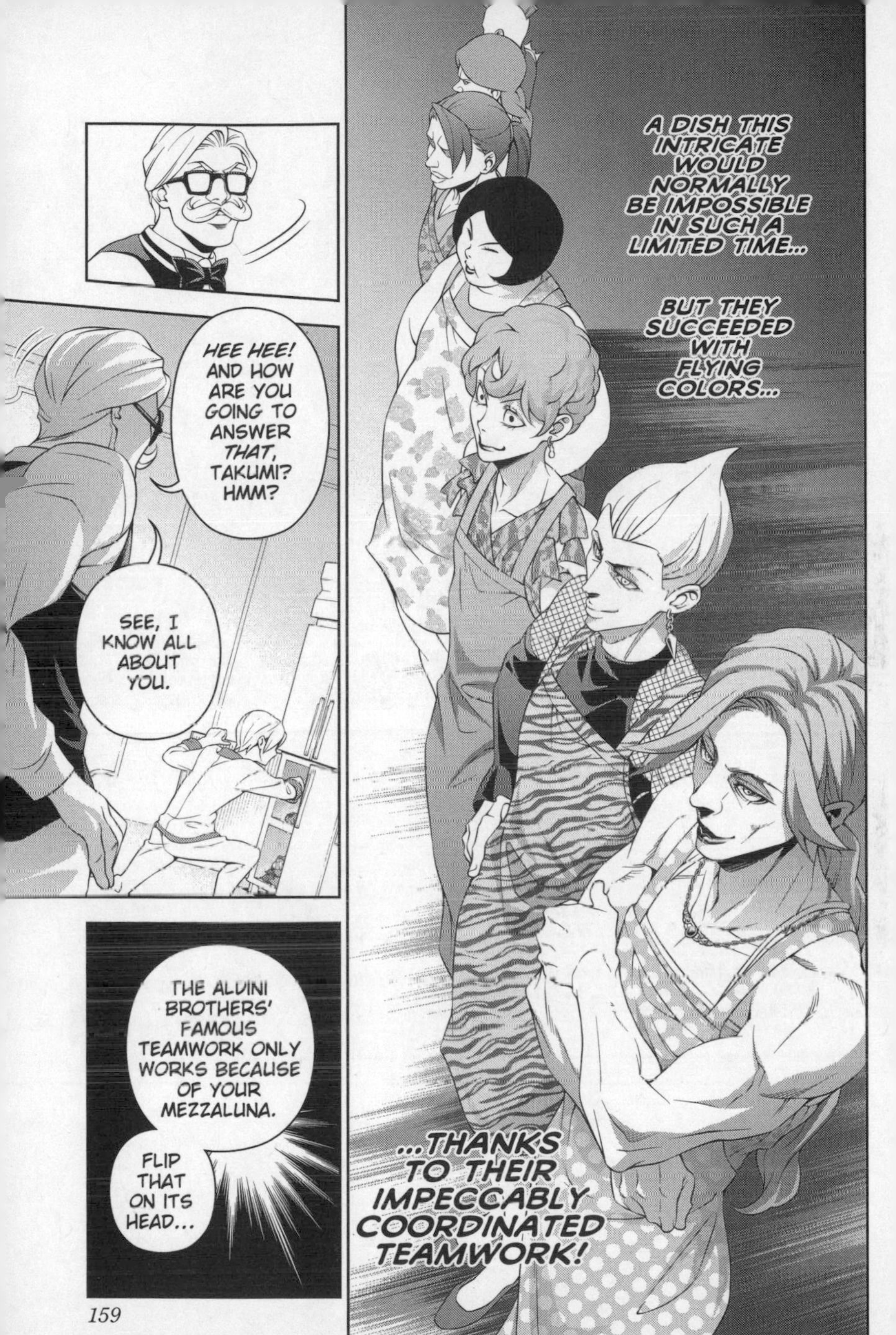
A DISH THIS INTRICATE WOULD NORMALLY BE IMPOSSIBLE IN SUCH A LIMITED TIME...
BUT THEY SUCCEEDED WITH FLYING COLORS...
...THANKS TO THEIR IMPECCABLY COORDINATED TEAMWORK!
HEE HEE! AND HOW ARE YOU GOING TO ANSWER THAT, TAKUMI? HMM?
SEE, I KNOW ALL ABOUT YOU.
THE ALDINI BROTHERS' FAMOUS TEAMWORK ONLY WORKS BECAUSE OF YOUR MEZZALUNA.
FLIP THAT ON ITS HEAD...

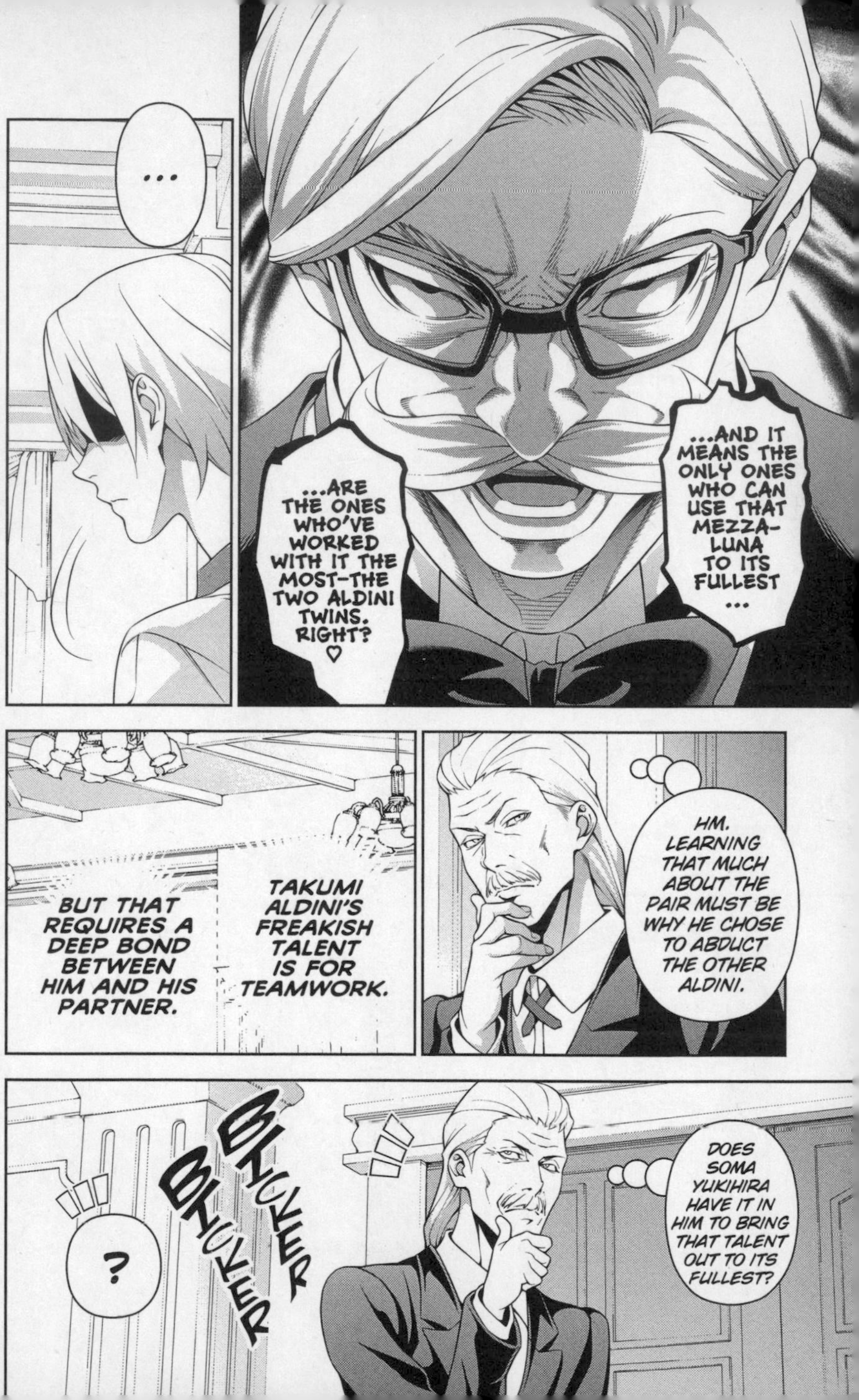
...AND IT MEANS THE ONLY ONES WHO CAN USE THAT MEZZA-LUNA TO ITS FULLEST ...
...ARE THE ONES WHO'VE WORKED WITH IT THE MOST—THE TWO ALDINI TWINS. RIGHT? ♡
...
HM. LEARNING THAT MUCH ABOUT THE PAIR MUST BE WHY HE CHOSE TO ABDUCT THE OTHER ALDINI.
TAKUMI ALDINI'S FREAKISH TALENT IS FOR TEAMWORK.
BUT THAT REQUIRES A DEEP BOND BETWEEN HIM AND HIS PARTNER.
DOES SOMA YUKIHIRA HAVE IT IN HIM TO BRING THAT TALENT OUT TO ITS FULLEST?
BICKER
BICKER
?

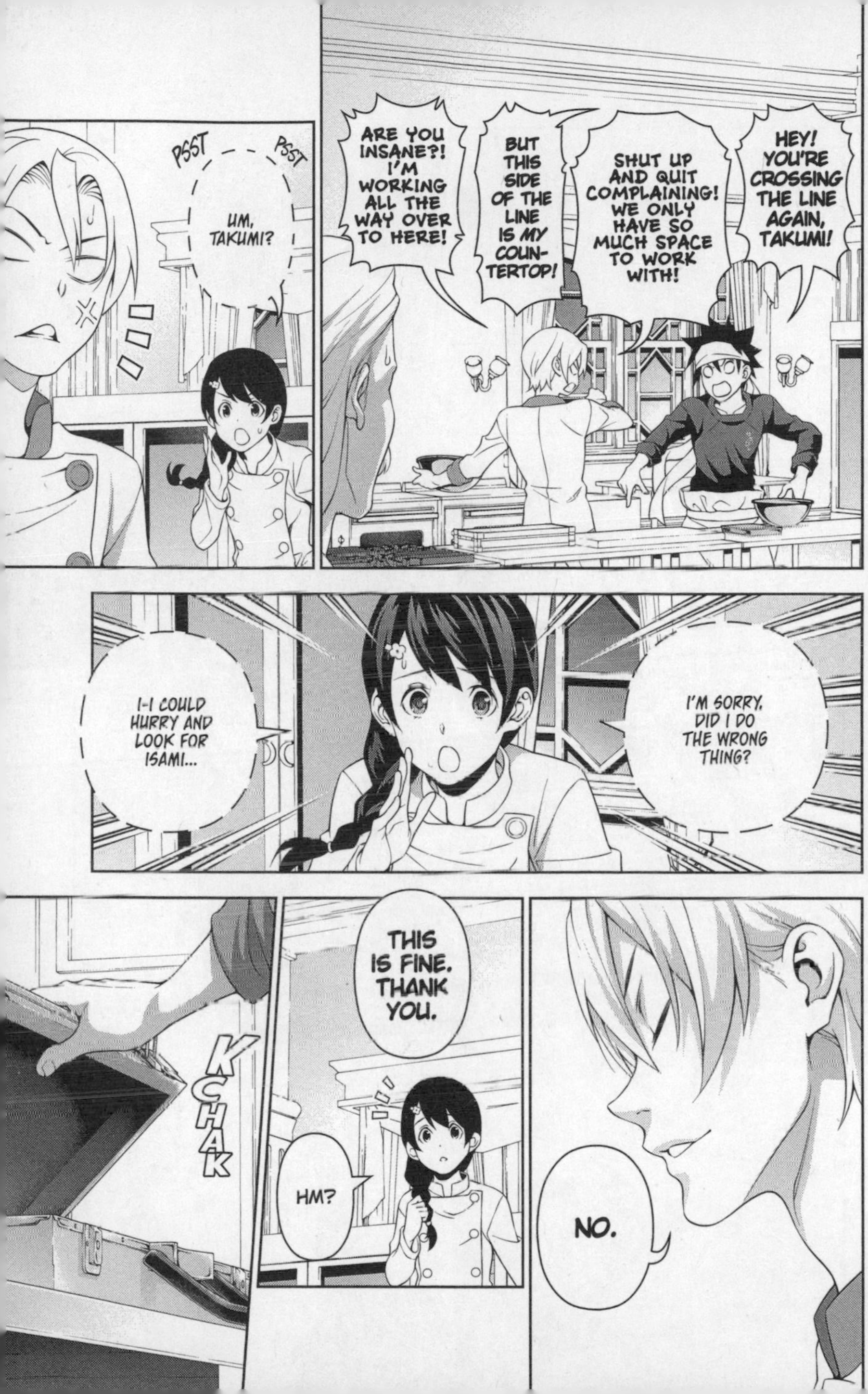
HEY! YOU'RE CROSSING THE LINE AGAIN, TAKUMI!
SHUT UP AND QUIT COMPLAINING! WE ONLY HAVE SO MUCH SPACE TO WORK WITH!
BUT THIS SIDE OF THE LINE IS MY COUNTERTOP!
ARE YOU INSANE?! I'M WORKING ALL THE WAY OVER TO HERE!
PSST
PSST
UM, TAKUMI?
I'M SORRY. DID I DO THE WRONG THING?
I-I COULD HURRY AND LOOK FOR ISAMI...
NO.
THIS IS FINE. THANK YOU.
HM?
KCHAK

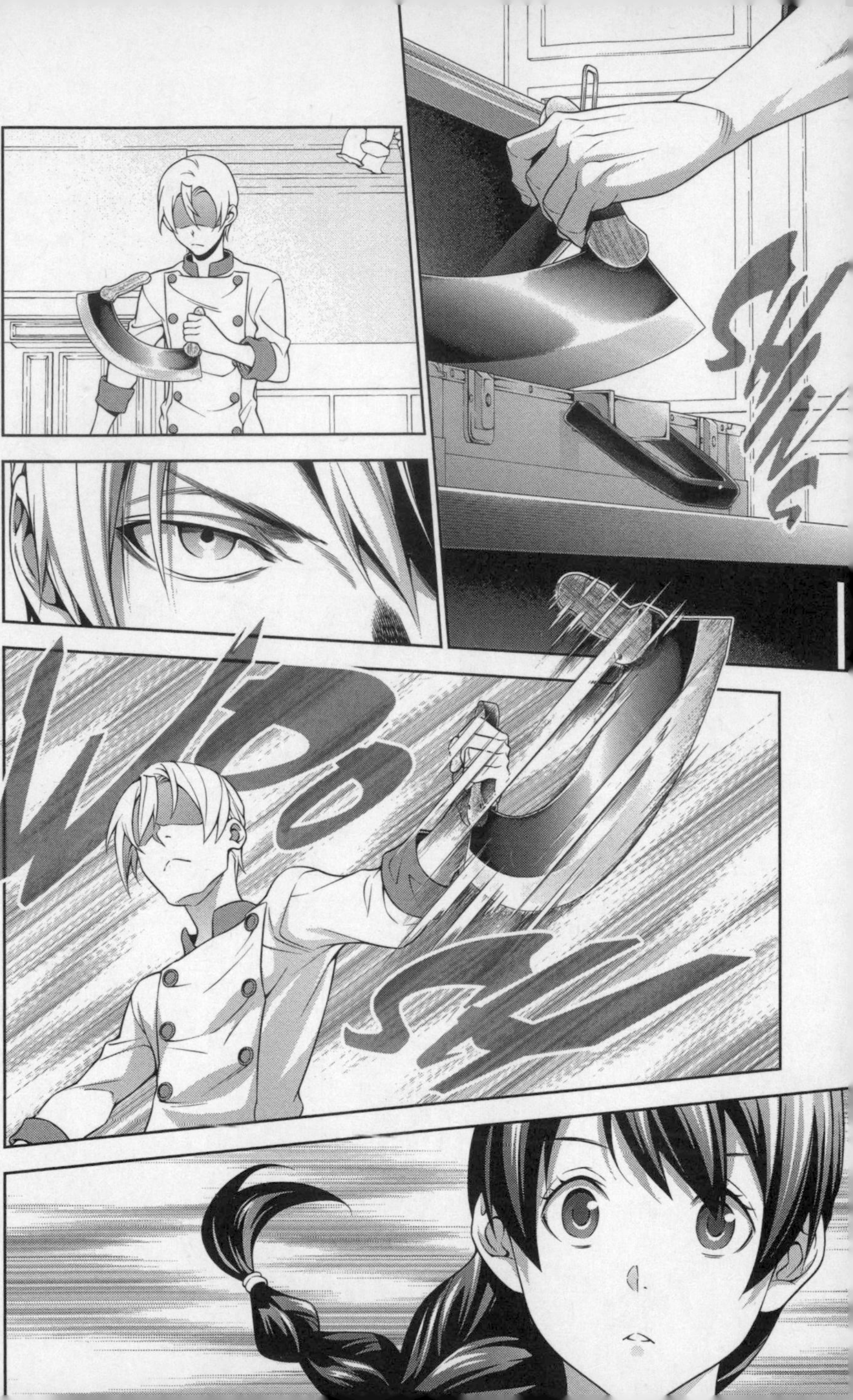
CHING
WOOSH

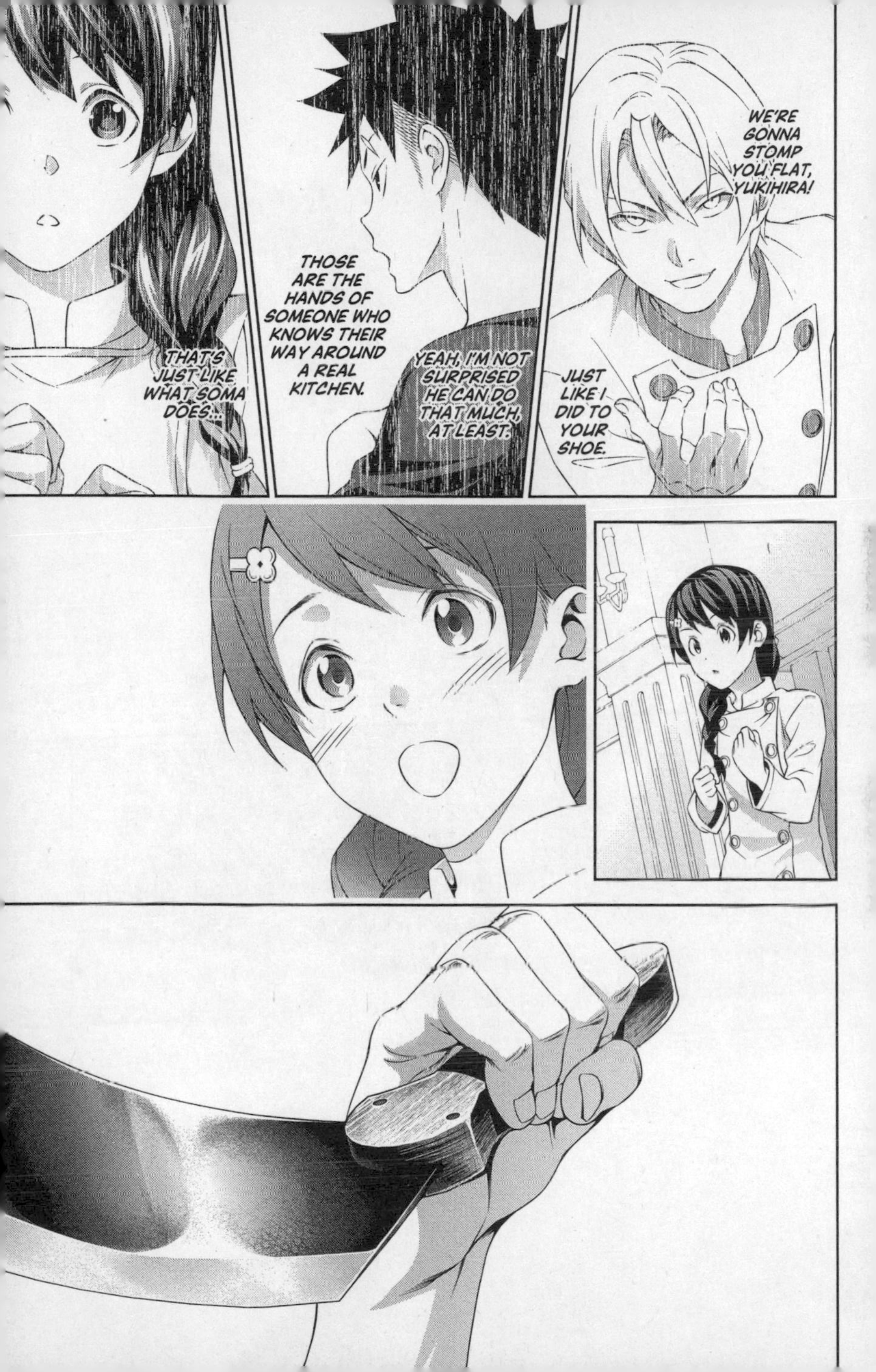
WE'RE GONNA STOMP YOU FLAT, YUKIHIRA!
JUST LIKE I DID TO YOUR SHOE.
THOSE ARE THE HANDS OF SOMEONE WHO KNOWS THEIR WAY AROUND A REAL KITCHEN.
YEAH, I'M NOT SURPRISED HE CAN DO THAT MUCH, AT LEAST.
THAT'S JUST LIKE WHAT SOMA DOES...

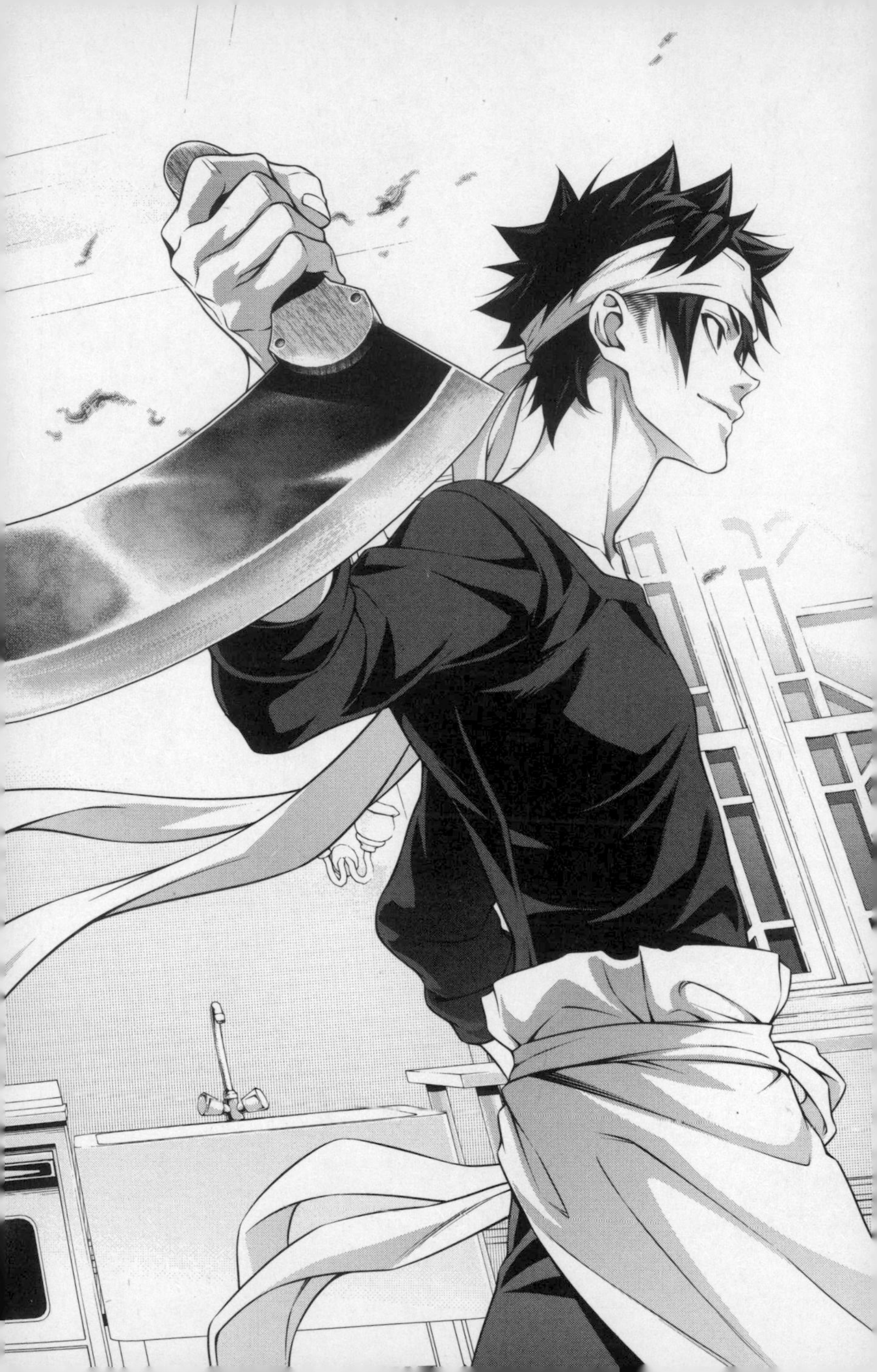

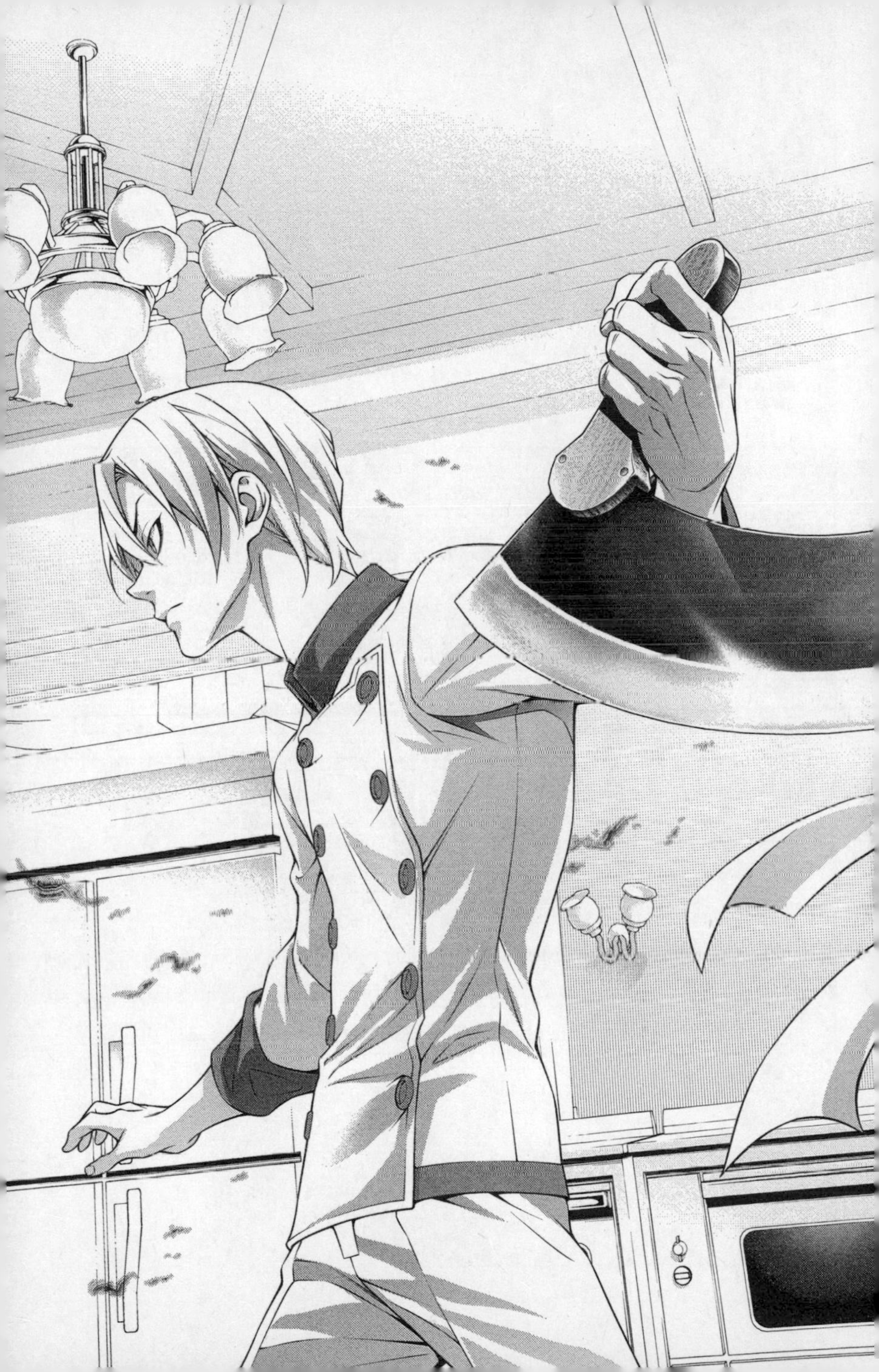

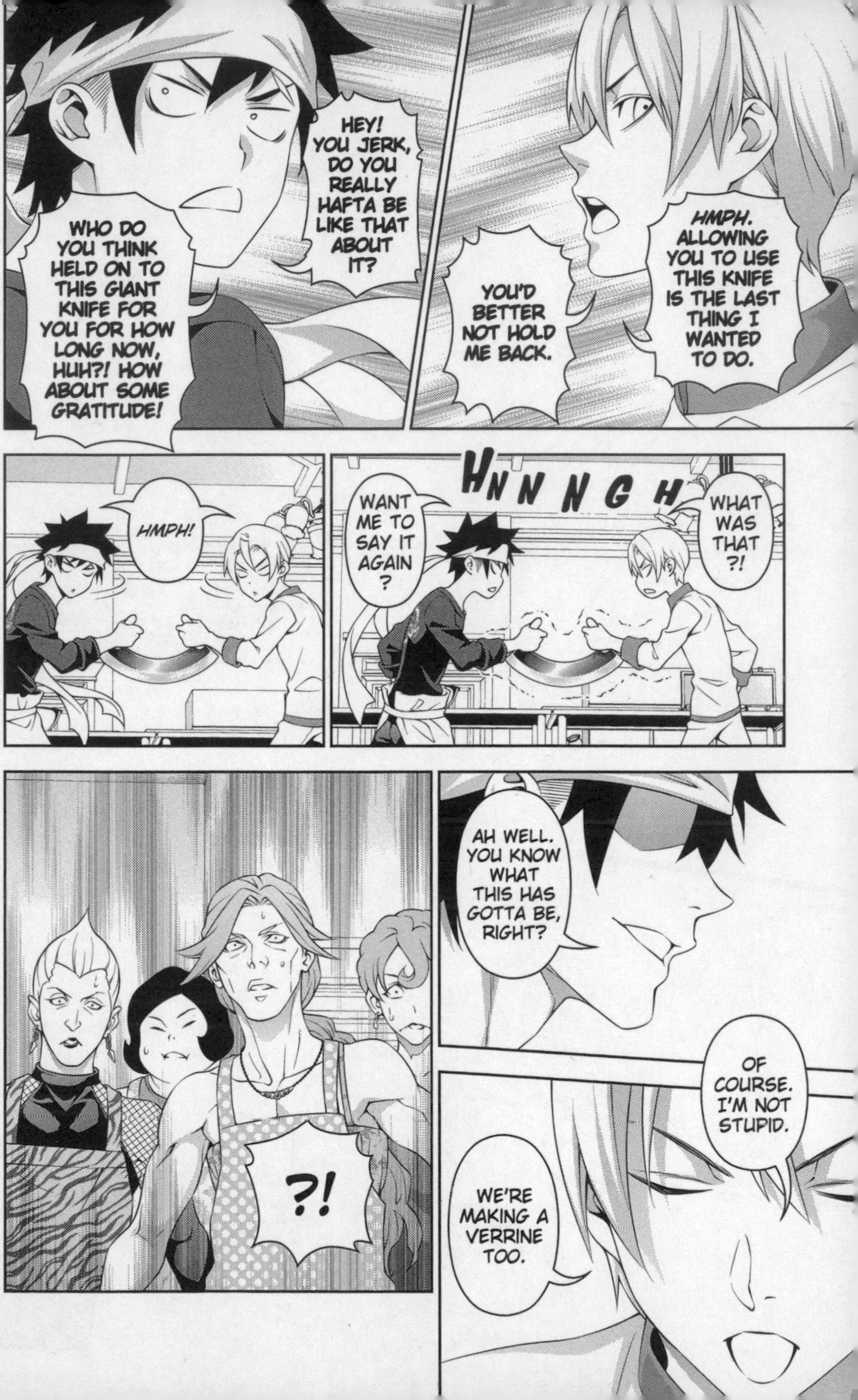
HMPH. ALLOWING YOU TO USE THIS KNIFE IS THE LAST THING I WANTED TO DO.
YOU'D BETTER NOT HOLD ME BACK.
HEY! YOU JERK, DO YOU REALLY HAFTA BE LIKE THAT ABOUT IT?
WHO DO YOU THINK HELD ON TO THIS GIANT KNIFE FOR YOU FOR HOW LONG NOW, HUH?! HOW ABOUT SOME GRATITUDE!
HNNNGH
WHAT WAS THAT ?!
WANT ME TO SAY IT AGAIN ?
HMPH!
AH WELL. YOU KNOW WHAT THIS HAS GOTTA BE, RIGHT?
OF COURSE. I'M NOT STUPID.
WE'RE MAKING A VERRINE TOO.
?!

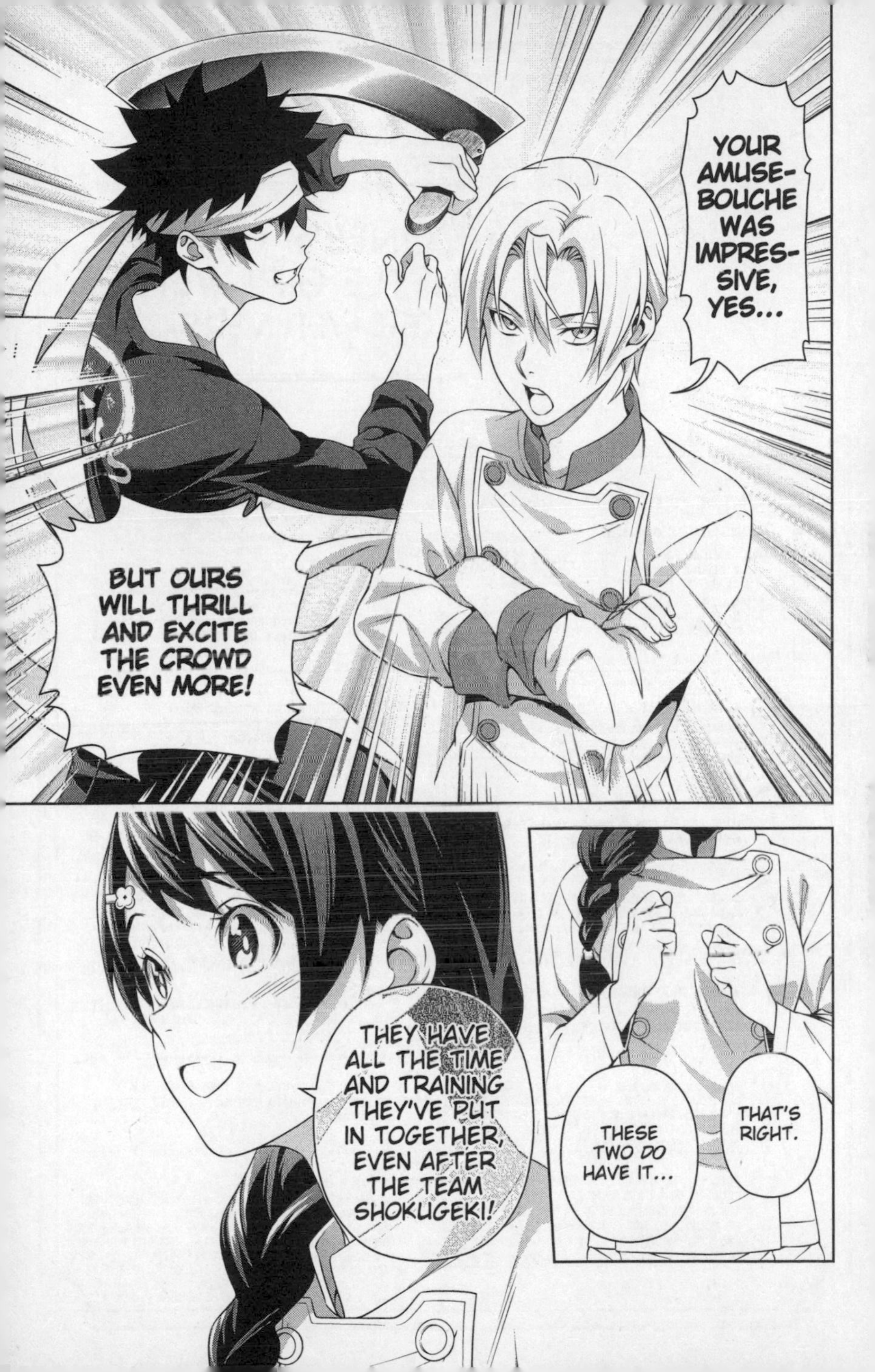
YOUR AMUSE-BOUCHE WAS IMPRESSIVE, YES...
BUT OURS WILL THRILL AND EXCITE THE CROWD EVEN MORE!
THAT'S RIGHT.
THESE TWO *DO* HAVE IT...
THEY HAVE ALL THE TIME AND TRAINING THEY'VE PUT IN TOGETHER, EVEN AFTER THE TEAM SHOKUGEKI!

ARTIST: YUTO TSUKUDA   RECIPE BY: YUKI MORISAKI

DON KAMA
HEE HEE! A PERFECT LITTLE DELIGHT TO SAVE FOR DESSERT.♡

VOLUME 34 SPECIAL SUPPLEMENT!

PRACTICAL RECIPE #3

ONEE'S GREEDY LITTLE GIRL VERINE <5-LAYER VERSION>

INGREDIENTS
(MAKES 5 GLASSES)

★SYRUP

2 TABLESPOONS EACH WATER, SUGAR, RUM

★BAVARIAN CREAM LAYER

200 CC MILK
50 CC CREAM
3 EGG YOLKS
4 TABLESPOONS SUGAR
5 GRAMS GELATIN POWDER
VANILLA EXTRACT

★MANGO MOUSSE LAYER

150 GRAMS MANGO
100 CC CREAM
5 GRAMS GELATIN POWDER
4 TABLESPOONS SUGAR
1 EGG WHITE

★STRAWBERRY JELLY LAYER

150 GRAMS STRAWBERRIES
3 TABLESPOONS SUGAR
3 GRAMS GELATIN POWDER

STORE-BOUGHT SPONGE CAKE, STORE-BOUGHT CHOCOLATE SPONGE CAKE, WHIPPED CREAM, FRUITS AS DESIRED

1) ★MAKE THE SYRUP★
IN A SMALL SAUCEPAN OVER MEDIUM HEAT, DISSOLVE THE SUGAR IN WATER. ALLOW TO COOL, THEN STIR IN THE RUM.

2) CUT THE STORE-BOUGHT SPONGE CAKE AND FIT IT INTO THE BOTTOM OF THE GLASSES. BRUSH GENEROUSLY WITH THE SYRUP FROM (1).

3) ★MAKE THE BAVARIAN-CREAM LAYER★
POUR THE MILK AND CREAM INTO A SAUCEPAN AND HEAT TO JUST BELOW BOILING.

4) PUT THE EGG YOLKS AND SUGAR IN A BOWL AND WHISK TOGETHER UNTIL IT MAKES A THICK, PALE-YELLOW CREAM. ADD (3) SLOWLY IN SMALL PORTIONS, MIXING UNTIL THOROUGHLY BLENDED EACH TIME. ADD VANILLA EXTRACT AS DESIRED. STRAIN BACK INTO THE SAUCEPAN FROM (3) AND HEAT ON LOW UNTIL THICKENED, STIRRING CONSTANTLY. TURN OFF THE HEAT, SPRINKLE IN THE GELATIN POWDER AND STIR UNTIL DISSOLVED. COOL THE BOTTOM OF THE SAUCE PAN IN AN ICE BATH AND STIR UNTIL VERY THICK. POUR INTO THE GLASSES OVER THE SPONGE CAKE, THEN PUT THE GLASSES IN THE REFRIGERATOR TO CHILL UNTIL FIRM.

5) CUT THE STORE-BOUGHT CHOCOLATE SPONGE CAKE AND CAREFULLY FIT IT INTO THE GLASSES OVER THE LAYER FROM (4). BRUSH THE SPONGE GENEROUSLY WITH (1).

6) ★MAKE THE MANGO-MOUSSE LAYER★
POUR THE CREAM INTO A BOWL AND WHIP TO SOFT PEAKS. PUT IN THE REFRIGERATOR TO CHILL.

7) BLEND THE MANGO AND HALF THE SUGAR TOGETHER INTO A PUREE IN A FOOD PROCESSOR. POUR THE PUREE INTO A SAUCEPAN AND HEAT TO JUST BELOW BOILING, STIRRING CONTINUOUSLY. TURN OFF THE HEAT, SPRINKLE IN THE GELATIN POWDER AND STIR TO DISSOLVE.

8) PUT THE EGG WHITE AND THE REMAINDER OF THE SUGAR INTO A BOWL AND WHIP INTO A MERINGUE.

9) COOL THE BOTTOM OF THE SAUCEPAN FROM (7) IN AN ICE BATH AND STIR UNTIL THICKENED. GENTLY FOLD IN (6) AND THEN (8). POUR INTO THE GLASSES OVER THE LAYER FROM (5). SMOOTH THE TOPS AND THEN PUT IN THE REFRIGERATOR TO CHILL UNTIL FIRM.

10) ★MAKE THE STRAWBERRY JELLY★
BLEND THE STRAWBERRIES AND SUGAR INTO A PUREE IN A FOOD PROCESSOR. POUR THE PUREE INTO A SAUCEPAN AND HEAT TO JUST BELOW BOILING, STIRRING CONTINUOUSLY. TURN OFF THE HEAT, SPRINKLE IN THE GELATIN POWDER AND STIR TO DISSOLVE. REMOVE FROM THE HEAT AND ALLOW TO COOL. ONCE COOLED, POUR IT INTO THE GLASSES OVER THE LAYER FROM (9). PUT IN THE REFRIGERATOR TO CHILL UNTIL FIRM. TOP WITH WHIPPED CREAM AND FRUIT AS DESIRED, AND DONE!

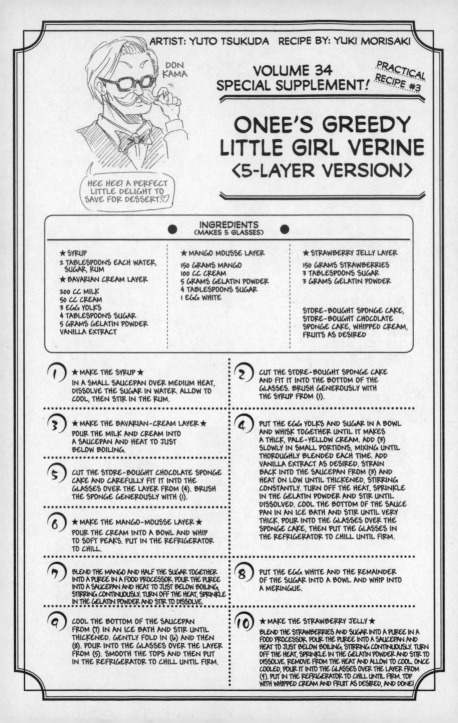

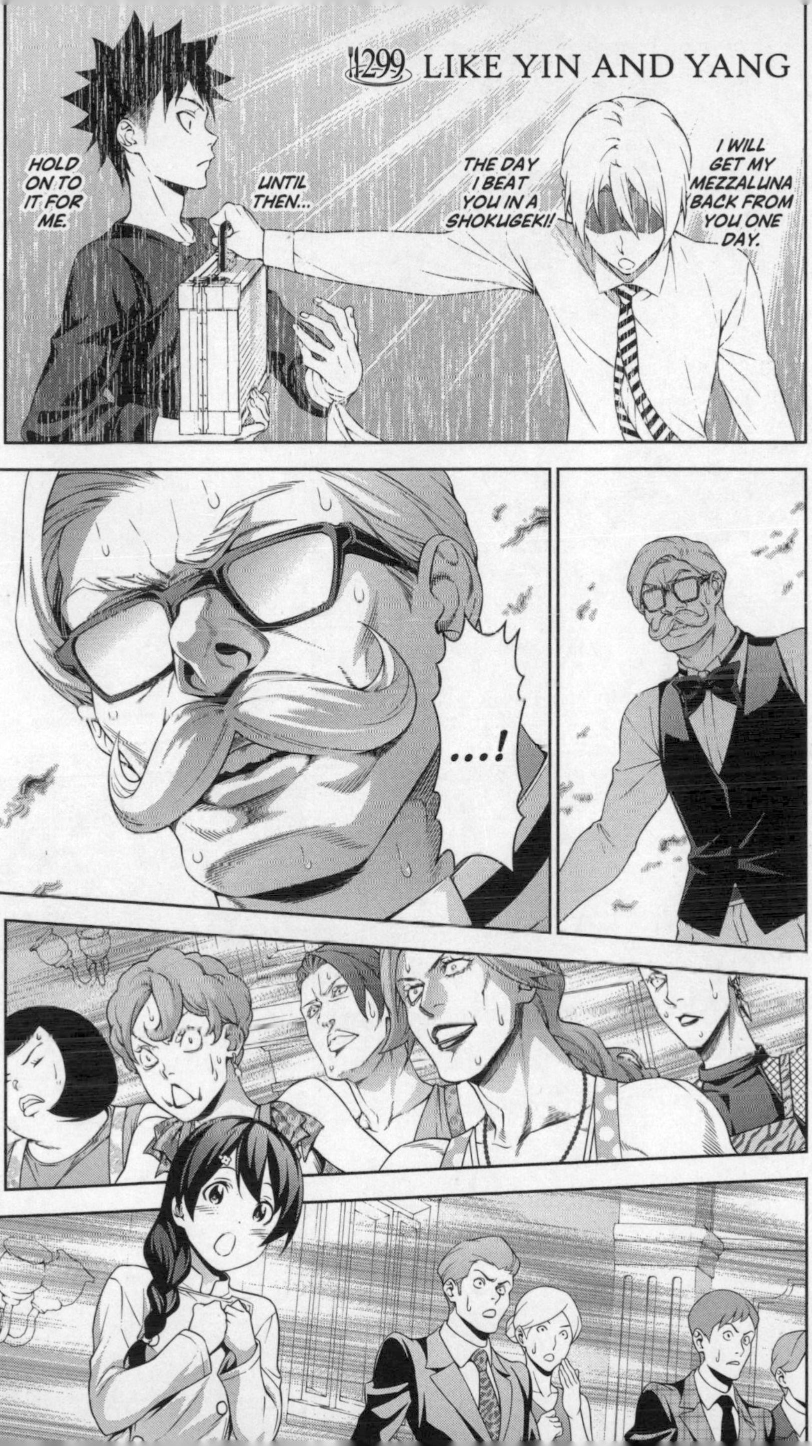
299 LIKE YIN AND YANG
I WILL GET MY MEZZALUNA BACK FROM YOU ONE DAY.
THE DAY I BEAT YOU IN A SHOKUGEKI!
UNTIL THEN...
HOLD ON TO IT FOR ME.
...!

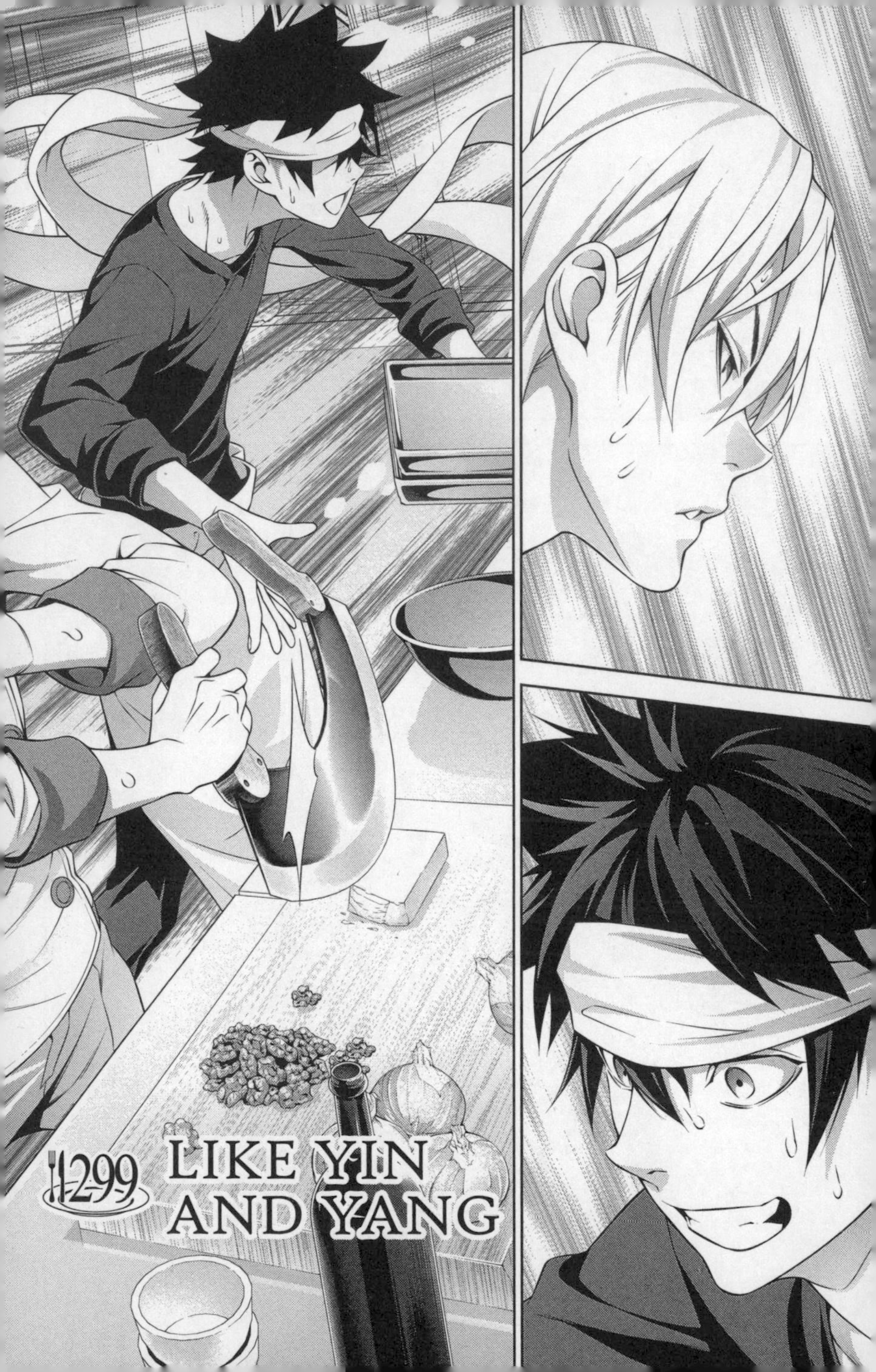
299
LIKE YIN AND YANG

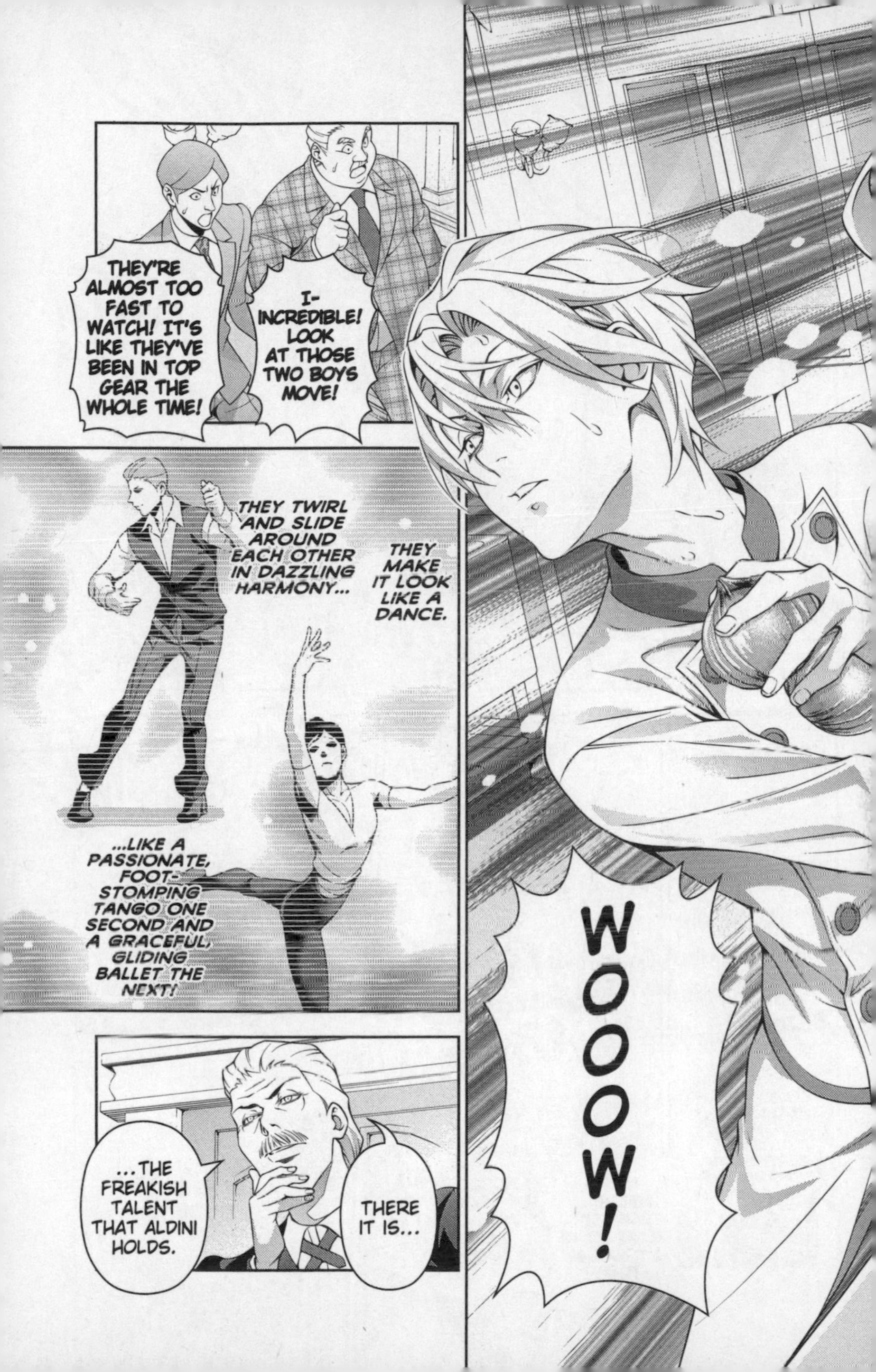
WOOOW!
I- INCREDIBLE! LOOK AT THOSE TWO BOYS MOVE!
THEY'RE ALMOST TOO FAST TO WATCH! IT'S LIKE THEY'VE BEEN IN TOP GEAR THE WHOLE TIME!
THEY MAKE IT LOOK LIKE A DANCE.
THEY TWIRL AND SLIDE AROUND EACH OTHER IN DAZZLING HARMONY...
...LIKE A PASSIONATE, FOOT-STOMPING TANGO ONE SECOND AND A GRACEFUL, GLIDING BALLET THE NEXT!
THERE IT IS...
...THE FREAKISH TALENT THAT ALDINI HOLDS.

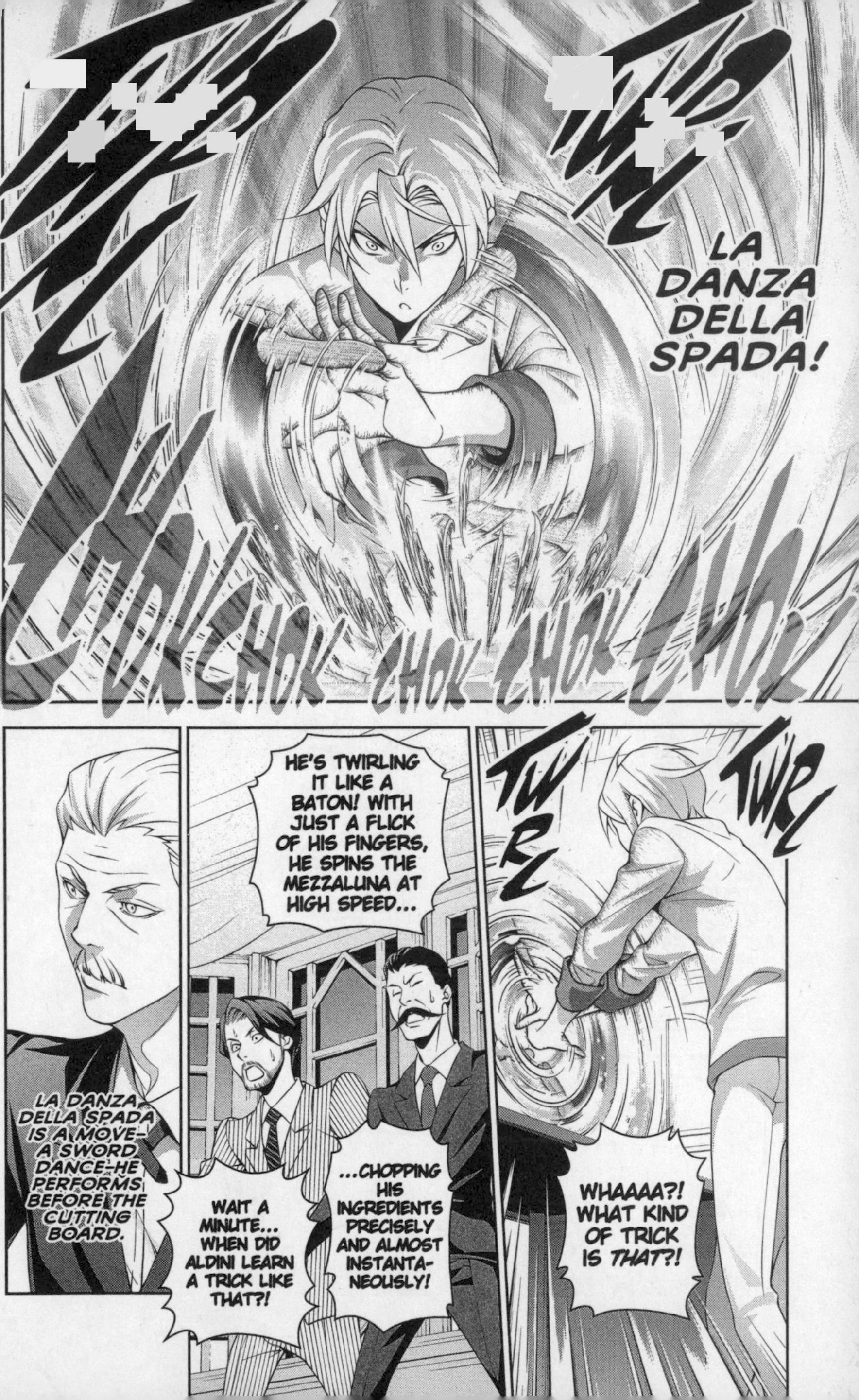
LA DANZA DELLA SPADA!
CHOKCHOK CHOK CHOK CHOK
TWIRL TWIRL
WHAAAA?! WHAT KIND OF TRICK IS *THAT*?!
HE'S TWIRLING IT LIKE A BATON! WITH JUST A FLICK OF HIS FINGERS, HE SPINS THE MEZZALUNA AT HIGH SPEED...
...CHOPPING HIS INGREDIENTS PRECISELY AND ALMOST INSTANTA-NEOUSLY!
WAIT A MINUTE... WHEN DID ALDINI LEARN A TRICK LIKE THAT?!
LA DANZA DELLA SPADA IS A MOVE—A SWORD DANCE—HE PERFORMS BEFORE THE CUTTING BOARD.

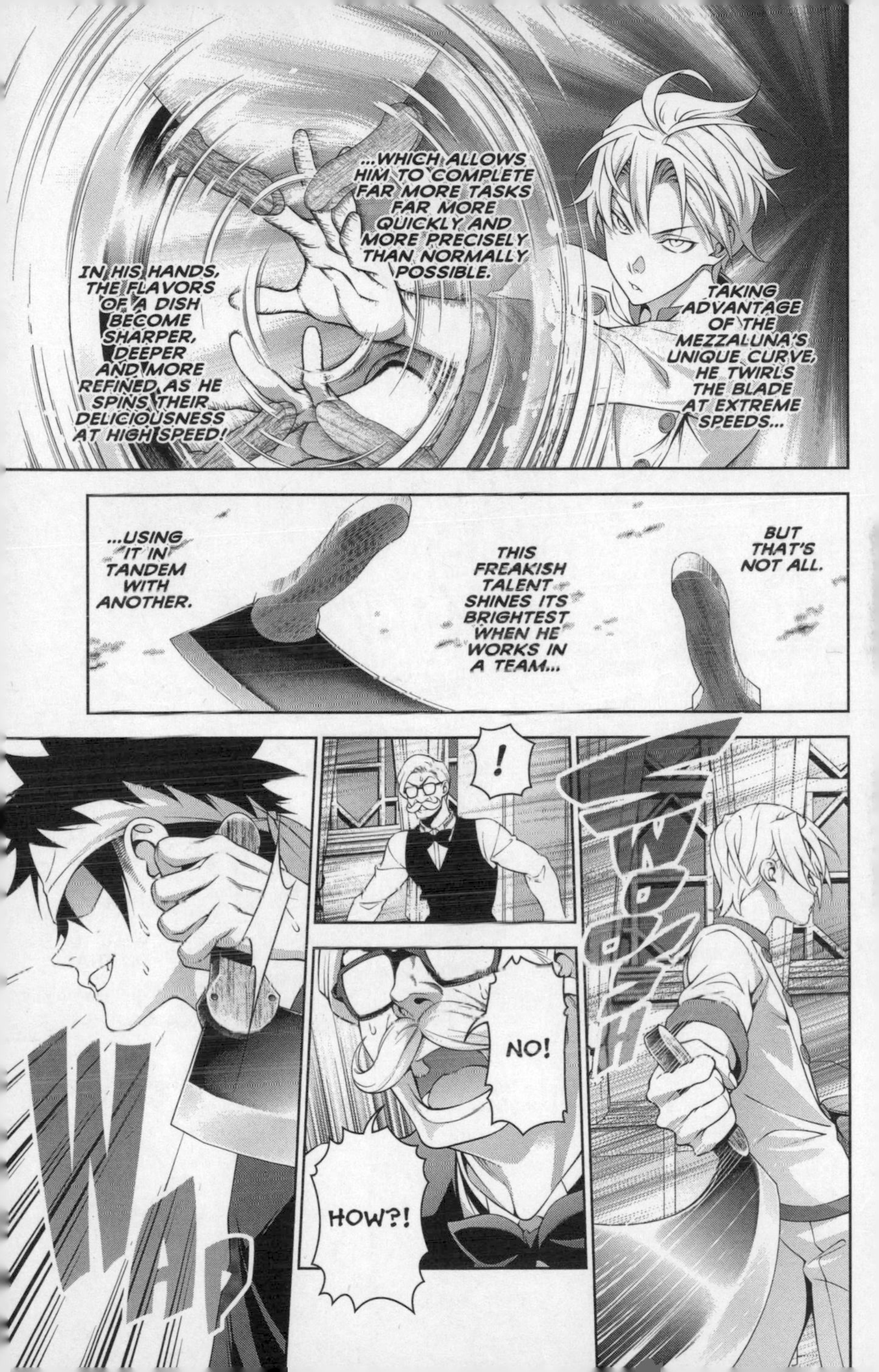
TAKING ADVANTAGE OF THE MEZZALUNA'S UNIQUE CURVE, HE TWIRLS THE BLADE AT EXTREME SPEEDS...
...WHICH ALLOWS HIM TO COMPLETE FAR MORE TASKS FAR MORE QUICKLY AND MORE PRECISELY THAN NORMALLY POSSIBLE.
IN HIS HANDS, THE FLAVORS OF A DISH BECOME SHARPER, DEEPER AND MORE REFINED AS HE SPINS THEIR DELICIOUSNESS AT HIGH SPEED!
BUT THAT'S NOT ALL.
THIS FREAKISH TALENT SHINES ITS BRIGHTEST WHEN HE WORKS IN A TEAM...
...USING IT IN TANDEM WITH ANOTHER.
!
NO!
HOW?!

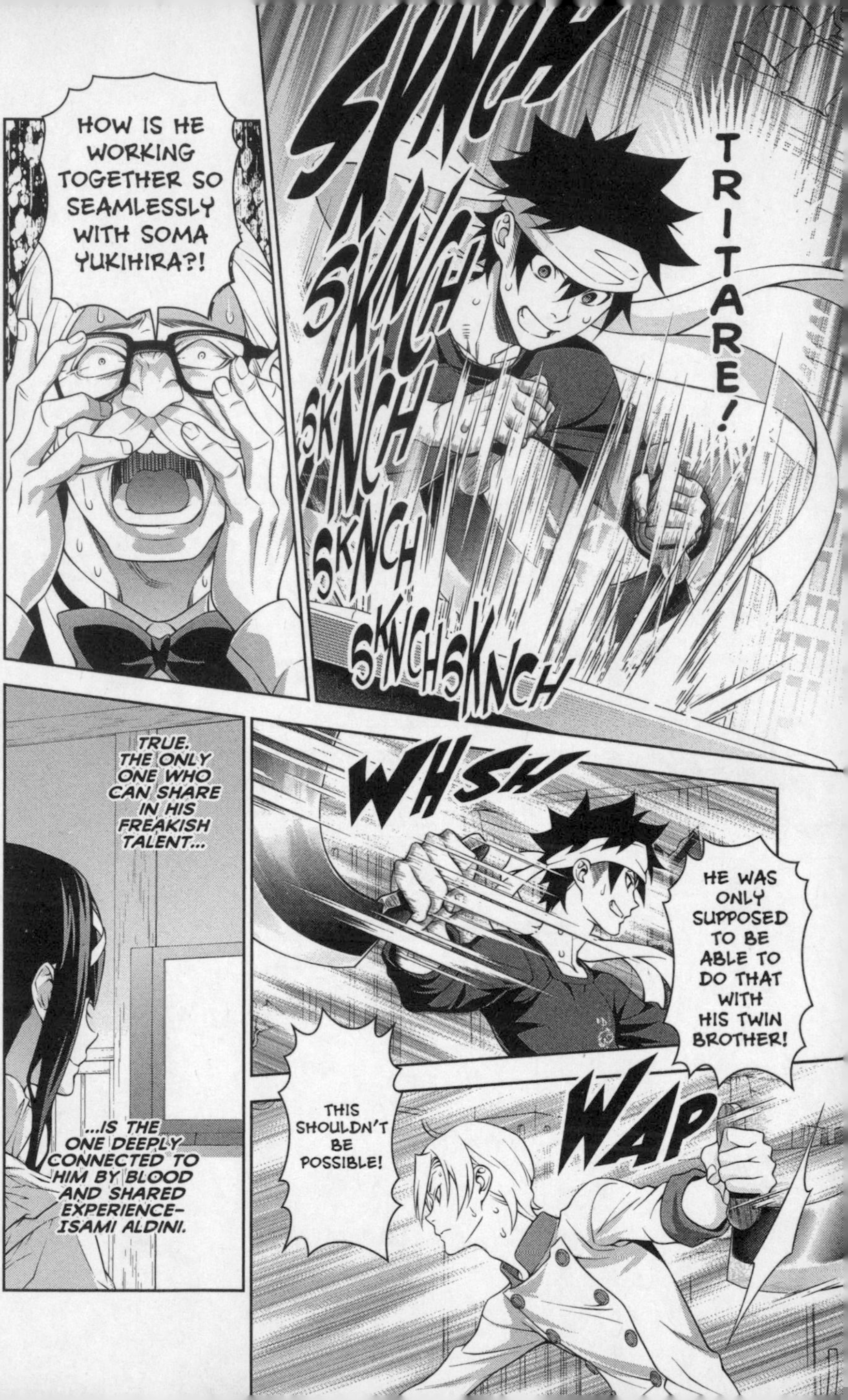
TRITARE!
SKNCH SKNCH SKNCH SKNCH SKNCH SKNCHSKNCH
HOW IS HE WORKING TOGETHER SO SEAMLESSLY WITH SOMA YUKIHIRA?!
WHSH
HE WAS ONLY SUPPOSED TO BE ABLE TO DO THAT WITH HIS TWIN BROTHER!
WAP
THIS SHOULDN'T BE POSSIBLE!
TRUE. THE ONLY ONE WHO CAN SHARE IN HIS FREAKISH TALENT...
...IS THE ONE DEEPLY CONNECTED TO HIM BY BLOOD AND SHARED EXPERIENCE-ISAMI ALDINI.

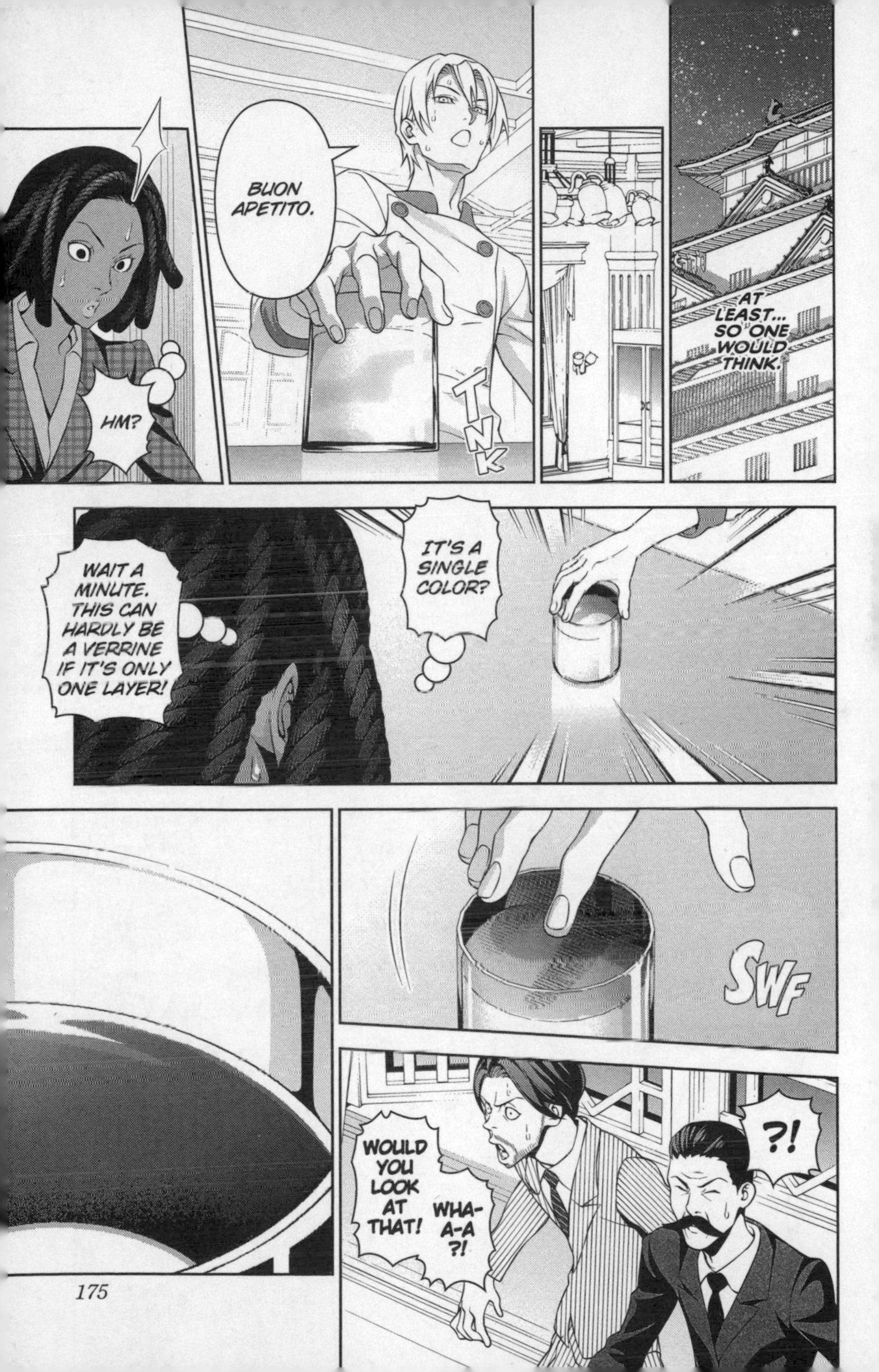
AT LEAST... SO ONE WOULD THINK.
BUON APETITO.
TNK
HM?
IT'S A SINGLE COLOR?
WAIT A MINUTE. THIS CAN HARDLY BE A VERRINE IF IT'S ONLY ONE LAYER!
SWF
?!
WHA-A-A ?!
WOULD YOU LOOK AT THAT!

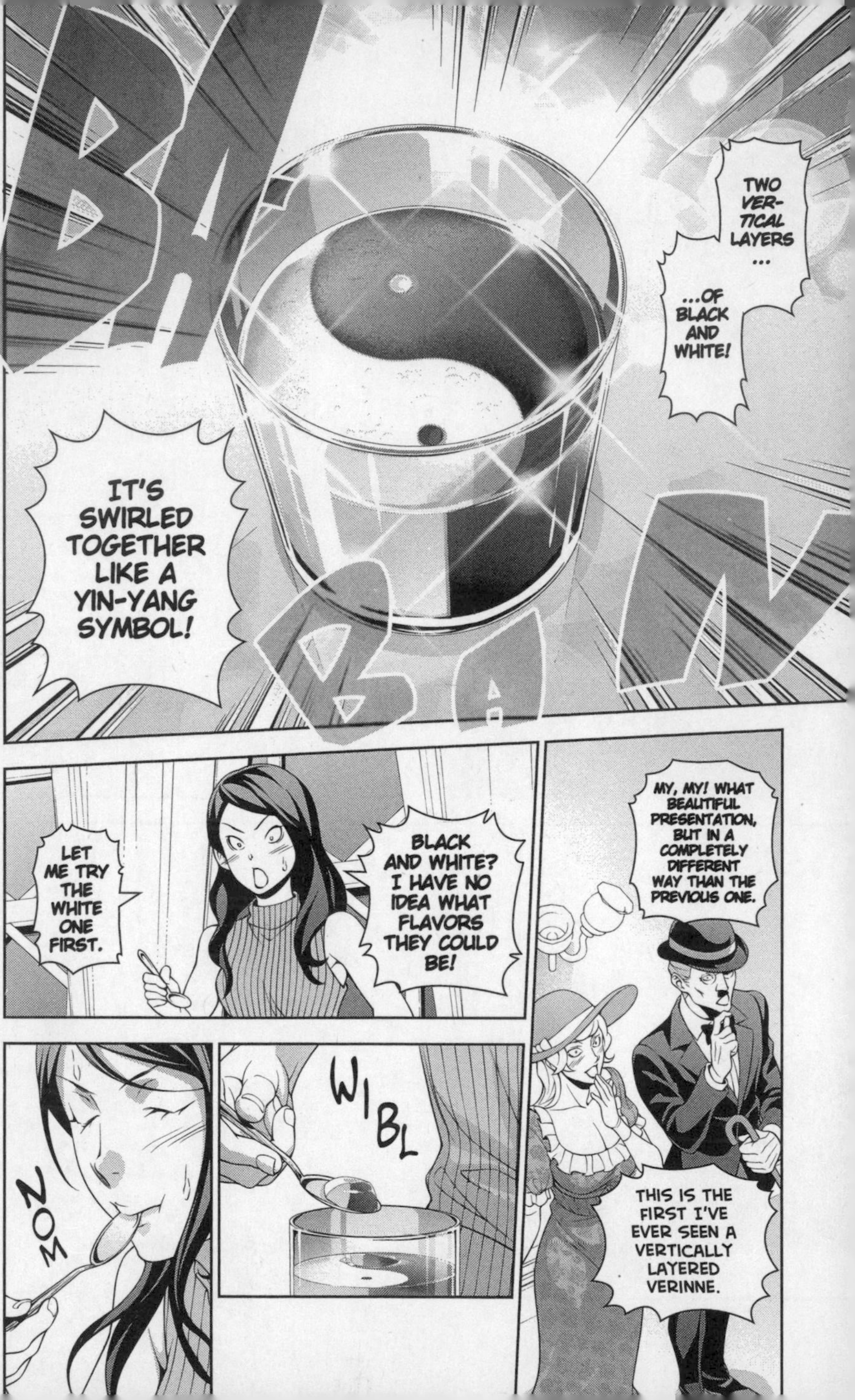
BA
TWO VERTICAL LAYERS...
...OF BLACK AND WHITE!
IT'S SWIRLED TOGETHER LIKE A YIN-YANG SYMBOL!
BAN
MY, MY! WHAT BEAUTIFUL PRESENTATION, BUT IN A COMPLETELY DIFFERENT WAY THAN THE PREVIOUS ONE.
THIS IS THE FIRST I'VE EVER SEEN A VERTICALLY LAYERED VERINNE.
BLACK AND WHITE? I HAVE NO IDEA WHAT FLAVORS THEY COULD BE!
LET ME TRY THE WHITE ONE FIRST.
WIBL
NOM

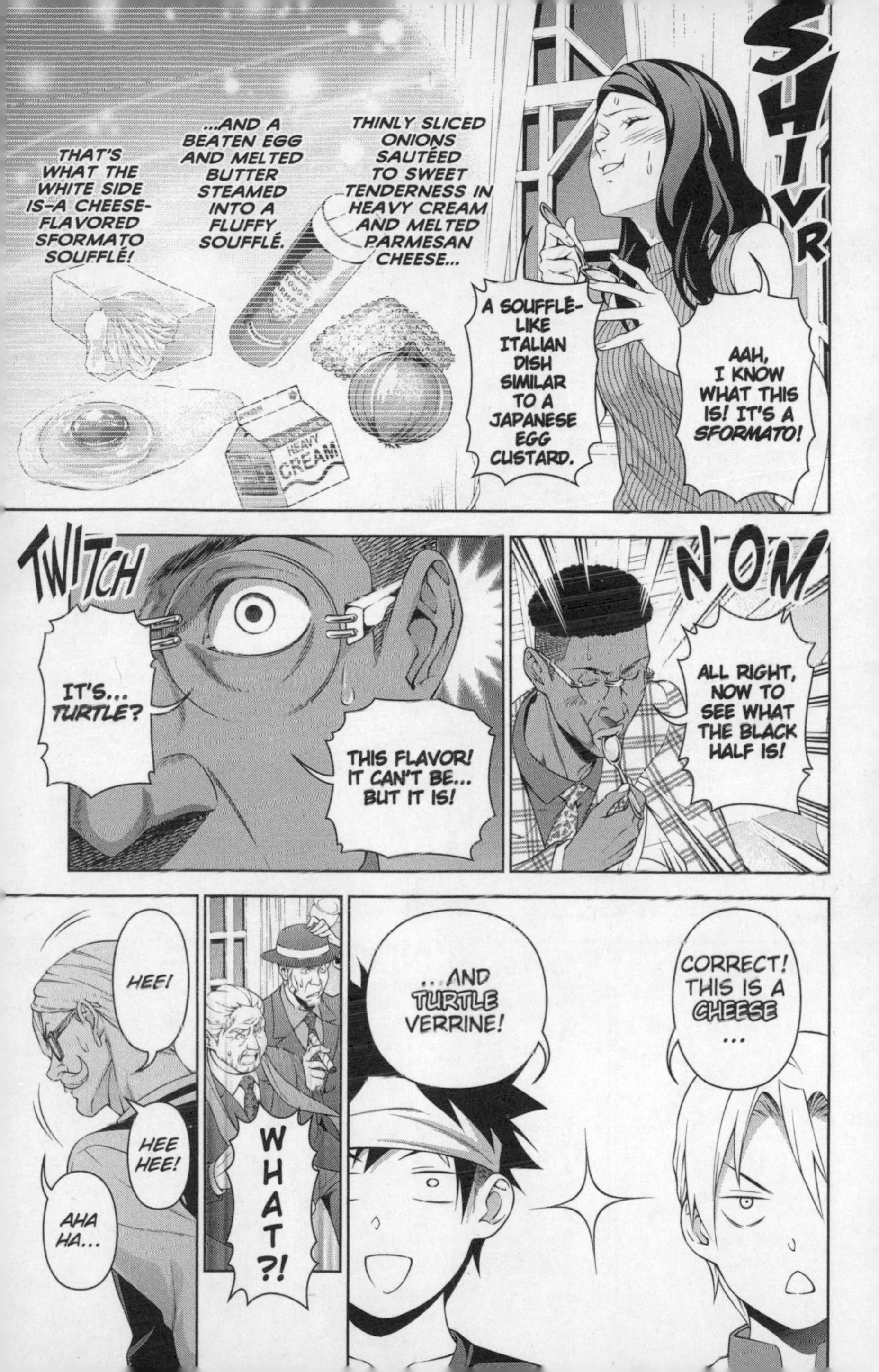
SHIVR
AAH, I KNOW WHAT THIS IS! IT'S A SFORMATO!
A SOUFFLÉ-LIKE ITALIAN DISH SIMILAR TO A JAPANESE EGG CUSTARD.
THINLY SLICED ONIONS SAUTÉED TO SWEET TENDERNESS IN HEAVY CREAM AND MELTED PARMESAN CHEESE...
...AND A BEATEN EGG AND MELTED BUTTER STEAMED INTO A FLUFFY SOUFFLÉ.
THAT'S WHAT THE WHITE SIDE IS—A CHEESE-FLAVORED SFORMATO SOUFFLÉ!
HEAVY CREAM
NOM
ALL RIGHT, NOW TO SEE WHAT THE BLACK HALF IS!
TWITCH
THIS FLAVOR! IT CAN'T BE... BUT IT IS!
IT'S... TURTLE?
CORRECT! THIS IS A CHEESE ...
...AND TURTLE VERRINE!
WHAT?!
HEE!
HEE HEE!
AHA HA...

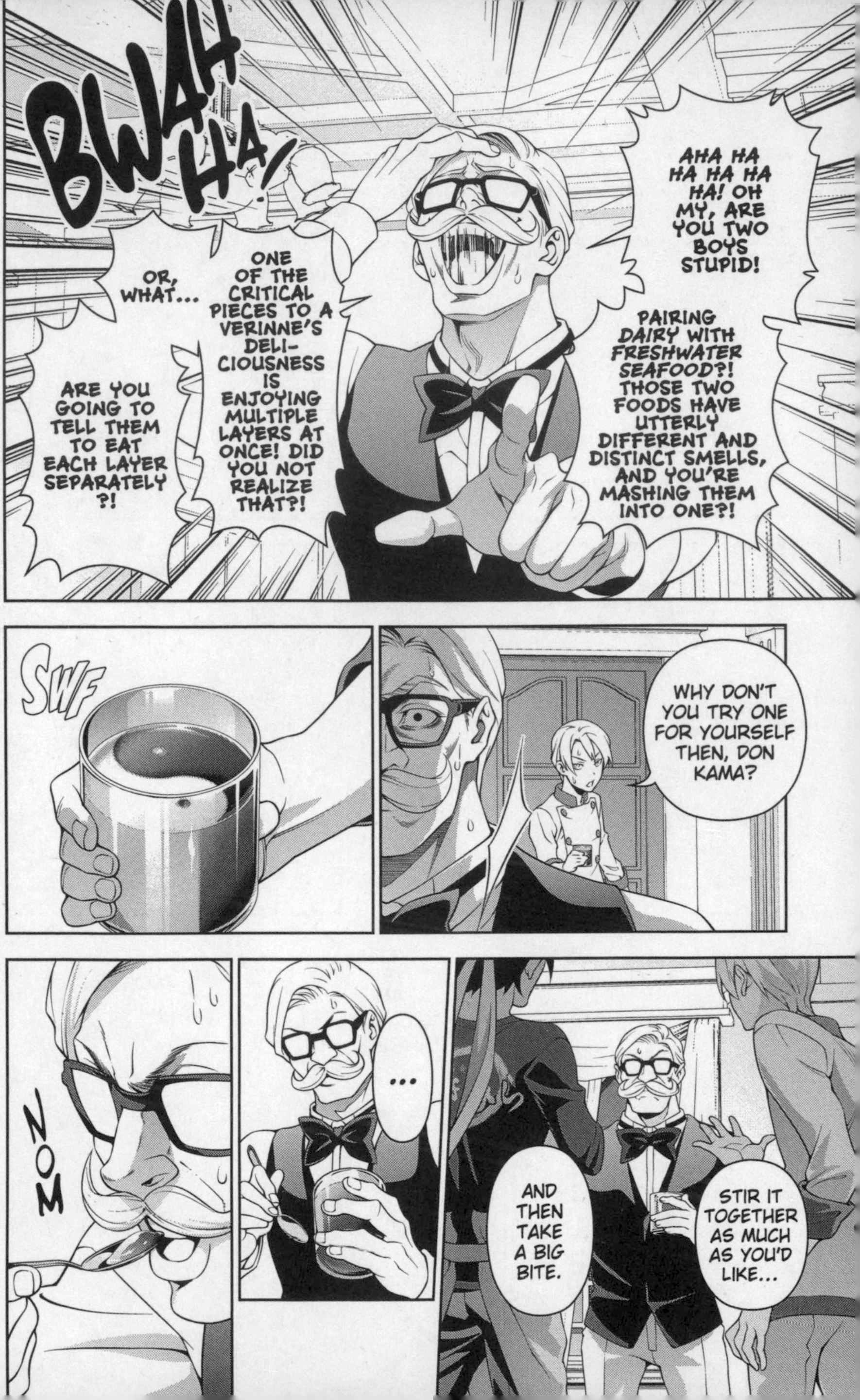
AHA HA HA HA HA HA! OH MY, ARE YOU TWO BOYS STUPID!
PAIRING DAIRY WITH FRESHWATER SEAFOOD?! THOSE TWO FOODS HAVE UTTERLY DIFFERENT AND DISTINCT SMELLS, AND YOU'RE MASHING THEM INTO ONE?!
BWAH HA HA!
ONE OF THE CRITICAL PIECES TO A VERINNE'S DELI-CIOUSNESS IS ENJOYING MULTIPLE LAYERS AT ONCE! DID YOU NOT REALIZE THAT?!
OR, WHAT...
ARE YOU GOING TO TELL THEM TO EAT EACH LAYER SEPARATELY?!
WHY DON'T YOU TRY ONE FOR YOURSELF THEN, DON KAMA?
SWF
STIR IT TOGETHER AS MUCH AS YOU'D LIKE...
AND THEN TAKE A BIG BITE.
...
NOM

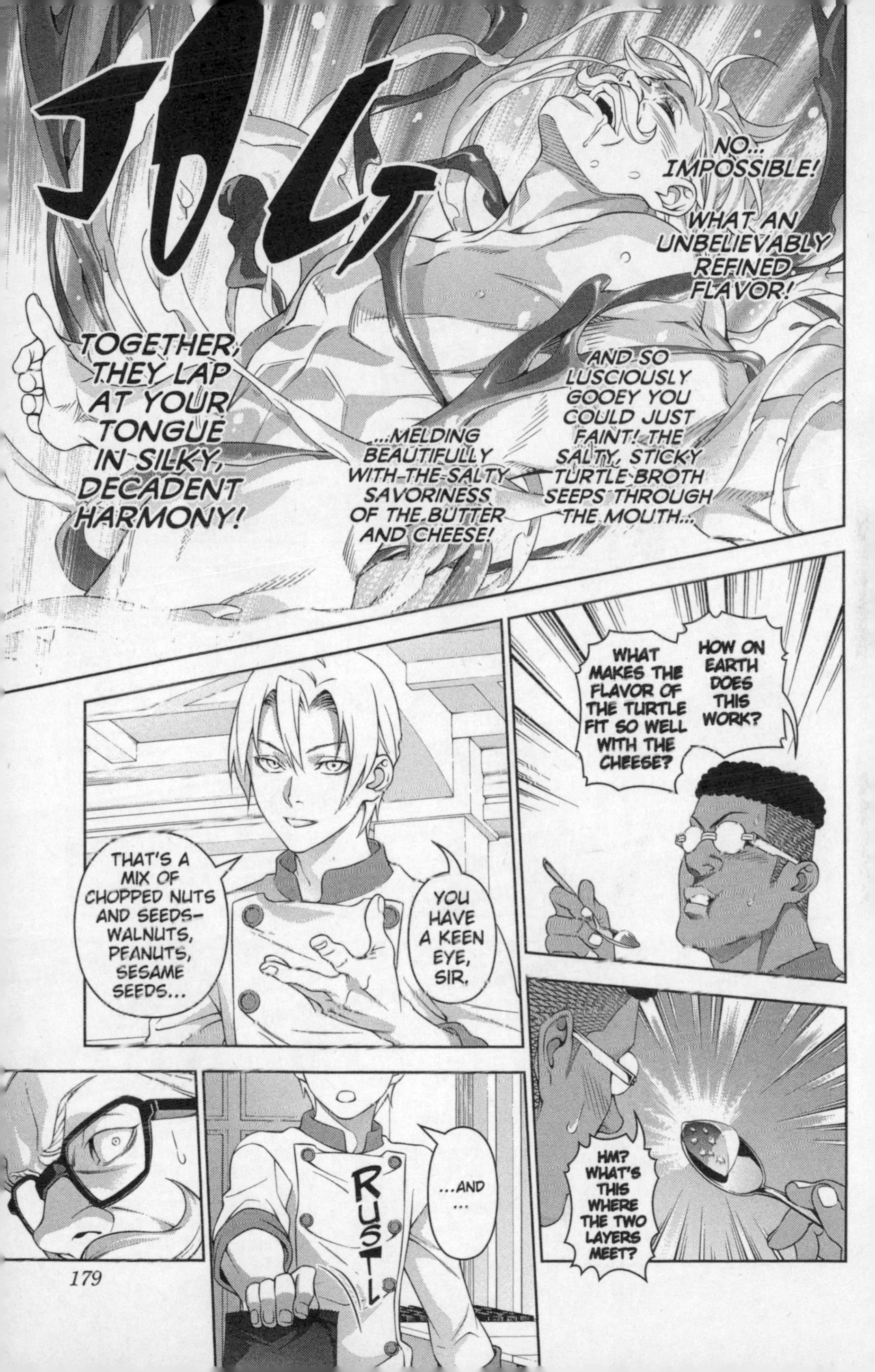
NO... IMPOSSIBLE!
WHAT AN UNBELIEVABLY REFINED FLAVOR!
AND SO LUSCIOUSLY GOOEY YOU COULD JUST FAINT! THE SALTY, STICKY TURTLE BROTH SEEPS THROUGH THE MOUTH...
...MELDING BEAUTIFULLY WITH THE SALTY SAVORINESS OF THE BUTTER AND CHEESE!
TOGETHER, THEY LAP AT YOUR TONGUE IN SILKY, DECADENT HARMONY!
HOW ON EARTH DOES THIS WORK?
WHAT MAKES THE FLAVOR OF THE TURTLE FIT SO WELL WITH THE CHEESE?
HM? WHAT'S THIS WHERE THE TWO LAYERS MEET?
YOU HAVE A KEEN EYE, SIR.
THAT'S A MIX OF CHOPPED NUTS AND SEEDS—WALNUTS, PEANUTS, SESAME SEEDS...
...AND ...
RUSTL

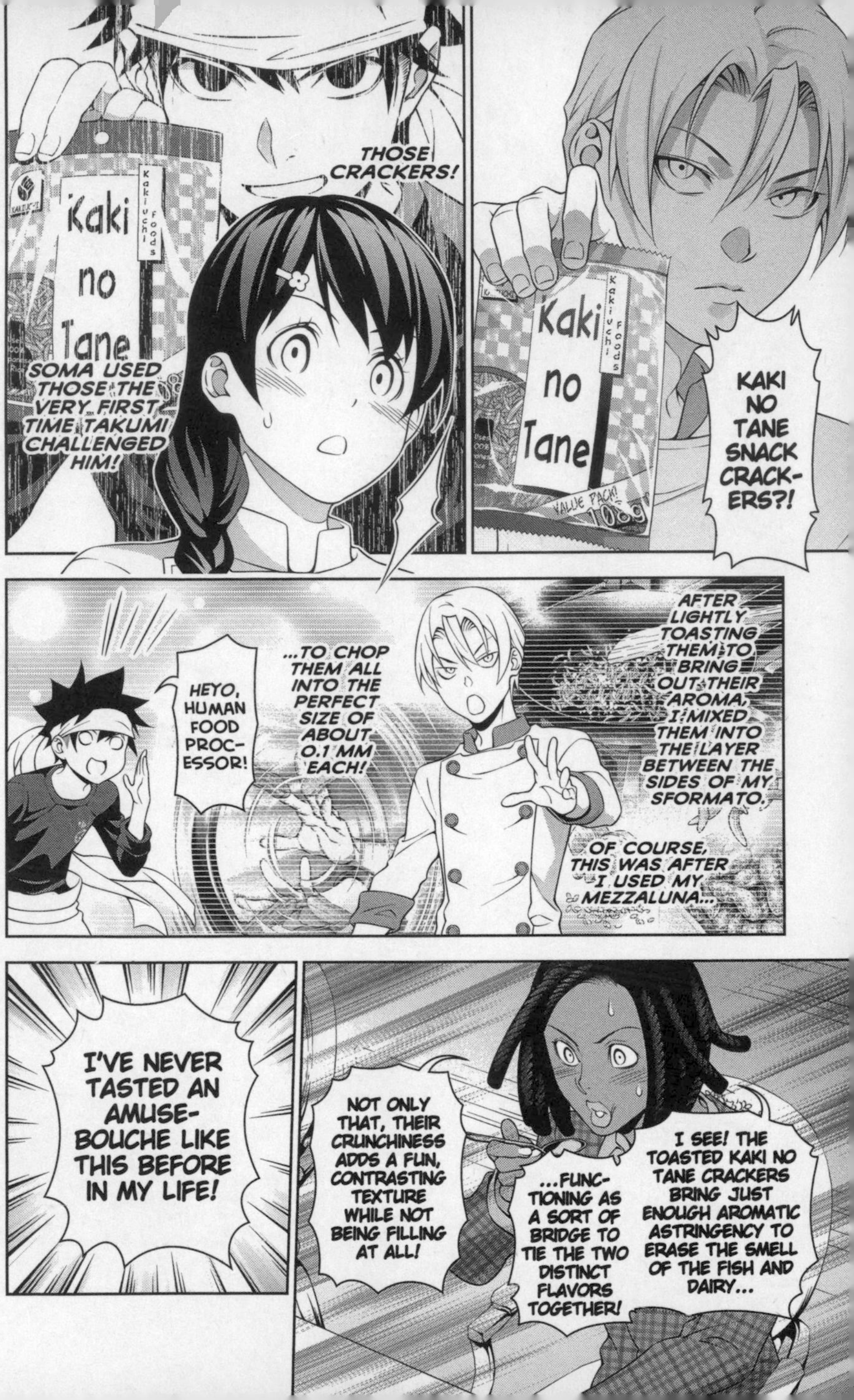
Kaki no Tane
Kakiuchi Foods
VALUE PACK! 100g
KAKI NO TANE SNACK CRACK-ERS?!
Kaki no Tane
Kakiuchi Foods
THOSE CRACKERS!
SOMA USED THOSE THE VERY FIRST TIME TAKUMI CHALLENGED HIM!
AFTER LIGHTLY TOASTING THEM TO BRING OUT THEIR AROMA, I MIXED THEM INTO THE LAYER BETWEEN THE SIDES OF MY SFORMATO.
OF COURSE, THIS WAS AFTER I USED MY MEZZALUNA...
...TO CHOP THEM ALL INTO THE PERFECT SIZE OF ABOUT 0.1 MM EACH!
HEYO, HUMAN FOOD PROC-ESSOR!
I SEE! THE TOASTED KAKI NO TANE CRACKERS BRING JUST ENOUGH AROMATIC ASTRINGENCY TO ERASE THE SMELL OF THE FISH AND DAIRY...
...FUNC-TIONING AS A SORT OF BRIDGE TO TIE THE TWO DISTINCT FLAVORS TOGETHER!
NOT ONLY THAT, THEIR CRUNCHINESS ADDS A FUN, CONTRASTING TEXTURE WHILE NOT BEING FILLING AT ALL!
I'VE NEVER TASTED AN AMUSE-BOUCHE LIKE THIS BEFORE IN MY LIFE!

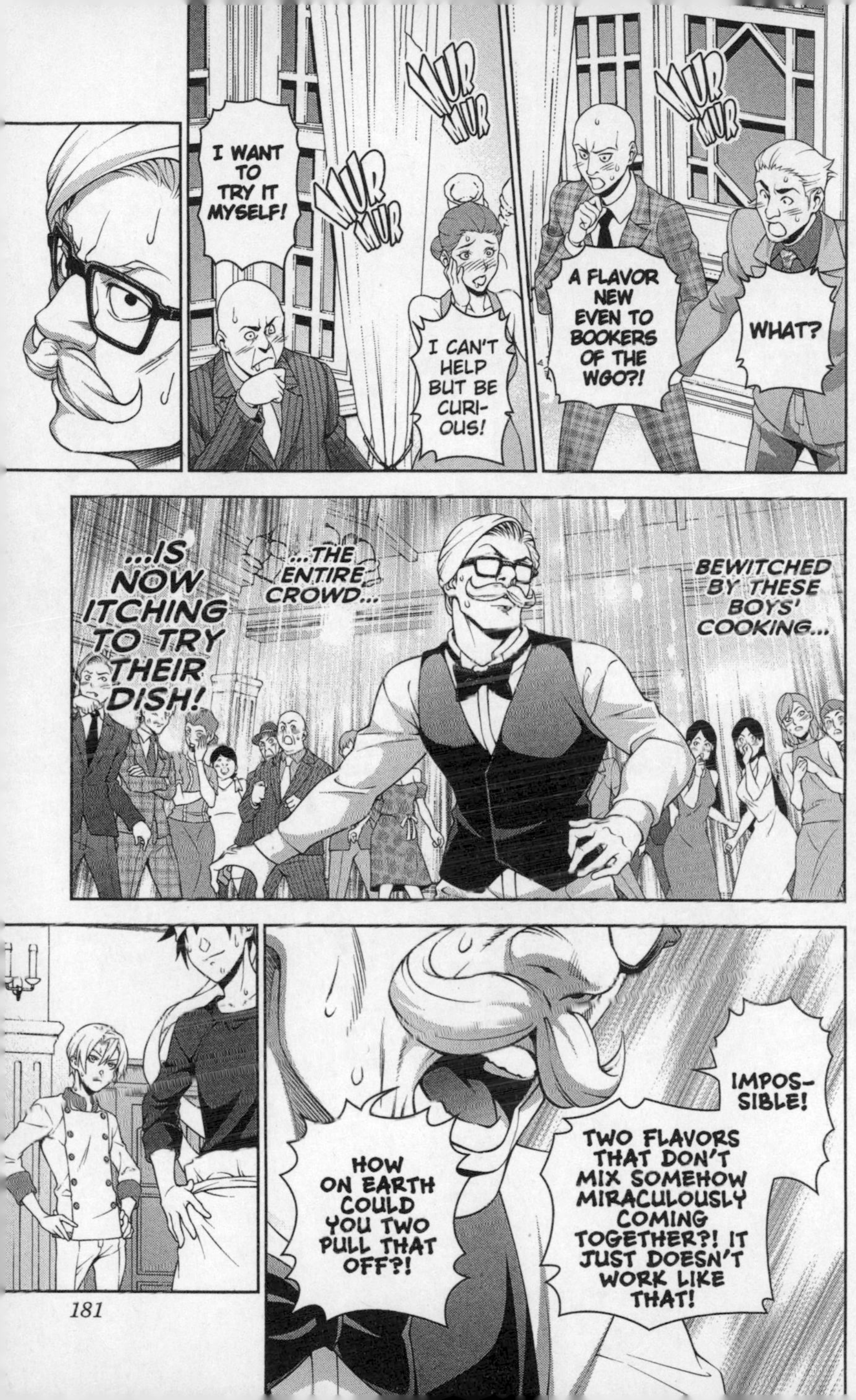
MUR MUR
WHAT?
A FLAVOR NEW EVEN TO BOOKERS OF THE WGO?!
MUR MUR
I WANT TO TRY IT MYSELF!
MUR MUR
I CAN'T HELP BUT BE CURI-OUS!
BEWITCHED BY THESE BOYS' COOKING...
...THE ENTIRE CROWD...
...IS NOW ITCHING TO TRY THEIR DISH!
IMPOS-SIBLE!
TWO FLAVORS THAT DON'T MIX SOMEHOW MIRACULOUSLY COMING TOGETHER?! IT JUST DOESN'T WORK LIKE THAT!
HOW ON EARTH COULD YOU TWO PULL THAT OFF?!

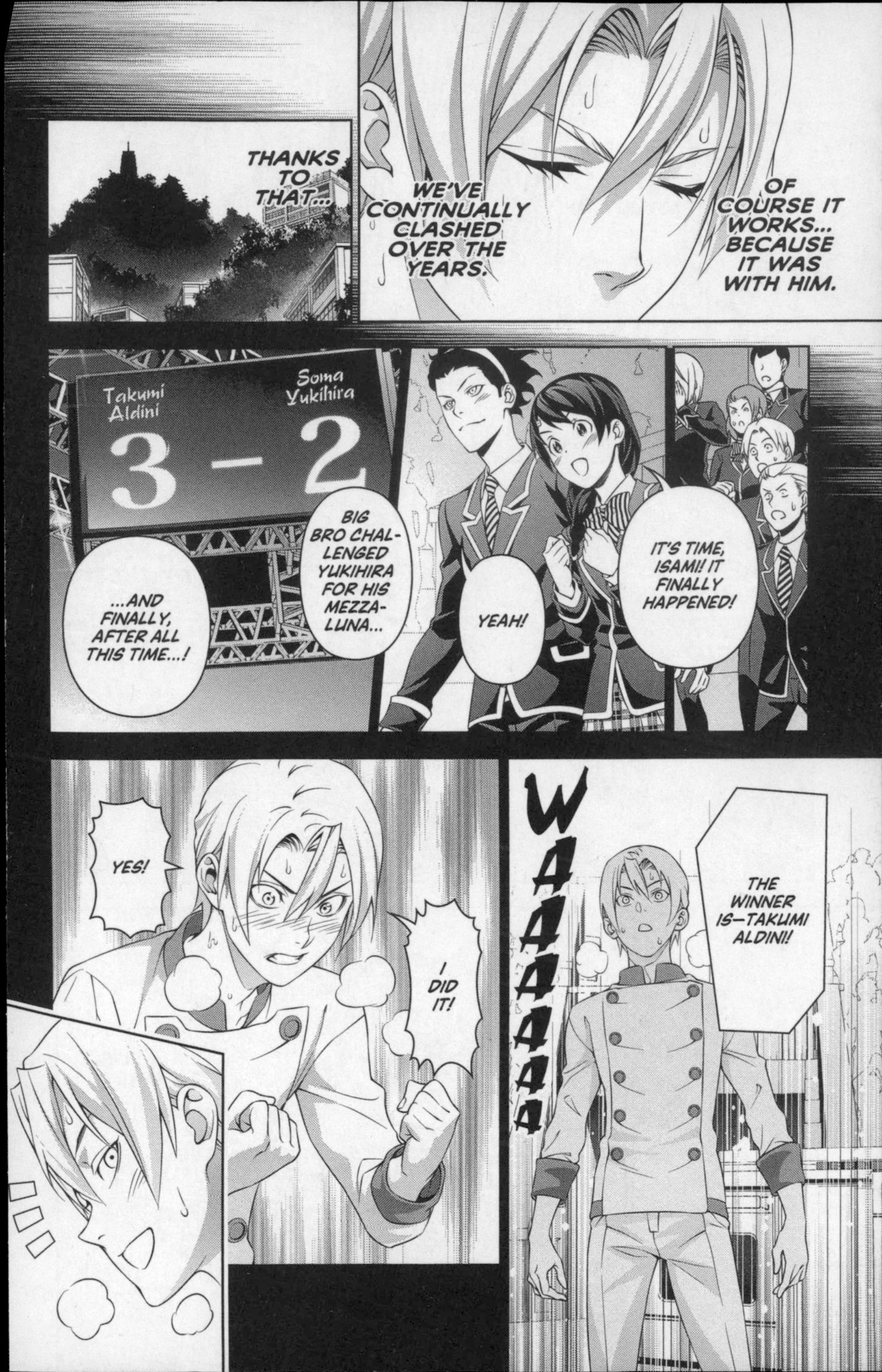
OF COURSE IT WORKS... BECAUSE IT WAS WITH HIM.
WE'VE CONTINUALLY CLASHED OVER THE YEARS.
THANKS TO THAT...
IT'S TIME, ISAMI! IT FINALLY HAPPENED!
YEAH!
BIG BRO CHALLENGED YUKIHIRA FOR HIS MEZZALUNA...
Soma Yukihira
Takumi Aldini
3 – 2
...AND FINALLY, AFTER ALL THIS TIME...!
WAAAAAAA
THE WINNER IS—TAKUMI ALDINI!
YES!
I DID IT!

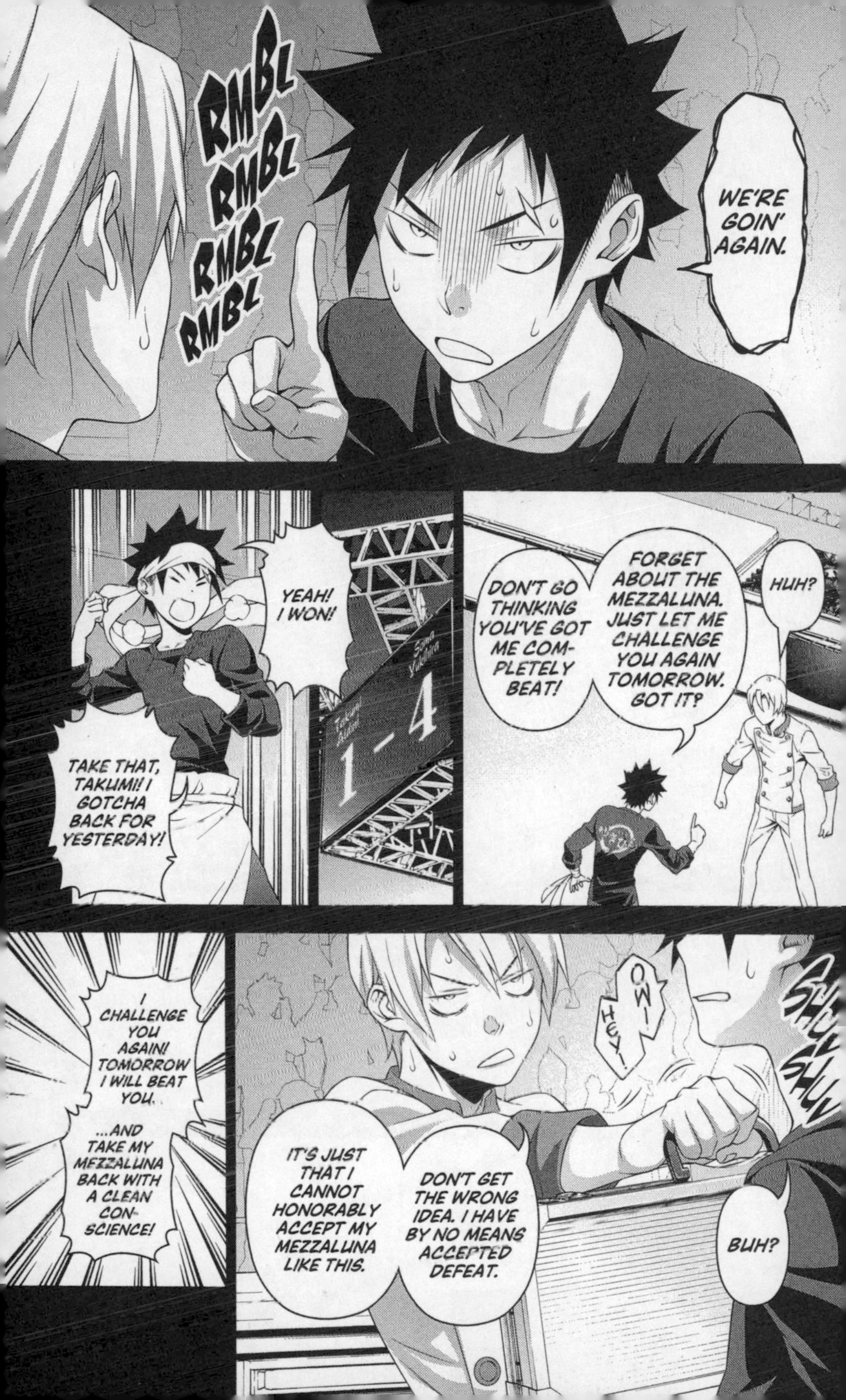
WE'RE GOIN' AGAIN.
RMBL RMBL RMBL RMBL
HUH?
FORGET ABOUT THE MEZZALUNA. JUST LET ME CHALLENGE YOU AGAIN TOMORROW. GOT IT?
DON'T GO THINKING YOU'VE GOT ME COMPLETELY BEAT!
YEAH! I WON!
1 - 4
TAKE THAT, TAKUMI! I GOTCHA BACK FOR YESTERDAY!
OW! HEY!
BUH?
DON'T GET THE WRONG IDEA. I HAVE BY NO MEANS ACCEPTED DEFEAT.
IT'S JUST THAT I CANNOT HONORABLY ACCEPT MY MEZZALUNA LIKE THIS.
I CHALLENGE YOU AGAIN! TOMORROW I WILL BEAT YOU.
...AND TAKE MY MEZZALUNA BACK WITH A CLEAN CONSCIENCE!

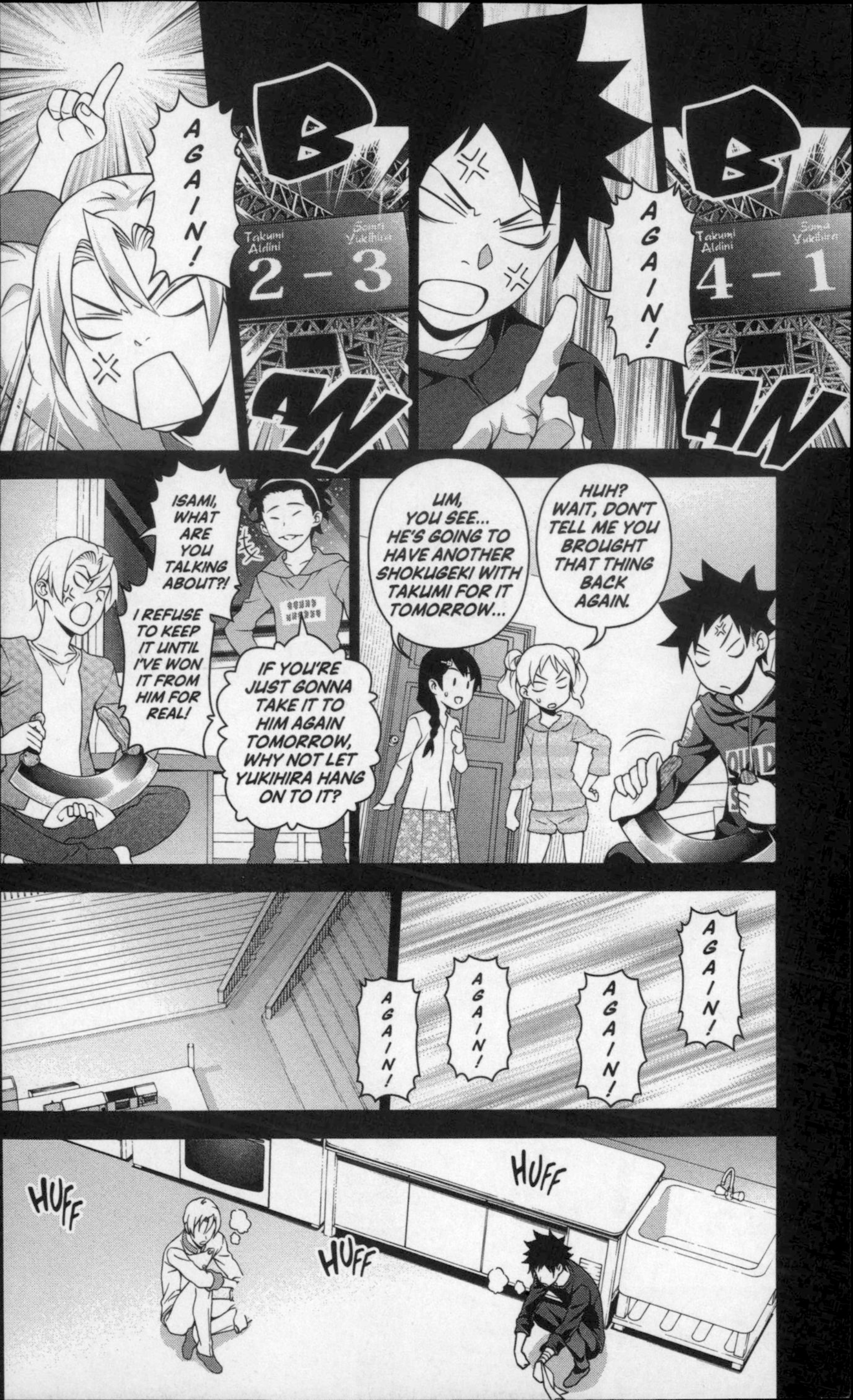
AGAIN!
Takumi Aldini
Soma Yukihira
4 - 1
BAM
AGAIN!
Takumi Aldini
Soma Yukihira
2 - 3
HUH? WAIT, DON'T TELL ME YOU BROUGHT THAT THING BACK AGAIN.
UM, YOU SEE... HE'S GOING TO HAVE ANOTHER SHOKUGEKI WITH TAKUMI FOR IT TOMORROW...
IF YOU'RE JUST GONNA TAKE IT TO HIM AGAIN TOMORROW, WHY NOT LET YUKIHIRA HANG ON TO IT?
ISAMI, WHAT ARE YOU TALKING ABOUT?!
I REFUSE TO KEEP IT UNTIL I'VE WON IT FROM HIM FOR REAL!
AGAIN!
AGAIN!
AGAIN!
AGAIN!
HUFF
HUFF
HUFF

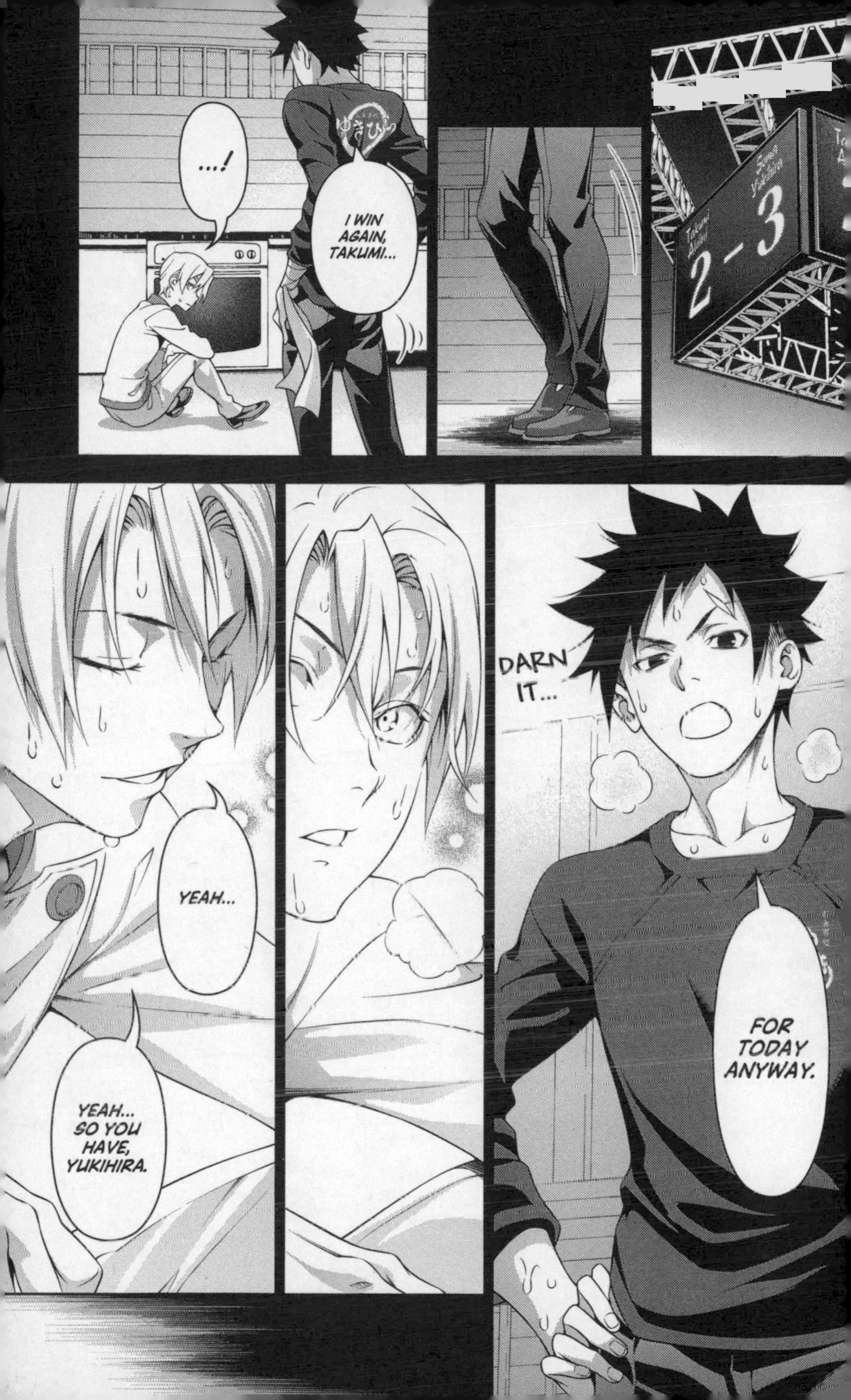
2 – 3
I WIN AGAIN, TAKUMI...
...!
DARN IT...
FOR TODAY ANYWAY.
YEAH...
YEAH... SO YOU HAVE, YUKIHIRA.

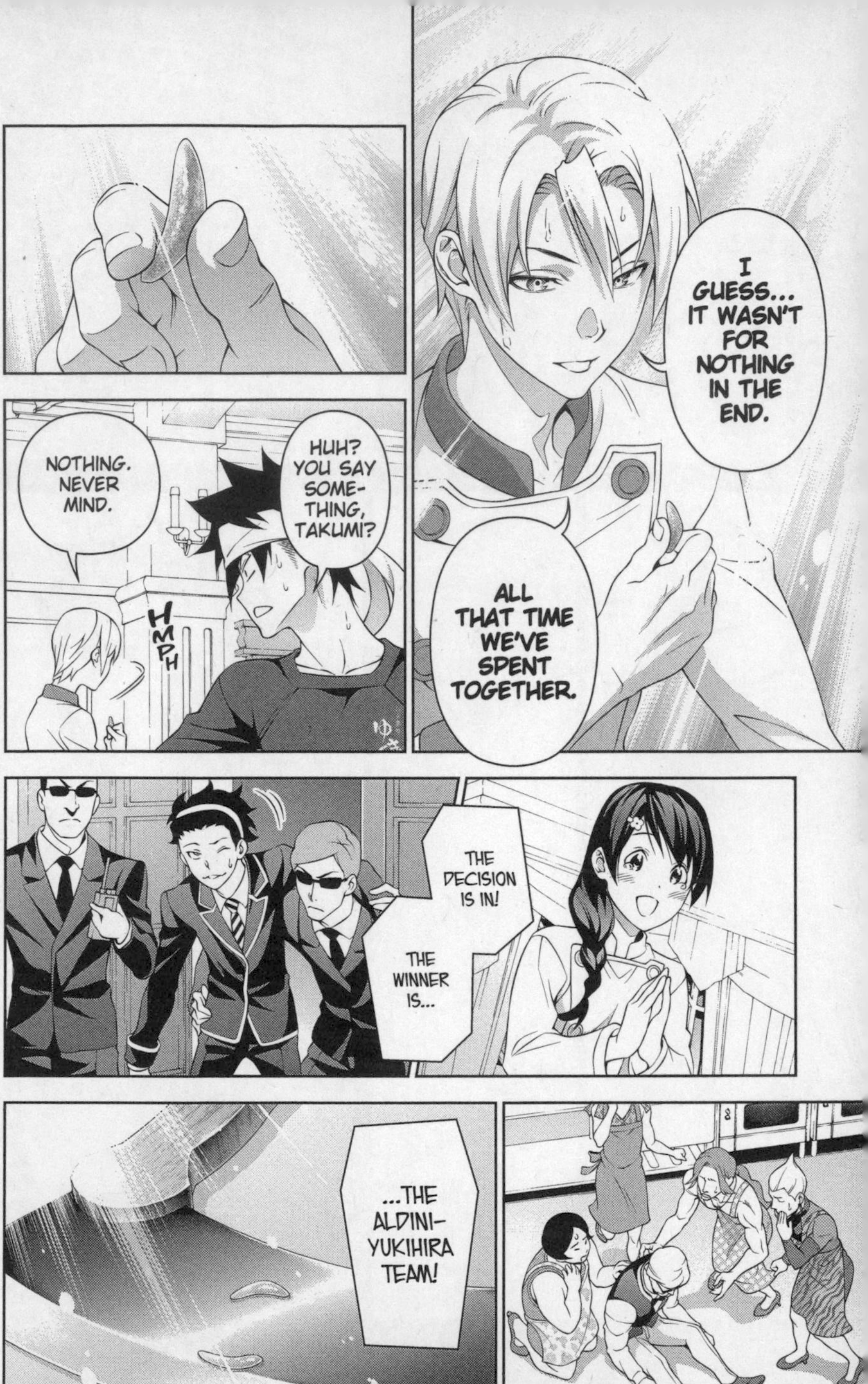
I GUESS... IT WASN'T FOR NOTHING IN THE END.
ALL THAT TIME WE'VE SPENT TOGETHER.
HUH? YOU SAY SOME-THING, TAKUMI?
NOTHING. NEVER MIND.
HMPH
THE DECISION IS IN!
THE WINNER IS...
...THE ALDINI-YUKIHIRA TEAM!

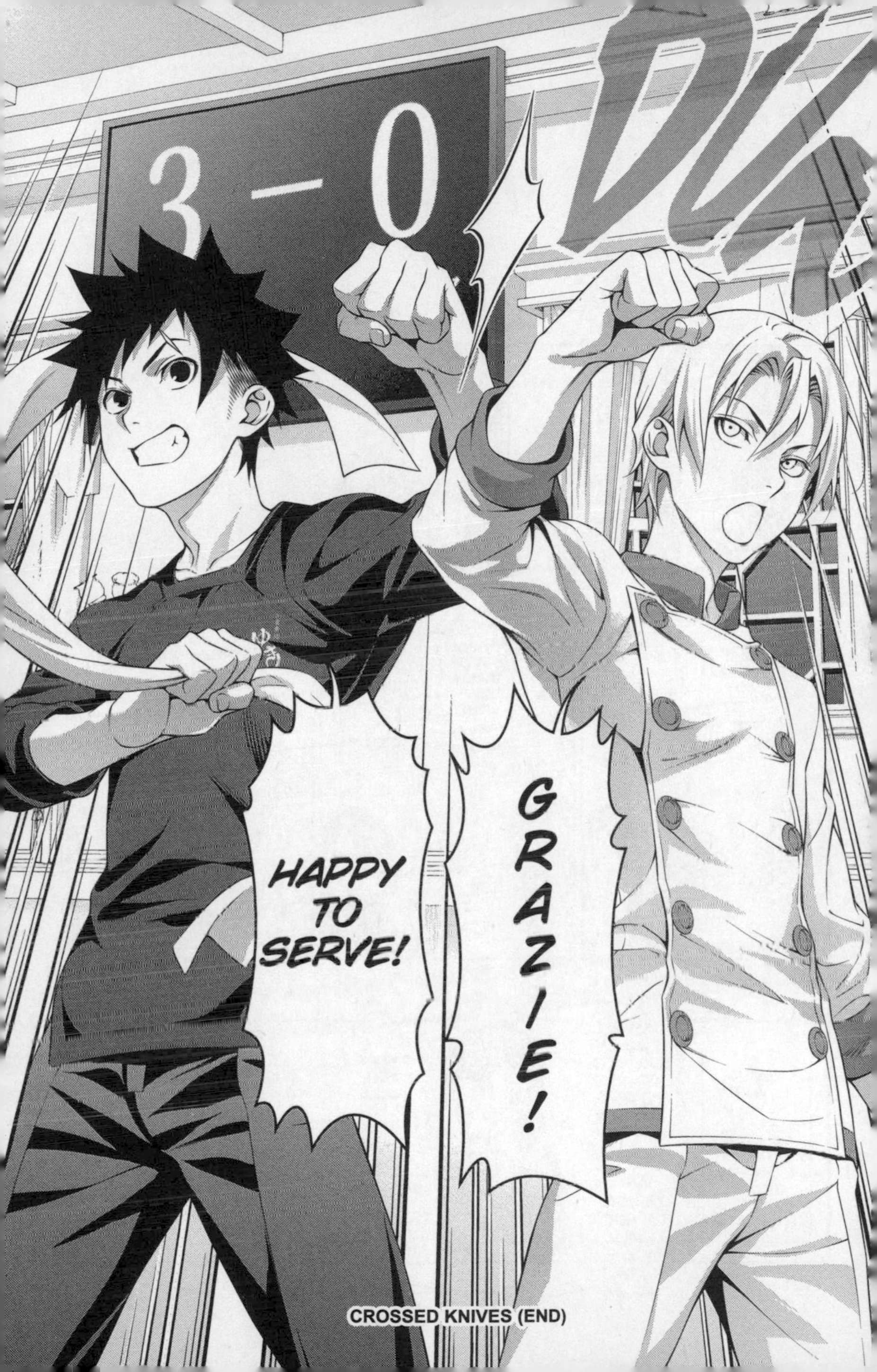
3 – 0
GRAZIE!
HAPPY TO SERVE!
CROSSED KNIVES (END)

SIDE STORIES FROM THE MAGAZINE

TREATED LIKE A CHILD?

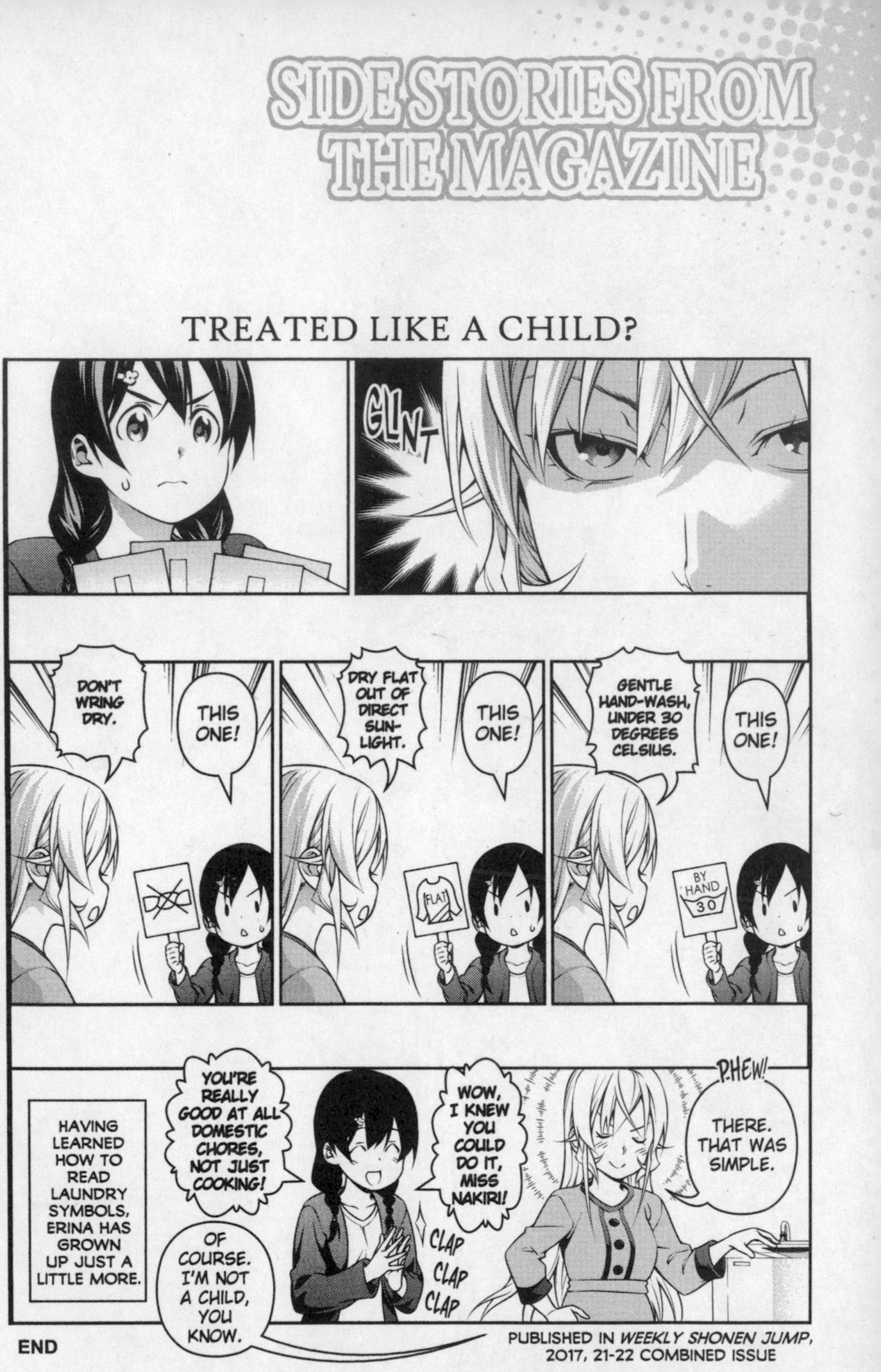

GLINT
THIS ONE!
GENTLE HAND-WASH, UNDER 30 DEGREES CELSIUS.
BY HAND 30
THIS ONE!
DRY FLAT OUT OF DIRECT SUN-LIGHT.
FLAT
THIS ONE!
DON'T WRING DRY.
PHEW!
THERE. THAT WAS SIMPLE.
WOW, I KNEW YOU COULD DO IT, MISS NAKIRI!
YOU'RE REALLY GOOD AT ALL DOMESTIC CHORES, NOT JUST COOKING!
CLAP CLAP CLAP
OF COURSE. I'M NOT A CHILD, YOU KNOW.
HAVING LEARNED HOW TO READ LAUNDRY SYMBOLS, ERINA HAS GROWN UP JUST A LITTLE MORE.

END

PUBLISHED IN *WEEKLY SHONEN JUMP*, 2017, 21-22 COMBINED ISSUE

A CHRISTMAS RECIPE

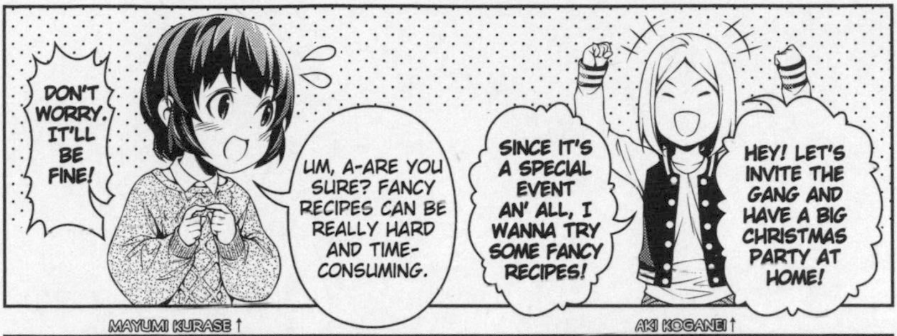
HEY! LET'S INVITE THE GANG AND HAVE A BIG CHRISTMAS PARTY AT HOME!
SINCE IT'S A SPECIAL EVENT AN' ALL, I WANNA TRY SOME FANCY RECIPES!
UM, A-ARE YOU SURE? FANCY RECIPES CAN BE REALLY HARD AND TIME-CONSUMING.
DON'T WORRY. IT'LL BE FINE!
AKI KOGANEI ↑
MAYUMI KURASE ↑

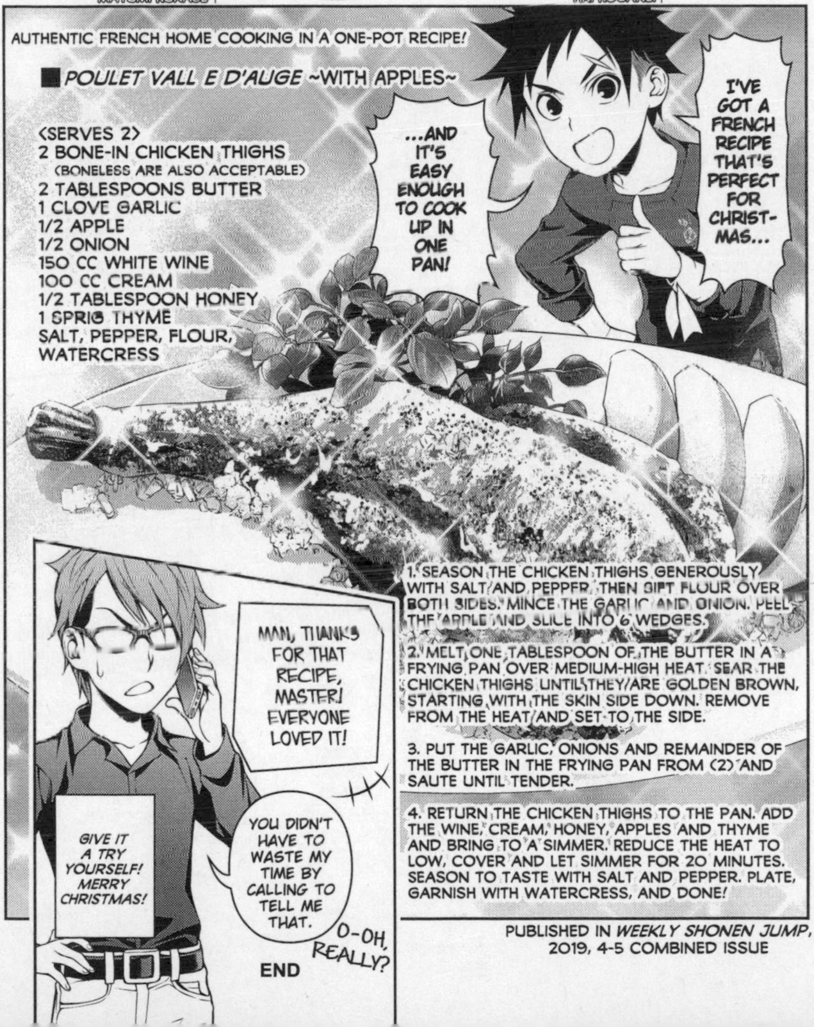
I'VE GOT A FRENCH RECIPE THAT'S PERFECT FOR CHRIST-MAS...
...AND IT'S EASY ENOUGH TO COOK UP IN ONE PAN!
AUTHENTIC FRENCH HOME COOKING IN A ONE-POT RECIPE!
■POULET VALL E D'AUGE ~WITH APPLES~
⟨SERVES 2⟩
2 BONE-IN CHICKEN THIGHS
(BONELESS ARE ALSO ACCEPTABLE)
2 TABLESPOONS BUTTER
1 CLOVE GARLIC
1/2 APPLE
1/2 ONION
150 CC WHITE WINE
100 CC CREAM
1/2 TABLESPOON HONEY
1 SPRIG THYME
SALT, PEPPER, FLOUR, WATERCRESS
1. SEASON THE CHICKEN THIGHS GENEROUSLY WITH SALT AND PEPPER, THEN SIFT FLOUR OVER BOTH SIDES. MINCE THE GARLIC AND ONION. PEEL THE APPLE AND SLICE INTO 6 WEDGES.
2. MELT ONE TABLESPOON OF THE BUTTER IN A FRYING PAN OVER MEDIUM-HIGH HEAT. SEAR THE CHICKEN THIGHS UNTIL THEY ARE GOLDEN BROWN, STARTING WITH THE SKIN SIDE DOWN. REMOVE FROM THE HEAT AND SET TO THE SIDE.
3. PUT THE GARLIC, ONIONS AND REMAINDER OF THE BUTTER IN THE FRYING PAN FROM (2) AND SAUTE UNTIL TENDER.
4. RETURN THE CHICKEN THIGHS TO THE PAN. ADD THE WINE, CREAM, HONEY, APPLES AND THYME AND BRING TO A SIMMER. REDUCE THE HEAT TO LOW, COVER AND LET SIMMER FOR 20 MINUTES. SEASON TO TASTE WITH SALT AND PEPPER. PLATE, GARNISH WITH WATERCRESS, AND DONE!
MAN, THANKS FOR THAT RECIPE, MASTER! EVERYONE LOVED IT!
YOU DIDN'T HAVE TO WASTE MY TIME BY CALLING TO TELL ME THAT.
O-OH, REALLY?
GIVE IT A TRY YOURSELF! MERRY CHRISTMAS!
END

PUBLISHED IN *WEEKLY SHONEN JUMP*, 2019, 4-5 COMBINED ISSUE

~BONUS SHORT~

YUKIHIRA THE DILIGENT

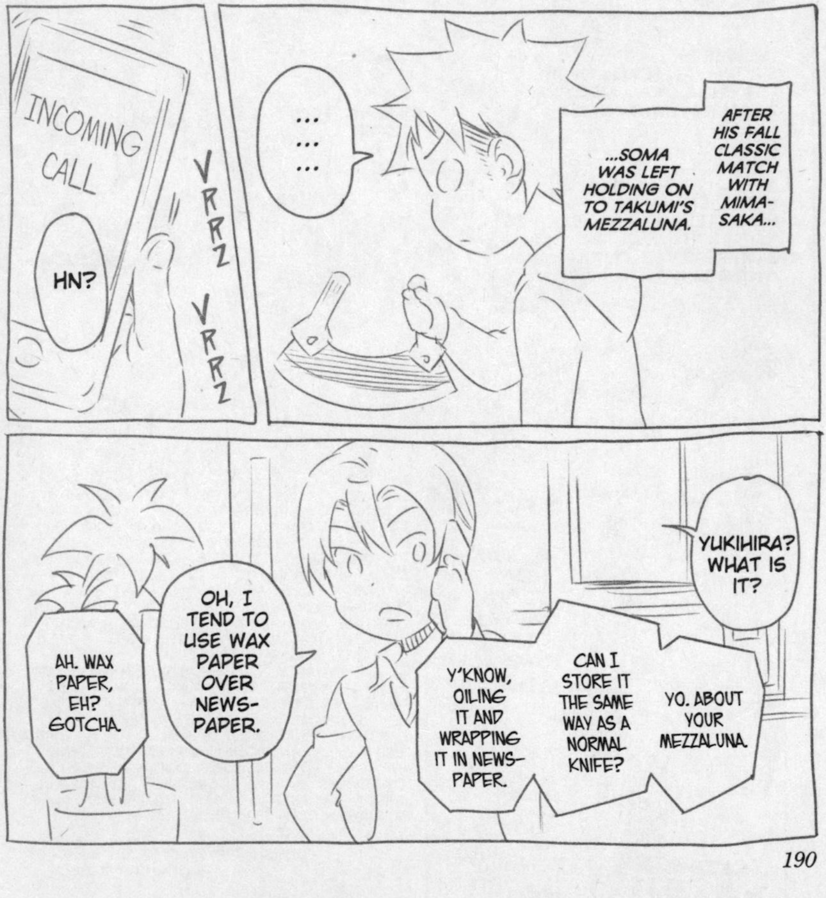
AFTER HIS FALL CLASSIC MATCH WITH MIMASAKA...
...SOMA WAS LEFT HOLDING ON TO TAKUMI'S MEZZALUNA.
... ...
INCOMING CALL
VRRZ VRRZ
HN?
YUKIHIRA? WHAT IS IT?
YO. ABOUT YOUR MEZZALUNA.
CAN I STORE IT THE SAME WAY AS A NORMAL KNIFE?
Y'KNOW, OILING IT AND WRAPPING IT IN NEWS-PAPER.
OH, I TEND TO USE WAX PAPER OVER NEWS-PAPER.
AH. WAX PAPER, EH? GOTCHA.

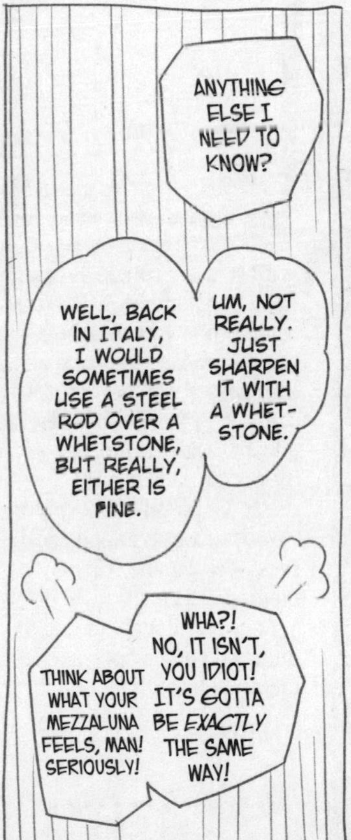
ANYTHING ELSE I NEED TO KNOW?
UM, NOT REALLY. JUST SHARPEN IT WITH A WHETSTONE.
WELL, BACK IN ITALY, I WOULD SOMETIMES USE A STEEL ROD OVER A WHETSTONE, BUT REALLY, EITHER IS FINE.
WHA?! NO, IT ISN'T, YOU IDIOT! IT'S GOTTA BE *EXACTLY* THE SAME WAY!
THINK ABOUT WHAT YOUR MEZZALUNA FEELS, MAN! SERIOUSLY!

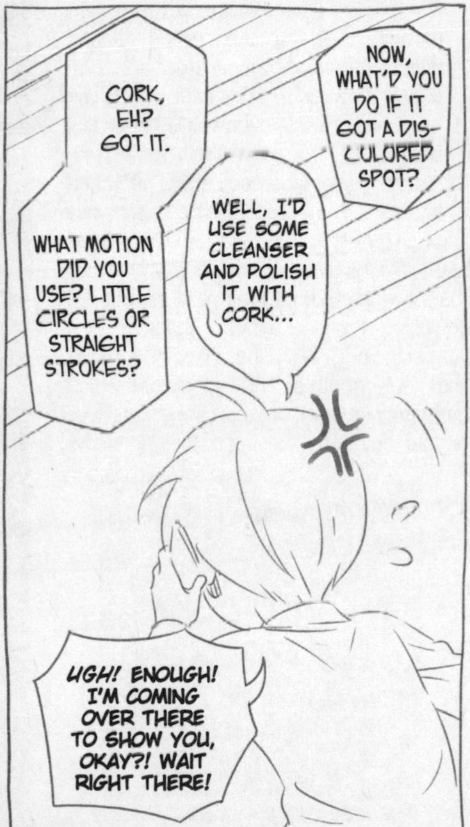
NOW, WHAT'D YOU DO IF IT GOT A DIS-COLORED SPOT?
WELL, I'D USE SOME CLEANSER AND POLISH IT WITH CORK...
CORK, EH? GOT IT.
WHAT MOTION DID YOU USE? LITTLE CIRCLES OR STRAIGHT STROKES?
UGH! ENOUGH! I'M COMING OVER THERE TO SHOW YOU, OKAY?! WAIT RIGHT THERE!

END

You're Reading in the Wrong Direction!!

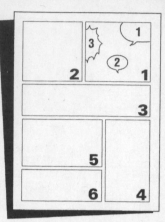

Whoops! Guess what? You're starting at the wrong end of the comic!

...It's true! In keeping with the original Japanese format, **Food Wars!** is meant to be read from right to left, starting in the upper-right corner.

Unlike English, which is read from left to right, Japanese is read from right to left, meaning that action, sound effects and word-balloon order are completely reversed... something which can make readers unfamiliar with Japanese feel pretty backwards themselves. For this reason, manga or Japanese comics published in the U.S. in English have sometimes been published "flopped"—that is, printed in exact reverse order, as though seen from the other side of a mirror.

By flopping pages, U.S. publishers can avoid confusing readers, but the compromise is not without its downside. For one thing, a character in a flopped manga series who once wore in the original Japanese version a T-shirt emblazoned with "M A Y" (as in "the merry month of") now wears one which reads "Y A M"! Additionally, many manga creators in Japan are themselves unhappy with the process, as some feel the mirror-imaging of their art skews their original intentions.

We are proud to bring you Yuto Tsukuda and Shun Saeki's **Food Wars!** in the original unflopped format.

For now, though, turn to the other side of the book and let the adventure begin...!

—Editor

THE HIGHEST RANKED OF ALL.